MICROPROCESSORS
IN INDUSTRY

MICROPROCESSORS
IN INDUSTRY

MICHAEL F. HORDESKI, P.E.

Control Systems Consultant
Siltran Digital
Atascadero, California

 VAN NOSTRAND REINHOLD COMPANY

Library of Congress Catalog Card Number: 83-17001
ISBN: 0-442-23207-1

Manufactured in the United States of America

Published by Van Nostrand Reinhold Company Inc.
135 West 50th Street
New York, New York 10020

Van Nostrand Reinhold Company Limited
Molly Millars Lane
Wokingham, Berkshire RG11 2PY, England

Van Nostrand Reinhold
480 Latrobe Street
Melbourne, Victoria 3000, Australia

Macmillan of Canada
Division of Gage Publishing Limited
164 Commander Boulevard
Agincourt, Ontario M1S 3C7, Canada

15 14 13 12 11 10 9 8 7 6 5 4 3 2 1

Library of Congress Cataloging in Publication Data

Hordeski, Michael F.
    Microprocessors in industry.

    Includes index.
    1. Microprocessors.   2. Automatic control.
I. Title.
TK7895.M5H67 1984   621.3819'58   83-17001
ISBN 0-442-23207-1

There exist limitless opportunities in every industry. Where there is an open mind, there will always be a frontier.

Charles F. Kettering

Preface

Microprocessors In Industry was written to provide the knowledge and design techniques that are required to apply microprocessors to the automation of industrial and commercial products as well as manufacturing and process control. The book relates the development of today's microprocessors to sensors, data-acquisition, and automatic control applications and provides a basis for the design considerations necessary to achieve a successful and efficient microprocessor application from initial design concepts to system manufacturing or sell-off.

The designer must have a thorough knowledge of microprocessors as well as the design techniques used to apply these devices. This text primarily relates the application of today's modern microprocessors for dedicated data-acquisition and automatic control when interfaced with various types of sensors and control elements. It is intended as a single-source reference book for the graduate engineer, but the various sections can also be presented at the undergraduate level. Discussions are included on the basic structure and technology of microprocessors, the various chips available, industrial sensors, data-acquisition, data conversion, interfacing, programming, control system elements, applications, and system design. This spectrum of topics is included to assist the reader not only in obtaining an understanding of the technology, but in applying the technology to actual product applications. Each chapter contains a number of review problems to provide the reader with a better understanding of the topics discussed.

Microcomputers are a popular topic in industry. In writing a book on microprocessors, it is important that any book have an originality that will justify it. Some books are written for software engineers with little hardware theory, while some books are written from the hardware viewpoint with very little software acknowledgement. This book attempts to rectify these shortcomings by treating both areas. Another unique path for this book is the mating of microprocessors with control hardware.

Chapter 1 considers the microprocessor structure. The basic building blocks are presented along with the methods used to perform the arithmetic and logical operations under program control, for the microprocessor is only one element in the microcomputer system. As a component, it allows new areas of industrial applications that were impractical before because of cost and size. These new areas of application can be considered to have a fundamental impact on the structure of the industrial control industry.

Memory is necessary in the microcomputer system to store programs and data used by the microprocessor. Thus, the first chapter presents an overview of the most common memory chips used in microcomputers systems: RAMs and ROMs. An analysis of the information flow in a typical microcomputer system is presented as well as an overview of instruction operations.

The development of microprocessors has been possible due to the advances in semiconductor process technology. Chapter 2 reviews modern semiconductor technology, with particular attention to those used in microprocessors. Integrated circuit techniques are discussed, and the important microprocessor and memory technologies are presented.

Chapter 3 considers the major characteristics of a number of popular microprocessor units. The chapter begins with a review of the evolution of microprocessors and then continues into the major product lines.

This chapter serves as a reference on microprocessor products. Much more detailed information is available from the manufacturers. This chapter discusses the general characteristics and their significance in an application to the user.

In Chapter 4, the major characteristics of transducers used in industrial applications are presented. Included in this chapter are the method of operation and operating ranges for temperature, pressure, and flow transducers.

Chapter 5 considers the types of data-acquisition circuits used in industrial applications and how to choose the best components for a particular application. The following topics are presented: single-channel systems, multichannel systems, multiplexing, sample-holds, signal-conditioning amplifiers, common-mode, isolation, and filtering. There is also an overview of plant-wide techniques. With the advent of distributed processing and computer networks, these are topics of high importance.

In order to process the data, it must be in digital form so that the data can be used for controlling a process, generating information for displays, or stored for future use. The basic method for getting the data into digital form is the analog to digital converter. Chapter 6 presents an overview of conversion methods along with their advantages and disadvantages. A review of binary codes is presented along with guides for applying converters. The chapter concludes with a number of synchro conversion techniques for ac measurement systems.

Interfacing the microprocessor is the subject of Chapter 7. The microprocessor interface is one of the most important elements in the microcomputer system. This chapter considers the hardware and software techniques required for a successful interface. Among the topics considered are interfacing the microprocessor with a data-acquisition system, microprocessor interface chips, programming the interface unit, and standard digital data interfaces. This is an important chapter, and the subject is one which may cause the most problems for the user.

Chapter 8 considers the control elements and the analysis of the total control system. The final element in the control system is the motor or solenoid used to provide the control function. The microprocessor is of little value to the industrial designer unless it can be used to modify the final control parameter. This chapter reviews the control techniques for solenoids and stepping motors. The control system analysis topics include closed and open loop control and system response characteristics. Much has been written on control theory and techniques, but this chapter emphasizes how the theory and techniques can be implemented when using a microcomputer.

Microprocessors will have a significant impact on all industries in the next five to ten years. As a low-cost product, microprocessors will cause the elimination of many competing technologies and products. The industrial firms that successfully use microprocessor technology will emerge with a larger share of the marketplace. Chapter 9 considers a number of important industrial application areas for microprocessors such as low-cost computers and controls, automotive devices, communicative networks, telephone switching, and process control. This chapter presents a real opportunity to the reader for developing even more unique applications. Emphasis is on industrial applications, including both the visible microcontroller/computer system and the buried microcomputer in an analytical instrument or other intelligent product.

The development of an operating microprocessor system starting with a microprocessor and associated parts can be a formidable task. Chapter 10 considers the hardware and software tools available to the designer. Also considered in this chapter are the techniques for selecting the best microprocessor and development path for the application. Included are these topics: development aids, hardware systems, software packages, assemblers, cross-assemblers, languages, editors, loaders, simulators, and PROM programmers.

This book would not have been possible without the help of many from a number of universities and industrial firms. I wish to thank those who have contributed the wealth of articles and books to this area of science and engineering. I am grateful to Dean Morris of the California Polytechnic State University for allowing me a forum to initially present many of the concepts illustrated in this book and to the students who attended these courses and provided valuable feedback during this initial development.

I am also indebted to those in the aerospace, automotive, communications, electronics, and process control industries who have supported me as a consultant and colleague. To those who have attended my seminars, I also wish to express my gratitude for their stimulation and insight.

I am especially grateful to the following individuals who through their discussions and writings provided inspiration and guidance in this fast moving technology: Robert Noyce and Gordon Moore of the Intel Corporation, Carver Mead of the California Institute of Technology, Harry Garland of Cromemco, Thomas Harrison of IBM, and Béla Lipták of Béla G. Lipták Associates, P.C.

A special thank-you is also due to Dulcy Peña who typed the entire manuscript as well as to Eli Peña who helped decipher my many rambling notes and to Larry Hager and Michael Gardner at Van Nostrand Reinhold and the rest of the staff there for their patience and support on this project.

MICHAEL F. HORDESKI, P.E.
Atascadero, California

Contents

MICROPROCESSORS IN INDUSTRY

1. Microprocessor Structure

COMPUTERS AND MICROCOMPUTERS

All computers have a central processor, some memory, and a way to bring data in and present it to the outside world. What is unique to the microcomputer is that the processor is usually on one semiconductor chip, and memory and input/output circuits may also be on that same chip, or the memory and the I/O circuits are at least on chips on the same circuit board.

Microcomputers are not only small but low in cost relative to larger computers. Typically, a microcomputer is used where there are only a few different tasks to perform or where the string of instructions (the program) is fixed. The range of input/output equipment to which the microcomputer is connected is limited compared to larger computers, and speed and efficiency may not be as important.

Microcomputers are found in microwave ovens, laboratory instruments (see Figure 1.1), machine tools, and electronic cash registers. High-speed punched card readers, line printers, and large magnetic tape or disk memories are not required in these applications. The input/output is limited to a keyboard with a digital display or a connection through a telephone line

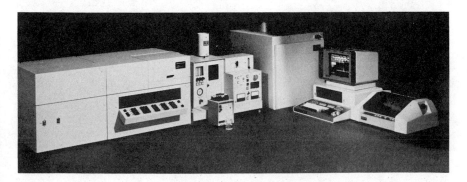

Fig. 1.1. An emission spectrometer which uses embedded microprocessors. (*Courtesy Perkin-Elmer Corporation.*)

to a larger computer. The program remains fixed; the task remains basically the same.

The larger computers, the "minicomputers," tend to handle a wider ranger of tasks. The minicomputer is usually contained in an enclosure about the size of a breadbox, and it may have a printing device and a magnetic tape output. It is capable of handling the paperwork for a small office—payroll, inventory, and other activities that can change from day to day. However, the line between microcomputers and minicomputers is changing, with some microcomputers approaching minicomputer performance. (See Figure 1.2.)

Larger than minicomputers are the "mainframe" computers, used in large offices such as insurance companies. These computers deal with large files of data such as millions of insurance policies. With mainframes, many magnetic disks and tapes are connected to the computer in order to store data, so the input/output scheduling can become a major task. Mainframe computers may be used to handle "scientific" computations such as those needed to produce the daily weather forecast for a section of the nation.

Fig. 1.2. This multiuser, multitasking transaction processing system is microcomputer-based. Yet it contains features previously available only on mainframes. (*Courtesy Intel Corporation.*)

Here, speed and efficiency in arithmetic, using computations far beyond what is found in most microcomputers, are needed.

The typical microcomputer application is the task that is small, relatively fixed, not too demanding of input/output paths, and requiring fast efficient arithmetic. (See Figure 1.3)

The typical microcomputer itself is a small box with a convenient mounting arrangement. It has its own self-contained power supply, along with terminals to which wires or cables are connected that lead to sensors and output devices such as keyboards, as well as temperature and pressure sensors, level

Fig. 1.3. Working in a chamber filled with nitrogen and using pressurized liquid Freon (lower insert), a robot cleans precision ball rotors (upper insert) used in submarine navigational systems. It is controlled by a microprocessor priced under $1000. (*Courtesy Rockwell International.*)

detectors, and flowmeters. Output devices include automatic typewriters, printers, video screens, electric motors, valves, solenoids, lighted displays, and actuators of various types.

The microcomputer may also "talk" to larger computers, floppy disks, magnetic tapes, remote terminals, and other peripherals.

MICROPROCESSOR COMPONENTS

Designing with microprocessors has become more of a programmer's task than a circuit designer's. Circuits fit together like blocks, while software tends to hold the blocks together. In this chapter, we will examine some of those blocks.

A microcomputer is a group of circuits, which include a microprocessor and other processing elements. It also has input/output lines for control and communications and enough memory to contain the programs. The micro-computer only needs a power source and a program in order to operate.

At the core of the microcomputer system is the microprocessor. It is the central processing unit (CPU) of the computer, and it has arithmetic processing circuits and control memory for its instruction set. (Even a simple micro-computer system and its microprocessor require a list of instructions, along with control of input/output operations and communications in order to perform a task. (See Figure 1.4) Although a CPU for a computer can be con-structed by utilizing various medium scale integration (MSI) functions such

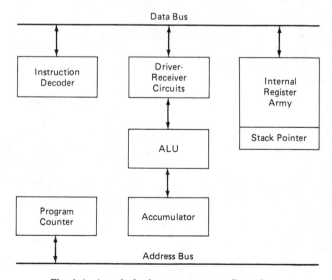

Fig. 1.4. A typical microprocessor configuration.

as registers, ALUs, and decoders, such a CPU may require hundreds of IC packages; it can, though, be tailored for a particular application. However, when the CPU is in large scale integration form (LSI), it becomes a microprocessor (also called a "processor-on-a-chip"). Unlike a custom-designed CPU, the functional characteristics of the microprocessor are fixed by the internal architecture. The only access available to a microprocessor is through the terminals of the package.

A microprocessor may be on a single semiconductor chip, or it may be on several interconnecting chips. The microprocessor performs the functions of instruction decoding from program memory and execution of the program, along with the synchronization and generation of control signals required for input/output operations. It tends to have the same functional configuration as any computer. The required functional blocks include an arithmetic logic unit (ALU) for processing instructions, an instruction decoder, register banks for temporary storage during arithmetic operation, and timing and control circuits such as clock oscillators, frequency dividers, and counters for sequencing (see Figure 1.5).

Memories are used to hold programs and any data that must be manipulated by the instructions. Programs are stored in the memory as a series of binary words, each word having from 4 to 16 bits, depending on the microprocessor used. Each word or series of words represents an instuction or data that the microprocessor will decode or act upon when that information is presented at the processor input.

The microprocessor communicates with the outside world via three paths—(1) the data bus, (2) the address bus, and (3) the control bus. The data bus is a group of parallel-line signals that permit bidirectional digital-data

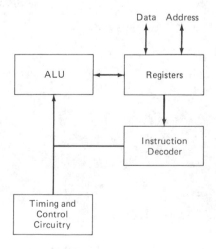

Fig. 1.5. Microprocessor components.

transfer. It may have 4, 8, 12, or 16 lines, depending on the microprocessor. Digital words transmitted over the data bus are either instructions for the processor, data to be manipulated, or the processed results of an operation.

A typical microprocessor like the 6800 has eight pins to which wires are attached for the movement of data into and out of the device. These eight wires constitute the data bus, and information can flow in both directions along the bus (during different times.) This technique is called "multiplexing."

In addition to the data bus the 6800 microprocessor also has a group of 16 pins, to which wires can be attached, that are used to move binary words called addresses; together they are called the "address bus." The address bus carries information outward only, from the microprocessor to memory and input/output chips. The signals on the address bus are used to select a certain part of memory or I/O section.

There is also a group of assorted control signals that enter and leave the microprocessor. Some of these may carry control signals back and forth between the microprocessor and the memory, and I/O chips. They are usually grouped together and called the "control bus." Other wires may go back and forth between the microprocessor and support chips. No connection is made directly to the registers, the ALU, or other internal components. Microprocessors have many of the features common to all computers. The characteristic that makes the microprocessor unique is that the CPU is contained in just a few integrated circuit packages. (A complete 6800 CPU board is shown in Figure 1.6.)

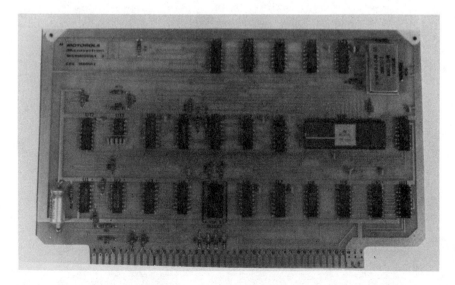

Fig. 1.6. This 6800 CPU board contains bus buffering and power reset circuits, clock circuitry, memory select logic, and timing and control for memory refresh operations. (*Courtesy Siltran Digital.*)

ARITHMETIC LOGIC UNITS

The arithmetic logic unit (ALU) can vary from a simple adder to a complex unit that can perform many arithmetic and logic functions. If the arithmetic logic unit cannot perform a function directly, several instructions may be necessary to produce the desired result.

Adders

The binary addition of all the combinations of two digits can be shown in a truth table. Only the 1 + 1 situation produces a carry. A two-input OR gate can accept these combinations as inputs and produce the correct sum as an output except when the 1 + 1 combination occurs. (See Figure 1.7.)

A circuit that will accept two inputs representing the augend and addend digits and produce output signals representing the sum and carry is known as a half-adder. The term half is employed since this adder circuit can only add together two variables at a time and does not consider the possible carry that might have occurred from the next lower bit. There are several ways of implementing the half-adder; two circuits are shown in Figure 1.8.

The correct addition of two numbers may be carried out by half-adders if several are connected together. For instance, the parallel addition of two third-order binary numbers is accomplished in Figure 1.9.

$$\text{Augend:} \quad X_3 = 1, X_2 = 1, X_1 = 1$$
$$\text{Addend:} \quad Y_3 = 1, Y_2 = 0, Y_1 = 1$$

Serial addition of two binary numbers may be accomplished using the circuit shown in Figure 1.10. The only additional element needed is a delay of one bit time to move any possible carry into the next higher bit time.

A full-adder circuit has three inputs and two outputs. The inputs are the addend, augend, and any possible carry from a preceding bit. The outputs are a sum and possible carry. Figure 1.11 shows a typical full-adder. Connecting full-adders together to form a parallel binary addition unit involves no extra circuitry and only one full-adder per bit. Figure 1.12 indicates the system of connecting full-adders in parallel for the addition of two 3-bit numbers. A full-adder can also be used for serial binary addition by using a one-bit delay to move the carry forward to the next bit time as shown in Figure 1.13.

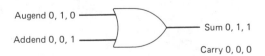

Fig. 1.7. Using the OR gate as an adder.

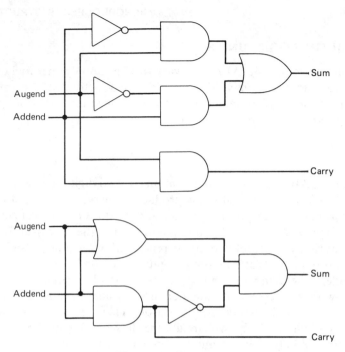

Fig. 1.8. Half-adders.

Addends and Augends

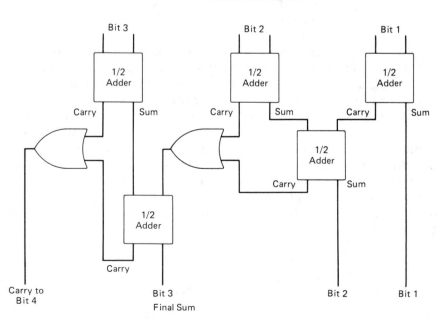

Fig. 1.9. Parallel addition with half-adders.

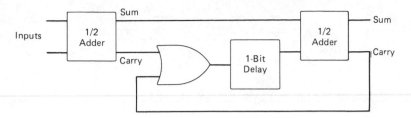

Fig. 1.10. Serial addition with half-adders.

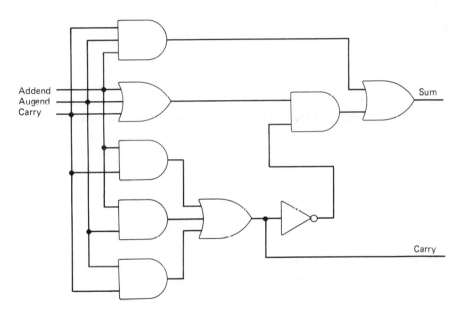

Fig. 1.11. Full-adder.

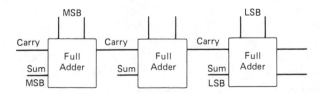

Fig. 1.12. Parallel adder using full-adders.

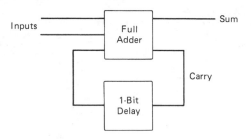

Fig. 1.13. Serial adder using a full-adder.

Subtraction

A subtracter circuit has a limited practical value since most computers subtract by the complementing and adding method using adder circuits. A more practical technique of subtraction is complementing, using full-adders.

It is more common to perform subtraction by complementing and adding since the adder circuits have already been mechanized for addition. The technique of performing subtraction by this method is to complement or invert the subtrahend before it enters the augend or addend inputs of the adder circuit. The parallel full-adder shown in Figure 1.11 may be used as a subtracter as shown in Figure 1.14.

These examples of designs for adders and subtracters indicate the basis for many arithmetic circuits in microprocessors for addition and subtraction. Other special circuits are used also, which are not included here. Note that an adder/subtracter circuit usually contains the necessary temporary storage registers to hold the individual operators and answer.

Often, the addend register serves as both an addend and answer store. It is then called the "accumulator register."

Multiplication

If speed is essential, then one can perform multiplication in one step. A "simultaneous" type multiplier for multiplying four bits in approximately one bit time would use seven full-adders and six half-adders. Most microprocessors use existing adder circuits in order to be hardware efficient.

There are several possible circuits for multiplication by repeated addition or by the shifting technique. Multiplication by repeated addition requires a counter. Figure 1.15 shows the technique used for repeated-addition multiplication. The value of the multiplicand is loaded into its register and the value of the multiplier is loaded into the multiplier counter. The multiplier counter is mechanized to start with an inserted count (the value of the multiplier) and then count down to zero. If 101 (5) is inserted, the counter will register 100 (4) at the next bit time, 011 (3) at the next bit time, and so on

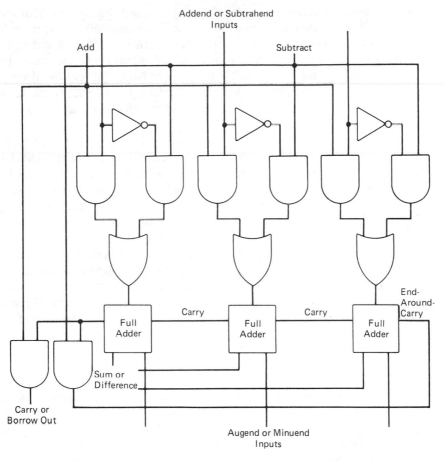

Fig. 1.14. Parallel adder and subtractor.

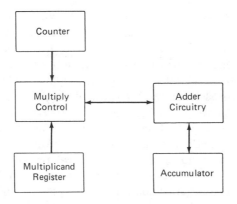

Fig. 1.15. Multiplication using repeated addition.

to zero. At zero, the multiply control switch is closed, halting the addition process. When the switch is open, the value in the multiplicand register is added to the existing value in the accumulator. The multiplicand and accumulator register outputs are the augend and addend inputs to the adder circuit. The accumulator always holds the answer from the last addition; it starts out with zero, and as the repeated addition continues, the accumulator increases. The accumulator needs to have as many flip-flops as the sum of the bits for both operators.

Repeated-addition multiplying is a time-consuming process for developing the products, but it is a simple method and requires only one extra device (the counter). This method produces answers as fast as they could ever be used by a human operator in a calculator application (about 150 to 1000 μs. for an average multiplication.) But the rest of the microprocessor circuits may need to use the products, and this time is too long for many real time applications.

The basic technique for multiplication by the "shifting method" requires additional control pulses (other than clock-pulses) that are developed in the control and timing section. The rule for multiplying by shifting indicates that for each step of the operation a "shift" occurs, whether an add takes place or not. This means that each step takes at least two bit times: one for adding or not adding and one for shifting.

Division

As with multiplication, a separate circuit can be used to do division. However, a simultaneous type of circuit for numbers of larger than 8–10 bits involves a large number of gates and subtracters. These circuits are used where speed is essential. But since division, like multiplication, can make use of existing adder/subtracter circuits, most microcomputers do not use straight dividing circuits.

Unlike the repeated-addition method of multiplication, where the value of the multiplier was loaded into a counter and counted down, the repeated-subtraction method of division loads the number of subtractions that take place into the counter. The counter then holds the answer.

The repeated-subtraction technique of division is shown in Figure 1.16. At the start, the dividend is loaded into the accumulator and the divisor into the divisor register. As each subtraction takes place, the value in the accumulator becomes smaller and smaller, finally reaching zero (or some remainder), and the value in the counter becomes larger and larger, finally yielding the correct quotient. The divider circuit does not stop when the accumulator reaches zero (or a remainder). The subtracter will try to continue subtracting beyond the point of zero remainder; when it does, the value in the accumulator becomes a negative quantity. The negative sign can be recognized

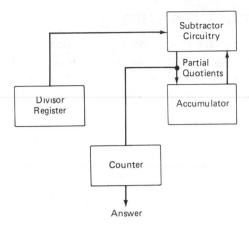

Fig. 1.16. Division using repeated subtraction.

with a "sign comparator." This stops the divide process and "adds-back" the overage.

The machine subtracts one step too far. When the negative value occurs, the machine adds-back the subtrahend and produces the correct positive remainder.

Often in dealing with large binary numbers, many of the arithmetic processes drop a few of the least significant bits in the answers. The final result may be in error but is usually more accurate than required.

Other circuits are used in microprocessors besides those described here.[1] Often a particular chip has control signals available from the "control and timing" section to regulate both the multiplication and division processes.

Circuits similar to those used to perform multiplication by "shifting-right" can also be employed in division, the only difference being the direction of the shift. The dividend is loaded into the accumulator and the divisor into another register, with an additional register provided to hold the quotient (See Fig. 1.17).

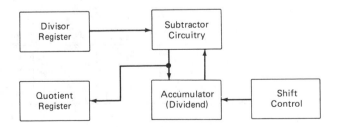

Fig. 1.17. Division using shifting.

MICROPROCESSOR REGISTERS

The idea of the register is important in microcomputers. A majority of operations inside the microcomputer are transfers of data from one register to another, sometimes between registers of different types; still these are just transfers of data. Memory can also be thought of as large groups of registers. Now that core memories have largely been replaced by chips, that is exactly what a memory is: a large group of registers.

Numbers are held inside the microcomputer in registers which are rows of flip-flop circuits, each with one output, that can be ON or OFF (see Figure 1.18).

A register can hold any number that has first been converted into a row of ON or OFF signals to represent a row of bits. There are several ways to represent a number as a row of bits, and we will consider this later.

Registers are connected to other registers, to other parts of the control section, and to external buses by means of internal buses. The registers and internal buses usually have the same word length as the rest of the computer system; but registers and internal buses with half or double the system word length are also used in some microprocessors. Signals generated by the instruction-handling section may place the contents of a register on a bus or the contents of a bus in the register.

The cost of registers and interconnections limits the number found in a microcomputer. Registers were once so costly that most systems used less than ten; the IBM 1130 and the DEC PDP–8 are examples with few registers. However, the rapid decrease in semiconductor chip prices and the increase of LSI technology, caused register costs to fall.

Newer computers may use dozens of registers. Chip sizes, though, have tended to keep the number of registers in microprocessors limited, but this is changing with the 16-bit chips that are now available.[2] When the CPU has a large number of registers, programs do not require as many transfers of data to and from the memory. This reduces the number of memory accesses and the size of the memory.

Figure 1.19 shows a typical set of registers in a microprocessor. Registers

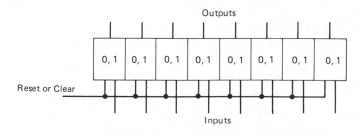

Fig. 1.18. The register as a series of flip-flop circuits.

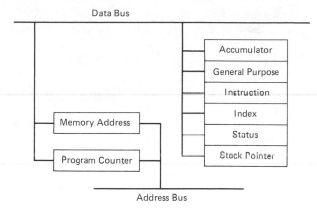

Fig. 1.19. Microprocessor registers.

have different purposes; some microprocessors allow the programmer to assign different functions to registers. Most registers, however, are permanently assigned.

Common uses for registers include:

- Program counter.
- Instruction holding.
- Accumulator.
- Index register.
- Condition code storage.
- Stack pointer.
- General purpose.

The Program Counter

The program counter (PC) holds the address of the memory location for the next instruction. An instruction cycle starts with the microprocessor placing the contents of the PC on the address bus, thereby fetching the first word of the instruction from the memory. Then the contents of the program counter are incremented so that the next instruction cycle will fetch the next instruction from memory. The microprocessor executes instructions sequentially unless an instruction (such as a JUMP or BRANCH) changes the program counter.

The program counter is of concern to the user since its contents can be changed, saved, or replaced by user instructions. This will cause the microprocessor to begin executing instructions in some part of the memory apart from where it had been executing; thus the user has control, using instructions, over what the processor will do next. Think of the contents of the program counter as a "pointer," or arrow, that points to a particular location in memory (see Figure 1.20).

In the 6800, the PC is a 16-bit register that holds the address of the instruction to be executed next. When it is time to "fetch" the next instruction from memory, whatever is in this register is presented to the memory, along with a command to read; an 8-bit "byte" from the memory, is then brought into the microprocessor. This byte is the instruction, or part of the instruction, since some instructions may require two or three bytes.

What happens in a microprocessor like the 6800 for a branch or jump instruction is this: instructions are directly in sequence in memory, so normally all the program counter has to do in order to step through the instructions is to keep incrementing itself by 1. When an instruction occupies more than one memory location, the program counter is directed to increment itself more than once for the instruction. The program counter in the 6800 is 16 bits long, so it can generate addresses for instructions for up to 65, 536 locations. When a branch or jump instruction occurs, the contents of the program counter are changed to a value that is carried along with the instruction (see Figure 1.21).

In a jump, this can be in any 16 bits of address, within the memory. In the 6800, a branch instruction is limited to eight bits, and this is not a general address; it is the distance—as a number of locations, forward or backward—that we wish to jump. This is the number that is to be added (algebraically) to the program counter.

The Instruction Register

An instruction register (IR) is used to hold the instruction until it can be decoded. The length of the instruction register is the same as the length of a

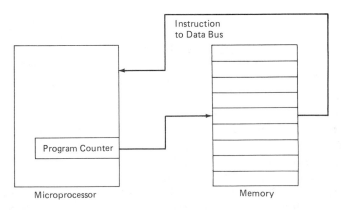

Fig. 1.20. The program counter acts as a pointer.

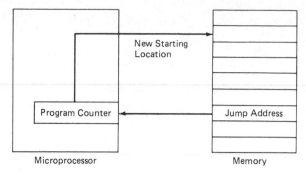

Fig. 1.21. Jump instructions change the program counter.

basic instruction for the microprocessor. Some devices use two instruction registers, and thus they can fetch and save one instruction while executing the previous one (this is called "pipelining"). The programmer can seldom access the instruction register in most microprocessors.

This instruction will "reside" in a read-only memory, or ROM, and it will be executed when the microprocessor reads it from the ROM, as part of a sequence of instructions (the program). If this particular instruction is eight bits—or one byte—long, then it occupies a single memory location in ROM. When it is read by the microprocessor, it becomes the signal for the microprocessor to go to a particular part of a smaller ROM that is part of the CPU chip and that contains "microinstructions" to control what is to be done (see Figure 1.22).

As instructions are read from the program memory of the microcomputer, the first part of the instruction, called the "opcode" or operation code (OP), is loaded into the instruction register, as illustrated in Figure 1.23.

The operation codes are addresses into the on-chip sequencer ROM that

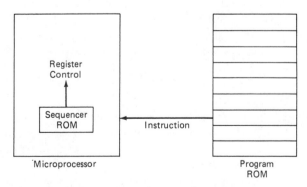

Fig. 1.22. Instruction to register control.

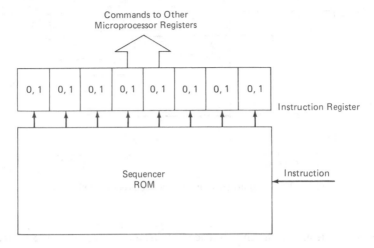

Fig. 1.23. Instruction register operation.

run the control lines for register clears, gate transfers, and other signals like telling the arithmetic unit when to shift.

The Accumulator

Accumulators are temporary storage registers for use during calculations. In most CPUs, the accumulator holds one of the operands in arithmetic operations. The CPU may also use the accumulator during logic operations, shifts, and other instructions. Accumulators are the most frequently used registers. Microprocessors like the 8080 that use single accumulator arithmetic programs tend to spend more time moving data to and from the accumulator. Other microprocessors such as the 6800 use several accumulators; consequently, programs do not need to move data around as much.

With only one accumulator, the program must save the first result and then recall it; with two accumulators, the program can perform the calculations separately. Each instruction in the two-accumulator machine must contain a code to identify which accumulator to use.

The Index Register

The index register is used to hold the addresses of important memory locations. This register can be incremented and loaded by various instructions. It functions as a pointer to direct the processor to an area of memory containing the necessary information.

A program can be simplified by having the index register act as a pointer to the memory locations. This manner of memory addressing is called indirect.

In its most general form, the pointer register is an internal register or any other memory location.

Such a revised program uses more memory space than if it used direct addressing. However, for long lists of numbers indirect addressing combined with an increment and compare loop shortens the number of instructions needed. But the instruction cycle for an indirect-address command is longer than for a direct-address instruction.

Another technique, used in more complex programs, is indexed addressing. Here, the correct data address is calculated by adding an offset value to a specified address. Usually, the offset is stored in the index register, and the specific address is obtained by direct or indirect addressing. As an example, if the index register contains 0005, and the instruction "Add (0A00) indexed" is used, the correct data address is obtained by adding the contents of the register to 0A00 to give the correct address, 0A05.

Some microprocessors have an indexed autoincrement indirect-addressing mode, where the correct address is obtained by adding the index register to the indirectly specified address; the register is then automatically incremented. Other processors manipulate the indirect address rather than an index register.

The Condition-Code Register

Condition-code or status registers hold 1-bit indicators (flags) that represent the state of conditions inside the CPU or the state of external conditions. The flags are the basis for computer decision-making. Some microprocessors use only one or two flags, while newer devices use several flags.

In some CPUs, flags may be changed or observed externally as serial input or output lines. Among the common flags used are the following:

CARRY. "1" if the last operation generated a carry from the most significant bit. The CARRY flag retains this information and handles the carry from one word to the next in multiple-precision arithmetic operations.

ZERO. "1" if the result of the last operation was zero. Useful in loop control or searching for a particular data value in a set.

OVERFLOW. "1" if the last operation resulted in an overflow. The distinction between carry and overflow is that the OVERFLOW bit shows if the result of an arithmetic operation has exceeded the capacity of a word or register.

SIGN. "1" if the most significant bit of the result of the last operation was 1 or negative, since "1" indicates a negative two's complement number. The SIGN bit is used in arithmetic and also in examining bits within a data word.

PARITY. "1" if the number of one bits in the result of the last operation was even or odd parity. PARITY is used in character manipulation for communications applications.

HALF-CARRY. "1" if the last operation generated a carry from the lower half-word. (Used in some 8-bit CPUs for BCD arithmetic.)

INTERRUPT ENABLE. "1" if an interrupt is allowed, "0" if not. The CPU can disable interrupts during startup or service routines. The programmer can disable interrupts during critical timing loops or multiword operations. The CPU can have as many interrupt enable flags as it has interrupt levels.

See Figure 1.24 for the structure of the condition codes register for the 6800.

The Stack-pointer Register

The stack-pointer register is a special register for keeping track of the next memory location available for a "stack."

We can explain a stack by analogy to a spring-loaded dish storage device like those used in restaurants: we place the dishes in one at a time, and their weight makes the stack of dishes sink into the well so that the last one in is the first one in position to come back out. This is the same way the computer stack works: as a word is written into the stack in the RAM, (using the stack pointer's contents as the address), the stack pointer is decremented to allow the next word to go into the next lower location or "above" it in the memory. Thus, the stack pointer keeps track of the next location into which a word should go in the stack as shown in Figure 1.25.

Stacks can be implemented two ways: (1) with a shift register, where a "push" corresponds to a shift in one direction and a "pop" corresponds to a shift in the other, or (2) with a RAM and the stack-pointer register.

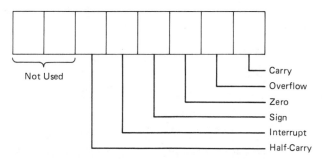

Fig. 1.24. 6800 condition codes register.

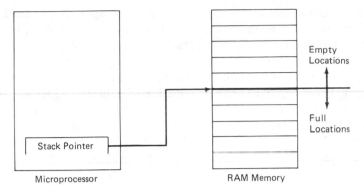

Fig. 1.25. Stack pointer operation.

Each time a subroutine call is made, the current contents of the program counter are stored in the stack. The loaded value is always placed on top of the stack and when a subroutine is completed, the top value from the stack is removed. Putting a word on the stack is often called a "push operation" and removing a word a "pop operation."

This saving may be done in a part of the RAM called the "stack." We can designate that part of the RAM for use as a stack, and the reading back from it is controlled with the addresses found in the stack-pointer register.

The shift-register approach is used where the stack is part of the processor chip; although faster than an off-chip register, it is restricted by the number of possible addresses it can hold. With the stack-pointer approach, the stack can grow to almost any size since external memory is used and more can be added if necessary.

Push and pop instructions can be powerful, particularly if they can operate on registers other than the program counter. In most cases, when the processor jumps to a subroutine, not only should the contents of the PC be stored, but also the contents of other registers. This is important if the processor is apt to be interrupted from its normal operation by a power drop or an interrupt signal from another device.

A major advantage of the stack is that we can add data to it (up to its capacity) without disturbing the data that is already there. If we store data in a memory location or register, we lose the previous contents of the storage place. So we can use the same memory location or register again if we save its contents somewhere else. We can use the stack over and over since its previous contents are automatically saved. The CPU can easily and quickly transfer data to or from the stack because the address is in the stack pointer and does not need to be part of the instruction. Thus, stack instructions can be short.

We use the last-in, first-out nature of the stack to our advantage to store subroutine return addresses. Each **JUMP TO SUBROUTINE** instruction moves a return address from the program counter to the stack. Each RETURN instruction fetches a return address from the stack and places it in the program counter. Then the program can retrace its path through the subroutines using the stack.

A disadvantage of stacks is the difficulty of debugging and documenting programs. Since the stack does not have a fixed address, its location and contents are difficult to remember. Lists of the current contents of the stack (called stack dumps) can be used as documentation. Errors in stack usage can be difficult to find; typical problems include removing items from the stack in the wrong order, placing extra items in the stack or removing extra items, and overflowing or underflowing the stack.

General-purpose Registers

General-purpose registers can have a variety of functions. Such registers serve as temporary storage for data or addresses. The programmer may be able to assign them as accumulator or even as program counters.

Another use for a general-purpose register is as a memory address register (MAR) to hold the addresses of data in memory. The addresses may be part of the instructions or may be provided by the program. Using a memory address register to increment the contents of a memory location is shown below:

Instruction 1—load memory address register with 300

MEMORY ADDRESS REGISTER = 300

Instruction 2—load accumulator from memory

ACCUMULATOR = 65   MEMORY LOCATION 300 = 65

The contents of memory location 300 are placed in the accumulator.

Instruction 3—add 1 to accumulator

ACCUMULATOR = 66

Instruction 4—store accumulator in memory

ACCUMULATOR = 66   MEMORY LOCATION 300 = 66

The contents of the accumulator are placed in memory location 300. Instructions 2 to 4 could be used to increment the contents of any memory location.

RANDOM-ACCESS MEMORIES (RAM)

The memory section of a microcomputer contains storage units, which usually consist of semiconductor cells. The storage units are binary, using two states to represent the values of zero or one. The memory is organized into "bytes," which are the shortest groupings of bits that the microcomputer can handle at one time, and "words," which have the same bit length as the microcomputer's data registers, data buses, and arithmetic unit. A byte usually consists of 8 bits, and a word may be from 4 to 16 bits in length. The memory is arranged sequentially into words, each one of which has its unique address. The address of a word in memory is not to be confused with memory contents. Memory location 0, for example, might contain any value. A memory word may represent a number, an instruction code, alphanumeric characters, or other binary coded information.

Memory Units

Communication between a memory unit and the microprocessor is achieved through control lines, address selection lines, and data input and output lines. The control signals specify the direction of transfer—whether a word is to be stored in a memory register (write) or whether a word previously stored is to be transferred out of a memory register (read.) The address lines specify the particular word chosen out of all the words available in that section. The input lines supply the information to be stored in the memory, while the output lines supply the information coming from the memory. A typical memory unit is shown in Figure 1.26.

A memory unit is specified by the number of words (M) it contains and the number of bits in each word (N) (as shown in Figure 1.25). The address selection lines select a particular word out of all the M words. Each word is

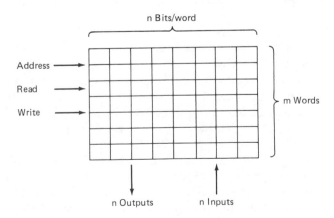

Fig. 1.26. A typical memory unit.

assigned an identification address, starting from 0 and continuing up to M-1. The selection of a specific word inside the memory is done by placing its address value on the selection lines or address bus. A decoder in the memory accepts this address and connects the paths required to select the word specified. Thus, K address bits will select one of 2^k = M words. Microprocessor memories may range from 1024 words, requiring an address of 10 bits, up to 1,048,576 ($= 2^{20}$) words or more, requiring an address of 20 bits.

(Let us refer to the number of words in a memory with the unit K. Where K refers to 1024 = 2^{10} words; then 1K = 1024 words, 4K = 4096 words and 64K = 65,536 words.)

Buses are uses to connect the microprocessor and memory. The address bus carries the address of the memory location and the read and write lines determine the direction of the transfer. Data buses carry the data between the units. Some buses may be physically the same; a single bus may carry data in different directions or carry data and addresses at different times. When a bus is used for more than one purpose it is said to be multiplexed. Additional control signals determine what is on the bus at a given time. Memories may contain either data or instructions, both of which are represented as binary numbers. A computer that uses the same format and memory for data and instructions is called a von Neumann machine after the mathematician.[3]

But how do we distinguish between an instruction or a piece of data? The answer is that the microprocessor will know what to expect at a particular time. If the program is in error, the microprocessor may interpret data as instructions.

Addressing

Let us now look at how we address the different devices external to the microprocessor: the memory and I/O chips that are the gateway to the outside world.

As we have said, all of these external devices are selected by the microprocessor by placing addresses on the address bus. In most 8-bit microprocessors, this bus consists of 16 bits, which are called A_0, A_1, A_2, and so on up to A_{15}—A_{15}, which is the most significant bit (MSB) of the address. The address can be thought of as a number that goes from 0 to 65,535; A_{15} is the left-most bit, with a weight of 32,768. A_0 is the least significant bit (LSB) with a weight of 1. The binary weights of the other bits fall between these extremes. When all the bits are a maximum, we get a total number of 65,535.

Binary numbers of 16 bits can be difficult to work with. It's also hard to think of the addresses in decimal form, because it takes an effort to convert between the decimal number and the pattern of 16 bits. It is usually necessary to work with the bit patterns in microcomputers, especially when designing your own mix of peripherals—all with peculiar addresses for the application. To wire up the address lines and debug the system, you usually have to be able to work comfortably with 16-bit addresses.

One technique that is used is to put the addresses in hexadecimal (or hex) form with a base of 16. The 16 bits are broken up into four groups of four bits each; then, a code of one letter or number is used to represent each group (as shown in Figure 1.27). An address that is 16 bits long can be given as four of these codes: for example FA34 or 05DC. These codes are easier to work with and remember. It is also easy to convert back and forth from the bit patterns.

To do such a conversion, try to visualize certain things in the conversion chart of the bit patterns and the letter/number codes as shown in Figure 1.28. Note that the first 4-bit patterns begin with 00; the next four with 01;

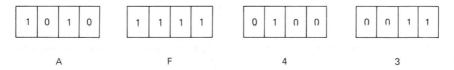

| 1 | 0 | 1 | 0 | | 1 | 1 | 1 | 1 | | 0 | 1 | 0 | 0 | | 0 | 0 | 1 | 1 |

A   F   4   3

Fig. 1.27. Hexadecimal representation for a 16-Bit address.

0	0	0	0	0
0	0	0	1	1
0	0	1	0	2
0	0	1	1	3
0	1	0	0	4
0	1	0	1	5
0	1	1	0	6
0	1	1	1	7
1	0	0	0	8
1	0	0	1	9
1	0	1	0	A
1	0	1	1	B
1	1	0	0	C
1	1	0	1	D
1	1	1	0	E
1	1	1	1	F

Fig. 1.28. Hexadecimal conversion.

the next four with 10 and the last four with 11. This is the sequence for a 2-bit binary number: 00, 01, 10, 11. Also notice that the groups of four (going down the table) start with 0, 4, 8, and C. Then the last two bits of each pattern go through the same sequence—00, 01, 10, 11—as you go through the set 4, 5, 6, 7. Next, look at the first two bits to get the starting point: 0, 4, 8, or C. Then use the last two bits to sequence from there. So 1011 is in the group that starts with 8, and it is the last one in that group, so it is *11*.

Starting with the letter/number code, first note the group, then write the first two bits; note where it is in the group, then write the last two bits.

Now we can easily convert from an address like "23FF" to its binary equivalent, 0010 0011 1111 1110 using hex codes.

Access Time

In a memory system, access time is the time difference between the time when a memory unit receives a read signal and the time when the information read from memory is available at its outputs. In a destructive read memory (such as magnetic core), information read out is destroyed during the reading process. However, it is automatically restored, but this requires an additional period of time. The sum of the access time and the restoration time is called the cycle time. In a nondestructive read memory, the cycle time is the same as the access time since no restoration is required. In a random-access memory, the access time is always the same regardless of the word's location in memory. In a sequential memory, the access time depends on the position of the word at the time of the request. If the word is just emerging from storage at the time that it is requested, the access time is the time necessary to read it. If the word happens to be in another position, the access time also includes the time required for all the other words to move through the output terminals. Thus, access time in a sequential memory is variable, and an average access time is used to specify the speed of reading data.

The mode of access of a memory unit is governed by the type of components used. In a random-access memory, the memory registers are thought of as being separated in space, with each register occupying one particular location. In a sequential-access memory, the information stored in some medium is not immediately accessible but is available only during certain intervals of time as in a shift-register memory.

Shift-registers for use as serial memories are available in SSI packages. The contents are recirculated via feedback loop from the output to the input. An M words by N bits sequential access memory is obtained from N shift-registers in synchronization, with each shift-register representing one bit of the word. The length of the shift-register will determine the number of words in the memory. Recirculating shift-register memories derive their address from a counter which determines the word emerging from the output terminals. Each word passes the output terminals, and the information is read out when the requested word is available at the output terminals.

Memory units which lose stored information with time or when the power is turned off are "volatile." IC memories are volatile because their cells require power to maintain the stored information. In contrast, a nonvolatile memory unit such as magnetic core or disk retains its stored information after power is removed. This is so because the stored information is determined by the direction of magnetization, which is retained when power is off. Microcomputers with volatile memories may use backup batteries or power supplies that continue to deliver power for some time after a power interruption occurs.

Semiconductor RAMS

A semiconductor memory is a collection of storage registers, together with circuits to transfer information in and out of the registers. When the memory can be accessed for information as required, it is a random-access memory, or RAM. Integrated circuit RAMs sometimes use a single line for the read/write control. One binary state specifies the read operation and the other state specifies the write operation. Enable lines are included in the IC to provide a means for expanding a number of packages into a memory with a larger capacity.

In a random-access memory, addresses are sent in as shown in Figure 1.29. An address enables a specific location on each data plane of the memory, allowing data to be written in or read out, depending on the state of the read and write enable lines.

The construction of a semiconductor RAM of M words with N bits per word consists of a $M \times N$ binary cell matrix along with the logic required to

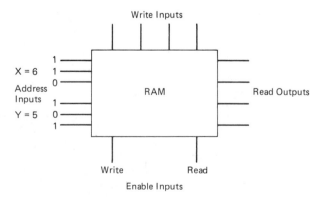

Fig. 1.29. RAM structure.

select a word for a write or read operation. The binary cell is the basic building block of a memory unit. The logic diagram of a typical binary cell for one bit of information is shown in Figure 1.30. The cell includes five gates and a flip-flop. Internally it is a 2-transistor flip-flop with multiple inputs. The cell of a memory unit is made small in order to pack as many cells as possible in the area available on the chip. The cell has three input lines and one output. The select input is used to select one cell out of all those available. With the select line true, a 1 at the read/write terminal allows a path from the output of the flip-flop to the read output. When the read/write terminal is 0, a bit at the input is transferred into the flip-flop. The input and output are disabled when the select line is false.

Note that the flip-flop operates without a clock pulse.

The circuit for a 4 × 3 RAM is shown in Figure 1.31. It has four words of three bits each for a total of 12 storage cells. Each cell contains the circuit of a binary cell similar to Figure 1.29. The address lines use a 2 × 4 decoder with a memory enable input.

When the memory enable is 0, all the outputs of the decoder are false and none of the words is selected. When the memory enable input is true, one of the four words is selected, depending on the bit combination of the two address lines. With the read/write at 1, (read) the bits of the selected word go through the OR gates to the output. The nonselected cells produce 0's at the inputs of the OR gate and thus have no effect on the outputs. When the

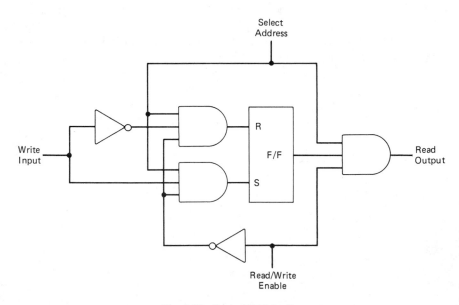

Fig. 1.30. Typical RAM cell.

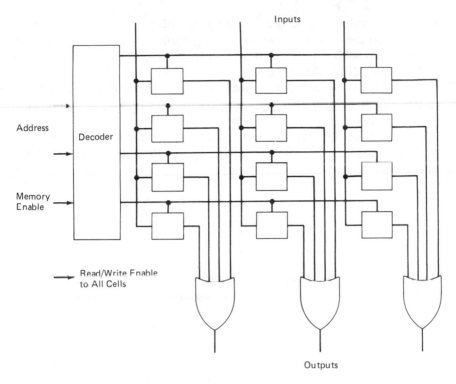

Fig. 1.31. 12-Word RAM

read/write control is 0, the data at the input lines is transferred into the flip-flops of the selected word. The nonselected cells in the other words are are disabled by their address selection line, so their previous values remain unchanged. When the memory enable is 1, the read/write line initiates the required read and write operations. An inhibited operation is obtained when the memory enable is 0. This condition leaves the contents of all words in memory as they were, regardless of the read/write control input. RAMs sometimes use cells with outputs that can be tied to form a wired-OR or a wired-AND function. Other RAMs may provide tristate outputs. These outputs are useful when a high impedance path is desired for isolation from the other integrated circuits in the microcomputer system.

READ-ONLY MEMORIES (ROM)

The read-only memory (ROM) is a memory unit that performs the read operation only; it does not have a write capability. This means that the binary information stored in the ROM is made permanent and cannot be altered by writing different words into it. A RAM is a general-purpose device with contents that can be altered during the computational process, but a ROM is restricted to reading words that are permanently stored in the device.

An M by N ROM is an array of cells organized into M words of N bits each as shown in Figure 1.32. A ROM has K address lines to select one of $2^k = M$ words of memory and N output lines, one for each bit of the word. An IC ROM can also contain one or more enable lines for expanding a number of IC packages into a larger capacity memory.

The ROM does not use a read-control line since at any given time, the output lines always provide the 1's or 0's selected by the address. Since the outputs are a function of only the present inputs (address lines) the ROM is classified as a combinational circuit. The ROM is constructed from decoders and a set of OR gates. The era of LSI has opened up many new horizons for ROMs. The LSI circuit allows extremely low cost digital elements. This is particularly true when the chip is in the form of arrays, such as random access or read-only memories. These arrays have a large number of functions per connection, which is the main driving force for LSI.

Semiconductor read-only memories are well-suited to the LSI manufacturing process and have received a great deal of attention in recent years due to the versatility of applications in which they can be used.

The coupling units commonly used between the input and output lines of the ROM are diodes and bipolar and metal oxide semiconductor (MOS) transistors. The presence or absence of an element at each of the intersections of the matrix determines the type of memory logic. Practically any active or passive electrical component can serve as a coupling element. Each of these, however, is subject to a number of tradeoffs with respect to cost, speed, reliability, and commercial availability. (The various criteria which affect the application of semiconductor ROMs, together with other types of memory, are discussed in Chapter 2.)

Since 1951, read-only memories have been widely used in data processing equipment to store data that seldom or never needs to be changed. One of the earliest uses was in the ENIAC computer to store multiplication tables.[5] Resistor matrices were used in the ENIAC.

Semiconductor ROMs are characterized by small volume, low cost, and nonvolatility. Like a RAM, the ROM can be addressed in a fixed time interval, regardless of location. Figure 1.33 shows a simplified arrangement of

Fig. 1.32. ROM structure.

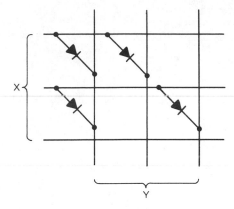

Fig. 1.33. Diode ROM.

ROM elements. The circuitry is much less complex than read/write memories and is ideally suited to MOS or bipolar manufacturing processes. Data storage is indicated by the presence or absence of a diode at the intersection point of the X and Y lines. Thus, any crosspoint may be identified as a "0" or "1" by making the X line positive and the Y line negative. A diode at the crosspoint will conduct, thus providing the readout. Both discrete or monolithic diode arrays can be used in ROMs. To program MOS arrays, the manufacturer uses a custom mask operation (with the mask being computer generated) to produce the required pattern of stored bits. ROM manufacturers provide forms on which users state the required contents. The data on these forms is translated to a computer program for automatic mask programming. There is also a variety of specialized ROMs for use in recurring applications. A block diagram of the organization of a typical ROM is shown in Figure 1.34.

PROGRAMMABLE READ-ONLY MEMORIES (PROM)

The extensive use of different programming techniques in the digital control and data processing fields creates the need for versatile read-only memories. Many kinds of ROMs have been proposed and a number of these have been put to practical use, and as they are used in various fields, the ROMs must usually be programmed to suit individual applications. If programming is carried out as a part of the manufacturing process, a special mask is required, yet this cost is justified only for large production requirements.

ROMs can be divided into two categories: (1) mask-programmed, (ROMs) and (2) field-programmed (PROMs). In either case, the data—usually on forms similar to a truth tables—is entered into the array. For masked programmed devices, the truth tables, on tapes or punched cards, are submitted

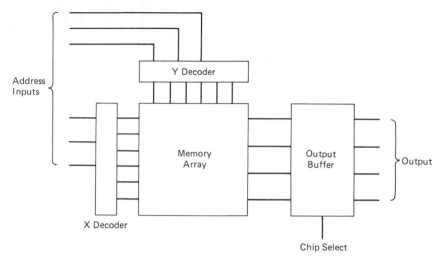

Fig. 1.34. ROM organization.

to the IC manufacturer, who uses them to prepare at least one of the photo-masks used for processing the IC wafers, and also to prepare the test program for testing the wafer. The presence or absence of the connections is established during the metallization process. Using computer-aided mask-making techniques, design costs and turnaround can be minimized, but the overall costs become large. In addition, it is not always possible to completely specify the memory configuration in the early design phases of the microprocessor system. Because of these limitations for mask-programmable ROMs, many designers have turned their attention to programmable ROMs (PROMs) in which the information pattern is recorded by the application of an electrical signal. The electrically programmable ROMs can be divided in two catagories: (1) ROMs in which a permanent change in the memory interconnection pattern is effected by an electrical pulse, and (2) reprogrammable ROMs in which a reversible change in active memory-device characteristics can be induced electrically. The PROM is preferred when a system design is tentative or where memory variability is a requirement. These field-programmable ROMs allow the user to enter data into devices as desired. This type of memory chip may be electrically programmable or electrically reprogrammable as shown in Figure 1.35. Field-programmable ROMs were initially of the fusible type.[6] Programming was accomplished by fusible links; connections represented by these links were opened for corresponding 1's or 0's by direct current in the appropriate circuit segments.

The disadvantage of the fusible-link system is that such memory chips cannot be reprogrammed. However, even though fusible-link programmable ROMs are more expensive, they do not require a special mask and are convenient for moderate quantity applications.

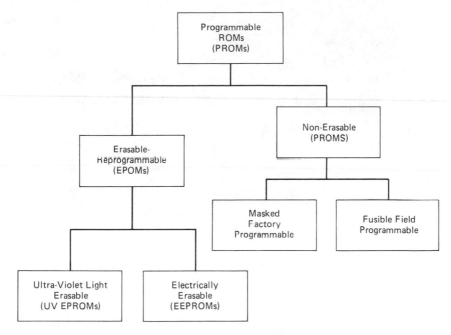

Fig. 1.35. Types of PROMs.

The other type of PROMs, known as electrically or erasable PROMs, are widely used and eliminate the disadvantages of the fusible PROMs. The reprogrammable feature permits the later correction of errors made during the write operation. These are basically charge storage devices which rely on the storage in a dielectric that is part of an insulated-gate field-effect transistor structure. The charge is removed by the application of ultraviolet light or an electrical pulse. The ultraviolet light devices require access to the lids of the devices, while the electrically erasable types only require electrical connections. (We consider the details of these devices in Chapter 2.)

A microprocessor system board for ROM or PROM memory components is shown in Figure 1.36.

MAGNETIC BUBBLE MEMORIES

In recent years, new techniques have been developed for microprocessor memory applications. Notable among these are, large scale integration using semiconductors and the magnetic bubble devices. Magnetic bubble memories (MBMs) have the capabilities of high bit density and large capacity per chip, and they may be also less expensive. Based on a solid state technology, they eliminate the mechanical motion associated with the present disk and tape systems. Long-term nonvolatility of the stored information is provided

Fig. 1.36. This 64K-byte memory board may use ROMs or PROMs. It has switch selectable address boundaries for assignment within a one megabyte address space. (*Courtesy Intel Corporation.*)

more easily than with most other semiconductor memories. The ability to store, transmit, and process information in the same medium reduces the problems of interconnections and signal conversion.

Bubble technology has reached the point where it may be destined to play a leading role in the future of computers.[7] The generation, propagation, and sensing of magnetic bubbles all involve action of the bubble domain with its magnetic environment.

Magnetic bubble memories are made by growing a thin layer of crystalline material which exhibits anisotropic (assuming different positions in response to external stimuli) properties on a nonmagnetic substrate. The magnetic domains in this anisotropic material tend to orient themselves in fields perpendicular to the surface of the material. When an external magnetic field is applied perpendicular to the crystalline layer, the magnetic domains position themselves in the same direction as the applied field. If any domains of the opposite polarity of this field exist in the material, they will form small cylindrical bubbles (see Figure 1.37). The stronger the applied field, the smaller the bubble. At a certain increasing field strength, these reversed domains vanish. A decreasing applied field allows them to increase in diameter until they have serpentine shapes. The applied perpendicular field is produced by permanent magnets on top of and below the bubble chip (see Figure 1.38).

The bubbles are mobile and travel across the memory by magnetic pole attraction. Short strips of permalloy on the surface, isolated from the bubble medium by a layer of silicon dioxide, are used to control bubble positioning. Applying the magnetic field in parallel with the device surface induces magnetic poles in these permalloy elements. Bubbles are then attracted by

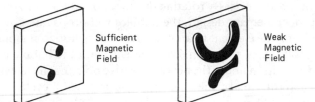

Sufficient
Magnetic
Field

Weak
Magnetic
Field

Fig. 1.37. Magnetic bubbles.

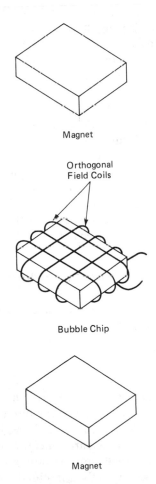

Magnet

Orthogonal
Field Coils

Bubble Chip

Magnet

Fig. 1.38. Magnetic bubble memory structure.

the poles of the magnets. By rotating the direction of the horizontal field and with the proper element design, the bubbles will propagate down a predictable path from one element to another. A rotating horizontal magnetic field varies the polarity of the permalloy element, with the bubble continuously moving to a position under the nearest positive pole. Each element is called a cell, and each rotation of the magnetic field is called a cycle.

Data is indicated by the presence or absence of a bubble in a cell, and data is propagated through the MBM like a shift register. Reading data requires detecting the presence of bubbles under the permalloy elements. A resistor bridge network compares the resistance of a detector permalloy element with that of a dummy element containing no bubble. Wrapping the MBM with two orthogonal coils and driving an ac current into each one 90° out-of-phase creates the in-plane rotating field. The field serves only for propagating bubbles, and normal operation would enable removing it when not required. However, without a horizontal component, the bubbles will tend to drift. To prevent this, the die in the package can be tilted 4 to 5° in order to create a constant horizontal component.

The electrical interface to the MBM is created through current loop functions. At specific points within a bubble track, conductors are deposited under the permalloy element in the form of single loops. Passing a pulse of current alters temporarily the level of the bias field under the permalloy element. The direction and the extent of the localized field, the direction of the horizontal field during the pulse, and the design of the permalloy element all determine how this pulse of current will affect the bubbles.

The essential current loop functions are as follows:

1. *Generate.* This inverts the bias field to allow the creation of a new bubble.
2. *Annihilate.* This intensifies the field and causes any bubble under the permalloy element to collapse.
3. *Transfer.* This moves bubbles residing on one track to an element in an adjoining track.

Compared to other architectures, single loop memories (see Figure 1.39) are simple to operate, since they require the minimum number of current loop functions and have a higher data access time. However, a single defective location in the loop makes the entire memory inoperative.

Dividing the memory into smaller minor loops gives an improved architecture. The added I/O tracks give only a minimal increase in the number of current loops (as shown in Figure 1.40). In this configuration, you read or write data in blocks or pages, where a block of data equals the number of minor loops. The block addresses refer to the location of one bit of data on any minor loop.

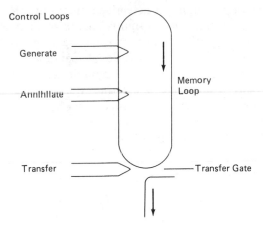

Fig. 1.39. Single-loop bubble memory architecture.

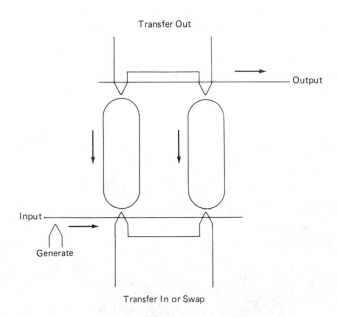

Fig. 1.40. Multiple-loop bubble memory architecture.

We can further enhance the efficiency of this configuration by removing the requirement to clear a block via the transfer-out function. The normal transfer-in function accumulates data onto the minor loops; a modified transfer gate function can use a swap function to interchange bubbles from one track to another. Any bubbles swapped into the input track would shift to the end where they generally collapse.

In a multiple-loop memory, a defective element in a minor loop affects only the operability of that loop. A significant increase in yield is obtained by discarding a number of minor loops in the testing process while still qualifying the device as a completely operational memory. A fixed percentage (5–10%) of the memory will always be unusable. Each memory device may have a unique loop error map that defines the unusable loops. The programmed memory controller will bypass those loops when reading data out of or writing data into the device. (A bubble memory board with automatic error correction is shown in Figure 1.41.)

MICROPROCESSOR OPERATION

We will now examine the operation of a typical microprocessor in detail by following the flow of information between the CPU and other devices during a typical instruction sequence. The structure of a typical microprocessor system (based on the PPS-4)[8] is shown in Figure 1.42. The microprocessor contains the ALU, an accumulator, program counter, instruction counter, a set of registers, and a number of driver/receiver circuits.

The section of the microprocessor that controls the sequence of instructions is the program counter (PC) and may also be called the program address register, memory address register, or program register in other microprocessors. The program counter is set to zero by a power-on reset line when

Fig. 1.41. A bubble memory board for 512K bytes of storage. Average access time is 48 ms. Power consumption is 32 watts. (*Courtesy Intel Corporation.*)

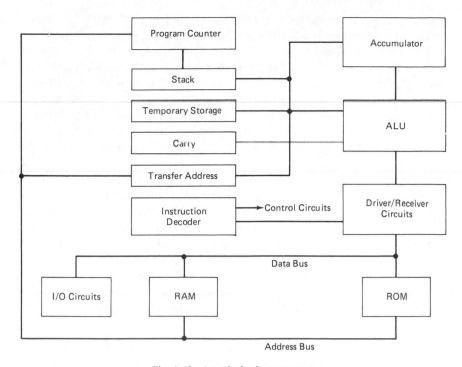

Fig. 1.42. A typical microprocessor.

power is turned on. The PC always contains the address of the next instruction.

The stack pointer holds instruction addresses during subroutine branching operations. The stack allows a multilevel nesting capability for storing the return program subroutine addresses; it contains three segments which are sequentially shifted to, and reloaded from, the accumulator for stacking of subroutine branches or auxiliary storage.

Arithmetic and logic functions are performed and processed in the section of the microprocessor that contains the accumulator register, the ALU, and the carry register. The accumulator is the primary working register for the microprocessor and the results of all arithmetic and logical functions are transferred here. The accumulator, ALU, and carry register provide a 4-bit parallel adder with carry-in and carry-out capabilities for words which are multiples of four bits.

Other registers include a register for the storage of data addresses and a register for temporary storage. The accumulator provides data for directly modifying sections of the data address register and an indirect path for modifying this register through the temporary register. Control flip-flops are used as status indicators, and they can be set, reset, and tested by the programmer. The carry register may also be independently set, reset, and tested, in addition to being used for arithmetic operations.

The microprocessor direct input/output capability using discrete input bits and discrete output bits. Inputs are loaded in groups of four bits into the accumulator, and an output buffer is loaded directly from the accumulator. The drivers and receivers provide an interface protecting the microprocessor, while at the same time they supply drive to power additional devices.

Figure 1.43 shows how the address defined by the program counter is supplied to the address bus to the program memory (ROM). This path is shown by the shaded lines. In a multiple-ROM system, the chip-select lines to each of the program memory of ROMs are coded so that only the ROM with the proper code will respond to the address from the program counter.

From the ROM, the instruction is supplied to the microprocessor (as shown by the shaded paths in Figure 1.44). A part of the instruction (the operation code) goes through the receivers directly to receivers which can also be supplied by data from the arithmetic section. The instruction is then decoded, and the microprocessor begins the execution process.

If the decoded instruction is not an input/output instruction, a signal is sent from the instruction decoder to indicate that data memory and not I/O

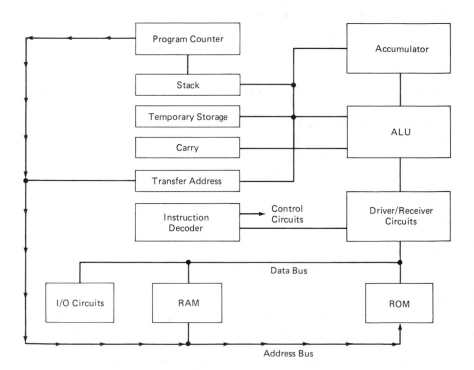

Fig. 1.43. Microprocessor ROM address selection.

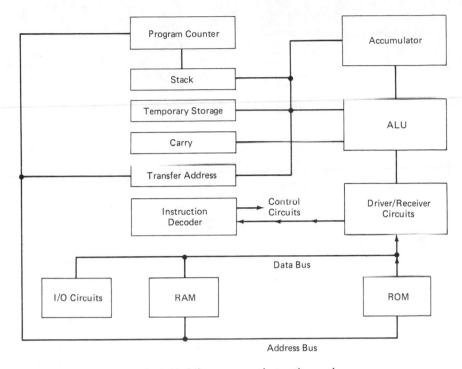

Fig. 1.44. Microprocessor instruction read.

has been selected. This path is shown in Figure 1.45. Also, during this time period, the transfer address register provides a data address to the address bus, which is the primary information flow path in Figure 1.45.

The data address is interpreted in a similar way as the instruction address was interpreted. The address is presented to all of the chips in a multiple-chip system and only the data memory circuit with the correct chip select code will respond. The proper coding is accomplished by wiring or logic switching of the chip-select lines.

The ROMs in this system can also be used for storing data that may be used throughout the program. If a ROM is used for data memory, it should not also be used for instruction memory, since it must be programmed to respond during data memory time and not program memory time. If the instruction to be decoded requires the contents of the accumulator to be written into memory, internal logic is used to allow the memory to write. During the correct time period, the selected memory cell will read out its contents and allow the new data to be written in. The RAM circuits will read the contents of the addressed data cell out on the data bus. After the RAM is enabled by a write signal, it will then write the information into memory obtained from the data bus. (This sequence is shown in Figure 1.46.)

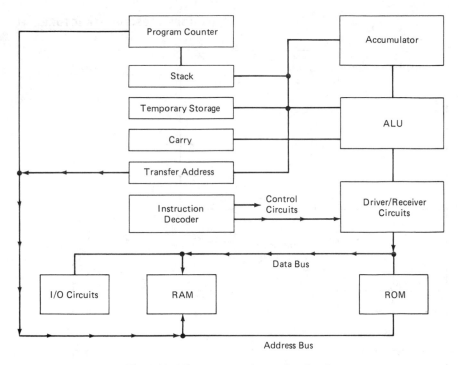

Fig. 1.45. Microprocessor instruction decode.

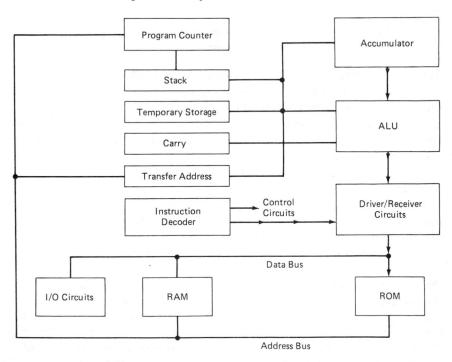

Fig. 1.46. Microprocessor accumulator write.

The program-counter register is either advanced by one count at this point or modified by the instruction being executed so that the cycle may be repeated in order to execute the next instruction. In actual microprocessor operation, the steps discussed so far tend to overlap. For example, the execution of instructions may be improved by allowing the address bus to address the next instruction while the data bus is being used for data transfer. (This is shown in Figure 1.47.)

During the next bus cycle, the address bus identifies the data location at the same time that the data bus transmits the next instruction as shown in Figure 1.48. The CPU uses a 4-phase clock cycle, and the events shown in Figure 1.46 occur during phase 2, while the events in Figure 1.47 events take place during phase 4. Phases 1 and 3 set all busses to the zero state while the internal processing required to complete the operations for instruction execution is performed.[9]

The timing cycle for the microprocessor is generated from a pair of signals which are obtained from a clock generator circuit that uses a quartz crystal as a frequency source. Two timing signals are used to generate the phases as shown in Figure 1.49. By outlining the two instruction periods of influence, we see that the instructions are overlapped in order to make better use of the bus system.

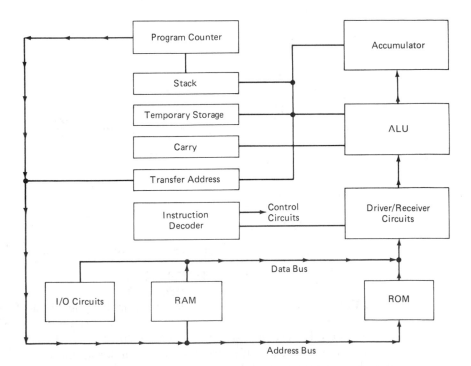

Fig. 1.47. Microprocessor accumulator read and ROM address selection.

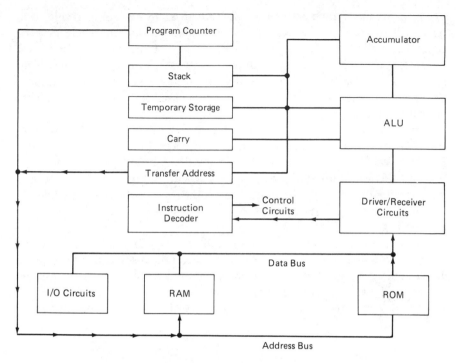

Fig. 1.48. Microprocessor RAM address selection and instruction read.

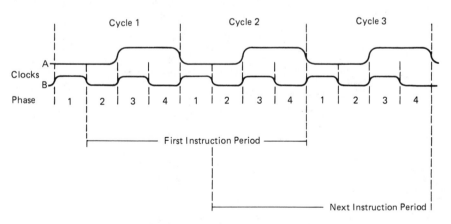

Fig. 1.49. Typical microprocessor timing.

A new instruction is obtained every clock cycle, and a single-cycle instruction is completed every clock cycle. The actual time to complete an instruction is dependent upon the specific instruction being executed. Even though there may be variations in the actual instruction times, these variations are transparent to the programmer and the system user.

INSTRUCTION OPERATIONS

We have examined how a typical microprocessor processes an instruction, along with some of the timing considerations involved. We will now examine how the instructions are used to provide the solutions to the processing tasks using the same PPS-4 microprocessor. Instructions and programming techniques used in microprocessor systems fall into seven basic functional groups. They are as follows:

1. *Data Transfers.* These are the methods of moving data from one point to another or organizing it for processing.
2. *Arithmetic Operations.* These may include binary or binary-coded decimal, or decimal manipulations.
3. *Logical Operations.* These include the methods for manipulating data as bits and the methods for obtaining logical functions of these bit combinations.
4. *Data Address Modifications.* These are the methods of modifying addresses in registers in order to facilitate data manipulation.
5. *Control Transfers.* These are the techniques such as interrupts for modifying the normal sequence of the program for conditional and unconditional branching.
6. *Register Manipulations.* These are the methods for storing data along with the manipulation of registers and individual segments of data within registers.
7. *Input/Output Operations.* These are the methods of using input/output instructions.

Subroutine usage—including the techniques for calling routines setting up data addresses, returning from subroutines, and the nesting of subroutines—may be used in conjunction with other operations.

Data Transfer

Typical data transfer instructions are shown below.[10]

MNEMONIC	DATA BUS OPCODE HEX AND BINARY	NAME	DESCRIPTION
LD	30–37 0011 0———	Load accumulator from memory (1 cycle)	The 4-bit contents of RAM currently addressed by the transfer register are placed in the accumulator. The RAM address in this register is then modified by the result of an EXCLUSIVE OR of the 3-bit immediate field 1 and the register contents.

(continued)

MNEMONIC	DATA BUS OPCODE HEX AND BINARY	NAME	DESCRIPTION
EX	38–3F 1100 1———	Exchange an accumulator and memory (1 cycle)	Same as LD except that the contents of the accumulator are also placed in the currently addressed RAM location.
EXD	28–2F 0010 1———	Exchange Accumulator and memory and decrement the transfer register (1 cycle)	Same as EX except RAM address in the transfer register is further modified by decrementing this register by 1. If the new contents are 1111, the next ROM word will be ignored.
LDI	70–7F 0111————	Load accumulator immediate (1 cycle)	The 4-bit contents (immediate field) of the instruction are placed in accumulator.

The first three instructions can be used to modify the transfer address register for the next instruction if desired by the programmer. To replace the contents of an address in RAM we could use the LD instruction followed by an EXD instruction, and to exchange the contents of two addresses in RAM we would use an LD instruction followed by EX and EXD instructions.

Arithmetic Instructions

Basic arithmetic operations are performed using the following instructions.[11]

MNEMONIC	DATA BUS OPCODE HEX AND BINARY	NAME	DESCRIPTION
AD	OB 0000 1011	Add	The result of binary addition of contents of accumulator and 4-bit contents of the RAM currently addressed by transfer register; replaces the contents of the accumulator. The resulting carry-out is loaded in the carry flip-flop.
ADC	OA 0000 1010	Add with carry-in	Same as AD except the carry flip-flop serves as a carry-in to the adder.
ADSK	09 0000 1001	Add and skip on carry-out	Same as AD except the next ROM word will be skipped (ignored) if a carry-out is generated.
ADCSK	08 0000 1000	Add with carry-in and skip on carry-out	Same as ADSK except the carry flip-flop serves as a carry-in to the adder.

MNEMONIC	DATA BUS OPCODE HEX AND BINARY	NAME	DESCRIPTION
ADI	60–6E 0110xxxx	Add immediate answer; skip on carry-out	The result of binary addition of contents of accumulator and a-bit immediate field of instruction word replaces the contents of accumulator. The next ROM word will be skipped (ignored) if a carry-out is generated. This instruction does not use or change the carry flip-flop. The immediate field 1 of this instruction may not be equal to binary 0000 or 1010.
DC	65 0110 0101	Decimal correction	Binary 1010 is added to contents of accumulator. Result is stored in accumulator. Instruction does not use or change carry flip-flop nor does it skip.

The add and the add with carry-in instructions are the most conventional arithmetic instructions found in microprocessors. The Add instruction can be used to initialize the adding operation for the first four bits of a number to be added, and it also may be used for additions that do not extend beyond four bits, which is the basic word length for the PPS–4 microprocessor. Any carry that may have existed from a prior operation is ignored, and the contents of the accumulator and the addressed memory cell are added to produce a 4-bit sum, with the carry bit set or reset as required. The Add with carry-in instruction is used to add successive groups of four bits using the carry from the previous four bits as an input to the Add operations. The prior carry and the contents of the addressed memory cell, along with the contents of the accumulator, are added together to form a new 4-bit sum with a new carry bit. The Add with carry-in instruction is used for a complete binary addition with the carry flip-flop set to zero before the first addition in the sequence. The ADSK and ADCSK are the primary arithmetic instructions for decimal arithmetic. The sum from adding two 4-bit numbers using these instructions is a binary 4-bit number with or without a carry depending on the digits used. If a carry is produced, these instructions cause the next instruction to be ignored and skipped. The ADI instruction adds a fixed constant to the accumulator. Addition of a constant 6 will convert binary arithmetic operations to decimal arithmetic. The ADI instruction can also be used to set up tests on the magnitude of the accumulator. For example, if ADI 5 is executed and no carry is produced, then the original number in the accumulator must have 6 or less.

The Decimal Correction instruction is a special version of the ADI instruction that causes 1010 to be added in all decimal addition and subtraction processes. It differs from the ADI instruction by allowing no skips to occur. This instruction can be used to correct the 4-bit sum in the accumulator to the binary-coded-decimal form as shown below in the following examples:

Example 1	4 + 5 = 9			
Decimal Addition	0 = Carry In		RC	: Reset Carry
4	0100 = 4		LD 4	: Load Accumulator
	110 = 6		ADI 6	: Add corrective 6
	1010			
+ 5	101		ADCSK: Add	
	11111 = 15			: No Carry, No Skip
	1010		DC	: Add + 10 Decimal Correction
9	1001			: Decimal 9 with Carry Ignore

Example 2	7 + 6 = 13			
Decimal Addition	0 = Carry In		RC	: Reset Carry
7	0111 = 7		LD 7	: Load Accumulator
	110 = 6		ADI 6	: Add Corrective 6
	1101			
+ 6	110		AD 6	: Add 6
13	1 0011			: Decimal 3 with a Carry = 13

Decimal subtraction can be performed in a similar fashion when a carry flip-flop is initially set to 1. The subtrahend is loaded into the accumulator and complemented and then the minuend is added using the ADCSK instruction to obtain a trial result. If a carry is produced, the trial result is the correct answer, but if no carry is produced, then a decimal correction is performed. This is shown below:

Example 1	8 − 3 = 5		
Decimal Subtraction	1 = Carry In	SC	: Set Carry to 1
	0011 = 3	LD 4	: Load Accumulator
	1100 = Complement of 3	COMP	: Complement 3
	1 = Carry In		
	1000 = 8	ADCSK	: Add
	1 0101 = 5 with carry		: Correct Answer

Both binary multiplication and division and decimal multiplication and division use repeated forms of additions and subtractions in the PPS–4 microprocessor. The digits are shifted, added, or subtracted the required number of times to obtain the solution.

Logic Operations

A set of logical instructions are used in this microprocessor for performing the logic operations required for problem solution. These are shown below:[12]

MNEMONIC	DATA BUS OPCODE HEX AND BINARY	NAME	DESCRIPTION
AND	OD 0000 1101	Logical AND	The result of logical AND of accumulator and 4-bit contents of RAM currently addressed by the transfer register replaces contents of accumulator.
OR	OF 0000 1111	Logical OR	The result of logic OR of accumulator and 4-bit contents of RAM currently addressed by the transfer register replaces contents of accumulator.
EOR	OC 0000 1100	Logical exclusive OR	The result of logic exclusive OR or accumulator and 4-bit contents of RAM currently addressed by the transfer register replaces contents of accumulator.
COMP	OE 0000 1110	Logical Complement	Each bit of the accumulator is logically complemented and placed in the accumulator.

The AND instruction will cause the contents of the accumulator to be modified depending on the contents of the addressed memory location. When there is a 1 in the corresponding bit positions of both words that bit position in the accumulator is retained as a 1. Any other combination in that bit will result in a zero in the corresponding bit position in the accumulator.

Example
AND
$$1100 = \text{Contents in accumulator}$$
$$\underline{0110} = \text{Contents in memory location}$$
$$0100 = \text{Logical AND result in accumulator}$$

The OR instruction causes the contents of the addressed memory location to be ORed with the contents of the accumulator. In the corresponding bit positions of the memory location and the accumulator, a single 1 will result in a 1, while two 0's will result in a 0. This is shown below:

Example
OR   1100 = Contents in accumulator
                        0110 = Contents in memory location
                        1110 = Logical OR result

With the use of the EXCLUSIVE OR instruction, the appropriate bit in the accumulator is set to 1 only when the corresponding bit positions in memory are different as shown below:

Example
EXCLUSIVE OR   1100 = Contents in accumulator
                        0110 = Contents in memory location
                        1010 = EXCLUSIVE OR result

The logical COMPLEMENT causes all of the bit positions in the accumulator to be set to their opposite value. If a particular bit position was initially a zero, it is set to one, and if the bit position were initially one, it is set to zero. This is shown below:

Example
COMPLEMENT   0101 = Contents in accumulator
                       1010 = COMPLEMENT result

Logical AND instructions can be used to test or reset individual bits in RAM. To test an individual bit in RAM, the contents of the accumulator are set to one in the desired bit position and to zero in all other bit positions. This may be done using a subroutine made up of a string of LDI instructions. To reset a bit to zero, the contents of the accumulator in all bit positions except the desired positions are set to one. Then the contents of the memory are ANDed with the accumulator and the result is stored in memory.

The logical OR instruction may be used to set bits in memory to one. The desired bit position is set to one in the accumulator with all other bit positions set to zero. The contents of the memory location are then ORed with the accumulator and the result transferred to memory.

The EXCLUSIVE OR instruction can be used for manipulating individual bit positions. For example, the individual bit positions may be inverted by loading the accumulator with all ones and then performing the EXCLUSIVE OR operation. The value in the accumulator is then stored in memory. The EXCLUSIVE OR instruction can also be used to test for equality between the contents of the accumulator and the contents of the addressed memory location. However, only if all the bits are identical will the contents of the accumulator remain zero.

The COMPLEMENT instruction is mainly used for performing subtraction operations as shown in the subtraction example.

Other Instructions

Microprocessor instructions may also be available for data address modifications, control transfers, register manipulation, and input/output operations. Typical instructions for input/output operations are shown below:[13]

MNEMONIC	DATA BUS OPCODE HEX AND BINARY	NAME	DESCRIPTION
IOL	IC 1st word 0001 1100 2nd word ——— ———	Input/output long (2 cycles)	This instruction occupies two ROM words and requires two cycles for execution. The first ROM word is received by the CPU and sets up the I/O enable signal. The second ROM word is received by the I/O devices and decoded for address and command. The contents of the accumulator inverted are placed on the data lines for acceptance by the I/O. At the same time, input data received by the I/O device is transferred to the accumulator inverted.
DIA	27 0010 0111	Discrete input	Data at the inputs to discrete are transferred to the accumulator.
DOA	ID 0001 1101	Discrete output	The contents of the accumulator are transferred to the discrete output register.

Input/output operations handle the transfer of data between the CPU and external devices or peripherals. The transfer may involve status and control signals as well as data. Input/output operations must reconcile timing differences between the CPU and the peripherals, format the data properly, and status and control signals. Irregular transfers can be handled with interrupts, that is, with control signals that receive the immediate attention of the control section and cause the suspension of normal operation. (We will consider the role of interrupts on input/output operations in Chapter 7.)

Jump and branch instructions allow a microprocessor to move about nonsequentially within a program. For instance, if a program contains three tasks, A, B, and C, and each is a complete section or subroutine, the microprocessor can be directed to perform them in any order. It is told where to go to in the program flow. This can be done by loading the PC with the address of the first instruction of the desired subroutine shown on top of page 52.

This type of jump or branch instruction is called an unconditional jump since the jump will occur no matter what external or internal conditions are present. A more powerful jump command—the conditional jump—will check internal and external conditions before jumping. Thus, after meeting one of the specified internal or external conditions, the program changes flow. For example, an instruction might be "If condition X is true, then

					PROGRAM B
0	JUMP TO		38		
1	4		39		
2	3		40		JUMP TO
3			41		0
4			42		3
	PROGRAM		43		
	A		44		
24					PROGRAM
25					C
26	JUMP TO		57		
27	6		58		
28	2		59		JUMP TO
29			60		2
30			61		9
	PROGRAM		62		END OF PROGRAM
	B				

jump to instruction X, otherwise perform the next sequential instruction." Status bits can serve as the check points for conditional jumps.

REFERENCES

1. Mead, C. and Conway L., *Introduction to VLSI Systems,* (Reading: Addison-Wesley, 1980).
2. Kraft, G. D. and Toy, W. N., *Mini/Microcomputer Hardware Design,* (Englewood Cliffs: Prentice-Hall, 1979).
3. Ibid.
4. Ibid.
5. Ibid.
6. Pro-Log Corporation, *PROM User's Guide,* (Monterey: Pro-Log, 1979).
7. Bernhard, R., Bubbles take on Disks, *IEEE Spectrum,* May 1980.
8. Rockwell International, *Parallel Processing System (PPS–4) Microcomputer,* (Anaheim: Rockwell International Microelectronic Device Division, June 1974).
9. Ibid.
10. Ibid.
11. Ibid.
12. Ibid.
13. Ibid.

EXERCISES

1. What is the largest product that can occur when two 8-bit binary numbers are multiplied?
2. Show how serial adding may be accomplished using half-adders.
3. Describe how the difference term from a half-subtractor circuit can be derived from an EXCLUSIVE OR gate circuit.

4. Draw a full-adder circuit using half-adders.
5. Draw the logic for a full-subtracter circuit.
6. Describe and discuss two methods that can be used for division.
7. List the registers in the basic microcomputer. State, in one sentence, the function of each register.
8. Describe how the expression below would be evaluated on a microcomputer having one accumulator and on a microcomputer having two accumulators.

$$A \times (B + C \times (D - E)$$

9. Which status bit would be used for the following:
   a. To check if a counter has been decremented to zero.
   b. To check if a binary addition resulted in an answer that could be represented in a single word.
   c. To determine if the result of a subtraction is positive.
   d. To determine if two numbers are both positive or both negative.
   e. To check if a number is odd or even.
10. If the last operation performed with an 8-bit word was an addition in which the operands were 2 and 8, what are the values of the following flags:
    a. CARRY
    b. ZERO
    c. OVERFLOW
    d. SIGN
    e. EVEN PARITY
    f. HALF-CARRY
11. How many bits long should the stack pointer be in the following cases?
    a. The stack is in the first 256 words of memory.
    b. The stack can be anywhere in a 16K memory.
12. A memory has a capacity of 65,536 words of 24 bits each. The instruction code is divided into three parts: (1) operaion code, (2) two bits that specify a processor register, and (3) an address part.
    a. What is the maximum number of operations that can be incorporated in the CPU if an instruction is stored in one memory word?
    b. Draw the instruction-word format, indicating the number of bits and the function of each part.
    c. How many processor registers are in the CPU and how many bits in each one?
13. A memory unit has a capacity of 8,192 words with 36 bits per word. The instruction code format uses 5 bits for the operation part and 13 bits for the address. Two instructions are packed in one memory word and a 36-bit instruction register IR is available. Describe the possible fetch and execute cycles for the CPU.
14. A CPU is available without a program counter. Instructions contain three parts: (1) an opcode, (2) the address of an operand, and (3) the address of the next instruction. The operation code consists of 6 bits and the memory has 8,192 words.
    a. How many bits must be in a memory word if an instruction is stored in one word? Draw the instruction word format.
    b. What other register is required in the CPU besides an operation register?
15. A computer has 16 processor registers and instructions, with four bits in the operation field. Show a possible instruction code format for an operation with the

content of any register with any other register and the result placed in any third register. How many bits are there in the instruction?

16. Explain how index registers can be used as pointers and counters in a microprocessor.

17. A first-in-first-out (FIFO) is a memory unit that stores information such that the item first in is the item first out. Show how a FIFO memory can operate with three counters: (1) a write counter—WC—that holds the address for the memory write operation; (2) a read counter—RC—that holds the address for the read operation; and a storage counter—SC—that indicates the number of items stored. The SC is incremented for every item stored and decremented for every item that is retrieved.

18. An 8-bit microprocessor communicates with up to 12^{16} words of memory. It has an 8-bit bidirectional data bus for the transfer of instructions, data, and addresses. A type of instruction format consists of three 8-bit words: the first word contains the operation field and the other two, the address field. Show the type of information (instruction, data, or address), the direction of transfer (to or from the microprocessor), and the number of times that the data bus is used in order to fetch and execute the following:

a. Load from memory to accumulator.

b. Store content of accumulator in memory.

2. Microprocessor Technology

INTEGRATED CIRCUITS

In this chapter, we will begin by considering the various types of semiconductor technologies used to create logic and memory elements, and then we will proceed to the logic and memory elements used to implement the microprocessor chips and the memory chips.

The integrated circuit (IC) is a single semiconductor crystal (called a chip) containing various electrical components such as transistors, diodes, resistors, and capacitors. These components are interconnected within the chip to form electronic circuits. The chip is enclosed in a metal or plastic package and connections are made to external pins to complete the IC. Individual components inside the package cannot be separated or disconnected, and the circuits are accessed only through the external pins. The benefits to be gained from ICs as compared to discrete components are as follow: (1) substantial reduction in size; (2) substantial reduction in cost; (3) reduction in power requirements; (4) higher reliability; (5) increased operating speed; and (6) the reduction of externally wired connections.

Integrated circuits fall into one of two categories; linear or digital. Linear integrated circuits operate with one continuous waveforms as found in such ICs as operational amplifiers and voltage regulators. Digital integrated circuits operate with binary signals as found in such ICs as gates, flip-flops, registers, and counters. Microprocessors use almost entirely digital integrated circuits, except for some emerging microcomputer chips which contain analog-to-digital converter circuitry.

THE INTEGRATED CIRCUIT EVOLUTION

Integrated circuit technology has moved rapidly in a period of 20 years from discrete solid state devices to Very Large Scale Integrated circuits (VLSI).

During the decade of 1960–1970, many applications of integrated circuits were evolutionary in nature, resulting in essentially the same type of equipment but with improved performance, and/or lower cost and smaller size. One example was the introduction of minicomputers using MSI in the late 1960s which had essentially the same computing power as some of the larger computers of earlier years.[1] Similar changes were taking place during this period in the factory; for example, each succeeding generation of control systems for machine tools, gained performance advantages over its predecessor. The first such equipment appeared about 1955, using electron tubes and electromechanical components; five years later, discrete transistors were employed. The third generation of equipment, introduced in 1967, utilized integrated circuits of small complexity using SSI (small scale integration).

As the degree of integration continued to increase into what came to be known as LSI (large scale integration), evolutionary developments began to occur. It became possible to fabricate complete system functions with one or several LSI chips, making possible products that simply were not feasible if constructed using other approaches.

A widely known example of LSI techniques leading to a new class of products was the hand-held calculator. The development of this product started during the 1960s.

Another example of the evolution due to LSI is in the area of memories. Memory components using magnetic cores had been used in digital computers since about 1953, yet the first memory components fabricated from semiconductor chips were much more expensive than magnetic cores. However, even though the complexity of semiconductor memory has increased steadily, the cost semiconductor memory has at the same time decreased below that of magnetic memory components through the use of improved technology and mass production.

These examples demonstrate some of the very successful applications of LSI technology. These examples also show a characteristic that they have in common: they were needed in large-volume applications. The earlier SSI integrated circuits and their successors, MSI (medium scale integration) circuits are basic building blocks that can still be used in a wide variety of applications, but as the degree of integration increased with LSI, the resulting circuits tended to be more specialized, with only one or possibly a few applications. If the specialized application, though, happens to involve a large volume of users (as was the case with the personal calculator and with the semiconductor memory chip, then fixed costs such as those of design and of developing test programs are amortized over a large number of chips, and the chip can be produced in large volume, which allows for the lowest cost. On the other hand, in applications that do not require a large volume of usage, costs are substantially larger for such specialized devices.

Integrated Circuit Families

Digital integrated circuits can be classified not only by their function but also by their particular logic circuit family. Each logic family has its own basic electronic circuit upon which all similar circuits and functions are developed. This basic circuit is either a NOR or a NAND gate. The topology of this basic circuit, that is, the electronic components employed and their interconnection, is usually used to derive the name of the family. Many different logic families of digital integrated circuits have been introduced commercially. The ones that are used in microprocessors are shown below:

TTL—Transistor transistor logic
IIL (I^2L)—Integrated injection logic
ECL—Emitter coupled logic
MOS—Metal oxide semiconductor
CMOS—Complementary metal oxide semiconductor

The two basic types of components that can be fabricated using integrated circuit technology are bipolar devices, which have two types of charge carriers, and unipolar devices, which have only one charge carrier. Bipolar technologies include transistor transistor logic (TTL), emitter coupled logic (ECL) and integrated injection logic (I^2L) among those that are used in microprocessors. A cross-sectional view of a bipolar transistor is shown in Figure 2.1.

The contacts are usually made of aluminum using an evaporation process. The buried layer is used to provide a more conductive path between the collector, base, and emitter regions. Figure 2.1 shows only one transistor; a microprocessor or memory circuit would have thousands of those transistors connected together to form the required logic elements.

Unipolar devices all use field-effect transistors made with MOS technology. The transistors are created on the surface of a small piece of silicon, called the substrate.

To make a MOS circuit, a single crystal of silicon must be grown. This crystal is then cut into thin circular slices called wafers. The crystal must be cut in a specific direction of the crystal lattice. Several hundred chips can be made from a wafer. (See Figure 2.2.) These chips may be used for microprocessors, memory, or other functions.

Transistors are created on the wafer by a photolithographic process similar to commercial printing. Positive and negative areas are made in the

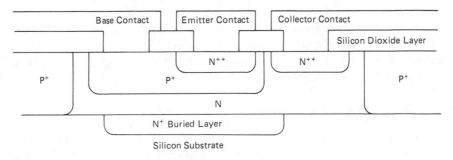

Fig. 2.1. Bipolar transistor.

Fig. 2.2. Intelligent peripheral controllers being produced from a wafer. (*Courtesy Rockwell International.*)

silicon by the addition of impurities through a process of masking and diffusion. This process is called doping. After the functions have been created on the wafer, it is tested using special test points which are on the edges and at the center. If the tests are successful, the wafer will be scribed and cut into individual chips. Each chip is then mounted in a package and connected through wires to the pads of the package. The IC is then subjected to further visual, electrical, and environmental tests. Then it is sealed and given a final test.

A PMOS transistor uses n-type silicon which is doped with p-type impurities in order to create the source and the drain of the transistor. Typical doping agents are boron and phosphorus. The areas to be doped with impurities are defined by a mask, which is made by the photolithographic process or the newer electron-beam process. The impurities are added to the exposed area of the wafer using thermal diffusion. An ion-implantation process can also be used to allow a more precise alignment, reducing the parasitic capacitance and improving switching speed.

Integrated Circuit Fabrication

We will now consider the actual fabrication of a single transistor in more detail.[2] The silicon wafer is manufactured by cutting a single crystal of silicon in the proper direction (for example, direction 111 of the lattice). A layer of oxide is then deposited on the silicon with a thickness of 5000 to 6000 Å, where 1 Å = 10^{-9}m. (See Figure 2.3, diagram B.)

The first mask is used to define the p-zones in the silicon. They are the source and drain areas of the transistor. A photosensitive emulsion is deposited on the silicon oxide, and a mask is used to print the areas which are to be doped. The oxide over the areas to be doped is then removed by chemical etching. (See Figure 2.3, diagram C.) Doping, using thermal diffusion, is then performed on the exposed areas which allows p-type impurities into the

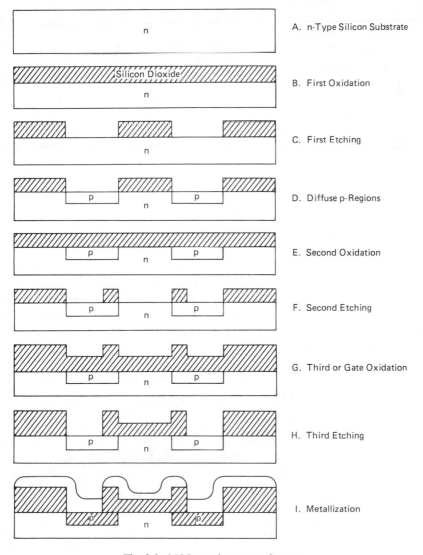

A. n-Type Silicon Substrate

B. First Oxidation

C. First Etching

D. Diffuse p-Regions

E. Second Oxidation

F. Second Etching

G. Third or Gate Oxidation

H. Third Etching

I. Metallization

Fig. 2.3. MOS transistor manufacture.

silicon (Figure 2.3, diagram D). Next, a layer of oxide is grown on top of the silicon as shown in Figure 2.3, diagram E.

Then, a mask is used to define the areas to be metallized. The oxide is then removed in these locations (Figure 2.3, diagram F). Another oxidation for the gate is performed in order to grow a thin layer of about 1000 to 1500Å (diagram G). A final oxide removal is performed to expose the source and the drain areas (diagram H), which are then connected to the rest of the circuit during metallization. (See Figure 2.3, diagram I.) For metallization, aluminum is deposited over the exposed areas, thereby connecting the source, gate, and drain to the other components of the circuit. The wafer is now ready for initial tests.

Small rectangles which are added on both sides of the chip and are called the pads. These pads are connected to the pins of the package. Usually gold wire is used to bond the pins to the pads. In this way, the chip is electrically connected to the pins of the IG package. The chip is also bonded to the package to hold it in place. The pins of the package can be directly inserted into the holes on the circuit board.

Microprocessors use 40 to 64 pins. Many testers have been limited to 40 pins. A typical test unit may cost $500,000, so the change to larger devices must be justified.[3]

TRANSISTOR TRANSISTOR LOGIC—TTL

The circuit for a TTL NAND gate is shown in Figure 2.4. This circuit uses four transistors and four resistors.

TTL is a saturated form of logic; during turn-on, both the emitter-base and collector-base junctions are forward biased which causes an accumulation of charged carriers in the base region. As the device is turned off, this charge must be discharged through the collector. The time required for this discharge results in a delay in turning the transistor off. All saturated logic experiences this storage time delay.

There are other versions of the TTL gate. Five versions are listed below, together with their propagation delay, power dissipation, and the product of these two parameters which serves a figure of merit.[4]

TTL VERSION	ABBREVIATION	PROPAGATION DELAY (NS)	POWER DISSIPATION (mW)	SPEED POWER PRODUCT	INPUT PULL-UP RESISTOR
Standard	TTL	10	10	100	4K
Low-power	LTTL	33	1	33	40K
High-speed	HTTL	6	22	132	2.8K
Schottky	STTL	3	19	57	2.8K
Low-power Schottky	LSTTL	9.5	2	19	25K

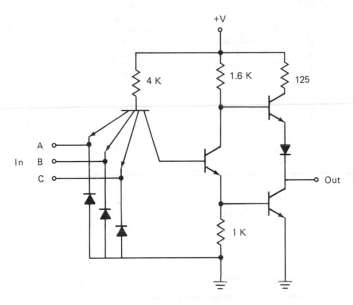

Fig. 2.4. TTL NAND gate.

The standard TTL gate was the original version of the TTL family. Improvements were made as TTL technology matured. In the low-powered version, the propagation delay was sacrificed to reduce power dissipation. In the high-speed version, power dissipation is increased to reduce the propagation delay. Schottky TTL increases the speed of operation without an excessive increase in dissipated power. The low-power Schottky version sacrifies some speed for reduced power dissipation. It compares with the standard TTL in speed but requires less power. The fan-out of TTL gates is 10 when the standard loads of the same circuit version are used. The noise margin is greater than 0.4 volt with a typical value of about 1 volt.[5]

INTEGRATED INJECTION LOGIC—I²L

A more recent development in semiconductor technology now being used in microprocessors is integrated injection logic (I²L) which is based on direct coupled transistor logic (DCTL). The problems of the older discrete component DCTL have been eliminated by using a single multiple-electrode transistor based on the structure shown in Figure 2.5. The n-substrate acts as the structure ground plane for connecting the grounded emitter transistor gates. The n-type layer which is grown on top of the substrate acts as both the grounded emitter region for the vertical NPN transistor and the grounded base region for the lateral PNP transistor.

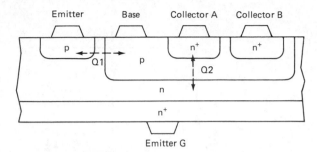

Fig. 2.5. I²L structure.

The resulting, relatively simple structure offers improvements in speed, power dissipation, and density, It is the newest bipolar technology to be applied to microprocessors. I²L uses saturated transistors, so the speed is slower than Schottky or ECL circuits.

The basic I²L circuit is shown in Figure 2.6. The lateral PNP transistor acts as a current source for the multiple emitter transistor that performs the inverting function.

When the input signal is high (open), injection current flows through *Q1* and turns on *Q2*. When the input signal is low (ground), the injection current is zero and *Q2* turns off. The magnitude of the injection current is set by the voltage *V* and *R1*. The injection current is given by:

$$I_I = \frac{V - Q1\,VBE}{R1}$$

The user of an I²L microprocessor is able to adjust the injection current, allowing a trade-off between speed and power consumption. When injection

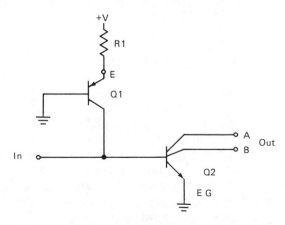

Fig. 2.6. Basic I²L circuit.

current is low, power consumption is low, but the speed of operation is reduced. Higher injection currents permit higher-speed operation, but with an increase in power consumption. Typical speeds as a function of injection current for an I²L microprocessor at room temperature are shown in Figure 2.7. I²L circuitry may be powered with a supply voltage as low as 0.8 V. Since the performance characteristics are controlled by the injection current, the voltage/resistance combination can be used to an advantage, and the low power consumption makes this an ideal technology for the consumer market. I²L, however, has not yet achieved the speed characteristics of TTL devices; it has been used for microprocessor bit-slice devices. An advantage, though, is the high integration level which may be achieved. Once high integration and high speed become real, I²L may become an important technology for portable microprocessor applications.[6]

EMITTER COUPLED LOGIC—ECL

Emitter coupled logic is nonsaturating by design, so storage time delays are avoided. In ECL, the transistors are biased to operate only in the linear region. The basic ECL circuit is shown in Figure 2.8.

The basic ECL circuit consists of a differential-amplifier input circuit. Emitter-follower circuits are used to restore the dc levels and provide the buffering to drive output lines. High fan-out is possible with ECL because of the high input impedance of the differential amplifiers and the low output impedance of the emitter-followers. Generated noise tends to be low because of the constant current drain of the differential-amplifier circuit. Gate delays of less than one nanosecond have been achieved, and operating frequencies for gates are close to one gigahertz. The basic circuit for the ECL OR–NOR gate is shown in Figure 2.9.[7] The circuit provides simultaneous outputs for

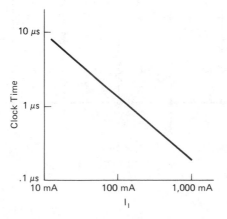

Fig. 2.7. I²L speed-power characteristics.

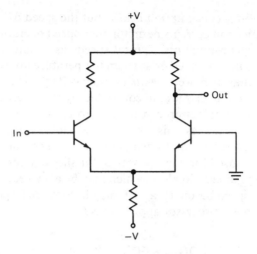

Fig. 2.8. Basic ECL circuit.

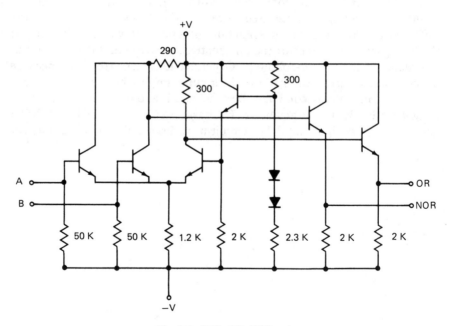

Fig. 2.9. ECL OR–NOR gate.

the OR function and its complement, the NOR function. Between the differential-amplifier and emitter-follower circuits is a network to set the differential-amplifier bias current.

The outputs of two or more ECL gates can be connected externally (with or without a resistor) to form a wire-OR function. This property can be utilized to form other logic functions by connecting the outputs of gates. Outputs of ECL gates are sometimes connected internally within the IC to form a dot-AND function. The wire-OR connection of two NOR gates produces the OR–AND–INVERT function. The internal dot-AND connection of two OR gates produces an OR–AND function.

The ECL family has a number of versions. The propagation delay ranges between 1 and 2 ns, depending on the version used. Power dissipation is about 25 mW, and fan-out is greater than 25. Noise margin is the lowest of all logic families at about 0.2 V.[8]

The fastest digital circuits in use employ ECL, and this has been the choice for most of the largest computers. ECL circuitry has also found some application in microprocessors, notably the 10800.

METAL OXIDE SEMICONDUCTOR TECHNOLOGY—MOS

A majority of the microprocessors being manufactured today use MOS (metal-oxide-semiconductor) rather than bipolar transistors in their integrated circuitry. The main advantage of MOS technology over bipolar technology is its higher density and lower production cost. The higher density of MOS allows more functions to be placed on a chip of a given size than can be attained using bipolar transistors. The unipolar devices which are used to fabricate MOS microprocessors are field-effect transistors (FETs) with p or n channels. A complementary type of MOS with both p and n channels (CMOS) is considered in the next section.

The basic structure of the MOS field-effect transistor is shown in Figure 2.10. Like a bipolar transistor, it is formed on a p- or n-type silicon substrate

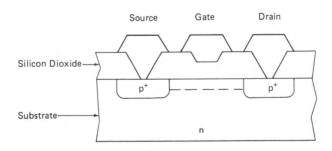

Fig. 2.10. MOS-FET structure.

that also serves as the supporting structure for the device. An oxide layer is formed on the silicon chip which serves as a protective layer against surface contamination. The source and drain are p or p + regions which are obtained by diffusing an impurity such as boron into the desired sections. The gate is usually aluminum and serves as the control element, covering an area from the source and drain. The oxide under the gate can be much thinner than the oxide on the rest of the surface in order to allow close control of the conduction characteristics between the source and the drain.

The channel refers to an area directly below the gate which connects the source and drain. When a voltage is applied to the gate, the field created will cause the channel to be converted into a p-region, thus allowing conduction. When a p-substrate is used as the body or support, the channel becomes an n-region when voltage is applied to the gate and the device is called n-type or NMOS instead of the PMOS device as shown in Figure 2.10.

Thus, we have the two basic types of MOS transistors that are used in MOS microprocessors, the p-channel transistors and the n-channel transistors. In the p-channel devices, the electrical carriers are holes, while in the n-channel devices the carriers are electrons. Both and p- and n-channel MOS amplifiers are shown in Figure 2.11.

The MOS field-effect transistor combines high impedance with the small size necessary for the fabrication of complex circuits on a small area of silicon. MOS technology developed as the ability to manufacture highly refined silicon wafers and the development of the planar process for making integrated circuits matured. The early PMOS devices had large variations in threshold conducting voltages which made interfacing between devices difficult. The threshold voltages tended to shift due to voltage bias changes or heat transients which made a large percent of devices behave erratically. A

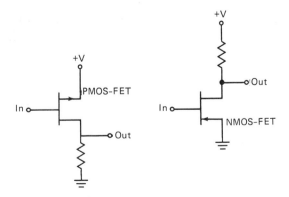

Fig. 2.11. Basic PMOS and NMOS transistor amplifier circuits.

significant advance occurred in processing with the control of sodium contamination during wafer fabrication. This was followed by additional controls on surface contamination and the addition of breakdown diodes in the gate structure to prevent transient voltage damage.

The earliest microprocessors used p-channel technology. However, this had two disadvantages. Holes have a lower mobility in silicon than do electrons; as a result, PMOS transistors are slower than NMOS devices. Also, PMOS circuits provide an active pull-up but they require a passive pull-down of external loads. NMOS amplifiers provide an active pull-down, which is more effective for driving the TTL interface circuits common in microprocessors. PMOS is the older technology; it was better understood and thus more economical, and it was used successfully in the first microprocessors. It provided good density (up to 15,000 transistors per chip). However, PMOS technology is slower compared to newer technologies, such as NMOS with its many variations. The main attraction of PMOS to manufacturers today is that it is a well understood process, and a complex device can be developed with a high probability of success at a lower cost than newer technologies. But while p-channel MOS technology provided a low-cost approach to early microprocessor designs, it is not used in designs today.

NMOS technology is the most widely used technology for microprocessors today. The first NMOS microprocessor was the 8080. The original 8080 was designed for a maximum clock frequency of 2 MHz.[9] Advances in n-channel technology now permit NMOS microprocessors to use clock rates as high as 12 MHz. An important point in MOS microprocessors is that the load resistors shown in Figure 2.12 comprises MOS transistors which are used as resistors. MOS transistors can be also classed as depletion-mode or enhancement-mode devices. Depletion-mode transistors are normally on and require a gate voltage in order to be turned off. Enhancement-mode devices are normally off and require a gate voltage in order to be turned on. The early NMOS microprocessors (such as the 8080) used enhancement-mode transistors for load resistors. This required a separate power supply to provide the gate voltage for the loads. Newer MOS microprocessors such as the 6800 use depletion-mode loads which eliminated the need for the extra power-supply voltage. These processors operate from a single 5-V supply using circuits as shown in Figure 2.12.

Since NMOS is faster than PMOS, and newer versions such as H-MOS and V-MOS give excellent density, NMOS is the most popular technology used to implement microprocessors today. The newer NMOS microprocessors achieve instruction execution speeds of the order of .5 μs. which is eight times faster than available PMOS microprocessors.

As MOS technology matured, device improvements evolved from the experimental stage to common production techniques. The silicon-gate MOS

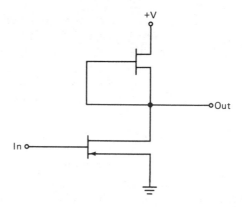

Fig. 2.12. NMOS-FET amplifier with depletion mode load.

device replaced the aluminum gate with a polycrystalline silicon region within the oxide layer. Although the silicon gate techniques required several additional processing steps, it allowed the following:

1. A higher conductance with lower gate voltage.
2. Reduced device capacitance for greater speeds.
3. Increased chip densities.

Ion implantation was used to obtain a greater control over the gate threshold voltage.[10] This process step adds dopant ions into specific regions on the chip and results in the ion-implanted channel as shown in the dashed line of Figure 2.10. A MOS logic circuit is shown in Figure 2.13. The gates act as the inputs to the circuit shown in the schematic diagram. The metallization pattern as seen from the top of the semiconductor chip is shown in order to illustrate how compact an actual MOS circuit can be constructed.

COMPLEMENTARY METAL OXIDE SEMICONDUCTOR TECHNOLOGY—CMOS

Another type of MOS transistor circuit used in microprocessors is the CMOS (complementary MOS) circuit. This circuit uses complementary transistors (one p-channel and one n-channel device) for active pull-up and pull-down of the load. This complementary structure allows one transistor to be off when the other is on, resulting in a very low power dissipation. CMOS also offers designers high noise immunity, large fan-out, and the use of inexpensive power sources.

The CMOS structure requires a more complex fabrication process (as shown in Figure 2.14). The p-channel device is formed directly from the n-type substrate. A p-doped tub must be created for the n-channel device

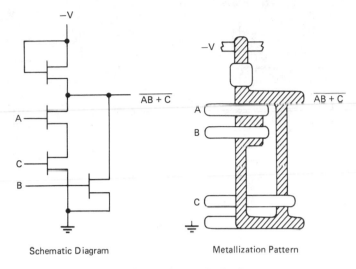

Schematic Diagram   Metallization Pattern

Fig. 2.13. PMOS logic circuit.

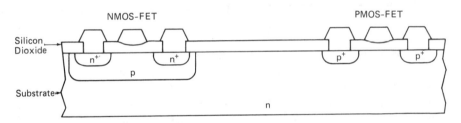

Fig. 2.14. CMOS IC structure.

which adds to the processing steps. Also, channel stops are required between the devices to prevent extraneous current flow between devices.[11]

In the standard MOS circuit (like the one shown in Figure 2.13), the upper transistor which acts as a load accounts for a significant amount of the power dissipation. In the CMOS circuits with p- and n-channel devices as shown in Figure 2.15, a complementary inverter is formed by applying an input to the gates of the two opposite polarity transistors. When a logical one is applied to this circuit, the upper p-channel transistor is off, while the lower n-channel device is conducting. The output is shorted to ground, and current from the supply is only the leakage through the p-channel device after the load capacitance is charged. When a logical zero is applied to the input, the upper transistor is on, while the lower device is off. The output is at $+V$ and the current will be a function of the load. If a similar high impedance MOS device is the load, the current will remain small.

The characteristics and advantages of CMOS technology are in between

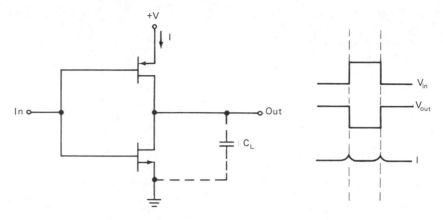

Fig. 2.15. CMOS operation.

those of NMOS and PMOS. CMOS is faster than PMOS, but slower than NMOS. Because it uses two transistors rather than one, CMOS offers less density than standard MOS. Its advantage is the very low power consumption and noise immunity (about 1.5 V). CMOS devices can operate between 2V and 12V.

CMOS technology is suited for avionics, aerospace applications, and other systems that require portability and/or a very low power consumption. Several commercial microprocessors using this technology are available. (We will consider them in the next chapter.) In addition to low operating power, a low-cost, unregulated supply is sufficient to operate most CMOS devices. However, since both n-channel and p-channel transistors are required, there is the disadvantage of having more processing steps involved in the manufacturing operation (two additional diffusions and photomasking steps). Also, more real estate is required for what are basically two separate MOS transistors.

CMOS is limited by substrate capacitances. To reduce the effect of this capacitance, CMOS devices can use an insulating substrate (usually sapphire). This technology is called silicon on sapphire (SOS). This extends the speed capability of CMOS into the lower range of transistor-transistor logic (TTL). The starting silicon layer is grown on a single crystalline wafer of sapphire. By a repeated process of producing silicon dioxide, etching, and diffusing, the configuration of Figure 2.16 is obtained. Unused silicon is removed from the substrate, leaving isolated islands of silicon that form individual n-channel and p-channel transistors. This structure almost eliminates the parasitic capacitance found in bulk silicon MOS circuits and may triple the speed of the device. In addition, the density of such SOS devices is greater by a factor of two to three over bulk MOS circuits. The major problem with SOS technology is the substantial cost required to produce the high-quality sapphire substrates needed.[12]

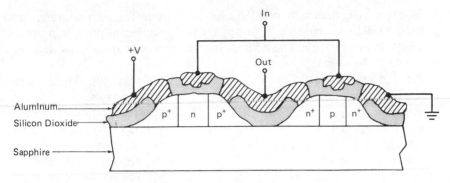

Fig. 2.16. SOS structure.

RANDOM ACCESS MEMORY TECHNOLOGY—RAM

RAMs are used in microprocessor systems for storing new results or new data for use in current processing operations. The memory cycle time is the same for any location addressed because there is no waiting or sorting time required as there is when data items are stored sequentially.

Bipolar random access memories use bipolar transistors arranged as flip-flops in the basic cell configuration shown in Figure 2.17. The memory, with its multiple emitter transistors, may be bit-organized or word-organized. If it

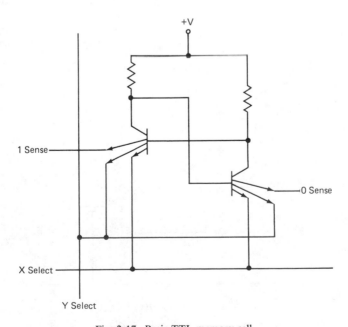

Fig. 2.17. Basic TTL memory cell.

is bit-organized, then only one data bit is provided for each address. In a word-organized system, the flip-flops are tied together in groups to obtain the desired word length. The address decoding circuits are usually included as a part of the chip.

A Schottky TTL memory can be made using a similar flip-flop arrangement with Schottky diodes used to isolate the transistor bases.

Semiconductor memories range from the higher speed bipolar to lower-speed, but higher-density MOS which are mainly used today for microprocessor storage. The industry is well along in bipolar technology, and the bipolar transistor has been the subject of extensive research and improvement for over 20 years. While the possibility of squeezing a few more picoseconds out of the bipolar designs may exist, its theoretical speed limits may already have been reached. In contrast, MOS—a newer technology—still holds the promise of substantially improved speed in its basic transistor.

Static MOS-RAMS

MOS memories use circuits of field-effect transistors to store the addressable sequences of binary information. A stable MOS memory cell is shown in Figure 2.18. It may be operated at any speed up to its rated maximum and does not require a periodic refreshing signal to maintain storage as in the case of the dynamic MOS memory cell.

The static MOS-RAM memory cell uses a flip-flop circuit with two MOS transistors which act as loads. The transistors are used to enable the sense

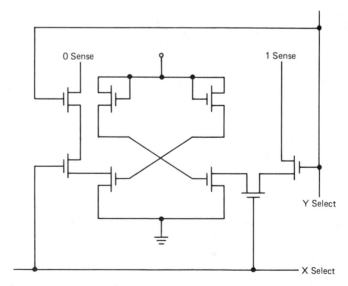

Fig. 2.18. Basic static MOS-RAM cell.

and select lines. The static memory cell is easy to drive and requires simpler external circuitry than does the dynamic MOS cell, but it tends to be more expensive due to its additional components when compared to the dynamic MOS-RAM circuit shown in Figure 2.19.

A static CMOS memory cell would use a similar flip-flop arrangement but the transistors which function as the loads are combined into a complementary circuit (as shown in Figure 2.15). The static CMOS memory allows low power dissipation with less density than standard MOS. It is also compatible with TTL logic for easy interfacing.

Dynamic MOS-RAMs

The three-transistor dynamic MOS cell of Figure 2.19 uses a shared read or write select line and separate read and write data bit lines.[13] The device capacitance shown in dashed lines is charged and discharged as a function of the write line. This type of MOS memory is less expensive to produce, but it requires additional circuitry for the refreshing operation.

MOS dynamic RAMs of 1024 bits were the first semiconductor memories to gain wide acceptance.[14] Built from p-channel MOS technology, these chips made large, solid state memory arrays possible. These dynamic memories used capacitive storage to hold each bit value and required periodic refreshing to retain data since the charge held in the capacitors leaked away. A three-transistor cell was used for each bit stored, and the 1024 bits were housed in about 20,000 sq. mils of silicon. This density first promised to displace core memories and make large semiconductor systems simple to implement. But it wasn't until even higher density products were introduced that the takeover began occurring. The first of the higher-density devices, the 4096-bit dynamic RAMs, provided quadruple the density. To make those higher-density and higher-speed RAMs possible, p-channel technology was abandoned and n-channel processing was used. N-channel

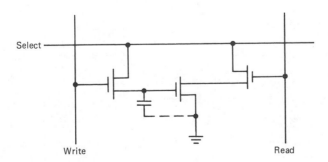

Fig. 2.19. Basic dynamic MOS-RAM cell.

technology allowed the low threshold voltages needed for TTL competitiveness and its speed was greater. It also permitted device densities to grow larger. Moreover, along with n-channel processing came a new cell design which permitted a bit to be stored with a single transistor and a capacitor, as shown in Figure 2.20[15].

Dynamic Cell Characteristics

With the two amplifying transistors eliminated, new sense amplifiers were developed to boost the small signal levels out of the memory matrix that dropped to millivolts. The most popular techniques use either a single-ended sense amp or a balanced differential sense amp. The balanced diff-amp, however, has become the dominant technique.[16]

The one-transistor cell is a minimal structure. The capacitor stores digital data as a high or low voltage, and the transistor connects the capacitor to a bit sense line. Conduction through the transistor is controlled by its gate, which is connected to the other gates in a row. When a row is enabled by the row decoder, all transistors in that row conduct and transfer the charge from their capacitors to the corresponding bit sense lines, destructively reading the data. Each column has its own sense amp to detect the charge and amplify the signal created by the charge. The amplifier signal is then at a full logic level.

During the destructive read, the transistors stay conductive, and part of the amplified signal is fed back to the cell input to refresh the cell. To maximize the signal fed to the sense amplifier means that the cell capacitance is made large and the bit/sense-line capacitance small. The two capacitances form a divider which attenuates the signal from the cell.

A double-level polysilicon process (as shown in Figure 2.21) helps maximize the cell capacitance, while cutting the bit sense line in half reduces its capacitance.[17] The sense amplifier is located in the center of the sense line and senses the differential voltage between the two halves of the line.

Once the amplifier design was proven, the 4096-bit RAM became a stan-

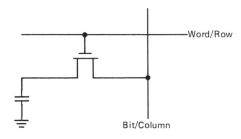

Fig. 2.20. Single-transistor MOS-RAM cell.

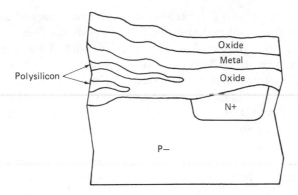

Fig. 2.21. Double-level polysilicon RAM structure.

dard memory component in 1973. Soon, newer chips reduced chip size from the original 19,000 mm² to 12,000 and cell size from 1.5 sq. mils to 1.008 sq. mils. Then came 16K RAMs, and cell size came down to 0.55 sq. mils. (Figure 2.22 shows this trend in cell reduction.)

Scaling

This cell size reduction has occurred using scaling in which the physical dimensions (length, width, and depth) are reduced by a scaling factor, $K,$ along with the operating voltage.[18] All the dimensions of a typical device are affected by scaling. To allow operation at 5 V when previous versions operated at 12 V, a device should have a K of 5/12. The most important advantage of scaling is that chip area goes down by a factor of K^2. At the same

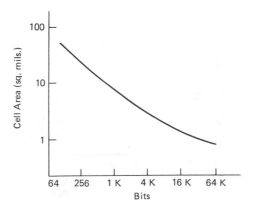

Fig. 2.22. Dynamic MOS-RAM cell size trends.

time, performance increases because smaller devices packed closer together have shorter propagation delays and less power dissipation.

Reliability, though, changes to some extent with changes in scale. Since power dissipation drops by a factor of K, voltage stress will decrease by a factor of K, and current density increase by a factor of $1/K$. This increase in current density should not affect reliability if conservative design guidelines are used. The field strength and power per unit area remain about the same. The performance for dynamic RAMs should improve as depicted in the graph of Figure 2.23.

Since access time is projected to shrink below 20 ns., dynamic RAMs will take advantage of continued improved processing and additional circuit innovations.

The leading edge of process and device technology has historically been applied to dynamic RAMs. The progress of the dynamic RAMs indicates what is down the road in other semiconductor memories and microprocessors as well.

Alpha Radiation Errors

A potential problem in memories is alpha radiation. No memory seems completely immune from alpha radiation, which is a special case of "noise" that can cause errors; positively charged alpha particles have been found to be a major source of "soft errrors" in 4K dynamic RAMs.[19] The phenomenon has also been observed in 16K dynamic RAMs and even in some static RAMs.

As signal levels inside memory and logic devices continues to shrink, other noise sources (thermal noise, for example) may be isolated as error

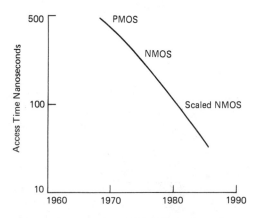

Fig. 2.23. Dynamic MOS-RAM speed trends.

generators, but the assumption is that not all errors can be prevented, which has sparked new interest in error correction and detection. Simple parity checks can spot single-bit errors, while more elaborate schemes such as the Hamming code can correct single-bit errors and detect double-bit errors. The Hamming code is gaining popularity as 16-bit microprocessors emerge, since the percent of overhead needed to perform the correction declines as word size increases. Five extra bits are required for an 8-bit word, while only six bits are needed to correct a 16-bit word. Error correction systems are a trend, and the logic necessary to perform this correcting is available in more and more ICs.

Recent Trends

An evolution in static RAMs has paralleled that of dynamic RAMs except that bit density is lower by a factor of four, since a static RAM cell occupies more silicon than a single-transistor dynamic RAM cell. A 16K × 1 dynamic RAM may use 21,000 sq. mils of silicon while a static RAM of one fourth the bit capacity occupies only 2 sq. mils less silicon.[20] A major portion of chip cost is silicon, so a static RAM costs about three to four times as much. But since a static RAM requires no externally applied control signals to maintain data, it is easier to use than a dynamic RAM. Designers of small memory systems find that the cost of implementing the multiplexed addressing and refresh control circuitry may offset the per-bit cost advantage of the dynamic RAM. To bring the cost effectiveness of dynamic RAM technology to the smaller memory system user, the quasi-static RAM has been developed. Here, a dynamic RAM is configured in a directly addressable byte-wide memory with an on-chip refresh scheme that is almost transparent to the user.

Another development not strictly limited to RAMs is the use of partially good devices. To lower the potential price per bit in a system, a memory device whose failure locations are known is used. Several techniques allow these devices to be usable: (1) identifying and bypassing the failures with a memory mapping scheme, (2) error-correcting the system, or (3) using only the totally good quadrants. As memories and die sizes increase, the impact of random defects also increases, thereby reducing device yields. Consequently, these partially good devices can be offered for sale with the use of this concept.

READ-ONLY MEMORY TECHNOLOGY—ROM

Read-only memories (ROMs) find a wide range of applications in the design of microprocessor systems. (See Figure 2.24.) Basically, a ROM generates the input-output relation specified by a truth table. It can implement any

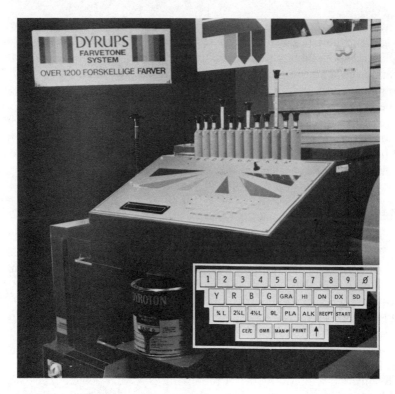

Fig. 2.24. This microprocessor-controlled colorant dispenser stores the paint manufacturer's color formulas in ROM. (*Courtesy Rockwell International.*)

combinational circuit with K inputs and N outputs. A ROM can also be used for the design of a sequential circuit, since a sequential circuit can be subdivided into a group of flip-flops and a combinational circuit. A register is used for the group of flip-flops and a ROM for the combinational circuit. ROMs are used for converting one binary code to another, for look-up tables for mathematical operations, for the display of characters, and for other applications requiring large numbers of inputs and outputs. They are also employed in the design of control units for CPUs. Here, they are used to store the coded information that represents the sequence of control variables needed for enabling the various CPU operations. A control unit that utilizes a ROM to store CPU control information is called a microprogrammed control unit.

Read-only memories are not new, although their use in the past has been limited. The original form of ROM was the diode matrix, which has been in use since the early days of diode production. Gradually, many technologies evolved for read-only memories. The rapid development of semiconductor

ROMs has produced a succession of faster, larger, and more flexible devices for use in code translation, character generation, microprocessor program storage (microprogrammed control), and look-up tables. Other than the semiconductor ROM, other types of ROMs include the capacitor matrix, inductance matrix, permanent magnet matrix, ferrite core matrix, magnetic film matrix, and others. Most of these are not fast enough to operate with today's microprocessors. Also, the limits of capacity of these memories are set by their physical size and electrical delay, but the main limitation to the use of these ROMs is their cost compared to semiconductor types.

ROMs are well-suited to LSI technologies. As the name implies, they are intended to store nonchanging information. (Although some ROMs can be written in or altered, this write time is relatively long.) The primary differences in various ROMs lie in the cell design, which can be divided into two types: permanent and semipermanent. The permanent read-only memory is fixed in construction so that any necessary change in data requires reconstructing at least a part of the device. In a semipermanent read only memory, data can be changed by modifying the changeable element.

Semiconductor ROMs can be constructed by either MOS technology or bipolar technology. The bipolar devices are faster and feature higher drive capability, whereas MOS circuits consume less power and space. The prime advantages of present day ROMs are their low cost, low power, fast access, and nonvolatility.

ROMs are used in microprocessor systems to read out stored code or data that is not subject to change. The data is programmed into the ROM during manufacture before delivery to the user. The fabrication process for these mask-programmed devices includes several steps such as photomasking, etching, and diffusing in order to create a pattern of junctions and interconnections across the surface of the wafer with a layer of aluminum or other conductor, and then to selectively etch away sections of the aluminum, leaving the desired interconnecting pattern. In the manufacture of these ROMs, the row to column contacts are selectively made by the inclusion or exclusion of aluminum connections during the final aluminum etch process.

Most of the advancements in ROM semiconductor memory are based on improvements in process, mask, and alignment technologies. The most rapid progress, however, continues to come from the drive for a wider range of applications, such as the users demand for low-cost read only memories for microprocessor program and other control applications. This has resulted in developments of various types of ROMs with the features of long-term nonvolatility and electrical reprogrammability. The design considerations of a high-speed integrated circuit ROM include minimum power dissipation, minimum propagation delay, minimum circuit area, and maximum reliability.

The circuit configuration is optimized in order to achieve fast switching and good driving capability without incurring excessive power consumption. The minimization of device area leads to reduced capacitance and higher speed. The reduced circuit area is achieved by a shrinkage of component area and also by reconsideration of logic organization and circuit designs. Moreover, the wide use of ROMs in the field requires certain basic properties such as electrical reprogrammability, high speed, and nonvolatility. However, the semiconductor ROM memories with custom masks need a long turn around time and are expensive to change.

The read-only memory, like the random-access memory, has gone through evolutionary changes in a short period of time. In a few years, programmable devices have evolved from expensive curiosities used in research to common microprocessor design elements. Innovations in bipolar and MOS technology have resulted in programmable and erasable programmable ROMs, called PROMs and EPROMs respectively. These two types of devices have greatly increased the usefulness and acceptability of read only memories microprocessor system applications.

PROM TECHNOLOGY

PROMs are an engineering development aid; they are a special form of semiconductor read-only memory. The PROM is similar in size and appearance to a ROM. But while the information in a ROM is written permanently during the process of fabrication, in a PROM, it is programmed after the chip is packaged using one of a number of built-in characteristics. Two processing techniques—fused links and avalanche-induced migration—are used with bipolar PROMs, while MOS reprogrammable PROMs or EPROMs employ one of a number of writing processes. Bipolar devices are usually selected for speed, having shorter access times compared to MOS devices. In contrast, MOS devices consume less power, and higher density parts are available with MOS technology. Programmable bipolar devices are limited to the nonerasable type, whereas most programmable MOS devices are erasable and reprogrammable. Programmable bipolar devices are available predominately as TTL Schottky devices, with a few devices offered in emitter coupled logic (ECL). Programmable MOS devices are fabricated in PMOS, NMOS, CMOS, and MNOS. Most programmable MOS devices are made to be compatible with + 5 V logic.

Programmable ROM devices fall into two categories: (1) those that are erasable and thus reprogrammable and (2) those that are not erasable.

The nonerasable PROMs involve some form of fusing process where a link is fused open or closed. The process involves an action which is basically irreversible, thus making this class of PROM nonerasable. There are three types of fusing technologies in use: (1) metal links, (2) silicon links, and (3) shorted junctions.[21] All fusible devices have a relatively short programming time.

Fusible link (FL) devices are completely nonvolatile, and once they are programmed they cannot be erased. Continued improvements in fuse technology have resulted in the following types of fuse material now in use: nichrome, platinum silicide, polycrystalline silicon, and titanium tungsten. All FL technologies are similar and are constructed using a structure like that shown in Figure 2.25. The fuse material is deposited as a thin-film link to the column lines of the PROM. The memory cell is constructed as a transistor switch. The fuses are "blown" during programming by saturating the transistor through the selection of the row and column by the decoding circuit. When the cell's transistor base is high and the column line near ground, a large current is switched through the transistor and through the fuse in the emitter leg. The emitter fuse link is open circuited by the current, resulting in the programming of the bit location. The PROM circuit for this device is shown in Figure 2.26.

A historical problem encountered in the use of metal link PROMs has been the regrowth of opened fused links over a period of time.[22] In the regrowth process, cells go from a programmed state back to the unprogrammed (closed) state. Manufacturers, however, have refined the process of programming of metal link devices to achieve improved yields as well as reliability.

Silicon link PROMs use notched strips of polycrystalline silicon material. Programming of these polysilicon fuses involves melting the links using a mechanism similar to that in metal fuses. During programming, a current of 20–30 mA is used to blow the fuse link. This current generates heat estimated at 1400°C. At this temperature, the silicon oxidizes, forming an insulating material around the open link. The use of silicon results in the absence of contact problems or difficulties caused by the use of a dissimilar material. Additionally, the use of silicon eliminates the existence of conductive materials in the open gap between the formerly linked polysilicon fuse ends.

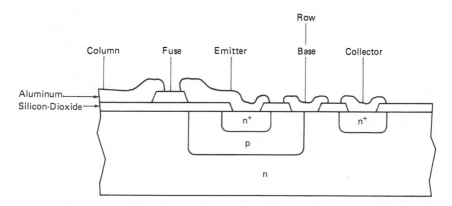

Fig. 2.25. Fusible link PROM cell structure.

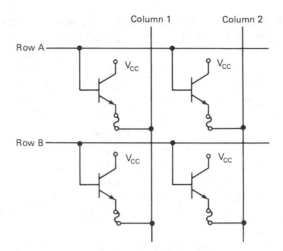

Fig. 2.26. Fusible link bipolar PROM.

Thus, growback is greatly reduced, although not completely eliminated. Manufacturers refer to improved reliability and simpler programming techniques with this technology. Of the various fuse materials used in PROMs, silicon fuses are preferred by the memory manufacturer because the silicon is a standard integrated circuit material and no contact problems or problems with dissimilar materials are encountered. The thickness of the silicon fuse used in PROMs is about 3000 Å, 15 times the thickness of a nichrome fuse. Resistivity of the silicon fuse is controlled by doping, as in standard integrated circuits.

Shorted junction devices are also referred to as the AIM (avalanche-induced migration) technology.[23] This device consists of two semiconductor junctions which appear as a high impedance circuit of back-to-back diodes as shown in Figure 2.27.

Generally an npn double-diffused transistor structure is used, with only the emitter and collector contacts metallized. As shown in Figure 2.28, the base is left open, forming the back-to-back diodes, D_1 and D_2. This structure is an irreversible process that occurs on the migration of aluminum through silicon to the diffused junction. D_2 is reverse biased, and the large flow of

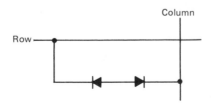

Fig. 2.27. Shorted junction or AIM PROM cell.

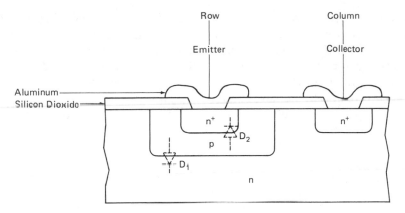

Fig. 2.28. Shorted junction or AIM PROM cell structure.

electrons in the reverse direction causes aluminum atoms from the emitter contact to migrate through the emitter to the base, thereby causing an emitter-to-base short. The avalanche technique requires a higher voltage and current than the fuse technique. The remaining junction is thus usable as a forward-biased diode and represents a programmed data bit.

The programming involved in implementing this type of technology requires precision. It is possible to program devices where the second junction is damaged making the PROM unusable. Note that the impedance of each link can be measured once it has been blown. This technique is not possible with open-circuit devices such as those described earlier. Thus, a potential advantage in reliability may result if the impedance is measured after the devices are programmed.

The permanence of fusible link PROMs is not practical if the PROM program is expected to be changed a number of times before it is complete. Therefore, erasable PROMs or EPROMs are more suitable for this purpose. All erasable PROMs are implemented using an isolated gate structure in a NMOS field-effect transistor. The isolated transistor gate has no electrical circuit connection and can store an electrical charge for indefinite periods under normal conditions. The stored gate charge becomes the memory mechanism for this device. However, under special conditions the charge on the isolated gate can be removed causing the contents of the memory cell to be erased. There are two types of erasable MOS-PROMs, ultraviolet-light erasable and electrically erasable.

EPROM Technology

The ultraviolet (UV) light erasable PROM uses a floating silicon gate which is erasable by ultraviolet light and reprogrammable after each erasure. The floating gate is located in the silicon dioxide layer (as shown in Figure 2.29), and it effectively isolates the source from the drain under normal operating conditions. During programming, a high negative voltage is applied which forces the junction of the desired cell into a breakdown condition; this results in the injection of electrons into the floating gate area. After the voltage is removed, the gate retains this negative charge since it is electrically isolated by the silicon dioxide layer. The negative charge on the gate results in forming a conductive inversion region in the substrate, which provides a channel between the source and drain, and it is the presence or absence of this conductive channel that determines if a one or zero is stored in the memory cell.

A lid is provided in the sealed package of the chip in order to allow erasure by illuminating the chip surface with ultraviolet light. The lids may be opaque or transparent in appearance, but they allow UV light to pass through for the erasing process. (See Figure 2.30) The technique for erasing UV EPROMs is to illuminate the window with an ultraviolet lamp which has a wavelength of 2537 Å. The UV source is placed at a distance of 2–3 cm from the lid, and the radiation is allowed to fall on the element for 10–45 minutes, depending on the type of device and source. The UV radiation raises the conductivity of the silicon dioxide and allows the floating gate charge to leak away. The erasing process is not selective, and results in resetting all cells in the device. Also, it may be necessary to check the UV source periodically since it may age with time, and its intensity may diminish, which means that an EPROM left to erase for the usual time may not be completely erased.[24] Incomplete erasure may result in increased access time or unstable bits.

UV EPROMs have been experiencing an increase in popularity; much of this is associated with their use in microprocessors. When properly erased and programmed, they have been shown to be reliable. This popularity has been noticed by the device manufacturers. Thus, most UV EPROMs are second sourced, and larger, faster, and easier to use devices have been appear-

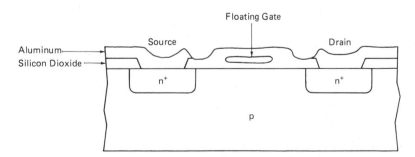

Fig. 2.29. UV EPROM structure.

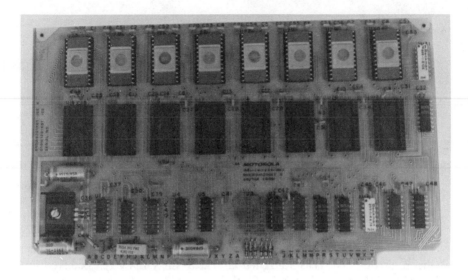

Fig. 2.30. A row of UV PROMs is shown in place in this microprocessor memory board. (*Courtesy Siltran Digital.*)

ing. UV EPROM technology is a popular choice for designs needing an erasable memory.

In some microprocessor applications, particularly in evaluating a new system, it is desirable to make changes in the memory content while avoiding the removal and replacement of the memory chips. In this type of application, the electrically erasable PROM (EEPROM) is well-suited.

EEPROM Technology

EEPROMs, also referred to as electrically alterable ROMs (EAROM), can be electrically erased and electrically written into. This alterability allows "in-circuit" programming where the device can be erased, written, and read without being removed from the circuit. There are two types of electrically erasable PROMs: (1) floating gate MOS devices and (2) metal-nitride-oxide-silicon (MNOS) devices.[25]

As shown in Figure 2.31, floating gate EEPROMs are similar to UV EPROMs, with the addition of a control gate. There is no quartz lid to allow erasing. The electrical control gate is used to control erasing and writing. Devices of this type, however, have to use a special voltage and complex voltage sequencing, making them impractical for in-circuit programming.

These gate EEPROMs had access times and data retention similar to UV EPROMs, and like UV EPROMs they were usually removed from the circuit

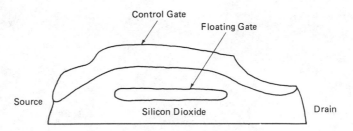

Fig. 2.31. EEPROM structure with control gate.

for erasing and reprogramming, although erase time was much shorter than for UV EPROMs—typically one minute or less.

A newer floating-gate tunnel oxide cell structure employs a mechanism called Fowler-Nordheim tunneling to write and erase data.[26] These devices erase and write by causing electrons to tunnel across a 200 Angstrom layer of silicon dioxide. The cells hold their charge in the same way as conventional EPROMs. Maintained at 125° C, they retain data for years. Operation is fully static, and refreshing is not required, regardless of read frequency. Byte erase/write or chip erase requires application of a 21-V pulse for 10 ms. Any 2K bytes of the device can be erased and rewritten in 20 ms. (The tunnel structure is shown in Figure 2.32.)

A comparison of the floating-gate tunnel oxide EEPROM characteristics with those of a UV EPROM are given below:[27]

	TUNNEL OXIDE EPROM	UV
Power Supplies		
Read Mode	+5 V	+5 V
Erase/Write	+5, +21 V	+5, +25 V
Write Method	Tunnel Injection	Hot Electron
Time/Word	10 ms	50 ms
Erase Method	Tunnel Injection	UV Light
Time/Word	10 ms	—
Time/Chip	10 ms	30 min
Access Time	250 ns	450 ns
Power Dissipation		
Active Mode	500 mW	550 mW
Standby Mode	100 mW	100 mW
Data Retention	10 Years	10 Years

Note that this EEPROM is quite similar in read performance to current EPROM memories, but with the ability to be electrically programmed in the field, without being removed from the system. Moreover, the device can be reprogrammed remotely via a radio or telephone link. This flexibility permits applications that were not possible with less flexible storage devices, along with advantages such as reduced systems downtime for program

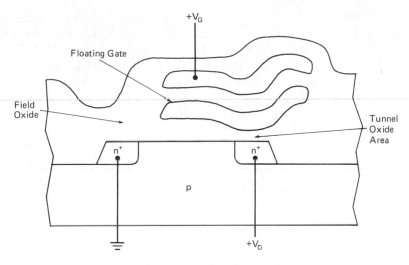

Fig. 2.32. Floating-gate tunnel oxide EEPROM structure.

changes, faster modifications for stored programs, and improved prototyp-
ing capabilities. Since the application of a 21-V pulse for 10 ms will erase or
write any byte of memory, the only hardware needed to interface to a microprocessor is a pulse generator and timer circuit.

It is expected that this new generation of devices may solve the past drawbacks for incircuit erasing and writing. If this does occur, it is anticipated
that these floating-gate EEPROMs will be the favorite for future designs.

MNOS memories utilize MOS transistors with thresholds that are altered
by applying a large gate voltage. Erase time is between 10–100 ms and write
time runs between 1–10 ms. Devices may use word, row, or chip-erasable
configurations. Serial addressing and output is also available.

MNOS memories have not been widely used. Although a variety of devices
has been available, problems in data retention and high cost due to the complex manufacturing process has limited their application.

BIPOLAR MICROPROCESSOR
TECHNOLOGY CONSIDERATIONS

To allow comparisons among the bipolar IC technologies, the natural gate
implementation can be used. The natural gate is a realization of a logical
operator which requires a minimum number of transistors while giving the
maximum speed. For TTL, this gate is a NAND; for ECL, it is a NOR.

The two major characteristics of a gate are power and speed. The figure of
merit is the speed-power product, with speed in nanoseconds (ns), power in
milliwatts (mW), and the product in picojoules (pJ). Another characteristic

parameter is the gate's fan-in. In many bipolar technologies, the fan-in is four. In the TTL family, NAND gates with one, two, three, or four inputs have the same speed and the same power, and the larger fan-in NAND gates also have larger speed-power products. Limited fan-in can be a limitation in arithmetic processors with long word lengths.

TTL technology first appeared in 1964 and was the most popular logic for over a decade. The original parts (standard TTL) had a 10-ns gate at 10-mW dissipation, and devices of this type still tend to be the least expensive. Two TTL subfamilies are also in wide use. One is the Schottky-TTL with 3-ns gates of 20 mW which is close to matching the speed and power of ECL. The second is the low-power Schottky (LS/TTL), which retains the speed of TTL but at a power dissipation of 2 mW.[28]

ECL is the fastest available technology; gate delay is 1 to 2 ns, and the speed-power product is 50 pJ.[29] Introduced in 1968, this technology has mainly been limited to applications that require very high speed such as mainframe computers and some signal processing equipment. Because of coupling effects, interconnections in ECL systems act like transmission lines which require careful termination and matching. Reliable ECL designs require properly designed multilayer printed circuit boards, which tend to be expenive. Since ECL devices are powered from a -5.2 V supply, they are incompatible with TTL circuits. Another problem with ECL devices is their excessive power dissipation of 25 to 60 mW/gate, which may require forced air cooling. The internal circuit of ECL uses a current-switching mechanism that uses a constant current drain from the power supply. The TTL logic family, however, uses voltage thresholds and causes noise from current spikes during switching from one state to another.

I^2L is a newer technology introduced in 1975 that has not yet matured like ECL and TTL. A gate with LS/TTL speed of 10 ns and power dissipation of 0.1 mW has been used. By 1980, a few high-density monolithic microprocessors have been implemented in I^2L and more can be expected in the future. I^2L devices are usually powered from 5-V power to retain TTL compatibility. But I^2L technology only needs 1 V to operate, since it uses current sourcing.

REFERENCES

1. Kraft, G. D., and Toy, W. N., *Mini/Microcomputer Hardware Design,* (Englewood Cliffs: Prentice-Hall, 1979).
2. Zaks, R., *Microprocessors,* Berkeley: Sybex, 1980.
3. Ibid.
4. Texas Instruments, *The TTL Data Book for Design Engineers,* (Dallas: Texas Instruments, 1978).
5. Ibid.
6. Zaks, *Microprocessors.*
7. Motorola, *Semiconductor Data Library,* Vol. 4, Series A, (Phoenix: Motorola, 1978).
8. Ibid.

9. McGlynn, D. R., *Microprocessors,* (New York: Wiley, 1976).
10. Ibid.
11. Zaks, *Microprocessors.*
12. Ibid.
13. Young, S., Memories, *Electronic Design,* October 22, 1978.
14. Ibid.
15. Ibid.
16. Ibid.
17. Ibid.
18. Ibid.
19. Hassberg, C., Trends in Microcomputer Storage, *Electronic Products,* June 1979.
20. Ibid.
21. Pro-Log Corporation, *PROM User's Guide,* (Monterey: Pro-Log, 1979).
22. Ibid.
23. Ibid.
24. Ibid.
25. Ibid.
26. Intel Corporation, *2816 E²PROM Data Sheet,* (Santa Clara: Intel, 1981).
27. Ibid.
28. Texas Instruments, *TTL Data book.*
29. Motorola, *Semiconductor Data Library.*

EXERCISES

1. TTL SSI gates come mostly in 14-pin IC packages. Two pins are reserved for power and ground, while the other pins are used for input and output. How many circuits are included in one package if it contains the following type of circuit: (a) inverters; (b) 2-input exclusive-OR gates; (c) 3-input OR gates; (d) 4-input AND gates; (e) 5-input NOR gates.

2. List the fan-out, power dissipation, propagation delay, and noise margin for the following logic families: TTL, STTL, ECL, NMOS, and CMOS.

3. What types of applications would require:
   a. A Schottky bipolar microprocessor?
   b. A I²L microprocessor?
   c. A CMOS microprocessor?
   d. An NMOS microprocessor?
   e. A PMOS microprocessor?
   f. ECL microprocessor?

4. Calculate the injection current for an I²L microprocessor with a 10-V power supply and a 100-Ω current limit resistor.

5. Find the injection current for an I²L microprocessor with a 5-V power supply and a 33-Ω current limit resistor.

6. Describe how a MOS circuit is fabricated.

7. Estimate the maximum clock frequency that can be used with an I²L microprocessor for an injection current of 500 mA. (Refer to Figure 2.7.)

8. Estimate the clock frequency that can be used with an I²L microprocessor when the power supply voltage is 30 V and the current limiting resistor is 270 Ω. (Refer to Figure 2.7.)

9. What are the basic characteristics of ECL technology?
10. Compare the utility of a RAM that is bit-organized with one that is word-organized.
11. Describe the technology commonly called Schottky TTL and draw the basic gate circuit.
12. Draw the block diagram of a complete static MOS-ROM.
13. Describe the type of bipolar PROM implementation technique known as shorted junction. What are its disadvantages?
14. Describe the approach to a reversable PROM in which one electrically alters the program using metal-nitride-oxide-silicon (MNOS) technology.
15. Describe how ROMs can be programmed in the field using equipment designed for this purpose. What are some ways for the programmer to determine the memory locations?
16. What problems can alpha radiation cause in memories?
17. What are the advantages of the tunnel-oxide EPROM over the UV EPROM?
18. Discuss the major factors that limit the amount of logic on a chip.
19. What is a natural gate?
20. What are the major cost factors for an electronic system? Discuss their relative importance in a small, high-volume microprocessor system.

3. Microprocessor Units

THE MICROPROCESSOR EVOLUTION

In this chapter, we consider the capabilities of the available microprocessor units and develop selection considerations for product applications. We begin with an overview into the evolution of microprocessor devices.

In the late 1960s semiconductor manufacturers began to consider the use of LSI circuits, and they began defining chips having the following characteristics:

1. High gate-to-pin ratio.
2. Regular cell structures.
3. Large markets.

The manufacturers began to exploit the semiconductor memory market, which fulfilled these criteria. These early semi-conductor RAMs, ROMs, and shift registers were used in calculator and CRT terminal products.

The First Microprocessors

The Intel 4004 was the first microprocessor. It was designed as the processing element of a desk calculator that was introduced in 1971. The 4004 was never designed to be a general-purpose computer. Its shortcomings in this area were soon recognized. However, it was the first general-purpose computing device in a chip to be on the market. Many other chips introduced at about the same time were called "microprocessors" but were, in fact, only calculator chips. Many of them used serial-by-bit arithmetic.

The 4004 replaced six custom chips. Because the first applications were known and easy to understand, instruction sets and architectures were defined in a short time with those specific applications in mind. As programmable computers, their uses were limited.

In 1969, Computer Terminal Corporation (today known as Datapoint) contracted Intel to do a memory stack chip for a processor that would be used in a CRT terminal.[1] Datapoint intended to build a bit-serial processor with TTL using shift register memory components. Intel proposed that the entire processor be implemented on one chip. This processor became the 8008 and, along with the 4004, was fabricated using PMOS, the current memory fabrication technology. Both microprocessors were complete CPUs on a chip with similar characteristics. But because the 4004 was designed for serial BCD arithmetic and the 8008 for 8-bit character handling, the instruction sets differed. Most of the instructions and register organization for the 8008 were specified by Datapoint. Intel changed the instruction set so that the processor would fit on one chip and added some instructions to make it more like a general-purpose CPU. Although Intel was developing the 8008 for a customer, they wanted the option of selling it to others. Memories were using 16- and 18-pin packages then, so they chose to use 18 pins for the 8008 rather than design a package for what was believed to be a low-volume product.

Thus, the ancestor of all 8-bit microprocessors was the 8008, which was introduced in 1972. Although it was not intended to be a general-purpose microprocessor, its introduction on the market was a success, even with its limited performance. This success motivated a number of leading semiconductor manufacturers to produce improved designs.

The Early 8-bit Microprocessors

In 1973, memory technology had advanced from PMOS to NMOS. At first, Intel decided to use the 8008 layout with the NMOS process for a faster 8008.[2] After a short time, the company decided to use a new layout which would enhance the processor; at the same time, they decided to use the new 40-pin package used by high-volume calculator chips. The result was the 8080 microprocessor.

The 8080 was the first chip designed specifically for the microprocessor market. It used all of the 8008 instructions, but not necessarily the same machine coding. This meant that software could be portable, but the actual ROM chips containing the programs would have to be changed. The main objectives of the 8080 were to (1) obtain a ten-to-one improvement in throughput, (2) eliminate 8008 shortcomings that had become apparent, and (3) provide new capabilities not found in the 8008. The latter included the handling of 16-bit data types, BCD arithmetic, enhanced operand addressing modes, and improved interrupt processing. Memory costs had come down and processing speed was increasing, so larger memory spaces seemed to be another goal.

Since the 8080 was designed as a successor to the 8008, it had to maintain compatibility. It included all the 8080 registers plus more and all the 8008 instructions plus more. The 8080 was the first powerful microprocessor introduced and was a best-seller. Several other microprocessors with similar performance were introduced on the market a year or more later.

Technically, the 8080 was not the best product; however, it had the highest sales of any standard microprocessor. This was due to a number of factors, one being the fact that it was introduced first. The second reason was that Intel was the first to invest in the development of support chips and of support software for its product. All of the 8080 competitors were introduced after a nine-month delay or more.

Motorola introduced the 6800 in 1974 as direct competition for the 8080. The design of the 6800 was inspired by the 8008, and by the prevalent mini-computer philosophy. The 6800 has almost the same internal architecture as the 8080, with some differences at the register level. The 6800 instructions reflect the fact that it was introduced later than the 8080. They are somewhat more complex but in general similar to those of the 8080. Either of these microprocessors can be faster, depending on the application used in the comparison.

Although the 6800 was the second best selling standard microprocessor in 1976,[3] motorola was not the only semiconductor manufacturer to examine the new market and introduce a competitor to the 8080. Many manufacturers entered the market; some technologies such as MOS brought direct competition for the 6800 (the 6500 family).

MOS Technology began with the production of a variety of microprocessors in 1975; this was the 650X family. Within the 650X family, there are important differences between the various family members.

One of the first devices, the 6502, had strong ties with the 6800 and can be considered a competitor. Its bus organization, internal registers, and instruction set were similar to the 6800. Support chips could be used for either the 6500 or the 6800. The 6502 was faster than the 6800, and with the chips introduced by MOS Technology, which combine memory and I/O, systems could be built with fewer chips. The low prices of these chips resulted in inexpensive small- to medium-sized systems, with processing power similar or greater than the 6800.

In 1975, the Signetics 2650 appeared. The 2650 is a powerful processor, but it is slower than either the 8080 or the 6800 for arithmetic computations. It has its own architecture and instruction set. Its design was guided towards communications rather than arithmetic or control processing. Using this philosophy, the address bus has its own processing unit, which allows it to compute complex and sophisticated addresses. These facilities for addressing memory allow the 2650 to be suited for memory word retrievals as required for word processing or accessing large chains of characters. The 2650 has its place in the market, even though it cannot compete with the 8080 or the 6800 for arithmetic-oriented applications.

The Rockwell PPS8 was introduced in 1975 to compete with the 8080 and the 6800. It is implemented in PMOS technology. In spite of the many features of the PPS8, it was on the market too late, since the set of support chips is extensive with a one-chip disk controller, display controller, and keyboard controller. These peripheral chips are incompatible with the 8080 and the 6800; as a result, neither those chips, nor the PPS8 had significant sales.

In 1971, Rockwell manufactured a number of calculator chips. Following an evolution similar to that of Intel, the PPS4 (4-bit chip) was introduced as the evolution of a calculator design. It was introduced late, and by the time it was becoming supported, 8-bit microprocessor designs were entering the field.

The Early Microcomputer Chips

One of the first complete microcomputers-in-a-chip the PPS4/1 was introduced in 1976. It had a number of input and output lines and included ROM, RAM, and clock on the chip, and it had a number of versions, depending on the amount of memory on the chip and the number of pins. The price in large quantities was set low for applications such as consumer items.

The MCP 1600 chip set from Western digital was introduced in the mid seventies. This is a microprogrammed unit using two chips. The MPU requires an external ROM for the microprogram. The set is used to implement the Digital Equipment LSI 11. Digital Equipment is now manufacturing its own chips including the LSI11 which is software-compatible with the PDP11.

In 1975, Texas Instruments introduced the TMS1000 family, a 4-bit microcomputor-on-a-chip. The TMS1000 family has ROM, RAM, and clock circuitry in a single chip and was designed for consumer applications and other volume products. The TMS1000 uses a number of control signals which are internally decoded by a PLA.[4] This allows the application to be coded in a way which is difficult to copy by competitors. It also replaces a larger amount of ROM for providing outputs in response to combinations of inputs. The TMS1000 is therefore suited to complex control in response to 4-bit inputs. It is not well-suited to processing of 4-bit streams. The price of the TMS1000 in quantity is very low. TI was also marketing at this time an I^2L bit-slice microprocessor, the SBPO 400 as well as its own version of the Intel 8080.

Improved 8-bit Microprocessers

National Semiconductor introduced the SC/MP in 1976 as its 8-bit design. SCMP stands for "simple-cost-effective microprocessor." It was designed as a simple microprocessor with only a few extra chips required and at a very low cost. A low-cost MPU, however, was not a sufficient feature to generate a large sales interest. The p-channel version was slow, and a new version was made available in n-channel technology to improve speed. This microprocessor is well-suited for simple applications where economy is desired, but it does not have the power of an 8080 or 6800. In 1976, National introduced another 8-bit microprocessor: its own 8080 unit.

Several of the original designers of the 8080 left Intel and started their own company, Zilog, which is now part of Exxon. Starting with a small number of people, Zilog achieved the size of a semiconductor manufacturing company. Its first major design was the Z80 which incorporated on a single chip the 8080, its clock, and system controller with additional facilities. It was compatible with 8080 software, and as fast as the fastest 8080. Thus, the Z80 provided additional facilities, compared to the 8080.

Higher speeds are possible with the Z80 due to the larger number of registers. Also the Z80 is ROM-compatible with the 8080, so an 8080 program, implemented in ROM, can be plugged into a Z80 system. It will not use any of the special features of the Z80, but it is compatible. The Z80 has two interrupt levels versus one for the 8080. It requires a single power supply instead of three. The Z80 created significant competition to the 8080, especially where an improvement in performance was significant. But, Zilog did not produce the many other family components or provide the same level of software support.

Meanwhile, Intel did not remain idle. In 1976, advances in technology allowed Intel to consider enhancing the 8080.[5] Their objective was a processor utilizing a single power supply and requiring fewer chips. The 8080 required an oscillator chip and a system controller chip. The new processor with those features added, the 8085, was designed to be compatible with the 8080 at the machine-code level.

Architecturally, the 8085 turned out to be not much more than a repackaging of the 8080. The major differences were the added features such as an on-chip oscillator, power-on reset, vectored interrupts, serial I/O, and a single power supply. The new instructions, were added to support the serial port and the interrupt mask. Several other instructions that were to be added were never announced because of constraints on the 8085 support software and the future 8086.

The 8085 does not offer some of the features of the Z80. It does not provide additional registers or multiple banks, and it does not provide dynamic refresh. However, it does provide interrupt levels which are not provided by the Z80.

Early 8-bit Microcomputer Chips

As technology evolved, it became possible to create a full 8-bit, single-chip microcomputer. The two-chip version of the F8 was the first true microcomputer using two-chips to be introduced. The F8 has an unconventional architecture and an unusual instruction set. This is due to historical evolution: the

2-chip F8 resulted from the specifications of a company for a custom chip built by General Instrument. The 2-chip F8 was later introduced as a product of Fairchild, and is essentially similar to the GI design. Since then, all of its functions have been implemented in a single-chip, the 3870, by Mostek and now by Fairchild. The target market for the chips is at the low-end: industrial and consumer applications.

Since the F8 was not designed from the start as a single-chip microcomputer, its instruction set may be harder to use than other traditional instruction sets. Programming may be more difficult at first. However, the cost of programming over a large number of units may be minimal. The essential consideration is the performance of the device and its price.

Competitors to the F8 appeared in the 8048 from Intel and the Z8 from Zilog. The 8048 architecture was derived from the 8080, but is not compatible with it. The 8048 has its own instruction set which is not the 8080 instruction set. It provides the capability of testing a bit within the accumulator and jumping to a location depending on the bit test. With a skilled programmer, the performance of the F8 can be close to the performance of the 8048. One of the versions of the 8048, the 8748, uses instead of ROM an EPROM, which is U.V.-erasable. It is erased with ultraviolet light and then reprogrammed. This can be an advantage during development. The Zilog Z8 is similar to the 8048 in that it is a single-chip microcomputer based on its parent the Z80.

Early 16-bit Microprocessors

The first 16-bit, single-chip microprocessor was introduced in 1974, when National offered its PACE unit, a one-chip version of the IMP16, a bit slice processor introduced in 1973.[6] PACE was a p-channel machine with a 10-μs instruction time, packaged in a 40-pin DIP. The PACE was to be a replacement for the IMP minicomputer CPU. The PACE instruction set was compatible with the IMP 16 instruction set, since the PACE used PMOS technology and was comparatively slow.

During this same period, General Instruments introduced the CP1600, which was a faster NMOS processor designed for a variety of minicomputer-like designs.

Also during the 70s the Data General MN601 implemented in one chip most of the slowest NOVA minicomputer. Minicomputer manufacturers had been facing the implementation of their own slow minicomputers by other companies using microprocessors. What is more, these implementations used a smaller number of components and resulted in a lower cost product. In order to compete, the minicomputer manufacturers had to produce their own LSI designs to reduce the number of parts and the cost.

This trend led Fairchild to announce the 9440 16-bit microprocessor, which implemented most of the functions of the NOVA 1200 CPU on one chip. It would then compete head-on with Data General products.

Most of these early 16-bit microprocessors were targeted at the minicomputer market. The newer ones aimed at establishing a market of their own.

Improved 16-bit Microprocessors

The first of the newer 16-bit chips was the Texas Instruments 9900. It has 16-bit multiply and divide operations in a 64-pin package.[7] The 9900 is used by Texas Instruments in their 990 minicomputer/microcomputer. Since Texas Instruments uses this chip as the CPU in their 990 system, any 9900 user has a minicomputer-like processor with the same instruction set as the 990.

Some of the characteristics of these early 16-bit microprocessors are shown in Table 3.1.

In 1978, Intel introduced a 16-bit NMOS processor, the 8086 (now called the IAPX 86). The 8086 was designed to offer power, speed, and features beyond the machines of the mid-70s. Throughput was increased an order of magnitude over the 8080; memory space was 16 times greater (one megabyte); and the number of I/O ports increased from 256 in the 8080 to 64K in the 8086. Other features included high-level language addressing, string manipulation, and full decimal arithmetic. The chip used 29,000 transistors on a die 27% larger than the 8080. This was made possible through the use of HMOS, a technology with tighter geometries that yielded smaller dice, lower power requirements, and faster processing.[8]

The 8086 instruction set is an expanded version of the 8080 instructions. Hence 8080 programs code can be converted to 8086 code.

The Z8000 appeared in 1979. However, it is not an enhancement of Zilog's Z80 family and has its own internal structure. The Z8000 uses a unique instruction set. The internal registers allow 32-bit doubleword operations. Traps for illegal addresses instructions can be used in debugging.

The Motorola 68000 was designed as a 32-bit wide machine; the external 16-bit bus is multiplexed from 32 bits inside. A 32-bit ALU is used along with 16 32-bit registers. The address bus uses 23 bits for addressing, providing a capability of 16M bytes.

It can be assumed that still wider bit sizes will be introduced in the future. However, the introduction time is speculative. Although densities are constantly improving, the cost and the design difficulties have been increasing steadily.

National Semiconductor has also announced a family of 16-bit microprocessors. The 16000 series consists of the 16008, 16016, and 16032 processors. The NS16008 and the NS16016 are similar, each offering an internal data bus 16 bits wide and a direct addressing range of 64K bytes. Either of these chips can operate in two modes:

Table 3.1 16-bit Microprocessors

	NATIONAL PACE	DATA GENERAL MN 601	GEN. INST. CP 1600	FAIRCHILD 9440	TEXAS INSTRUMENT 9900
Technology	PMOS	NMOS	NMOS	13L	NMOS
Instructions	50	NOVA 3 Instr.	87	NOVA 1200	69
Cycle Time (μs)	8 to 10	2.4 to 10	2.4	1 to 2.5	1.5
Direct Addressing (bits)	16	16	16	16	16
Registers	4	4	7	4	RAM (16)
Package (pins)	40	40	40	40	64
Power Supply (V)	$+5, -12$	$-4.25, +5, +10, +14$	$+12, +5, -3$	$+5, +1$	$-5, +5, +12$
Features	Compatible IMP 16	Emulator NOVA 3	—	Emulator NOVA 1200	Mult/Div

1. Native mode in which the two processors have 100 instructions and are compatible with the 16032;
2. 8080 mode which allows emulation of the 8080, with a speed four times the 8080.

The 16016 has a 16-bit data bus, while the 16008 has an eight-bit data bus for use in systems with 8-bit-wide memory and peripheral devices. The 16032 has an address range of 32M bytes using a memory management unit (MMU). The 16032 has an internal data bus that is 32 bits wide.

The characteristics of these later 16-bit microprocessors are shown in Table 3.2.

16-bit Microcomputer Chips

A single chip 16-bit microcomputer has been announced by Texas Instruments. The 9940 single-chip microcomputer has an instruction set compatible with the 9900 microprocessor.

The 16-bit single-chip microcomputer represents a technical solution to the pin count problem since the microcomputer integrates the memory on the chip, it does not require an address bus; therefore, these pins are available for input-output functions.

Bit-Slice Devices

Bit-slice devices should not be properly classified as microprocessors, but the term "microprocessor" is often applied to bit-slice devices since they are LSI components which implement some of the functions of a CPU. Yet they are not complete CPU's. Still, popular usage labels them as microprocessors.

The bit-slice device is a section of an arithmetic logic unit along with its data paths. It may include registers, the ALU, multiplexers, and buses. It does not include the control section. This part of a bit-slice system is implemented with other devices and is generally microprogrammed as shown in

Table 3.2 16-bit Microprocessors

	8086	Z8000	68000	16008/ 16016	16032
Instructions	95	110	61	100	100
Registers	14	16	16	8	8
Package (pins)	40	48/40	64	40	48
Address Range (bytes)	1M	48M	64M	16M	16M
Addressing Modes	24	6	14	9	9
Clock Frequency	4–10 MHz	2.5–3.9 MHz	5–8 MHz	10 MHz	10 MHz

Figure 3.1. The complete microprocessor requires a significant number of devices which make bit-slice systems larger and more expensive than single chip microprocessors. The usual size for bit-slice devices is four bits. Bit slices are used for building the most powerful processors in use.

The use of bit-slices started from the search for processing speed. To implement the fastest possible speed, designers turned to the fastest technologies, such as low-power Schottky.

In the early 70s a number of companies introduced ALU slices. These were not bit-slice devices but 4-bit ALU slices, which were used to implement 8- or 16-bit ALUs, since a bit-slice also includes all of the multiplexers, buses, registers, and flags. Implementing four 4-bit ALU slices in parallel resulted in a 16-bit ALU.

Early Bit-Slice Chips

National Semiconductor was the first to introduce a bit-slice device. The GP/CP set used PMOS technology to implement the IMP series which was influenced by the Data General Nova minicomputer. The result was the 16-bit IMP16 minicomputer which used four slices plus control elements (CROMs). These chips implemented a complete minicomputer with a small number of chips, but unfortunately they were very slow. The GP/CP may be considered the grandfather of bit slices.

Intel then introduced the first bipolar bit-slice, the 3000.[9] The 3000 was

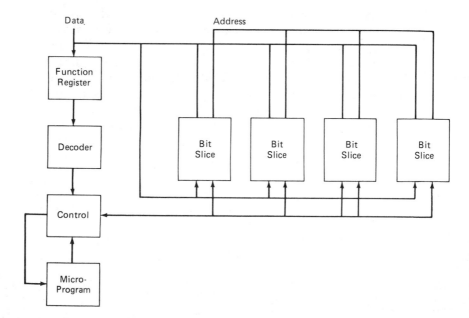

Fig. 3.1. Bit-slice structure.

fast, and it was the first bipolar design in a bit-slice. But it operated only on two bits and required more components than a 4-bit slice. Its instruction set was limited, although it was equipped with a large number of buses. Another feature of the 3000 was that it was horizontally microprogrammable. Thus, a microinstruction specifies events within several fields simultaneously. It is then possible to execute many operations simultaneously and achieve high speeds provided that the programmer takes advantage of it. Unfortunately, many progammers did not because they were discouraged by the complexity involved and considered this a disadvantage.

Monolithic Memories then introduced the 5701/6701 as the predecessor of the standard 4-bit design in use today. The MMI5701 was designed as an emulation of the Data General Nova. MMI produced boards using a bit-slice design with the 6701 which replaced a Nova board by using fewer components, with 10% more speed. The introduction of the 2901 by AMD replaced the 5701/6701 by offering the same functions at even higher speed.

Modern Bit-Slice Chips

The Advanced Micro Devices 2901 has become the standard 4-bit-slice. The 2901 architecture is essentially the same as the 5701, but with a few improvements. Its speed is much higher. Other improvements of the 2901 over the 5701 are an extra bit in the microinstruction field, resulting in twice as many microinstructions, and an external connection on the internal bus.

The Motorola ECL component, the 10800, achieves a very high speed, with a cycle time of 55 ns. But it requires an external register chip, which increases the component count and reduces the effective system speed. With a higher integration, this technology could become a most efficient implementation of bit-slice devices for fast applications.

Texas Instruments has introduced the 0400, followed by the 0401, the first bit-slice device implemented in I²L technology. I²L (integrated injection logic) is a bipolar technology which is characterized by bipolar speed and a low power consumption. A summary of the major characteristics of these bit-slice devices appears in Table 3.3.

Fairchild has introduced a number of devices in the 9440 family that are not complete bit-slice devices but are more than ALU slices. They are intermediate and can be used for CPU designs. The 2901 design has become the standard for 4-bit slices. As the newer technologies are improved, this design will be displaced.

INTEL MICROPROCESSORS

The Intel 4004, which was the first microprocessor, was rapidly replaced by an improved version—the 4040. In order to preserve the software investment of the 4004, the 4040 instruction set was made compatible with the 4004, but

Table 3.3 Bit-Slice Microprocessors

	NATIONAL IMP	INTEL 3000	MMI 5701	AMD 2901	MOTOROLA 10800	SBP0400
Bits	4	2	4	4	4	4
Technology	PMOS	Schottky	Schottky	Schottky	MECL	12L
Instructions	4 + shift	Minimal	36	36	Complex	16
Cycle Time (ns)	9200	100	200	95, 125	55	1000
On-Chip Registers	7	12	16	16	—	7
memory register	—	YES	—	—	—	—
EXT Accumulator	—	—	YES	YES	—	—
stack	YES (16)	—	—	—	—	—
status	YES	YES	YES	YES	YES	YES
package	24, 40	28	40	40	48	40

the 4040 offers a number of improvements.[10] It has an interrupt capability and a larger number of internal registers. The register banks can allow a fast interrupt response. When an interrupt occurs, (provided there are no more than two interrupt levels), one can switch from one bank of registers to the other. The program counter and the status word are not repeated within the register banks, which would require additional instructions to be executed for switching.

Intel 4040

The basic architecture of the 4040 is shown in Figure 3.2. The device is organized around a 4-bit internal data bus which interconnects the internal registers. Input and output functions are performed by a 4-bit bidirectional data bus which interfaces with the input/output pins. The accumulator is used as a latch for storing data that is ready to be processed by the ALU, or for receiving data that has already been processed. A temporary register, (T), (not under user control) is used to temporarily store data which has been transferred from another register in the microprocessor.

The address registers operate as a last-in first-out pushdown stack. The address stack uses a program counter with seven levels. The address registers are 12 bits wide and are multiplexed to the 4-bit internal bus by a stack multiplexer. The register bank consists of 4-bit general-purpose registers, which can be used in pairs for 8-bit storage. These registers can be used during interrupt processing for saving status variables as already discussed, and during addressing in order to provide indexed capabilities.

The instruction register stores the next instruction to be executed by the processor. Instructions may be either 8 bits or 16 bits in length. The instruction register is 8 bits wide, so a one-word instruction will be executed in one instruction cycle, while a two-word instruction will take two instruction cycles.

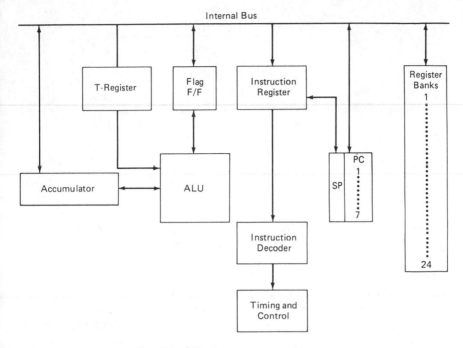

Fig. 3.2. 4040 microprocessor architecture.

The instruction decoder decodes the bit pattern of the instruction from the instruction register by translating it into a sequence of machine operations using the timing and control circuitry which in turn controls the internal operations of the 4040. A two-phase clock input is used in the 4040 to develop the synchronization signals which are transferred to the internal elements of the CPU.

A basic 4040 system is shown in Figure 3.3. A 4289 memory interface is used with 1-of-8 decoder for connecting a ROM. As a 4-bit microprocessor, the 4040 is intended for applications such as calculators, games, appliances, and simple control applications.

Intel 8008

The 8008 is the first-generation 8-bit microprocessor that was introduced in early 1972. It was the second of the first generation processors, following the introduction of the 4004 in late 1971. The 8008 is fabricated using the PMOS process and is compact for an 8-bit microprocessor packaged in an 18-pin dual in-line package.

Address information is multiplexed over the 8-bit bidirectional data bus. At the beginning of each machine cycle requiring a read-from or write-to

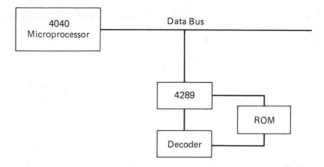

Fig. 3.3. Basic 4040 system.

memory, the address information is put on the data bus at the beginning of the cycle. The address information must be saved or latched by external circuitry.

The instruction set consists of scratch-pad-register instructions, accumulator instructions, transfer-of-control instructions, input/output instructions, and processor-control instructions. The 8008 was a low-cost microprocessor, but the low cost was achieved with low performance. Since p-channel technology is slower than other technologies, multiplexing the address information on the data bus reduced performance even further. The minimum time to execute a single instruction with the standard 8008 was $20\mu s$. (The architecture of the 8008 is shown in Figure 3.4.)

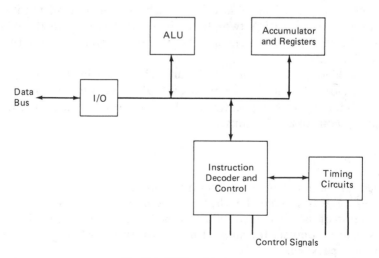

Fig. 3.4. 8008 architecture.

Intel 8080

One of the most popular microprocessors, was the Intel 8080. The 8080 is an 8-bit n-bannel MOS device which is packaged in a 40-pin DIP. It is based on the older 8008 architecture, but it is capable of much more sophisticated applications. The architecture of the 8080, like the 8008, is organized around an 8-bit internal data bus (as shown in Figure 3.5). Compared to the 8008, the 8080 has the following additional capabilities:

1. Decimal arithmetic.
2. External stacking.
3. Direct memory access.
4. Increased instructions and addressing modes.

One of the limitations of the 8008 was its limited stack depth. The use of an external stack in the 8080 provides improved design flexibility, while the direct memory access feature allows peripheral devices to access the busses

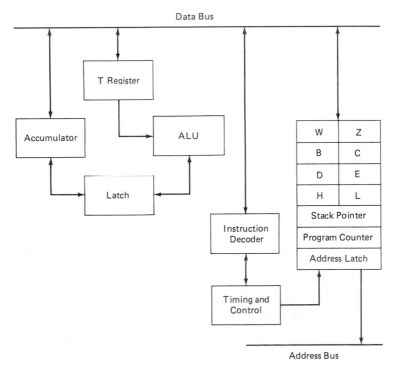

Fig. 3.5. 8080 architecture.

for direct memory data transfers without interferring with processor operation. A decoder as shown in Figure 3.6 is necessary to synchronize the operation of the 8080 with the rest of the system.

The 8080 processor requires + 12, + 5, and −5 V supplies. Clock speeds from 500 KHz to 2 MHz can be used; however, prolonged operation at the maximum speed may affect device reliability. If high operating temperatures are to be experienced, reliability can be maintained by operating at slower speeds during these high temperature periods. If a switching system is used to change the operating speed, it can also be used to speed up processor operations for short periods when data is liable to back up during busy periods. An additional consideration is the drive capability of the 8080 when connected to TTL outputs. Since the 8080 is a MOS device, only one TTL load can be safely connected to each output. If additional drive is required, circuitry for driving the external loads must be added.

Intel 8085

The 8085 is a faster version of the 8080. It has an on-chip clock along with a system controller to provide cycle status information. It is software compati-

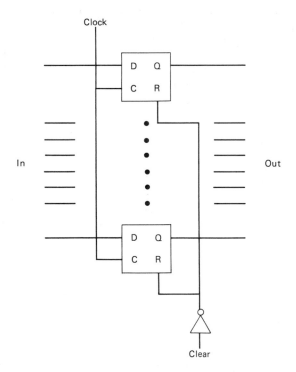

Fig. 3.6. 8080 status decoding.

ble with the 8080, and it operates with a 1.3 μs instruction cycle for the A configuration. The 8085 uses two additional instructions:

RIM: read interrupt mask
SIM: set interrupt mask

The major value of 8085 lies in the special chips which are available for a minimal 8085 system. These are memory and I/O combinations, and they connect directly to the 8085 without the need for any additional components. They allow a complete 8085 system to be assembled with just three chips. Thus, we have a microprocessor with the same power as the 8080, while requiring a minimal number of chips for a system. The limitation of the system is the amount of memory contained in these memory and I/O combinations: 2K words of ROM and 256K words of RAM. But for small- or medium-sized systems, the 8085 is a leading contender. A comparison between the 8080 and the 8085 appears below:

	8080	8085
CPU	3 chips: 8080 + 8228 + clock	1 chip
Speed of Execution	2.μs to 1.3μs (8080 A-1)	1.3 μs
Memory Access Required	300 ns	450 ns
Power Supplies	3	1
Instruction Set	78	8080 + 2 instructions
Interrupts	1	5
Serial I/O	0	1

Intel 8021

The Intel 8021 is an 8-bit parallel microcomputer chip in a 28-pin package.[11] The n-channel silicon gate chip contains a 1K x 8 program memory, a 64K x 8 data memory, an 8-bit timer/event counter, 21 input/output lines, and oscillator and clocking circuitry. The block diagram for the 8021 is shown in Figure 3.7. The chip has a bit handling capability and will perform either binary or BCD arithmetic. The 8021 program memory is mask programmable with no provisions for external expansion. All locations in the data memory are indirectly addressable, with eight locations being directly addressable.

Intel 8048 Family

The 8048 is a self-sufficient 8-bit parallel computer fabricated on a single chip using the n-channel silicon gate MOS process. The 8048 has a 1K x 8 program memory, a 64K x 8 RAM data memory, 27 I/O lines, and an 8-bit

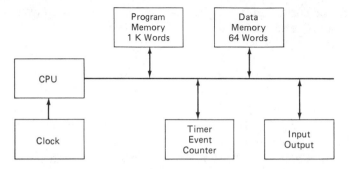

Fig. 3.7. 8021 microcomputer chip.

timer/counter with oscillator and clock circuits. For systems that require extra capability, the 8048 can be expanded with standard memories. The 8035 is the equivalent of an 8048, but without program memory.

Three interchangeable pin-compatible versions of this microcomputer exist: (1) the 8748 with user-programmable and erasable EPROM for prototype and preproduction systems, (2) the 8048 with factory-programmed mask ROM program memory for low cost, high volume applications, and (3) the 8035 without program memory for use with external memories.

The 8048 has bit handling capability as well as facilities for both binary and BCD arithmetic. The instruction set consists mostly of single byte instructions with no instructions over 2 bytes in length. The 8048 family characteristics are summarized below:[12]

	8021	8035	8039	8048	8049	8748
Resident Program Memory (bytes)	1K ROM	none	none	1K ROM	2K ROM	1K EPROM
Resident RAM (bytes)	64	64	128	64	128	64
Number of I/O Lines	21	27	27	27	27	27
Number of Pins	28	40	40	40	40	40

The 8048 was designed for single-chip applications and does not suffer from having to be compatible with more powerful predecessors.

The program memory of 1K x 8 can be expanded. But expanding the memory affects the hardware configuration drastically. Expanding the 8048 moves the device into the general purpose control market.

In addition to expansion, the program memory can be completely external to the device. This requires a multichip system but allows more complete emulation during development.

The 8048 uses a register-oriented architecture with two banks of 8-bit registers in the 64K x 8 RAM. The selected bank operates with the accumulator using a somewhat incomplete set of instructions (incompleteness is due to a lack of compare and substract operations). There is a full set of increments and decrements, and all of the registers, except the accumulator, may be decremented with a jump if not zero.

The data memory is a 64K x 8 RAM. Two register banks and the 8-level stack reside in the RAM, leaving half of the locations available as scratch pad. RAM operations can be done with indirect register addressing using either of two registers in the selected register bank. The same operations that can be performed with the registers may also be performed with RAM locations except for the decrement operations.

Intel 8022

The 8022 is another member of the Intel group of single-chip 8-bit microcomputers.[13] It is designed for low-cost, high-volume applications which involve analog signals, capacitive keyboards, and/or large ROM space. The 8022 addresses these applications by integrating additional functions on-chip, such as A/D conversion, comparators, and zero-cross detection.

The 8022 includes 2K bytes of ROM, 64K bytes RAM, 28 I/O lines, an on-chip A/D converter with two input channels, an 8-bit port with comparator inputs for interfacing to low voltage capacitive touchpanels or other non-TTL interfaces, external and timer interrupts, and zero-cross detection capability. In addition, it contains an 8-bit interval timer/event counter, an oscillator, and a clock.

The 8022 can be used as a controller as well as a basic arithmetic processor. It has bit-handling capability plus binary and BCD arithmetic. The instruction set consists mostly of single byte instructions and has extensive conditional jump and table lookup capability. The 8022 contains an on-chip hardware implementation of an 8-bit analog-to-digital converter with two multiplexed analog inputs. The A/D converter uses the successive approximation technique and provides an updated conversion once every 40 μs using a minimum of software.

Intel 8051 Family

The 8031/8051/8751 are stand-alone single-chip computers fabricated with depletion-load, n-channel, and MOS technology.

The 8051/8751 contain a nonvolatile 4K x 8 read only program memory; volatile 128K x 8 read/write data memory; 32 I/O lines; two 16-bit timer/counters; five-source, two-level, nested interrupt structure; serial I/O port for multiprocessor communications, or full duplex UART (universal asynchronous receiver transmitter); and on-chip oscillator and clock circuits. The

8031 is identical, except that it lacks the program memory. The 8051 can be expanded using standard TTL compatible memories.

The 8051 microcomputer, like its 8048 predecessor, was designed as a controller or a basic arithmetic processor. It has facilities for binary and BCD arithmetic, as well as bit-handling capabilities. The instruction set consists of 44% one-byte, 41% two-byte, and 15% three-byte instructions. With a 12-MHz crystal, 58% of the instructions execute in 1 μs and 40% in 2 μs, while multiply and divide require 4 μs. Among the other instructions added to the 8048 instruction set are subtract and compare.

The 8031 is a control-oriented CPU without the on-chip program memory. It can address 64K bytes of external program memory in addition to 64K bytes of external data memory. For systems requiring extra capability, each device in the 8051 family may be expanded. The 8051 is an 8031 with the lower 4K bytes of program memory filled with on-chip mask programmable ROM, while the 8751 has 4K-bytes of UV erasable ROM.

Intel 3002

The Intel 3002 is an early 2-bit-slice microprocessor that used Schottky bipolar technology to achieve the first fast cycle times.[14] The 3002 central processing unit was combined with the 3001 microprogram control unit to form a two-chip microprocessor system based on user-generated microcode stored in the microprogram memory. The two components were combined with memory and peripherals for the first high-speed controllers and processors. Each 3002, however, represented only a 2-bit-slice, so devices were connected in parallel to form processors of the desired word length. (The basic architecture for the 3002 is shown in Figure 3.8.)

In the 3002, the microfunctions were controlled by a function bus which instructed the decode unit to select the ALU functions to be performed, to generate scratch pad register addresses, and to control the A and B multiplexers. A microfunction action could be a data transfer, a shift, an increment or decrement, a test for a specified condition, an initialization for a specified condition, an addition or subtraction in two's complement, a bit mask, or a program counter operation.

The 3001 used a technique in which the microinstruction field specified conditional tests on bus inputs and registers. The unit used a row and column addressing method which allowed a jump from one location unconditionally to any other location within that row or column, or conditionally to specified locations in a single operation. This allowed processor functions to be executed in parallel with program branching. (The 3000 system configuration is shown in Figure 3.9.)

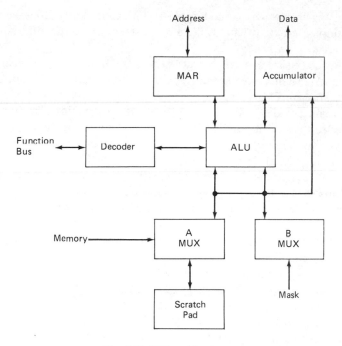

Fig. 3.8. 3002 architecture.

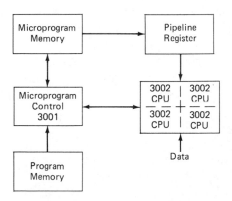

Fig. 3.9. 3000 system configuration.

Intel 8086

The 8086 is a 16-bit microprocessor based on the 8080. The 8086 uses silicon-gate HMOS technology for faster performance and an expanded 8080 structure.[15] Basically, it is an improved, 16-bit version of the 8080. The 8080 multiplexed bus has been expanded into a 16-bit external bus. Like the 8080, the instructions are byte-oriented. (The basic structure of the 8086 is shown in Figure 3.10.)

The 8086 consists of two separate processing units: (1) an execution unit, or EU, and (2) a bus interface unit, or BIU, connected by a 16-bit ALU data bus and an 8-bit Q bus. The EU obtains instructions from the instruction queue, maintained by the BIU, and executes instructions using the 16-bit ALU. Execution of instruction involves maintenance of the status and control logic, manipulation of the general registers and instruction operands, and manipulation of segment offset addresses. The EU accesses memory and peripheral devices through requests to the BIU, which performs all bus operations for the EU. This involves generating the physical addresses from the segment register and offset values, reading operands, and writing the results.

The execution unit and the bus interface unit operate independently of each other, enabling the 8086 to overlap instruction fetch and execution. While the 8086 is decoding the current instruction, the bus interface unit (BIU) fetches the contents of the next sequential memory addresses and loads them into the queue. If the current instruction is not a branch instruction, the next instruction is available to the processor's execution unit (EU) upon completion of the current instruction without the need for a memory access. If the current instruction is a branch instruction, the next instruction is fetched from memory. The queue decreases address bus/data bus idle times by prefetching data, thus increasing processor speed.

The 8086 register structure is similar to the 8080's. The 8086 execution unit contains four 16-bit pointer and index registers and four 16-bit data registers that are addressable on a byte basis. These eight registers are used to provide

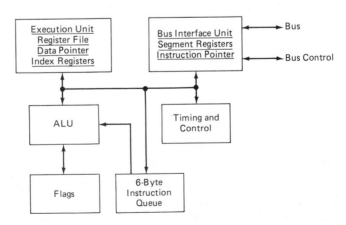

Fig. 3.10. 8086 architecture.

compact coding at the cost of flexibility. The BIU contains one 16-bit instruction pointer, which holds the offset of the next instruction to be fetched. This pointer is updated by the BIU but is not directly accessed by the program. The BIU also contains four 16-bit segment registers for segment base addressing, which allows access of up to four 64K-byte segments at a time. The EU also contains six 1-bit status flags and three 1-bit control flags.

The 8088 is an 8086 with an 8-bit data bus. An 8088 microcomputer board is shown in Figure 3.11.

MOTOROLA MICROPROCESSORS

Motorola 6800

The Motorola 6800 is an 8-bit NMOS single chip microprocessor. The architecture of the 6800 is shown in Figure 3.12. The microprocessor has three 16-bit registers and three 8-bit registers that are available to the programmer. Another register, the instruction register, is used for temporary storage of instructions for the instruction decoder.[16]

Two 8-bit accumulators are used to hold operands and results from the arithmetic and logic unit (ALU). The A accumulator serves as the primary accumulator, while the B unit functions as a secondary accumulator. The 6800 performs all arithmetic computations using one of these registers. The index register is a 2-byte unit for storing data or 16-bit memory addresses for use in the indexed mode of addressing. The program counter is a 16-bit, 2-byte register which points to the current program address.

The stack pointer register serves the same function for subroutine linkage as the stack pointer in the 8080. It contains the address of the next available

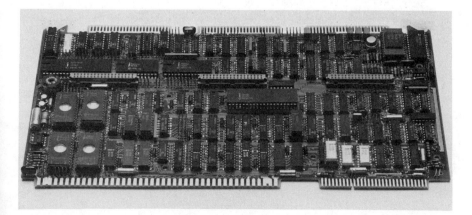

Fig. 3.11. This 8080 industrial microcomputer board contains all the parts needed for many complex industrial control applications. (*Courtesy Intel Corporation.*)

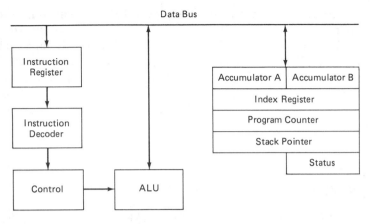

Fig. 3.12. 6800 architecture.

location in a last-in-first-out pushdown stack. The stack itself is normally a RAM.

The condition code register is an 8-bit register used to indicate the results of an ALU operation such as negative (N), zero (Z) overflow (V), carry from bit 7 (C) and a half-carry from bit 3 (H). These bits are used to test conditions for conditional branch instructions. Bit 4 of the condition code register is used as the interrupt mask bit (I). Unused bits of this register are always ones. (These bit positions are shown in Figure 3.13.)

The 6800 uses an 8-bit bidirectional data bus for transferring data to and from memory and peripheral devices (see Figure 3.14). The address bus is 16 bits wide, and when the bus is turned off, it acts as an open circuit for direct memory access (DMA) operations.

When compared to the 8080, the 6800 has an apparent advantage because of the use of depletion-mode loads. The 8080 requires three voltages: + 5V, −5V, + 12V. Since the 8080 was introduced at a time when Intel was using a dynamic memory technology, the three levels were considered necessary.

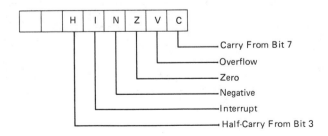

Fig. 3.13. 6800 status register.

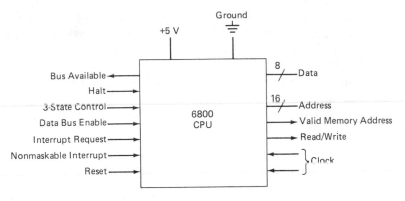

Fig. 3.14. 6800 signal interface.

The 6800 by contrast, requires only one voltage. This frees two pins on the package and requires a simpler power supply. Because of the lack of pins, the 8080 must use the data bus to propagate status information during state T1 of each machine cycle, and it is necessary to multiplex the data bus externally, which is done with the 8228 system controller. In most applications, however, the 8080 does not require an extra component relative to the 6800.

The 6800 uses two arithmetic flags, one for carry and one for overflow. The overflow occurs during 8-bit arithmetic and the flag signals that a previous computation is outside the range provided by an 8-bit two's complement number. A flag condition is produced when two positive numbers are added and a negative number results or when two negative numbers are added and a positive number results. This flag can be used to detect error conditions as shown:

```
LDA  A  X1   : load accumulator, A = X1
ADD  A  X2   : add, A = X1 + X2
BVS  OVFW : branch if overflow
```

The sequence transfers control to OVFW if the sum of $X1$ and $X2$ produces an overflow. The overflow flags can also be used to compare two values and determine which is greater. If $X1$ minus $X2$ is positive and no overflow results, then $X1$ is greater or equal to $X2$. If $X1$ minus $X2$ is negative and no overflow results, then $X1$ is still greater than or equal to $X2$. In all other cases, $X1$ is less than $X2$.

The 6800 has a software interrupt instruction (SWI) that can be used to decrease memory requirements. This instruction uses a subroutine address stored in hexadecimal locations FFFC and FFFD.

The following rules can be helpful when laying out programs for the 6800:

1. For frequently used variables, use memory locations 0–255 for storage and pass parameters between routines. Direct addressing is then maximized, which reduces storage space and is faster compared to extended addressing.
2. Use the index register as much as possible to further reduce extended addressing.
3. Structure subroutines so that they are near the calling routine in order that branch-to-subroutine instructions can be used instead of jump-to-subroutine instructions.

With direct addressing, the first 256 memory locations can be operated as general registers which allows more operations than the 8080, although these instructions require two bytes with a memory reference.

Motorola 6802

A second version of the 6800 is the 6802. This chip includes all of the features of the 6800 along with an on-chip clock-oscillator and 128 bytes of RAM. The RAM locations are at hex addresses 0000 to 007F, with the first 32 bytes at addresses 0000 to 001F having a low power mode for memory retention during power outages. The 6802 can be used with a 6846 timer for a complete system for simple control applications in just two packages.

Motorola 6809

The 6809 is a 16-bit internal version of the 6800; it uses an extended 6800 instruction set with instructions like 8 by 8 bit multiply, and it has 16-bit modes with mnemonics the same as used for the 6800. The op codes differ so that object code cannot be directly transferred from 6800 to 6809, but the programs can be reassembled with a 6809 assembler in order to provide more efficient program resulting from the improved internal structure of the 6809. A stack pointer defined by the user has been added, as well as another index register and a page register. The 6809 also has a number of long branch instructions which were absent in the 6800.

An additional addressing mode in the 6809 is auto-increment addressing. This capability improves the software in sequential indexing applications since index updating commands are not required. A new SYNC instruction stops the processor until an interrupt occurs to resume processing. This instruction can be used to synchronize the processor to real time events in a system.

The instruction set has fewer instructions than the older 6800; however, the 6809 has more powerful commands that replace the multiple instructions of the older processor. The 59 instructions include 16-bit arithmetic, extended range branches, enhanced pointer register manipulation, and auto-increment/decrement operations with any of four pointer registers.

Motorola 6801

The Motorola 6801 microcomputer is an expandable chip which contains 2048 bytes of mask-programmable ROM, 128 bytes of RAM, a 16-bit counter/timer, a UART, 31 parallel I/O lines, and an expanded instruction set of the 6800. The 6801 is object-code compatible with the 6800. It has improved execution times of some instructions plus new 16 and 8-bit instructions. It is expandable to a 64K words.

The basic architecture of the 6801 microcomputer is shown in Figure 3.15. In addition to the 6800 CPU on the chip are the program memory, scratch pad memory, counter, clock oscillator, UART, and I/O ports.

Besides code compatibility with the 6800 processor, there are 10 new instructions. Added are instructions for performing 8-bit multiplication, double-precision addition, double-precision load operations, and double precision subtraction. There are also some new shift, rotate, and index register operations.

The 6803 is similar to the 6801 except that it doesn't have on-chip ROM storage, and some of the port lines are used as a multiplexed data and address bus. The 6803 has a 16-bit counter/timer, 13 parallel I/O lines, UART, clock, and a 128-byte RAM.

Motorola 10800

The Motorola 10800 4-bit slice uses emitter coupled logic (ECL) to achieve high-speed performance. A 48-pin quad-in-line package is used, and both lateral and vertical expansion are allowed. Lateral expansion can be used to increase the bit length in increments of 4 bits, while vertical expansion can be

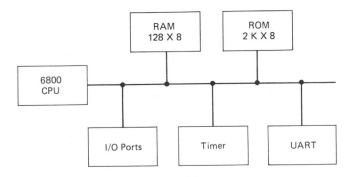

Fig. 3.15. 6801 microcomputer.

used to increase throughput by pipelining. The 10800 system structure is shown in Figure 3.16.

The 10800 arithmetic logic unit is combined with a microprogram control unit, a timer unit, and a memory interface unit for the microprogrammed system. The memory and register file complete the configuration.

The ALU components include a 4-bit adder which uses a shift network and accumulator for arithmetic operations. A latch and multiplex system are used to control data flow within the ALU, and bus control logic is used to control the flow of data over the input and output busses. (The architecture of the 10800 is shown in Figure 3.17.)

The 10801 microprogram control unit was designed as a component for the 10800 microprocessor system, but it may also be used as an independent device for controller applications. The 10801 contains bit control registers which are expandable to any number of bits. It also contains a control memory address register and a 4-bit, 4-deep LIFO stack register for subroutine nesting. Sixteen address control functions are used for jumps (which may be conditional or unconditional) and for subroutine control. This chip also has an internal instruction register, a repeat register, and a 4-bit status register.

A single 10801 allows addressing of 256 words using row and column jumps. Two chips allow addressing for 65,536 words. A two-chip system also allows eight-way branching for three separate branch inputs. Multiple-chip operation uses the extender bus.

The 10803 memory interface unit is used as an interface between memory and processor for generating memory addresses and routing data. It contains an ALU for generating memory addresses, which may also be used as the prime ALU in a simple system. It contains the memory address register, the memory data register, and a set of four 4-bit register files for minimum systems. The 10803 can perform 17 transfer or store operations for data manipulation, as well as 12 register/bus/ALU functions.

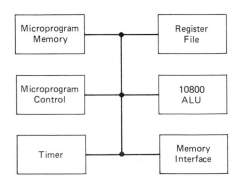

Fig. 3.16. 10800 system structure.

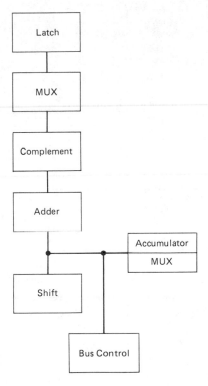

Fig. 3.17. 10800 components.

The 10802 timer unit contains a 4-phase counter with a start synchronizer for the sensitive ECL circuits. The phases are programmable as well as the phase time. One control function allows the microprocessor to be stopped through a routine for diagnostic testing.

Motorola 68000

In the Motorola 68000, the external 16-bit bus is multiplexed from the 32 bits inside.[17] A 32-bit ALU is used. The 16 32-bit registers of the 68000 are partitioned into eight address registers and eight data registers. (The 68000 structure is shown in Figure 3.18.)

The CPU is centered around the microprogram-controlled execution unit. Control store area size is minimized by the use of a two-level control structure. First, machine instructions are produced by sequences of microinstructions in the microcontrol program. These microinstructions are actually addresses to nano-instructions in the nano-control program. This memory contains a set of machine-state words that control the execution unit. Infor-

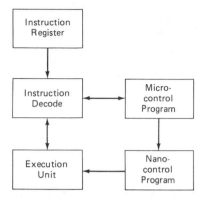

Fig. 3.18. 68000 structure.

mation that is timing-independent bypasses the control programs and is transmitted directly to the execution unit. About 22.5K bits of control memory is used, 50% less than required for a one-level implementation.

Since the two-level structure increases access time, an effort has been made to reduce this effect by using a pipelined architecture, in which the instruction fetch, decode, and execute cycles are overlapped.

The 68000 uses eight 32-bit data registers, seven 32-bit address registers, and two implied 32-bit stack pointers. The data registers can be addressed as byte, word, or double-word registers. The address registers are used for 32-bit base addressing, 32-bit software stack operations, and word or long word address operations. The stack pointers are used for the 32-bit base addressing and word or long word address operations. The 68000 uses a 32-bit program counter and a 16-bit status register.

ZILOG MICROPROCESSORS

Zilog Z80

The first Z80 appeared in April 1976. By using a depletion-mode load and n-channel MOS fabrication, only a single + 5-V power supply is required for this microprocessor. The Z80 does not multiplex status information on the data bus, as is done with the 8080. It is contained in the same 40-pin DIP that is used for the 8080.

The Z80 architecture is shown in Figure 3.19.[18] An accumulator register is used to store data from the accumulator. This additional register tends to improve response time during interrupts. The temporary registers, *W* and *Z* have been replaced with a set of temporary registers for the general registers: *B, C, D, E, H,* and *L.* This set of temporary registers also improves the interrupt response time. The Z80 microprocessor has four 16-bit registers, a pro-

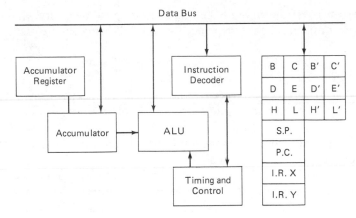

Fig. 3.19. Z80 architecture.

gram counter which provides the same functions as in the 8080, a stack pointer like the 8080 to hold the address of the next available location in the last-in-first-out (LIFO) stack stored in RAM, and two index registers X and Y.

A clock generator is on the CPU chip along with circuitry for dynamic RAM refresh capability. There is also a special register for controlling interrupts. This allows the microprocessor to operate in a mode where an indirect call to memory may occur from an interrupt. The added special purpose register can be used to hold the upper 8 bits of the indirect address, while the lower 8 bits is furnished by the interrupting device.

Comparison of the Z80 with the 8080

The Z80 is based on the 8080; it has the same hardware and software of the 8080 plus some additional hardware and software features. For example, programs written for the 8080 may be run on the Z80. The internal architecture of the Z80 is quite similar to the 8080, with the major difference being that there are over twice as many internal registers. The instruction set of the Z80 consists of 158 instructions, including the 78 instructions of the 8080.

However, compatibility between the Z80 and the 8080 instruction sets is less than perfect. One difference in the instruction sets is in the Z80 parity/overflow flag. The Z80 uses an expanded version of the 8080 parity flag which can indicate bit parity or arithmetic overflow. The flag is used as a parity flag whenever the Z80 performs logical operations and as an overflow flag when arithmetic operations are performed. The 8080 always uses the flag for parity.

If an overflow occurs, the Z80 sets the parity/overflow flag but the 8080 ignores the overflow and sets the flag according to the parity which is odd. To correct this problem, a sequence like the following can be used.

```
LD  A, 120   : load accumulator, A = 120
ADD  104     : add, A = 120 + 104
JP  PE, Z80  : jump to location Z80 if parity is set
JP  PO,  8080 : jump to location 8080 if parity is reset
```

This sequence branches to location Z80 if executed on the Z80 and to location 8080 if executed on the 8080.

The relative address jump instructions of the Z80 represent an improvement in the instruction set. The six instructions, JR, JR C, JR NC, JR NZ, JR Z and DJNZ can be used to reduce program size in many applications. Jumps in almost any sequence can be replaced with the relative address jumps saving one byte for each jump. The only problem is that the relative address jump takes more time to execute if the condition is met and the jump is performed. A JP instruction requires 10 cycles while a JR instruction requires 12 cycles. The 20% increase may be critical in a routine with many jumps and interrupts. There, the extra byte of memory can be used to save processor time.

The Z80 allows more shifts than the 8080. In the 8080, a common shift sequence for shifting left is:

```
LD  A,D : load accumulator, A = D
OR  A    : OR accumulator to clear carry
RLA      : shift accumulator left
LD  D,A : load to put answer back in D
```

The Z80 does with one instruction:

```
SLA  D : shift register D left
```

This capability may be used to create a multiword shift.

Z80 Applications

Microprocessors like the Z80 are used to implement front-end processors in minicomputers. The microprocessor replaced the hard-wired logic which used to interface the minicomputer to remote communications hardware. Typical microprocessor tasks include: bit detection, signal qualification, character assembly, character detection, modem status, buffering, error handling, protocol management, message acknowledgement and handling, file management, and transaction handling. A basic Z80 system for asynchronous communications operation is shown in Figure 3.20. The Z80 and the UART provide the complete interface between the minicomputer and modem.

Expanding this concept into a distributed microprocessor system for synchronous communication operation results in the configuration shown in Figure 3.21. The Z80 and random access memory now provide the interface between the minicomputer and a system bus. Connected to the bus are additional microprocessors with specialized tasks for a number of modems and communications lines.

Zilog Z8

The Z8 single-chip microcomputer shown in Figure 3.22 provides an on-chip ROM of 2048 bytes, a RAM of 124 bytes, 32 I/O lines, two counter/timers and a programmable UART.[19] I/O is software configurable on some ports and dedicated on others. One port is set up as four-input and four-output lines; another has eight lines which are bit programmable as inputs or outputs; still another port is programmable in four-bit sections, while the fourth

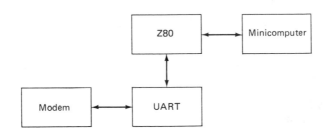

Fig. 3.20. Z80 minicomputer interface for asynchroneus operation.

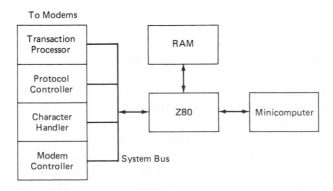

Fig. 3.21. Z80 minicomputer interface for synchronous operation.

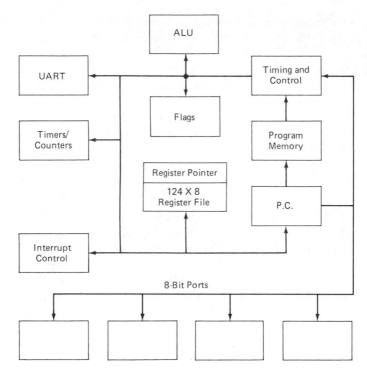

Fig. 3.22. Z8 structure.

port is byte programmable. Up to 64K bytes of external memory may be addressed by the processor which also contains a 64K byte ROM test memory.

Zilog Z8000

The Z8000 is a 16-bit microprocessor with an instruction set based on an expanded Z80 instruction set.[20] Z80 users must use a translator to convert programs to the Z8000. Although the Z8000 uses a different architecture, both processors are register oriented, and the addressing modes of the Z80 are a subset of the Z8000 modes. The Z8000 also has more instructions, a greater addressing space, and more powerful instructions. To make full use of the Z8000, the user should recode Z80 programs for the Z8000 rather than translating for most applications.

The Z8000 is a random-logic-based CPU; its structure is shown in Figure 3.23. An internal 16-bit data bus is used for internal addressing and data communication. Instructions are fetched over the bus interface and executed by the instruction control unit. Throughput is enhanced by lookahead pipelining, which allows prefetching of the next single-word instruction or the first word of the next multiword instruction.

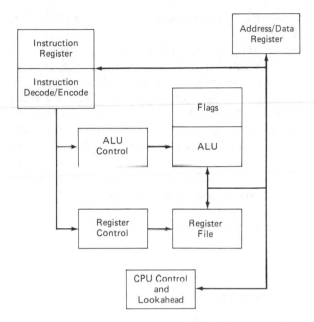

Fig. 3.23. Z8000 structure.

The Z8000 is available either in a 40-pin package or a 48-pin package. The 40-pin Z8000 is able to address 64K of memory, while the 48-pin device will address 8 megabytes of memory. In the Z8000 units, addresses are expressed in bytes. Single bytes are read and written using the byte/word output line. The eight megabytes of directly addressable memory is split up as 128 segments, each of 64K bytes. The CPU generates information which enables the address range to be increased by separating code, data, and stack spaces. External logic is used for this extension.

TEXAS INSTRUMENTS MICROPROCESSORS

In this section Texas Instruments microprocessor products are considered, concluding with the 99000 16-bit chip.

Texas Instruments TMS 1000 Family

The Texas Instruments TMS 1000 series is a family of 4-bit devices that use PMOS technology and include the ALU, ROM, and RAM on a single semiconductor chip.[21] The user's application determines the ROM pattern which is produced during manufacture. The 1000 and 1200 units use 1K-bit instruction ROMs. The 1070 and 1270 units are designed to interface with high voltage displays; otherwise they are identical to the 1000 and 1200 devices.

The 1100 and 1300 units provide twice the ROM and RAM capacity of the 1000 and 1200.

The architecture for the 1000 series appears in Figure 3.24. The ROM holds the program which is used to control data input, processing, storage, and output. All data processing is done by the ALU, with temporary storage in the 4-bit accumulator. Data storage in the 256-bit RAM is organized as sixty-four 4-bit words. The words are grouped into four 16-bit files which are addressed by a two-bit register. Decode logic is a programmable logic array (PLA) which is changed by mask tooling. Thirty programmable-input NAND gates are used to decode the eight bits of each instruction word. Each gate output selects a combination of 16 microinstructions and these are used to control the ALU, status, and write inputs to the RAM.

Device operation is determined by the sequence of the 1,024 eight-bit instructions. There are 16 pages of instructions with 69 instructions per page. The instruction set is modified by a tooling step similar to that used for the ROM.

Texas Instruments 9900

The Texas Instruments 9900 microprocessor is a single-chip, 16-bit CPU that is available in a NMOS silicon-gate version or an I²L equivalent.[22] The 9900 design has a 16-bit capability on both address and data busses. The busses use a parallel configuration that allows access to 16-bit words in one cycle. The basic architecture of the 9900 is similar to some minicomputers. There are no general purpose registers in the CPU itself; instead, the general registers are found in memory. All data goes directly from memory to the ALU or to special purpose registers for interrupts or data status and then

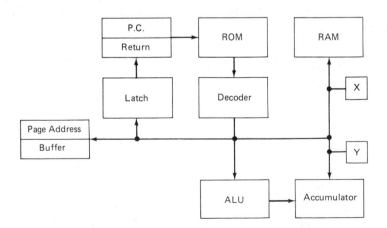

Fig. 3.24. 1000 microcomputer architecture.

back to memory again. Thus, since all data resides in external memory, register capacity is not limited by on-chip register capacity. This system can also save time during interrupts since register data does not have to be saved, but it can also slow processing speed for arithmetic calculations.

The heart of the chip is the ALU as shown in the architecture of Figure 3.25. Three internal registers are accessible to the user. The PC (the program counter) contains the address of the next instruction. This address is referenced by the processor for fetching the next instruction from memory which is then incremented. The status register is used to contain the previous state of the processor including the interrupt mask level and information pertaining to the instruction operation.

The work space pointer register is a 16-bit register that holds the address of the first general register in memory, RO. A work space register file uses 16 memory words of the general memory. Work space registers can hold data or addresses, and they function as accumulators, address registers, operand registers, or index registers. During the execution, the processor addresses as a register in the work space by adding the register number to the contents of the work space pointer register and then initiating a memory for the word.

The work space system may be useful when there is a change from one program environment to another due to an interrupt or a subroutine. With a conventional register arrangement, at least part of the file must be stored and reloaded. A memory cycle is used to store or fetch each word. The 9900,

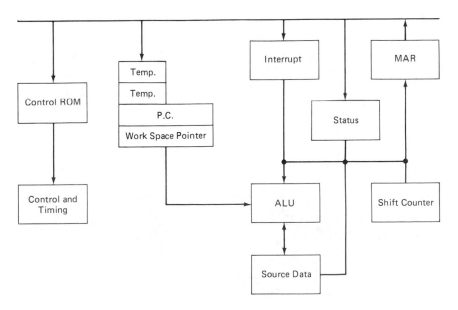

Fig. 3.25. 9900 architecture.

however, goes through a change of program environment by exchanging the program counter, the status register, and work space pointer register in three stores and three fetch cycles. After the exchange, the work space pointer holds the starting address of a new 16 word work space for the new routine. Time can also be saved when returning back to the original program environment.

The instruction set of sixty-nine 16-bit words provides 26 arithmetic, logic, and data manipulation instructions; 14 internal register-to-memory operations; 5 data transfer commands; and 24 control functions. Instructions include binary multiply and divide, as well as programmed DMA I/O capability.

The instruction set is more powerful than any 8-bit microprocessor, but since it is word-oriented, memory requirements must be larger; the 64-pin package also tends to increase costs.

Memory access is organized so that any 16-bit memory address can specify the location of one byte of data. The memory space for 9900 system is 65,536 bytes which is organized as 32,768 sixteen-bit words. Access to memory is via 15 bits on the memory bus for all 32,768 words. The 16th bit is maintained in a register in order to specify the byte which the processor must use during instruction execution. During byte operations, the unused byte is held, and at the end of an instruction the two bytes are merged and returned to memory.

The 9900 does not use a stack like other microprocessors for subroutine return addresses. One normally saves each return address in a general register like *R11* if only a few subroutine calls are required. For applications with many subroutine levels, storage in RAM may be used.

A small 9900 microprocessor system is shown in Figure 3.26. The memory contains a 16-bit by 1,024 word ROM system and 256 by 16 RAM system.

Both the TMS9900 and SBP9900A are 16-bit microprocessors with non-

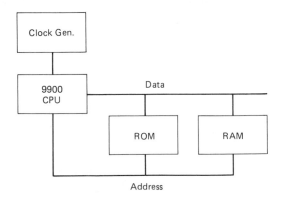

Fig. 3.26. Minimum 9900 system.

multiplexed data and address buses. The TMS version is the silicon gate NMOS device. It requires a four-phase clock. The SBP unit is an I²L equivalent that requires just a single-phase clock input. The I²L unit also permits the supply current to be adjusted so that power consumption can be reduced (as discussed in Chapter 2).

Texas Instruments 9940

The 9940 single-chip microcomputer was designed to be compatible with the 9900 family of microprocessors. It copies the memory-oriented architecture of this family.

This compatibility may be an advantage to those who are familiar with the 9900 series, but it may be a disadvantage to those not familiar or prepared to handle it. The program memory is a 1K x 16 ROM, which is not expandable. An erasable reprogrammable version is also available.

Data memory is a 64K x 16 RAM divided into four work space areas. The work space concept is useful in a multiprocessing environment where a portion of memory can be used for each task; the processor can change tasks by switching to a new work space area in memory.

The 9940 provides an extensive I/O structure for a single-chip device. It has 32 general purpose I/O lines, and it has provisions for expansion to 256 additional lines. The 9940 has a serial I/O system designed for multiple-processor applications, which can be useful in distributed processing applications. The 9940 has an internal 14-bit binary counter that may be used as a timer or event counter.

Texas Instruments SBP 0400

The Texas Instruments SBP 0400 is a 4-bit slice microprocessor that uses nonisolated I²L technology. SBP stands for Semiconductor Bipolar Processor. It is microprogrammable with up to 512 microinstructions and uses a single-phase clock. The 4-pin package draws 200 mA at 0.85 volts and the current drain can be adjusted to be as low as 1 μA for low clock rates.

This processor contains about 1,450 logic gates which would be equivalent to 30 or 40 standard TTL packages, and it contains the functions required for 4-bit parallel processing except for sequence controls. (The architecture of the 0400 is organized as shown in Figure 3.27.) The ALU has 16 functions with full carry-lookahead logic. It receives inputs from a multiplexed A port and a multiplexed B port. The eight general purpose registers have access to the A port while the data-in bus has access to the A or B ports or the working registers. The output from the ALU is multiplexed and transferred out or along the data bus to the general registers or the working register and its extension. The eight-word general register file includes a program counter and

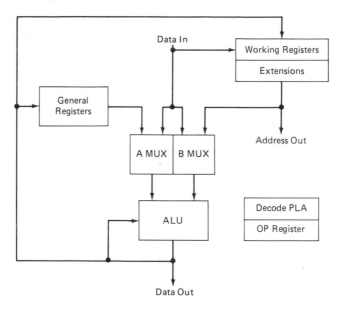

Fig. 3.27. SBP 0400 architecture.

incrementor, and the working register and extension can handle either single- or double-length operations.

A programmable logic array (PLA) is used to define the instruction set by the user. Up to 512 operations can be programmed into this on-chip array compared to 50 to 100 instructions for the typical fixed instruction set microprocessor. The user can define an instruction set that is unique to a particular application. Each instruction uses a 9-bit operational select word as an input to the PLA, which is operated under the clock to decode this input into a specific operation for the 20-bit operation register. The control word in the operation register then provides commands to the ALU, the general and working registers, and the bus lines for executing the machine operation. The PLA concept can allow greater system security and integrity because it is programmed at the factory and it would be difficult to copy the software instruction set; thus, the developed software remains proprietary with the developers. The PLA technique also allows emulation of larger systems.

The chip architecture is expandable in 4-bit multiples. A 16-bit machine can be made up with four chips (as shown in Figure 3.28). A multichip system like this uses parallel access to control, data, and address functions, along with carry-look-ahead capability. A 16-bit system as shown can be used to emulate low-level minicomputers.

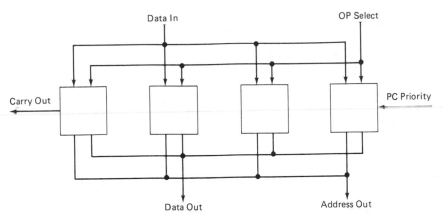

Fig. 3.28. 16-Bit SBP 0400 circuit.

Texas Instruments 99000

The TI 99000 uses n-channel, silicon-gate, scaled MOS (SMOS) circuitry and runs on a 6-MHz microinstruction cycle. These microinstructions, or machine states, carry out the instructions. Using code-compression the control ROM decodes the assembly-language instructions into a 162-bit control word.

NATIONAL SEMICONDUCTOR MICROPROCESSORS

National Semiconductor SC/MP

The National Semiconductor SC/MP (simple, cost-effective microprocessor) was an 8-bit PMOS processing unit. The SC/MP used a 16-bit memory bus for addressing up to 64K bytes of memory with four address pointer registers. The basic components of the SC/MP unit are shown in Figure 3.29. A preprogrammed, programmable logic array (PLA) is used for instruction decoding.

The SC/MP ALU has 8-bit binary ADD, AND, OR, and EXCLUSIVE OR operations and can perform two-digit BCD additions. The pointer registers are 16 bits long; one register serves as the stack pointer and the others can be used by the programmer. The chip operates on a single power supply of + 10 to + 14 volts and uses a 40-pin package. The single supply voltage can allow direct interfacing with CMOS components.

The instruction set for the SC/MP is smaller than most 8-bit microprocessors. There are 40 basic instructions. Addressing modes in SC/MP include

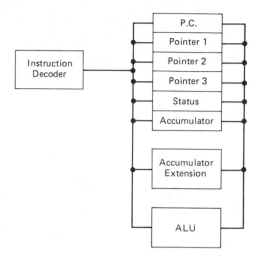

Fig. 3.29. SC/MP architecture.

indexed addressing, auto indexed addressing, immediate addressing, and extension register addressing.

SC/MP is a page-addressed unit, as the program counter is incremented to fetch the next instruction. First, the lower 12 bits are changed, and then the page is changed as shown below:

UPPER 4 BITS	LOWER 12 BITS	
0	000	Page 0
0	FFF	
1	000	Page 1
1	FFF	
2	000	Page 2
2	FFF	
•	•	•
•	•	•

The page system requires extra care for addressing memory. If a NOP instruction is placed in memory location 0FFF and a branch provided to that location, the next instruction after the branch is executed at 0000 not 1000. This is sometimes referred to as wrap-around addressing.

SC/MP treats the input/output interface in the same way as external memory. The external hardware detects a reference to an address and responds with the desired data or signal. This is known as memory-mapped input/output control and is used in other microprocessors.

The accumulator extension register can be used for serial input and output, while the extension register will function as a serial shift register using the SIO instruction. A serial input (SIN) and the serial output (SOUT) are controlled by the SIO instruction, which shifts the contents of the register right by one bit; the last bit position is the output to SIO. The vacated bit position on the left is filled from the serial input line.

Since SC/MP has no special instructions to call subroutines, the routine address must be loaded into a pointer register to provide a branch to the subroutine. To call subroutine YYY, we use:

LDI H(RET) · load to set P2 for return
XPAH 2   : exchange to set P2 for upper byte
LDI L(RET) : load for lower byte
XPAL 2   : exchange for lower byte
JMP YYY   : call YYY

To use this sequence, the subroutine must be on the same page as the call. To return control from the subroutine, use:

XPPC 2 : exchange program counter with P2

For nested calls, a push-down stack can be developed from the pointer registers. Let pointer 1 be the address of the push-down stack in the random access memory; then, P1 will contain the address of the next usable location on the stack. Next, P3 can be used for the address of the subroutine call. This stack approach is similar to the one used in the 6800 or 8080 microprocessors. For pushing an entry on the stack, use the store instruction:

ST @1(P1) : store to push accumulator and increment stack pointer

For popping items off the stack

LD @−1(P1) : load to pop accumulator after stack pointer decrement

The stack builds upward in memory instead of down as with the 6800 or 8080. A downward stack pointer always points to the top position of the stack, while an upward stack pointer points to the next usable location to be used for temporary storage.

SC/MP Applications

A simple SC/MP system can be constructed with three integrated circuit packages (as shown in Figure 3.30). The timing capacitor is connected to the CPU for clock timing, and a ROM and RAM complete the system along with

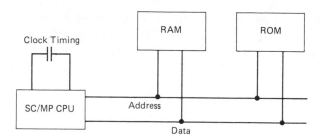

Fig. 3.30. Basic SC/MP microcomputer system.

the power source. This system has three serial data input ports and four serial data output ports for applications like games, traffic controls, simple industrial controllers, appliances, and vending machines.

The input/output capability of the SC/MP unit may be increased by adding the three CMOS devices (as shown in Figure 3.31). To increase the number of serial data input and output ports we have added the following to the system:

1. A hex D flip-flop.
2. An 8-channel digital multiplexer.
3. A 1-to-8 demultiplexer.

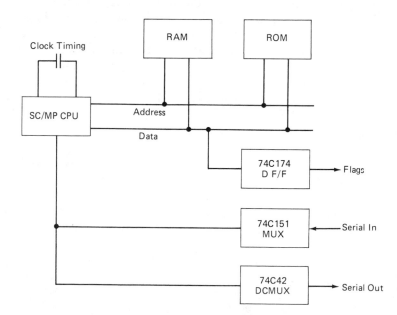

Fig. 3.31. Expanded SC/MP microcomputer system.

This system has four latched control flags and can address 4-K bytes of memory. It can be used to implement industrial controls with up to eight loops or to implement complex traffic controllers.

The SC/MP has a feature in its delay instruction that is useful in control interfaces. The delay instruction can be used to program delays for control input/output timing for an interface (as shown in Figure 3.32). For this serial interface, SIN is the receive data line and SOUT the send data line. A single control word communication contains a start bit; data bits, and a stop bit. The delay instruction may be used to cause a delay of time according to the following formula:

$$delay = 13 + 2* \text{ accumulator} + 514* \text{ displacement}$$

The SC/MP chip has two control lines which allow implementation of a multiprocessor system. The CPUs are tied together through two enable control lines. When a CPU requires the bus, it requests access to the bus and then waits for a bus enable signal. Until the CPU receives this signal, it waits with its address and data busses in the high impedance state. This provides the user with the flexibility of adding extra processors in order to achieve additional throughput without changing the processor or software.

The SC/MP II or INS8060 microprocessor is an NMOS version of the original SC/MP PMOS microprocessor.

National Semiconductor IMP 5750

The National IMP 5750 register and arithmetic logic unit (RALU) was a microprocessor element utilizing p-channel enhancement mode, silicon gate technology.[23] It provided a 4-bit slice of the register and arithmetic portion of a general purpose controller/processor. RALUs could be stacked in parallel for longer word lengths. Each RALU provided 96 bits of storage in the form of 4 bits in each of 7 general registers, a status register, and a 16-word last-in-first-out (LIFO) stack. The arithmetic and logic unit performed ADD, AND, OR, and exclusive OR operations.

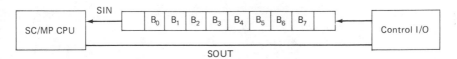

Fig. 3.32. SC/MP programmed timing delays.

National Semiconductor INS8900

The INS8900 is architecturally similar to the PACE PMOS microprocessor, but this NMOS processor is recommended for all applications instead of the PACE. The microprocessor uses an on-chip, 10-word stack, indirect addressing, 8- or 16-bit data operation memory-mapped I/O, four accumulators, and vectored interrupts.

The architecture shown in Figure 3.33 for the INS8900 and PACE provides the 10-word stack as well as four general-purpose registers and a 16-bit status and control flag register. A minimal system consists of the CPU, the clock, and memory.

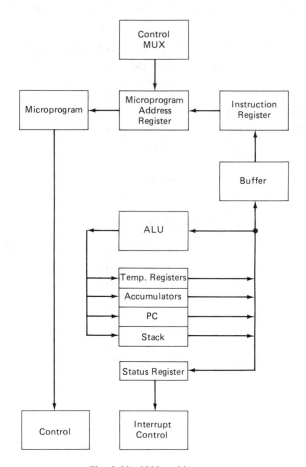

Fig. 3.33. 8900 architecture.

National Semiconductor NS16000 Family

National Semiconductor has also announced the NS16000 microprocessor chip family.[24] The 16008 and 16016 are 8080 code compatible. The 16008 is designed for 8-bit systems while the 16016 has a 16-bit data bus. The 16032 has an internal 32-bit ALU bus and a direct address range of 16M bytes using 24-bit address pointers. Unlike the 16032, and 16016, the 16008 cannot be used with an MMU to increase the address space beyond 64K.

The 16000 family offers symmetric addressing, including top-of-stack, memory-relative, external, and scaled. This provides modular software capabilities, permitting a user to develop software packages independent of other packages and without regard to individual addressing. This can provide flexibility in system design and lower programming costs. (The 16000 system structure is shown in Figure 3.34.)

FAIRCHILD MICROPROCESSORS

Fairchild F8

The Fairchild F8 is a multichip NMOS microprocessor system which is designed around a bus architecture. The heart of the system is the CPU chip. When this is combined with the program storage unit (PSU) which contains a

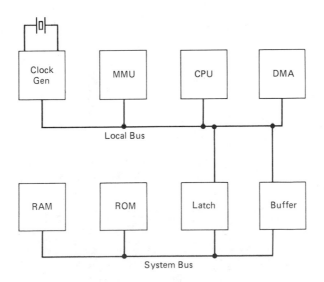

Fig. 3.34. 16000 system structure.

masked ROM, along with timing and interrupt control, a minimal system configuration is obtained. A memory interface unit contains the memory address registers and address bus, which are not in the CPU unit. A DMA chip has the hold and wait circuitry required for direct memory access. The basic device family is shown in Figure 3.35.

The CPU chip contains 64 bytes of scratch pad memory which may eliminate the need for random access memory in simple control applications. The scratch pad can also serve as a work space for simple calculations without transferring the data to external memory. The F8 CPU architecture is shown in Figure 3.36.

A potential problem can occur in systems with chips of both one and two data counters. This can happen in systems that contain both PSU chips (one data counter) and memory interface chips (two data counters). As the data counter is loaded, all DCO counters are loaded, but when the data counter exchange instruction is used (XDC) the chips with only one counter ignore this, while in the other chips the data is exchanged between DC0 and DC1. Careful use of the exchange instruction in these systems is required to prevent erroneous memory addresses.

F8 Applications

Combining a F8 CPU and PSU results in a two-chip system which may be used as a simple controller (as shown in Figure 3.37). The CPU recognizes inputs from the control panel keyboard and from sensors located on the controlled item and then produces output signals for motor control use. The PSU provides the control program storage along with the interface for the

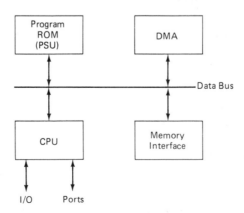

Fig. 3.35. F8 family.

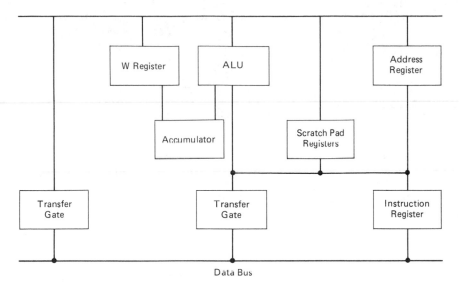

Fig. 3.36. F8 architecture.

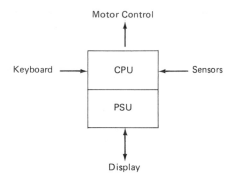

Fig. 3.37. F8 controller.

display unit. In contrast, a hard-wired logic system might require more than 250 components for a simple controller such as this. The system shown has about 50 components which includes 28 devices for the display function and power.

A more complex F8 system in Figure 3.38. This system uses one CPU and two PSUs along with a memory interface unit for connecting a RAM to the system. The CPU accepts inputs from the system sensors and produces outputs for the system motors. One PSU interfaces with the printer and the

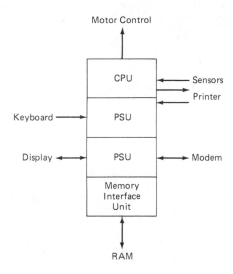

Fig. 3.38. F-8 expanded controller.

keyboard input terminal. The rest of the PSU input/output ports are shared by a display unit and modem. This system approaches a small minicomputer in complexity and utility, but it is more flexible with fewer parts and a lower cost.

A multiprocessor system may also be used if additional functions are required. A typical system might use a common memory interface and RAM with CPUs to provide control signals to individual controllers for floppy disk, magnetic tape, and CRT display units. The use of the multiprocessor concept results in a system which may cost about half compared to conventional implementations with concurrent operations allowed for all devices connected to the controllers.

Fairchild 3870

The 3870 is the single-chip microcomputer version of the F8; it uses the F8 microprocessor along with a 2K ROM.[25] It consumes less power using a 5 V supply instead of 12 V. Besides the 2K of ROM, the device has 64 bytes of scratch pad RAM, a programmable timer, and 32 bits of I/O.

The 3870 structure is shown in Figure 3.39. The instruction register receives the operation code of the instruction to be executed from the program ROM over the data bus.

The program and any constants are stored in the program ROM. When a ROM access is desired, an address register is gated to the ROM address bus and the ROM output is then gated to the main data bus.

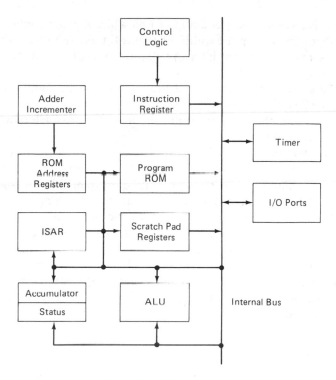

Fig. 3.39. 3870 architecture.

The accumulator is the principal register for data manipulation; it provides one of the inputs to the ALU for all operations, and then the result of the operation is stored there. The status register holds the five flags shown in Figure 3.40. An interrupt control bit is used to enable interrupts. If this bit is set and an interrupt request is made to the CPU, the interrupt is acknowledged and processed when the first nonprivileged instruction is complete.

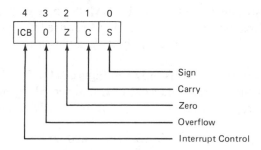

Fig. 3.40. 3870 status bits.

The timer is an 8-bit binary countdown unit which is programmable in one of three modes: interval, pulse width, or event. If there is both a timer interrupt request and an external interrupt request, the timer request is given priority.

The 3870 executes the same instruction set as the F8 family of chips. However, the STORE instruction is not used in the same way since the ROM addresses are within the range of the data counter. The STORE may be used to increment the data counter.

For total software compatibility, the 3871 input/output circuit should be used instead of the older 3861 PIO. Also, the interrupt control bit of the status register is automatically reset when an interrupt is acknowledged. But when an external reset is recognized at the start of a machine cycle, the old contents of the stack register are lost since the program counter is then pushed into the stack. The new address in the stack may not be the address of the instruction to be executed next. If this is likely to occur, a hardware priority circuit can be used to inhibit external resets during critical times.

The binary timer may be used for interval timing, external pulse width measurement, or external event counting. External timing functions are shared wih the external interrupt input and selected by the control port.

Fairchild 9440

The 9440 is a 16-bit microprocessor fabricated with the Isoplanar I^{2}L process (I^{3}L). Housed in a 40-pin DIP, all of the 9440's software is compatible with the Nova minicomputer made by Data General Corp.

The architecture shown in Figure 3.41 varies from that of the Nova, although the 9440 performs the same instructions. The 9440 uses a 4-bit ALU to process data and has an on-chip clock generator.

OTHER MICROPROCESSORS

General Instruments 1600

The General Instruments 1600 is a 16-bit NMOS single-chip microprocessor that uses ion-implantation. Ion implanting produced a device with a cycle time of 400 nanoseconds, and the capability to add two 16-bit numbers in 3.2 μs.[26]

The architecture of the 1600 is shown in Figure 3.42. The chip is organized around a 16-bit bidirectional internal bus. Connected to the bus is the instruction register, the ALU, the input/output buffers, and eight 16-bit general-purpose registers.

Assembler/simulator routines for the 1600 are available on larger machines. These will accept assembly language statements in order to produce relocatable, linking object code. The microprocessor environment

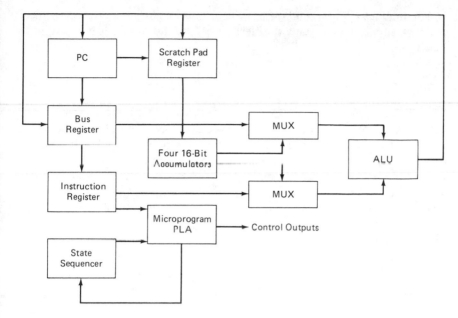

Fig. 3.41. 9440 architecture.

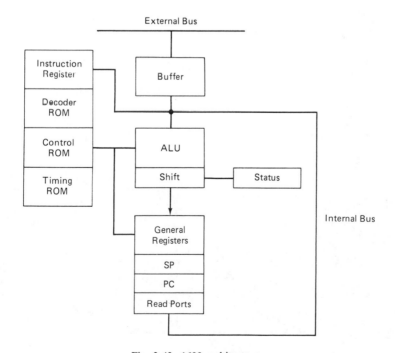

Fig. 3.42. 1600 architecture.

which includes all input and output operations can be simulated on the host machine to allow debugging and testing before the system is committed to hardware.

RCA 1800 Family

The RCA 1800 series of microprocessors is based on CMOS technology. The 1802 is an 8-bit silicon gate CMOS device that has an on-chip single-phase clock.[27] The CMOS unit requires a minimal power supply. It may be operated with unregulated supplies over a wide voltage range. Noise immunity is high, and there is compatibility with other logic families such as TTL and NMOS. The power requirements can be lowered at slower operating speeds in order to allow the use of small batteries in remote or isolated applications.

The 1802 architecture is shown in Figure 3.43. The register file uses sixteen 16-bit scratch pad registers. Registers in the array are designated and selected using a 14-bit code from one of the 4-bit designator/registers, *P, X,* or *N.* The transfer of any register may take one of three paths:

1. To the external memory with the higher order byte first.
2. To the accumulator.
3. To the increment/decrement circuit where it is processed and then stored back in the selected register.

These three paths can operate independently, in different combinations during the same machine cycle.

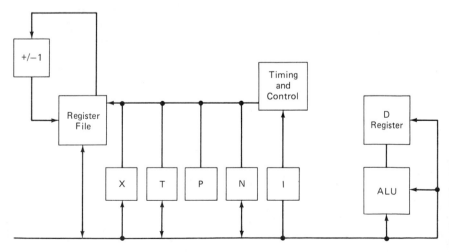

Fig. 3.43. 1802 architecture.

The registers in the file can be used as program counters, as data pointers, or as scratch pad locations for holding data. When a register is used as the main program counter, its register number must be stored in the P register. Other registers in the array can then be used as subroutine program counters. When a call is required, the contents of the P register are changed by an instruction which allows the call to be made.

Figure 3.44 shows how a basic 1802 system with ROM, RAM, and input/output is configured.

Signetics 2650

The Signetics 2650 is a single-chip 8-bit microprocessor that uses the ion-implanted n-channel silicon gate process. It has 576 bits of ROM and about 250 bits of registers.

The 2650 architecture is shown in Figure 3.45. Instructions are read in the CPU from the data bus and loaded into the instruction holding and data bus registers. The instructions are then decoded using ROM along with decode logic.

The ALU can be used for Boolean and combinatorial shifts as well as arithmetic operations. It operates in a parallel mode on 8-bit words using a carry-lookahead system. The address adder is used for incrementing the instruction address register and calculating the operand addresses for the indexed and relative addressing modes. A general purpose stack and subroutine stack for return addresses are mechanized with RAM. The general purpose stack may hold up to eight 15-bit addresses for eight-level nesting operations. For instruction and operand addressing, separate 15-bit registers are used.

About 40% of the 75 instructions apply to arithmetic; another 30% apply to branch operations, while the remaining instructions are used for input/output operations and status. Automatic incrementing and decrementing of index registers is allowed using the arithmetic indexed instructions. All branch instructions except those for indexed branching are conditional. The

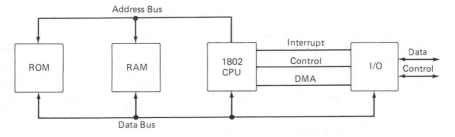

Fig. 3.44. Basic 1802 configuration.

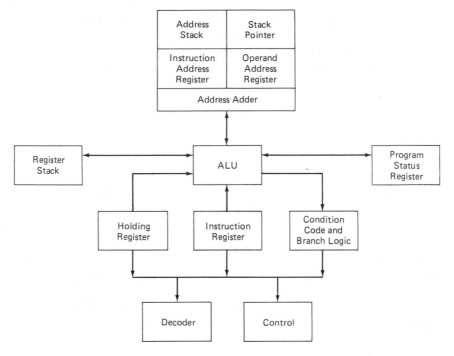

Fig. 3.45. 2650 architecture.

register-to-register instructions are one byte long and register-to-memory instructions are two or three bytes long. The register-to-memory instructions may use either immediate or relative addressing modes.

A simple 2650 terminal application uses 256 bytes of ROM and 1024 bytes of RAM to interface with a Teletype unit. The ROM holds bootstrap loader and driver programs.

AMD 2901

The Advanced Micro Devices (AMD) 2901 is a 4-bit slice unit that uses TTL technology. It is designed for use as a high-speed element in controllers and other applications. The 2901 uses a 40-pin package and consumes 925 mW at 5 V. Instruction word size is 9 bits, and the chip uses a single-phase clock with clock speeds of to 10 MHz.

The basic structure for the 2901 is shown in Figure 3.46. The 2901 uses a 16-word 4-bit RAM, a high-speed ALU, and the Q register along with associated shift, decode, and multiplex circuitry. The microinstruction word is organized in three groups of three bits each which are used to select the ALU source operands along with the function and destination registers.

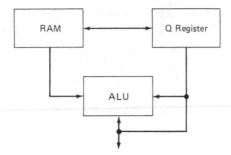

Fig. 3.46. 2901 structure.

Data outputs from the ALU may be routed as an output of the device, or they can be stored in the RAM or the Q register, which is used as an accumulator or holding register. The primary purpose for the Q register is multiplication and division operations.

A 16-bit ALU may be simply assembled with this device by cascading in parallel four slices. For efficiency in arithmetic operations, a carry-lookahead unit can be added. Outputs are provided for using a 2902 carry-lookahead-generator or similar device. A ripple-carry configuration can also be used.

The major complexity and limitation of this device lies in the control section, which includes control logic, loop counter, and bus multiplexers. (The architecture of a 2900 bit-slice system appears in Figure 3.47.) However, the

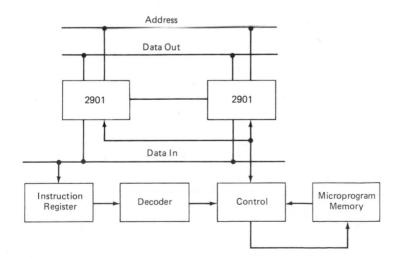

Fig. 3.47. 2900 bit-slice system.

complexity of the external control required to build such a system has been decreasing with the introduction of new control devices. The main use of bit-slice devices has been in building large CPUs, using components that reduce the number of parts over other types of logic. Such bit-slices have become the major design tool for fast CPUs. A typical CPU implemented with the 2901 bit-slice device can achieve speeds of 300 ns for 32 bits.

The AMD2901 is second-sourced by a number of manufacturers. It has been used in a number of minicomputer designs as well as military processors.

MOS Technology 6500

The MOS Technology 6500 microprocessor series are 8-bit devices produced using n-channel MOS with silicon-gate processing. Ten CPU devices are available, with various options including addressable memory (4K to 65K), interrupts, and on-chip oscillators and drivers. These ten CPU devices are software compatible among themselves and bus-compatible with the 6800 series. Six of the family use on-chip clock oscillators in which a single input from a crystal or RC oscillator circuit provides the time base. The other four devices are designed for multiprocessor applications where some flexibility in clock timing is desired. A pipelined architecture is used for improved speed. The architecture can be divided into two sections, as shown in Figure 3.48: (1) a register section which contains the ALU and registers and (2) a control section containing the decode logic and timing.

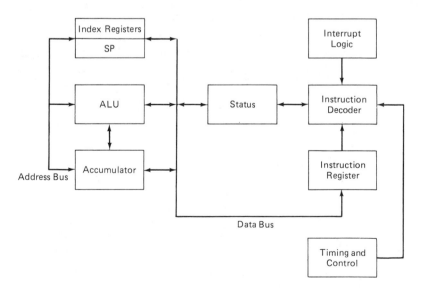

Fig. 3.48. 6500 architecture.

There are several types of peripheral devices for the 6500. A peripheral interface adapter (PIA) provides two 8-bit bidirectional ports and four control or interrupt lines. Another type is called a versatile interface adapter (VIA). In addition to the PIA, it also contains two interval timers, along with a shift register and latch for serial-to-parallel and parallel-to-serial conversion. These devices also include handshaking capability for data transfers in multiprocessor systems. (This is shown in Figure 3.49.)

The Rockwell 6500/1 combines the 6502 microprocessor with 2048 bytes of ROM, 64 bytes of RAM, 32 bidirectional I/O lines, four interrupts, and a 16-bit programmable counter/timer. The 6500/1 single-chip microcomputer has a separate pin for RAM power, which may be used to maintain data in the RAM on 10% of the total power for the chip. The programmable 16-bit counter/timer can operate as either an interval timer, pulse generator, or event counter. The chip layout for a CMOS version of the 6500 series is shown in Figure 3.50.

MICROPROCESSOR ANALYSIS

The selection of a microprocessor is a crucial step in the design of a system. The selection should be based upon established criteria such as cost, system flexibility, and compatibility. Other criteria which should be considered include availability or viability, support hardware and software, and expansion or upgrading. For example, is the microprocessor commercially producible or available on a large enough scale for the application? With a complex device such as a microprocessor, this is not always easily demonstrated. More than one microprocessor has been announced before it was realized that it could not be produced at a profit. That is one reason why only established microprocessors should be treated for many designs.

Also, if the production volume of the microprocessor is large, there should be second sources for the microprocessor in order to ensure that pro-

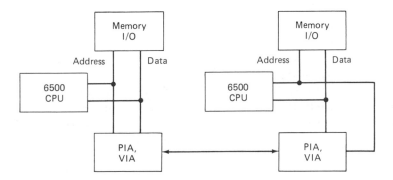

Fig. 3.49. 6500 multiprocessor configuration.

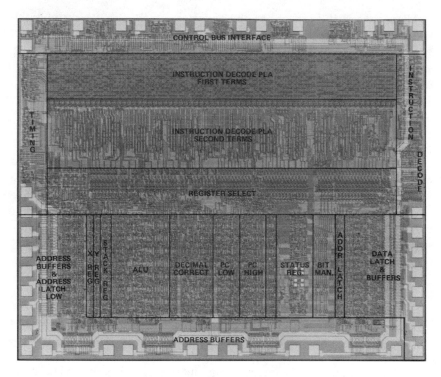

Fig. 3.50. This CMOS version of the 6500 microprocessor uses a programmable logic array (PLA) for instruction decoding. (*Courtesy Rockwell International.*)

duction schedules can be adhered to. Support hardware and software include development hardware such as simulators, software aids and assemblers, and programming and design training for the particular microprocessor selected. System expansion or upgrading allows the completed system to be adapted to improved devices when microprocessors are redesigned so as to make them more competitive with newer microprocessors. With upgrading capability designed into the system, the user can improve product performance without having to change microprocessors or microprocessor families. An essential criterion in evaluating a microprocessor system is whether it can really exist since a system requires other chips beyond the microprocessor itself for support: memory chips, I/O chips, interface chips, and device controllers. The complete system should include as few components as possible in order to keep the cost of the design low. Once the functions of the system are defined, it then becomes a simpler task to consider which of the microprocessors are available, along with the required LSI components, for completing the design. Other criteria must then be considered as we will discuss below.

There are constraints on each end of the microprocessor application spectrum, but for logic replacement the important factor is cost, for data processing, throughput is usually critical. Cost and throughput tend to be as diverse as the range of microprocessors.

All microprocessor architecture is aimed at reducing the cost of hardware such as printed circuit board space, interconnects, cabling, and power supplies. But a data processing architecture is aimed at improving throughput as its main objective.

Speed Considerations

If we consider throughput as a measure of processing information per unit time, then speed is a measure of how rapidly that is accomplished. Thus, throughput is the measurement of productivity. Speed can increase the throughput, but greater processing volume is also attained by increasing information paths.

Microprocessor timing begins with an instruction-fetch and execute cycle (as shown in Figure 3.51.) This cycle involves the basic processing elements: an incrementing program counter, a program memory, and an instruction register. The program counter sends an address to the program memory; then, the word selected from memory is transferred to the instruction

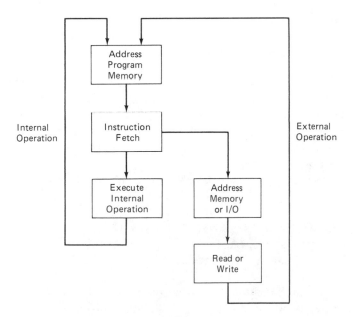

Fig. 3.51. The basic processor cycle.

register, and the decoding and execution of the word as an instruction takes place.

In the basic cycle, at least three distinct intervals are required. If the execution state is expanded to show both internal and external instruction execution, it is observed that external memory or I/O operations require two time states. This results in a minimum of four states for external instructions. The expanded external cycle consists of two similar repeated operations (as shown in Figure 3.51). The address time state may be either the program address during instruction fetch or the memory or I/O address during the execution cycle. The internal instruction execution can occur during the succeeding address state. This results in an overlapped cycle where internal executions are performed at the same time as the next instruction state. The overlapped cycle is one method employed by most processors in order to gain speed.

Instruction Formats

All instruction formats use an operation (OP) code which defines the basic operation. In general, all instructions must also address one or more elements to be operated on. The addressing is either implied by a unique OP code or it specifies the desired elements. The elements to be operated on may be either internal registers or bits, or external memory or I/O. The number of elements that can be operated on by an instruction is related to the architecture of the processor and the instruction word size.

The two architectures that determine the instruction formats are (1) register-oriented processors and (2) memory-oriented processors. Register-oriented processors use the instruction formats to address internal registers, while memory-oriented processors use the instruction format to select the modes for addressing memory. The 8-bit microprocessors with a limited instruction word size have to choose between the two architectures. The 8080 favors a register architecture, while the 6800 favors a memory architecture. The 16-bit microprocessors processors have an instruction word size large enough for both architectures.

We have seen that there are basically three categories of instruction operations:

1. Data Movement (Registers, Memory, I/O).
2. Arithmetic and Logic.
3. Control (Machine or Program).

Variations on these basic operations tend to be a function of the architecture orientation towards registers or memory. More powerful processors have instructions that combine the basic operations. However, the limited instruction size of many 8-bit processors does not lend itself to many combinations.

Addressing Considerations

Most instructions address some element upon which to operate. The element may be a bit, a register, or memory location. When the instruction involves movement of data, two addresses, a source, and a destination are required. Most processors are implemented with a central register (the accumulator); some instructions imply an operation with the accumulator.

When an I/O or memory operation is performed external to the CPU, explicit addressing is necessary to select the external location. One way to select the external location is to obtain the address directly from the instruction. This is called "direct addressing." Direct addressing is the most basic type of external addressing, but it is often the least efficient.

In addition to direct addressing, several nondirect methods are used for external addressing. These nondirect methods can be grouped as follows:

- Indirect.
- Indexed.
- Relative.

Since all addresses must have a source, some other element other than the instruction register must be used for all nondirect addresses. The elements commonly used are internal registers, memory locations, or the program counter. The nondirect addressing methods when used with the different addressing elements combine to give the microprocessor more flexibility and power in addressing.

Benchmark Programs

If the microprocessor task to be performed is specific enough, it may be possible to establish a benchmark program. Benchmark programs are typical programs or tasks written to test the speeds of the processors which are being considered. The benchmark concept is an important method for performance comparison.

A benchmark can be a sample program or simple routine or operation mix which can be used to compare the performance of different processors. Since processors utilize different instruction sets, the benchmark programs are specified using flow charts. As an example of a benchmark program consider a simple program or test or poll a peripheral device. Figure 3.52 illustrates a flow chart for performing a polling function, labeling the data obtained, and storing it in memory. The program is simple, and the blocks of

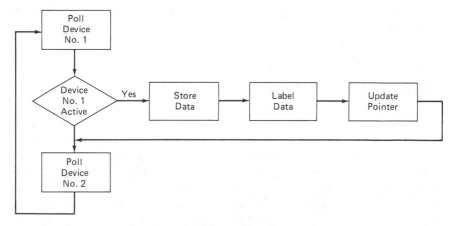

Fig. 3.52. Benchmark program flow chart.

the flow chart represent machine functions in this example. From the flow chart, a program for the particular microprocessor can be coded and run, or a timing memory size analysis can be computed based on execution times and instruction bytes. Thus we would obtain these two key performance parameters: (1) the number of memory bytes occupied by the program or task and (2) the speed of execution of the program of task.

The relative importance of these parameters depends on the application, but a benchmark can establish a quantitative measurement for making a comparison. A complex program or actual operational application may contain numerous routines and conclusive information is not always drawn from simple benchmarks. In most cases, programs are a mix of different operations and it is not easy to establish a single benchmark. One must then use judgement or, if time and resources are available, actual simulation. It has been found in practice that the large majority of tasks to be performed by microprocessors can be performed by any standard 8-bit or 16-bit microprocessor, although in many cases involving more difficulties and more memory for the program. When comparing microprocessors, an 8-bit by 8-bit multiplication may be faster on one, while an 8-bit by 16-bit multiplication may be faster on the other, due to design differences.

Benchmark Comparisons

Figure 3.53 shows the results of a benchmark test using a sample program like the flow chart in Figure 3.52. The results reflect tests of available microprocessors.[28] In this task, microprocessor C requires the least amount of processing time but it also uses the smallest amount of memory for the benchmark program. Microprocessor D, on the other hand, uses more

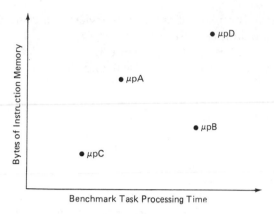

Fig. 3.53. Typical benchmark test results.

memory and requires the most processing time. Processing power favors an 8-bit design over a 4-bit one. If minimizing cost is the most important goal, 4-bit microprocessors should be considered. However, the domain of small to medium application problems are dominated by 8-bit microprocessors.

Figure 3.54 shows some benchmark results using 8-bit microprocessors.[29] The program consists of the movement of a block of data using a sequence like the following:

```
SET  UP   MOV              : move data to register A
          MOV              : move data to register B
          MOV              : move data to register C, (character move)
          LOOP      MOV    : combine data in register A with B
          LOOP  1          : loop to register C
          EXIT
```

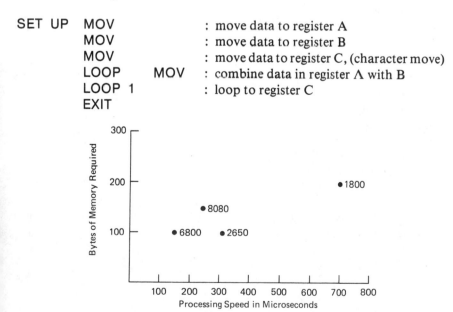

Fig. 3.54. 8-Bit microprocessor benchmark results.

Other criteria consisted of interrupt servicing, arithmetic operations, searching, or monitoring. Test results for these criteria are shown in Table 3.4. The totals have been plotted in Figure 3.54.

In a separate benchmark the 8080, 6800, and 9900 were compared for five program tasks:[30]

1. Input/output handler.
2. Search for characters.
3. Go-to routine.
4. Right shift by five bits.
5. Move a block of characters.

The handler brings in a character from a device such a modem, tests for end-of-character, outputs the character, and returns control to the main program. The search checks a table of 40 characters in memory for a specific character and generates the address of the matched character, or in the case

Table 3.4 8-Bit Microprocessor Benchmark

	8080	6800	1800	2650
BLOCK DATA MOVEMENT				
Bytes of instruction	18	15	22	10
Setup time	13.5	8	60	4.8
Move time/character	23.5	20	36	26.4
SERVICING AN INTERRUPT				
Bytes of instruction	8	2	15	13
Service time	42	22	72	52.8
ADD OF "N"				
DECIMAL DIGITS AND STORE				
Bytes of instruction	22	17	79	17
Setup time	17.5	7	114	7.2
Add time/byte	29	28	216	50.4
SEARCH FOR CHARACTER STRING				
Bytes of instruction	21	22	23	16
Setup time	5	3	36	4.8
Search time/character	29.2	29	48	40
MONITOR 8 DATA CHANNELS				
Bytes of instruction	34	30	28	30
Setup time	8.5	—	24	—
Throughput	71.1	61	84	98.4
TOTAL				
Bytes of instruction	103	86	167	86
Total program execution time (μs)	249.3	178	690	284.8

of a nonmatch generates a zero address. The go-to routine tests a control byte to determine which table vector will control a transfer. The right shift routine shifts a 16-bit word to the right by five places and fills with zeros from the left. The move sequence moves a block of 64 characters anywhere in memory to another location anywhere in memory. The program memory requirements in bytes, along with the number of assembler statements required and the task execution times are shown in Table 3.5.

In a similar manner we can compare the operational speeds of the newer 16-bit microprocessors which have been improved over the previous generation. If we let the shortest execution time be 400 ns for the 8086, 750 ns for the Z8000, 500 ns for the 68000, and 300 ns for the 16032, we get the execution times shown in Table 3.6.

Although the speed of instruction is an important selection criterion, we must use the data listed for the four microprocessors with caution. Throughput is a function of the exact instruction sequence, and of displacements, data lengths, clock frequency, and other factors. Overall, the 68000 is the fastest for branch operations. For data transfers, the 16032 and 68000 are faster than the 8086 and the Z8000.

Additional Considerations

Another technique that can be useful in selecting a microprocessor for a particular application is to analyze a number of issues, both technical and nontechnical, and rate the microprocessors accordingly. The various factors can then be given a weight for the application being considered and the optimum choice can be computed. A rating of the four microprocessors from 1–10, with 10 being the highest, is given below:

	8086	Z8000	68000	16000
Speed	7	8	9	9
Number of Registers	7	8	9	9
Address Range	7	9	9	8
Compatibility Earlier Microprocessors	9	8	8	8
Support Chips	9	7	6	5
Multiprocessing Capability	8	8	8	7
Second Source	9	9	9	6

Special criteria may have to be considered for nonstandard customer requirements. If low power consumption is essential, then a CMOS design might be required. An I^2L design might also be considered in this case.

For military designs, it is necessary to consider microprocessors which have the required environmental characteristics. Many microprocessors are available in an M version for the extended temperature range, and some of

Table 3.5 Benchmark Results

	PROGRAM MEMORY REQUIREMENTS (BYTES)			ASSEMBLER STATEMENTS			EXECUTION TIME (μs)		
	8080	6800	9900	8080	6800	9900	8080	6800	9900
Input/output handler	28	17	24	17	7	9	79	49	71
Character search	20	18	22	9	8	8	760	808	661
Computer go-to	17	14	12	11	8	5	145	145	98
Shift right five bits	19	20	10	12	9	3	137	81	22
Move block	16	34	14	9	16	4	1262	2246	537
TOTALS	100	103	82	58	48	29	2838	2401	1389

Table 3.6 16-Bit Microprocessor Benchmark

OPERATION	DATA TYPE	8086	Z8000	68000	16032
Register-to-Register Move	Byte/Word	0.40	0.75	0.50	0.30
	Double-Word	0.80	1.25	0.50	0.30
Memory-to-Register Move	Byte/Word	3.40	3.50	1.50	1.00
	Double-Word	6.80	4.25	2.00	1.40
Memory-to-Memory Move	Byte/Word	7.00	7.00	2.50	1.60
	Double-Word	14.00	18.50	3.75	2.40
Add Memory to Register	Byte/Word	3.60	3.75	1.50	1.10
	Double-Word	7.20	5.25	2.25	1.50
Compare Memory to Memory	Byte/Word	7.00	7.25	3.00	1.80
	Double-Word	14.00	9.50	4.00	2.60
Conditional Branch	Branch	1.60	1.50	1.25	1.40
		0.80	1.50	1.00	0.70
Modify Index Branch if Zero	Branch	2.20	2.75	1.25	1.30
Branch to Subroutine	Branch	3.80	3.75	2.25	2.50

the other military specifications. However, few microprocessors are qualified to the specifications of the 38510 JAN program.

In this chapter, different microprocessors have been presented and evaluated. However, selecting the proper microprocessor is not as difficult as it might appear. When an overwhelming criterion exists such as very high speed, or extremely low cost, or power consumption, the choice is restricted. When there is no overwhelming criterion, the choice is usually a compromise. The criteria presented in this section should allow narrowing down the number of microprocessors to be considered. An essential consideration to consider is that if the most significant parameter is not overwhelming, then consider convenience or efficiency. One of the main obstacles in using microprocessors, especially for the first time, is not technical complexity but programming the system. There, the selection of the proper microprocessor rests on the difficulty of programming it. Selection criterion then becomes the need for a high-level language, or compatibility with a language or an instruction set familiar to the user. If the user is skilled in the use of a assembly language that microprocessor family will be easy to use. Another important criterion may be sufficient support. Support includes hardware and software facilities. Support also means the availability of persons familiar with the components who are accessible to the user, that is, the availability of engineers and experienced individuals who can support the effort. This often means the difference between the success or failure of a development project schedule.

REFERENCES

1. Morse, S. P., Ravenel, B. W., Mazor, S., and Pohlman, W. B., Intel Microprocessors—8008 to 8086, *Computer,* October 1980.
2. Ibid.
3. Zaks, R., *Microprocessors,* Berkeley: Sybex, 1980.
4. Texas Instruments, *TMS1000 Series MOS/LSI One-Chip Microcomputers,* Manual No. CM 122-1, Dallas: Texas Instruments, November 15, 1975.
5. Morse, et. al.
6. National Semiconductor, *MOS Integrated Circuits,* Santa Clara: National Semiconductor, April 1974.
7. Texas Instruments, *TMS9900 Microprocessor Data Manual,* Dallas: Texas Instruments, December 1976.
8. Morse, et. al.
9. Intel, *Component Data Catalog,* Santa Clara: Intel, 1978.
10. Ibid.
11. Intel, *Component Data Catalog,* Santa Clara: Intel, 1981.
12. Ibid.
13. Ibid.
14. Intel, *Component Data Catalog,* 1978.
15. Morse, et. al.
16. Motorola, *M6800 Programming Manual,* Phoenix: Motorola, 1975.
17. Motorola, "M68000 Microprocessor User's Manual", Austin: Motorola, 1980.
18. Zilog, *Z80 CPU Technical Manual,* Cupertino: Zilog, 1976.
19. Zilog, *Z8 MCU Microcomputer, Product Specification,* Cupertino, CA: Zilog, 1979.
20. Zilog, *Z8000 User's Guide,* Cupertino, CA: Zilog, 1980.
21. Texas Instruments, *TMS1000 Manual.*
22. Texas Instruments, *TMS 9900 Manual.*
23. National Semiconductor, *MOS Integrated Circuits.*
24. National Semiconductor, *The NS16000 Family of 16-Bit Microprocessors,* Santa Clara: National Semiconductor, 1981.
25. Fairchild Camera and Instrument Corporation, *F3870 Fairchild Microcomputer Family,* Mountain View, CA: Fairchild Camera and Instrument Corporation, 1977.

26. General Instrument Corporation, *Series 1600 Microprocessor System,* Hicksville, NY: General Instrument Corporation, 1975.
27. RCA, *COSMAC Microprocessor Product Guide,* Somerville, NJ: RCA, 1977.
28. Hordeski, M. F., *Microprocessor Cookbook,* Blue Ridge Summit, PA: Tab, 1979.
29. Ibid.
30. Ibid.

EXERCISES

1. How is address information handled in the 8008 microprocessor?
2. How does the 8080 indicate an interrupt?
3. How does the 8080 indicate that status information is available on the data bus?
4. Describe the hold, wait, and halt states of the 8080 microprocessor.
5. What control lines of the 6800 microprocessor are used to initiate an interrupt? Discuss the function of these lines.
6. Discuss the difference between the INT and the NMI inputs of the Z80 microprocessor.
7. What is the purpose of the 8228 chip?
8. How many words of memory space can be directly addressed by each of the following microprocessors:

   a. 8008   b. 8080   c. Z80   d. F8
   e. Z8000   f. 8086   g. 68000

9. A. What technology is used in the manufacturing of each of the following microprocessors:

   a. 8008   b. 8080   c. 6800   d. Z80
   e. Z8000   f. 8086   g. 68000

   B. Discuss the effects of the technology upon the microprocessors above.

10. What microprocessors would the following sizes of memories require? Assume that we access each byte.

    a. 78K bytes   b. 64K bytes
    c. 12K bytes   d. 1100K bytes

    Does the choice of microprocessor change if you wish to access separate words? Is the choice dependent on the length of the word?

11. Discuss the basic structure of the 8086.
12. What are the basic characteristics of the following microprocessors:

    a. 3000   b. 5701
    c. 2901   d. 10800

13. Select a 16-bit microprocessor discussed in this chapter and discuss its: (a) data bus, (b) address bus, and (c) control bus functions.
14. Consider a small microprocessor application that includes a clock circuit, a programmable timer/event counter, and a small ROM memory. What components are economical to use only if planned quantities are in the high 1000s? What if typical markets for such microprocessors involve quantities of 10,000 or 100,000? In such quantities, the cost of the components is expected to be on the order of $10 or $12. Can this be achieved?

15. One 4-bit single-chip microcomputer on the market today is the TMS1000, which has many family members depending on the amount of memory on-board the chip. The device uses mask-programmed ROMs. For what types of applications is it intended?

16. The direct address sizes supported by the various 16-bit microprocessors are considerably different, making some machines more suitable for different applications. Text editing, for example, generally requires less memory than data base management, and memory requirements increase in direct proportion to the number of users simultaneously on-line. With this in mind, define the best application areas for the 8086, Z8000, and 68000. What are some other important considerations?

17. Should an advanced microcomputer be instruction-set compatible with an existing minicomputer? Would the use of all this software help to solve programming problems?

18. The 3000 was particularly suited to complex control in real time sophisticated processes. It has been used in complex controllers and in many avionic applications for signal processing. What was one of the major programming disadvantages of the 3000, a disadvantage that also allowed it to be used in these applications?

19. Some specialized microprocessors have a small customer base. The architecture and instruction set of these devices therefore become familiar to only a small number of users, but this limitation does not result in the same habit-forming trends as with the standard microprocessor chips. What are the advantages and disadvantages of these specialized chips?

20. The characteristics of particular microprocessors are described in reference manuals published by the manufacturers. These manuals assume that the reader is familiar with the concepts of hardware and software architectures. Although the architectures are different, what are some properties that microcomputers have in common?

21. In order to compare microprocessors, one basis of comparison would be to execute a standard program on the microprocessors that are to be compared. Is a standard test such as this feasible? Is it valid?

22. Why is it unlikely that many new designs in 4-bit microprocessors will be introduced now? What are the obvious advantages of 8-bit and 16-bit designs? Is compatibility with existing instruction sets or architecture important? Is it possible to consider more complex designs?

23. Is it possible that 16-bit microcomputers in a single chip will be available? Discuss your answer. Make a prediction about other, more complex devices.

4. Industrial Sensors

TRANSDUCER CHARACTERISTICS

In this chapter, we examine typical transducers, or sensors, which might be used in a microprocessor system. A transducer is a device for determining the value of a quantity, condition, physical variable, or phenomenon. Generally, the purpose served by the transducer is to ascertain the magnitude of some particular phenomenon under investigation, and the value determined by the transducer is generally, but not always, quantitative. The measurement consists of an information transfer from an accompanying energy transfer. Energy, however, cannot be drawn from a system without altering its behaviour. Thus, all measurements affect the quantity being measured. The measurement is, therefore, a combination of applied physics (the energy conversion) and applied data processing (the information transfer).

Transducers use a number of techniques to extract information via this energy transfer. In a piezoelectric transducer, energy is converted into a change in electrostatic charge or voltage generated by certain crystals when mechanically stressed. The stress is developed by compression or tension forces, or by bending forces exerted upon the crystal directly by a sensing element or by a mechanical member linked to a sensing element (this and other transducer techniques are shown in Figure 4.1).

In photoconductive transduction, energy is converted into a change in resistance of a semiconductive material by a change in the amount of illumination incident on the material. In light-intensity transducers, the resistance change is a result of a change in illumination intensity. In other transducers, the change in incident illumination is controlled by a moving shutter or mask between a light source and the photoresistive material. The shutter can be mechanically linked to a sensing element such as a pressure bellows or a seismic mass.

In photovoltaic transducers, energy is converted into a change in voltage when a junction between dissimilar materials is illuminated. This principle can be utilized for the direct measurement of light intensity. It is also used in other transducers with the mechanical means to change the intensity of illumination from the light source.

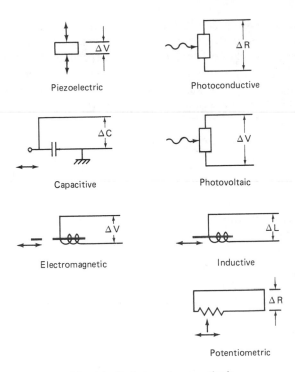

Fig. 4.1. Basic transducer methods.

Capacitive transduction uses energy which is converted into a change of capacitance. Since a capacitor consists essentially of two conductors or plates separated by an insulator, the dielectric, a change of capacitance can occur when a displacement of the sensing element causes one conductive surface to move toward or away from the other conductive surface. In some cases, the moving plate is the sensing element, such as a diaphragm or seismic mass. In some transducers, both plates are stationary and the change occurs in the dielectric, such as the proportions of a liquid or a gas in the space between the surfaces.

Electromagnetic transducers use energy which is converted into an electromotive force (voltage) induced in a conductor by a change in magnetic flux in the absence of any excitation. This transducer is self-generating. The change in magnetic flux is accomplished by a relative motion between a magnet or piece of magnetic material and a coil with a ferrous core.

In the inductive transducer, energy is converted into a change of the self-inductance of a coil. This is usually caused by a displacement of the coil's core, which is linked or attached to a mechanical sensing element. A resistive or potentiometric transducer works in much the same way.

The most commonly used transducers detect either temperature or pressure changes. Some temperature transducers such as the filled system thermometers or bimetallic sensors convert the thermal expansion of a liquid or solid into the proportional temperature signals. Others use resistors, diodes, thermistors, or thermocouples to sense temperature changes by monitoring the changes in conductivity or voltage.

TEMPERATURE TRANSDUCERS

For any temperature measurement application, there may be one particular type of sensor which fulfills the necessary performance and economic requirements better than all others. In the past, industry as a whole has been slow to change its methods of temperature instrumentation, relying instead on proven methods.

In the development of automatic control systems for industrial processes, the increased accuracy of measurements meant more successful and more economical operation. When computer-control or remote readouts are involved, long lines often lead to difficulty when using low output sensors. This is the area where resistance thermometers can best be used, with their high output and linearity.

Resistance Temperature Detectors

Resistance temperature detectors (RTDs) operate on the principle that the resistance of a material to electric current flow is temperature dependent. The resistance of metals used as sensing elements increases with increasing temperature (see Figure 4.2), while most semiconductor materials decrease in resistance. One component of the total resistivity is due to impurities and is known as residual resistivity. This component is lowest for the pure metals. The residual resistivity can change if the RTD is used at too high a temperature, or if the wire is contaminated by the environment or materials in contact with the wire.

Tungsten is a popular material for RTDs. It has good resistance to high nuclear radiation levels along with platinum. Tungsten's mechanical strength allows fine wires to be made, resulting in sensors with higher resistance values.

The International Temperature Scale has been defined by a pure platinum resistance thermometer from the triple point of hydrogen (13.81 K) to the freezing point of antimony (630.74° C).[1] The R/T relationship of platinum is well-known, reproducible, and linear over a wide temperature range. Platinum is chemically inert and not easily contaminated. It does not readily oxidize and can be used up to 1500°C. However, it is generally more expensive than other resistance temperature sensors, although some industrial grades are competitive.

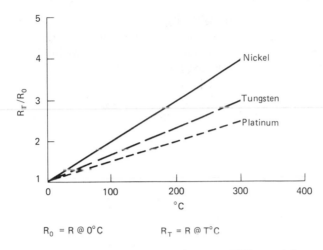

Fig. 4.2. Temperature dependence of common RTD materials.

Thin-film platinum temperature sensors are made by depositing a thin film of platinum on an insulating substrate. This construction technique yields high resistances and small sensing elements with fast response times. The construction techniques used are similar to those used to manufacture ICs. Platinum wire RTD elements generally are delicate and thermal cycling can cause aging, while thin-film platinum deposition and laser trimming results in a small, rugged thermal sensor at a lower cost. But problems in applying the high purity films can cause the R/T relationship to behave differently from pure, annealed, strain-free platinum. The temperature coefficient at room temperature is typically in the range of 30 to 80% of pure platinum, and the residual resistance tends to be much higher. Instability of calibration and variation of the resistance-temperature relationship from one specimen to another are other potential problems.

These thin-film detectors combine the precision of platinum detectors (with accuracy and repeatability typically less than 0.01°C) with the small sensing tip and more rapid response time of thermocouples. The devices use a glass encapsulated platinum layer on a ceramic substrate measuring 10 × 3 × 1 mm. The rapid response times are from a large surface area-to-volume ratio along with the excellent thermal conductivity of the thin ceramic substrate.

Thermistors

Thermistors are semiconductors with a resistance that varies rapidly with temperature. The materials are usually sintered mixtures of sulfides, selenides, and oxides of metals such as nickel, manganese, cobalt, copper, and iron. These mixtures are formed into small glass-enclosed beads, disks,

or rods. They have high resistivity and high negative temperature coefficients of resistance. (The resistance-vs-temperature characteristics appear in
Figure 4.3; these characteristics are not linear.) It is difficult to maintain narrow resistance tolerances during manufacture.[2]

Thermistors are relatively inexpensive. They are available in small sizes
and can be obtained with high resistance values. Properly aged, calibration
stability is equal to well-made wirewound elements. Because of the nonlinear
relationship, however, numerous calibration points are necessary.

Transistors

Transistors can also be used as temperature sensors.They operate with circuits designed to take advantage of the change in emitter-to-base voltage
with temperature rather than a change in resistance. An accurately
characterized silicon transistor may be specified as a temperature transducer. Producing a linear change in voltage over the -40 to $150°C$ operating
range, these devices use the predictable correlation which exists between
temperature and the transistor base-to-emitter voltage (V_{be}). The voltage
change is approximately 2m mV/°C. The sensors have a usable 400 mV
variation. Accuracy is $\pm$ 2%, or 5°C. The thermal time constant for the
sensors is rated at 3 seconds in flowing liquid and 8 seconds in moving air.
Junction devices such as these require a stable constant current source.

IC Temperature Transducers

A variety of IC temperature transducers that use complete circuits along
with the sensor itself are available. Laser trimming, coupled with low-cost

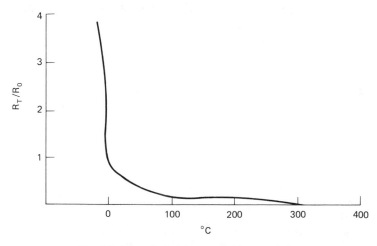

Fig. 4.3. Thermistor temperature characteristics.

integrated circuit techniques results in a precalibrated temperature transducer.[3] In applications below 150°C, linearization circuitry, references, precision amplifiers, and compensators are not required. Operating as a current source, these transducers output one microampere per degree Kelvin. Trimming of the internal calibration film resistors is performed during manufacture. As a result, ±0.5°C accuracy and linearity within ±0.3°C over full range are possible. Output impedance is greater than 10 MΩ for the rejection of hum, ripple, and noise. The high output impedance also makes these transducers useful in remote sensing applications with lines that can be hundreds of feet in length. The sensor can also be powered directly from 5-V logic, thus allowing multiplexing in most microprocessor control systems.

ICs that output temperature changes as frequency variations are also available. Voltage-to-frequency converter chips can operate as digital pulse output temperature transducers. They can be trimmed for Celsius, Kelvin, or Fahrenheit measurements with external components.

Thermocouples

A thermocouple circuit consists of a pair of wires of different metals joined together at one end, (the sensing junction), and terminated at their other end by a reference junction.

A thermoelectric potential is produced when there is a temperature difference between the two junctions. Figure 4.4 shows the thermal EMF produced by typical thermocouples. The values are based on a reference temperature of 0°C. The most common thermocouples are chromel-alumel, iron-constantan, copper-constantan and chromel-constantan.[4] Tables show-

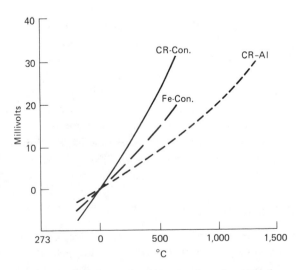

Fig. 4.4. Typical thermocouple temperature characteristics.

ing the thermal EMF vs temperature, based on standard materials, have been developed for most thermocouples by the National Bureau of Standards, the Instrument Society of America, and many manufacturers. They are usually based on a reference temperature of 0°C. Similar tables can be derived for other reference temperatures.

The common laboratory method of using an ice bath for the reference temperature has its limitations when measurements must be made frequently or continuously. Common replacements for the ice bath are (1) automatic icepoint references, (2) automatic references at temperatures other than 32°F (most commonly 150°F), and (3) electrical compensators—an ambient-temperature couple using a bridge circuit with ambient-sensitive elements. Of the three, the electrical compensator is the most economical for single-channel applications. Typical accuracies are $\pm\frac{1}{2}$°F.

The oven-type of reference is used to reference a number of thermocouple channels. Oven-type references, as well as ice-point references, provide an economic advantage over compensators where a number reference couples are required with a high channel-to-channel electrical isolation.

A major problem with thermocouples is spurious and parasitic EMFs in the leads. This effect is primarily responsible for the difference in precision between thermocouples and resistance thermometers. Slight differences in the state or composition of a wire will produce Seebeck EMFs anywhere a temperature gradient exists. These problems are most severe where the gradient on the leads is changing. Annealing reduces the effect but does not eliminate it. Most manufacturers recommend periodic recalibration of thermocouples in order to offset the temperature distribution.[5]

Thermal Pyrometers

When temperatures are too high to allow a thermocouple or other temperature-sensing element to be used, other methods are available. All hot bodies emit radiant energy with an intensity that bears a relation to the absolute temperature of the emitting surface. Radiation pyrometry measures the radiant heat emitted or reflected by a hot object. Practical radiation pyrometers are sensitive to a limited wavelength band of radiant energy.[6] The operation of thermal radiation pyrometers is based on blackbody radiation concepts and has made possible the measurement of automatic control of temperature under conditions not feasible with other temperature sensing elements.

PRESSURE TRANSDUCERS

Pressure transducers find many uses in aerospace, automotive, chemical, and civil engineering, as well as hydraulics, transportation, power generation, medicine, and other application areas. Pressure transducers are frequently used to measure altitude and water depth. For example, although atmospheric pressure decreases with increasing altitude, the relationship is not linear; the density of air and temperature decrease rapidly as altitude increases. Values for pressure-vs-altitude can be found in tables. Measurements taken by satellites are used to compute the barometric pressure-vs-altitude relationship. Ambient pressure increases with water depth, but is affected by density changes due to temperature variation and by the salinity of ocean water. When corrections for these variables are not considered, the average seawater depth may be calculated on the basis of 0.445 psi per foot of depth, and the average freshwater depth can be calculated on the basis of 0.434 psi per foot of depth.

Almost all electrical-output pressure transducers sense pressure with a mechanical sensing element. The elements are generally thin-walled elastic members, such as plates, shells, or tubes, which offer a surface area upon which the pressure can act. When the pressure is not balanced by an equal pressure acting on the opposite surface, the element will deflect. This deflection is then used to produce an electrical change in the transduction element.

The most common sensing elements are shown in Figure 4.5. The sensing elements shown measure a differential pressure, but transducers can be designed to measure differential, gauge, or absolute pressure depending on the reference pressure maintained in the reference side of the sensing element. The reference side of an absolute-pressure transducer is evacuated and sealed. Gauge pressure is measured when ambient pressure is allowed on the reference side. These configurations are shown in Figure 4.6.

Potentiometric Transducers

The potentiometric pressure transducer was first available in 1914, and it is still used today due to its low cost and connection simplicity. The potentiometric transducer consists of a resistance element either wirewound or

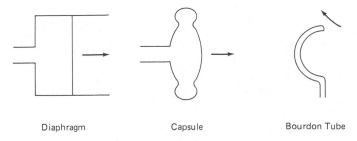

Diaphragm   Capsule   Bourdon Tube

Fig. 4.5. Pressure sensing elements.

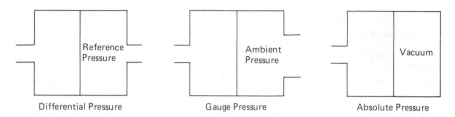

Fig. 4.6. Pressure reference configurations.

deposited conductive film, and a movable slider or wiper which is connected to the mechanical sensing element. The motion due to a pressure change results in a resistance change. Depending on the design of the potentiometer, the output can be linear, sine, cosine, logarithmic, or exponential. A typical potentiometric pressure transducer is shown in Figure 4.7.

These transducers can be used with ac or dc, and no amplification or impedance matching may be required. Other advantages include low manufacturing cost and high output with high input voltages.

The disadvantages of potentiometric transducers include finite resolution, mechanical friction, and limited life. They may also develop noise with wear. They require a relatively large displacement and have slow response time, and they are sensitive to shock environments.

Typical transducers have an accuracy of $\pm 1\%$. Their pressure range is 5 to 400 psi, but high pressure devices are available up to 10,000 psi. Specialized devices are also available within the following ranges: resolution 0.2%, linearity $\pm .4\%$, hysteresis .5%, and temperature error $\pm .8\%$. Advanced instruments can offer $\pm 0.25\%$ end-point accuracy for demanding environments.

Trends in potentiometric pressure transducers have been in two directions: (1) miniaturization with relaxed tolerances; and (2) the application of control systems to supplement the force of a diaphragm or capsule. This allows the use of low-resolution multiturn potentiometers.

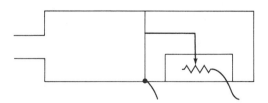

Fig. 4.7. Potentiometric pressure transducer.

Strain-Gauge Transducers

Strain-gauge transducers convert a pressure change into a change in resistance due to a mechanical strain. Usually four or sometimes two arms of a Wheatstone bridge are used for temperature compensation.

The pressure-sensing element can be a flat or corrugated diaphragm, or a straight tube since the deflection required is small. The strain-sensor gauges can be mounted right on the tube which is sealed at one end. A pressure differential causes a slight expansion or contraction of the tube diameter. Other designs use a secondary sensing element or auxiliary member as the deforming member. Available strain-gauge elements include:

1. Unbonded metal-wire gauges.
2. Bonded metal-wire gauges.
3. Bonded metal-foil gauges.
4. Bonded semiconductor gauges.
5. Integrally diffused semiconductor gauges.

Unbonded wire elements are stretched and unsupported between a fixed and a moving end. The wire is usually looped one or more times over supporting posts. They tend to have higher sensitivity, but are more sensitive to vibration. Nichrome and platinum are two materials used.

Bonded elements are attached permanently over the active element, and they are less sensitive to vibration.

Foil and semiconductor strain elements are usually bonded or deposited so that the semiconductor or foil and diaphragm appear as a single part. Semiconductor types feature larger output than wire types, but they tend to be more temperature sensitive.

Diffused semiconductor strain gauges used in pressure measurement devices are based on the technology of integrated circuits. A sensing element is made by diffusing a four-arm strain-gauge bridge into the surface of a single crystal silicon diaphragm whose diameter and thickness is varied according to pressure range and application. The silicon has excellent mechanical properties, being elastic and free from hysteresis. The bonded gauges have high gauge factors and give relatively high outputs at low strain levels.

This basic sensor is built into an encapsulated transducer or transmitter by using manufacturing techniques such as electrostatic or thermal compression bonding and electron beam welding. Operational ratings such as shock, vibration, and overload are typical of high quality microcircuit devices. The combined linearity and hysteresis accuracy is typically less than 0.06%. The low-mass silicon diaphragm gives fast response, and minimum acceleration sensitivity. In cases where the pressure media are not compatible with silicon, stainless steel, hastelloy, or other materials are used as isolating diaphragms.

The full-scale output of a four-element strain-gauge bridge, for a pressure transducer using metal wire or foil gauges, is 50–60 millivolts for bonded gauges, and 60–80 millivolts for the unbonded gauges, using 10-V excitation. The compensating and adjusting resistors reduce the output to about 20–30 millivolts for bonded and 30–40 mV for the unbonded gauges. These resistors permit zero and balance adjustments, full-scale adjustment, thermal zero-shift compensation, thermal sensitivity-shift compensation, and also shunt calibration.

Semiconductor strain-gauge transducers have a higher output, in the order of 200–400 mV for 5–7 mA excitation. Most designs have a limitation on the excitation voltage and produce a full-scale output using internal circuitry in order to reduce the voltage to the level required for the proper bridge operation. They also use a constant current to provide some thermal compensation. In order to obtain TTL output levels, an amplifier must be used for all metal and many semiconductor strain gauge transducers. Many IC designs use integral amplifiers, which also provide compensation functions.

The advantages of strain-gauge transducers are (1) fast response times, (2) good resolution, (3) minimal mechanical motion, (4) good accuracy (5) predictable compensation for temperature effects, (6) low source-impedance, and (7) freedom from acceleration effects (bonded type). Disadvantages include (1) obtaining zero output at zero pressure due to residual bridge unbalances, (2) high vibration errors when unbonded types are used for the range lower than 15 psi (3) low output levels (4) isolation of excitation ground from output ground, and (5) signal-conditioning requirements.

Strain-gauge pressure transducers are available from 0.3–100,000 psi with accuracies of 0.25–0.5%. Accuracies of up to 0.05% are also available at premium prices. (See Figure 4.8.)

Inductive and Reluctive Transducers

Inductive transducers use pressure to move a mechanical member which alters the self-inductance of a single coil. The inductance is changed by the relative motion of a core and an inductive coil (as shown in Figure 4.9). Inductive single-coil transducers have been used in L-C tank-circuit oscillators, where they formed the frequency-control. Their use has diminished, though, because of difficulties in compensating for temperature effects, which required a matching of core and windings materials for temperature-vs-permeability characteristics.

Reluctive transducers use the ratio of the reluctance of two coils and are

Fig. 4.8. This portable digital pressure transfer standard uses a strain-gauge transducer. It has an accuracy of 0.05%. (*Courtesy Volumetrics.*)

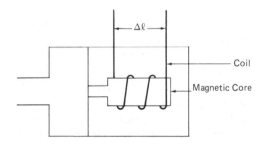

Fig. 4.9. Inductive pressure transducer.

less sensitive to temperature effects than one-coil elements. They use a small motion of 0.003 in. to yield an ac output voltage of about 100 mV.

In the diaphragm-type of variable-reluctance pressure transducer, a diaphragm of magnetic material is supported between two symmetrical inductance assemblies. The diaphragm deflects when there is a difference in pressure between the two input ports. This tends to increase the gap in the magnetic flux path of one core and to decrease the gap in the other; the reluctance varies with the gap. The overall effect is a change in inductance of the two coils. The inductance ratio L_1/L_2 is usually measured in a bridge circuit to produce a voltage proportional to the pressure difference.

Most manufacturers of reluctive transducers offer dc-to-ac-to-dc conversion circuitry in separate or integral packaging. Reluctive transducers with dc excitations of 28 and 5 V are available for absolute, gauge, and differential pressure measurements. Typical range is 1 inch of water to 12,000 psi.

The performance of reluctive transducers, with or without dc-to-dc converters, is comparable in most respects to the best available versions of other transducer types. Static-error is typically ± 0.5% with nonlinearity producing the major portion of error. Errors due to hsyteresis and nonrepeatability can be below 0.2%. Proof pressure ratings of greater than six times range are available. However, errors can also be introduced by stray magnetic and electric fields.

Most ac transducers operate at a carrier frequency in the range of 60 Hz to 30 KHz. When dc conversion is used, the internally-generated carrier frequency may be much higher, permitting smaller coils and capacitors in a smaller package.

Temperature effects are minimized by similar sensing element and coil materials. Temperature errors are typically 1 or 2% up to 100°F. Pressure transducers without dc conversion operate over a wide temperature range with an upper limit of 350°F. The solid-state components of dc converters may limit the operating temperature of this transducer to less than the ac version. Frequency response is flat from 50 to 1000 Hz, but it depends on the particular design.

The reluctive transducer lends itself to operation with many types of fluids, including corrosive media.

Variable-reluctance pressure transducers, particularly the diaphragm type offer the ability to withstand shock and vibration environments along with good overload tolerances. The dynamic response allows use in liquid as well as gas systems due to high natural-frequency.

The linear variable differential transformer (LVDT) uses a movable core attached to the pressure sensing element. Depending on the particular sensing element and linkage, transducers of this type may be more sensitive to vibration and mechanical wear.

Piezoeletric Transducers

Piezoeletric pressure transducers use a crystal to generate a charge or voltage when mechanically stressed. Many transducer designs use a diaphragm which deflects with pressure in order to produce the stress on the crystal.

Piezoelectric pressure transducers can operate over a wide temperature range with small temperature errors.

The ability of the piezoelectric sensor to respond rapidly to applied shock levels may become a limiting factor in some high-level applications. An application of high-level shock can produce a voltage that may overload signal-conditioning circuitry for 50 or more times the shock duration causing a data loss during this time.

Since the output of a piezoelectric crystal is small and the impedance high, a high-impedance amplifier is required to record the output. A common configuration is an operational amplifier with capacitive feedback to compen sate for capacitance due to cable length. Integrated-circuit techniques permit the amplifier to be placed inside the transducer case. Typical pressure ranges in which these devices can operate are 5 to 10,000 psi.

Capacitive Transducers

Capacitive pressure transducers employ a metal diaphragm, with a metal plate positioned on one side of the diaphragm. Deflection of the diaphragm changes the capacitance between it and the fixed plate. An ac signal across the plates is used to sense the change in capacitance, or the capacitance change is used to alter the frequency of an oscillator circuit.[8] The advantages of capacitive transducers are small size, high-frequency response, and high temperature operation. Moreover, they have the ability to measure both static and dynamic quantities. Their shortcomings include a sensitivity to temperature variations, high-impedance output, and complexity of associated circuitry. Capacitance transducers must be reactively as well as resistively matched. Long lead lengths and loose leads can cause a variation in capacitance. It is usually necessary to locate a preamplifier very close to the transducer.

The total range is 0.01 to 10,000 psi with a typical accurancy of 0.25%; premium units are available with accuracies to 0.05%.

Some capacitive transducers utilize materials such as quartz. The sensor consists of two thin quartz disks, each having a platinum electrode on its inner surface. The disks are fused at their periphery to form a capsule, with the electrodes separated by a 0.002 in. gap. When a vacuum is drawn inside the gap, absolute pressures of up to 30 psi are measured. Gauge pressures of up to 30 psi can also be measured with one port vented to the atmosphere. The quartz device can provide an accuracy of ± 0.05%, full scale. A 5V TTL output is available.

New types of digital pressure transducers are being introduced to take advantage of the accuracy and readability of digital readouts. Some use sensors such as bellows as the primary sensing device with analog-to-digital conversion circuitry.[9] Others may use a bourdon coil pressure sensing element and optical encoder.[10] These are mounted on a common shaft which rotates 270° in proportion to applied pressure, thereby providing a direct BCD, or serialized output, to a readout device which displays pressure in digital form. The outputs are compatible with microcomputers, as well as the monitoring and recording equipment in many chemical, paper, and similar industrial applications.

The digital pressure instruments form an important part of the product range. By using selected transducers, high performance instruments are produced which can be used to calibrate other pressure transducers or gauges. Such instruments can be supplied giving the digital display in any pressure units. (See Figure 4.10).

FLOW TRANSDUCERS

No manufacturing process can get along without measuring the flow of some of the materials involved. These may be fuel, gas, cooling water or process air. Or they may be process liquids and gases, or the product itself.

When one has to specify a flow sensor, there is a wide variety of devices from which to choose. Flow sensing elements which respond directly to the flow-rate of a fluid fall can be placed in three general categories:

1. A section of a pipe or duct contains a restriction which produces a differential pressure proportional to flow-rate. The differential pressure (Δ_p) is then measured with a pressure transducer.
2. A mechanical member responds to moving fluid by rotating or deflecting, or by displacement in a tapered tube.
3. One of the fluid's physical characteristics interacts with the sensing element.

Head Meters

The flow-sensing elements in the first group are called head meters because the differential pressure across two points can be equated to the head or the height of the liquid column. The elements are characterized by a constant area of flow passage. The venturi tube, flow nozzle, orifice plate, pitot tube, and other restricted sections are included in this group. (The pressure transducers used to measure flow with these sensing elements are described in the previous section, "Pressure Transducers.")

Other differential pressure sections that are used include elbows, which are useful for viscous fluids, and loops which can be used for pulsating flows and slurries.

Fig. 4.10. This digital pressure sensor uses a bourdon coil sensing element and an optical encoder. (*Courtesy Siltran Digital.*)

Variable-Area Meters

A variety of different mechanical flow-sensing elements are used in flow transducers. Variable-area meters use a float (called a "rotameter") in a tapered section of tubing, a spring-restrained plug, or a spring-restrained vane. The displacement of these elements causes the area of flow passage to vary while the differential pressure or head remains constant. The displacement is measured in order to provide an output proportional to the flow-rate.

Some types of variable-area meters use the deflection of vanes measured with strain-gauge bridges. The vane in these flowmeters is usually installed perpendicular to the flow. A wedge-shaped vane has been used with strain-gauges for air turbulance measurements.[11]

Turbine Flowmeters

The turbine flowmeter uses moving fluid to turn a turbine wheel, and the speed of the rotor varies with the flow-rate. Turbine flowmeters supply the flow information as a precise number of pulses for the volume of fluid displaced between the rotor blades. The relationship is linear, within limits, for flow-rate and viscosity. This linearity may be ± 0.25% of rate, and repeatability can be 0.02% of rate.[12] Bearing friction, fluid and magnetic drag, and swirl in the fluid stream, can cause deviations in the behavior of the transducer.

The transducer case must be made of a nonmagnetic metal. The amplitude of the output voltage from the coil is dependent on the gap between the pole piece and turbine blade tips. Most turbine flowmeters use an electromagnetic coil of the permanent-magnet type. The turbine blades are then made of a ferroelectric material. An accuracy of 0.5% can be achieved. A turbine meter installation with pickup electronics is expensive in comparison with most head meters. The advantages of turbine meters, though, include:

1. High pressure and high flow measurement capabilities over a wide temperature range.
2. Good flow range.
3. High accuracy and repeatability.
4. Short approaches required.
5. Quick response.
6. Can be converted to mass flow by compensating equipment.

The disadvantages include the following.

1. Abrasive materials can wear out bearings.
2. High viscosities can affect measurement.
3. Pulsating flow or water hammer may cause damage.
4. High cost.

Fluid Characteristics Sensors

A number of different types of flow sensors use the fluid characteristics interacting with a sensing element. For example, a heated wire in a hot-wire anemometer will transfer more of its heat as the flow-velocity of its surrounding fluid increases. The resultant cooling of the wire causes a resistance decrease. A fluid containing a small amount of radioactivity will cause an increase in ionization current for an increasing flow-velocity. A mildly conductive fluid flowing through a transverse magnetic field will produce an increasing voltage for an increasing flow-velocity. When the boundary layer of a moving fluid is heated by a small heating element, the convective heat transfer to a temperature sensor located downstream from the heater will increase with increasing flow-velocity.

Transducers which convert flow-rate into a change of resistance use the fluid characteristics. The resistive element may respond to temperature changes in three transducer types: (1) the hot-wire anemometer which is a specialized device primarily for air-flow measurements, (2) the thermal and boundary-layer flowmeters that use resistive transduction, and (3) the oscillating-vortex flowmeters.

Hot-Wire Anemometers

The hot-wire anemometer has a wire element normal to the flowing stream which is heated electrically. Cooling by the flow changes the resistance of the wire as a function of the flow-velocity. Other forms maintain the wire temperature constant and measure the current required to maintain the temperature; this current is then a function of the flow. Such instruments can measure mass flow as long as the product of the thermal conductivity, specific heat, and density remain constant.[13] This is true for many gases at low pressures as this meter has the greatest application in the measurement of low flow-rates of gases. They are also used for gas velocity determinations. They are sensitive to flow changes but tend to be expensive. Anemometers are widely used in air conditioning, in weather stations, and around cooling towers.

Nucleonic Flowmeters

Flow instruments have been developed which utilize radioisotopes and the detection of nuclear radiation. One type uses a source mounted to the outside of the pipe some distance upstream from the detector. The source neutrons collide with the atoms of the moving fluid and cause particle and electromagnetic radiation to be emitted. Most of the emitted radiation occurs at the source location, but some is emitted as the fluid passes the detector. The number of counts produced by the detector are an indication of the flow-rate of the fluid. Another type of nucleonic detector obtains an output by adding minute amounts of a radioactive trace element to the fluid.

Nucleonic flowmeters offer no obstruction to the fluid and are useful for the measurement of difficult fluids such as multiphase variable composition fluids, slurries, and suspensions.

Electromagnetic Flowmeters

Electromagnetic flowmeters follow Faraday's Law that relative motion, at right angles between a conductor and a magnetic field, induces a voltage in a conductor. This voltage is proportional to the relative velocity of the conductor and the magnetic field. An electromagnetic flowmeter is made with a nonmagnetic tube and uses a conductive liquid. On the tube are magnetic coils which, when energized, provide a magnetic field through the full width of the tube. As the liquid moves through the magentic field, a voltage is generated proportional to the flow-rate.

Because electromagnetic flowmeters directly sense liquid velocity, the entire cross-sectional area of the pipe must be full.[14] There should be no entrained gas. Any gas bubbles carried by the liquid will be measured as liquid, resulting in a measurement error.

The meter's output is in microvolts to millivolts. Proper installation and grounding are required for accurate flow measurement. These flowmeters are unaffected by changes in liquid density or viscosity. Turbulence of the liquid and variations in piping have very limited effects.

One limiting factor, though, is the requirement that the conductivity of the fluid be greater than about 10^{-8} ohm/cm^3. In addition, the presence of mixed-phase fluids may cause major measurement errors. DC coil excitation is rarely used, since it can cause electrolysis is a conducting fluid. However, the linearity of output voltage with flow-rate is a significant advantage, as is the absence of any obstruction in the pipe.

Piezoelectric, Sonic, and Ultrasonic Flowmeters

Piezoelectric flowmeters were originally developed for aerospace applications in the 1950s. One design uses two transducer pairs in order to establish an upstream and a downstream sonic path diagonally across the fluid (as shown in Figures 4.11 and 4.12). The difference in propagation velocity (the doppler effect) between the two paths is then related to the flow-rate.[15]

Sonic and ultrasonic flowmeters are used with liquids or sonically conductive slurries through pipes or open channels. They are used in water and waste sewage plants, industrial process plants, and power stations.

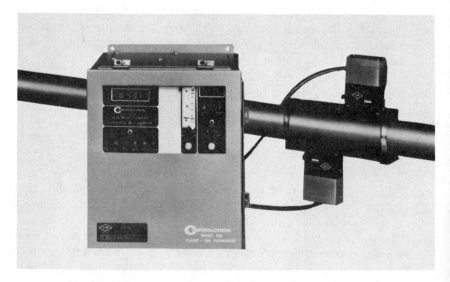

Fig. 4.11. A clamp-on ultrasonic flowmeter is shown installed on a closed pipe. (*Courtesy Controlotron Corporation.*)

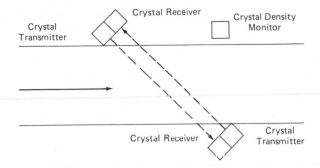

Fig. 4.12. Ultrasonic flowmeter (doppler type).

REFERENCES

1. Liptak, B. G. and Venczel K., eds., *Process Measurement Instrument Engineers' Handbook,* Radnor: Chilton, 1982.
2. Ibid.
3. Mendelsohn, A., Temperature Transducers, *Electronic Products,* May 1979.
4. Liptak and Venczel.
5. Ibid.
6. Ibid.
7. Ibid.
8. Ibid.
9. Sandford, J., Eyeballing Pressuring, *Instruments and Control Systems,* November 1976.
10. 3D Instruments, *Direct Drive Digital Pressure Transducers,* Huntington Beach: 3D Instruments, 1978.
11. Hall, J., Solving Tough Flow Monitoring Problems, *Instruments and Control Systems,* February, 1980.
12. Liptak and Venczel.
13. Ibid.
14. Ibid.
15. Ibid.

EXERCISES

1. a. What common materials are used in resistance temperature detectors?
   b. Define the temperature coefficient of each.
2. What is the resistance range of most commercial resistance temperature detectors at 0°C?
3. Describe how a thermistor differs from a resistance thermometer.
4. A change in line resistance between a thermocouple and an indicator has no effect under what conditions?
5. The scale of a millivoltmeter connected to a thermocouple can be calibrated to read temperature directly for what conditions?
6. The temperature of a pump housing is to be measured while the pump is operating. Required accuracy is ± 10°F, range is + 40 to + 300°F, and time constant is up to 8 seconds. Readout equipment is in a temperature-controlled area 50

ft. from the pump. Describe a system to measure and record pump housing temperatures on a sampled basis for quality control. Justify your choice of sensor and computer equipment.

7. The temperature of a mildly corrosive and conductive liquid is to be measured as the liquid enters the pump in problem 6 above. Required accuracy is ± 8°F, range is 0 to 300°F and time constant is 2 seconds. Describe a continuous monitor and alarm system for a series of 13 similar pumps with output to a digital modem. Design the system for maximum reliability without redundant equipment.

8. What pressure reading is obtained when the reference side of a sensor is evacuated?

9. Describe the operation and characteristics of a potentiometer pressure transducer.

10. What are the advantages of a strain-gauge transducer over a potentiometer transducer in a microprocessor control system?

11. What are the advantages of a semiconductor strain-gauge over a metallic strain-gauge in a high-volume, low-cost application?

12. What are the advantages of piezoelectric pressure sensors over other types in a low-cost, low-volume application?

13. The pressure of liquid oxygen flowing through a high-pressure duct must be found. Required accuracy is + 1%°F, range is 200 to 300°F psi, and time constant is 0.8 seconds; a proof pressure of 600 psig is required; flow-rate is 60 to 150 gpm. Describe a monitoring system for a local microprocessor alarm-control system located within 20 feet of the pressure duct.

14. Describe how the venturi tube can be used for liquid-flow measurement.

15. Compare the operation and construction, as well as the advantages and disadvantages, of the venturi tube and orifice plate.

16. Water is flowing down a vertical pipe 6 ft. long. The pipe has a diameter of 4 in. If the quantity of water is 300 gallons/min. nominal, with expected variations of ± 30, describe a flow-monitoring and pumping-control system using a low-cost microprocessor.

17. Describe, with the aid of a diagram, the operation of measuring liquid-flow in an open channel by means of a simple microprocessor system.

5. Data-Acquisition

THE DATA-ACQUISITION PROBLEM

Data acquisition is typically concerned with the collection and processing of analog sensor data into digital form for any or all of the following purposes:

1. Storage for later use.
2. Transmission to other location.
3. Processing to obtain additional information.
4. Display for analysis or recording.

Data can be stored in raw or processed form; it might be retained for short or long periods, or transmitted over long or short distances, or displayed on a digital panel meter or a cathode ray tube (as shown in the system of Figure 5.1).

Data processing can range from simple value comparisons to complicated manipulations. Its purposes may be for collecting information, converting data to a more useful form, using the data for controlling a process, performing calculations, separating signals from noise, or generating information for displays. In this chapter, we consider some of the data acquisition configurations that have proven useful in the past, and we will discuss some of the considerations involved in the choice of configuration, components, and other elements of the system. We will then discuss the use of digital data communications for remote microcomputer networks. Next, we will address the aspects of remote multiplexing in microcomputer networks, including distributed control. Finally, we will look at the impact of distributed control on system designs in the future.

Data-Acquisition Considerations

The systems design should begin with the choice of sensor. If the systems engineer has a part in the selection of the transducer, this can go a long way towards easing the design task. For example, in monitoring or controlling

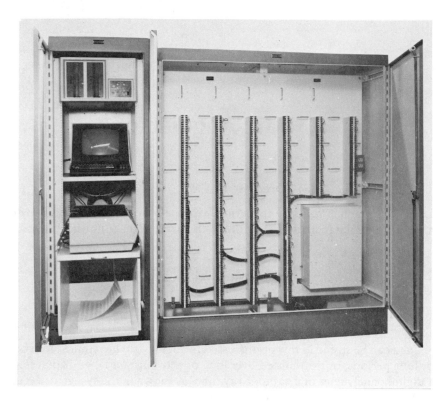

Fig. 5.1. This data acquisition system is used for monitoring generator temperatures. RTD's or thermocouples are terminated in the larger cabinet while the smaller cabinet houses the recording equipment. (*Courtesy Volumetrics.*)

motor shafts, the designer may have the choice of signals from three different position-sensing approaches: shaft encoders, synchros, or potentiometers. Temperature measurements may be made with thermocouples or thermistors, while force can be measured by strain gauges, or obtained by integrating the output from accelerometers.

To accommodate the sensor voltage for analog-to-digital conversion, some form of scaling and offsetting may be performed with an amplifier. To convert analog information from more than one source, additional converters or a multiplexer will be necessary. To increase the speed at which information may be accurately converted, a sample-hold may be used, and to compress analog signals, a logarithmic amplifier might be used.

If transducer signals must be scaled from millivolt levels to an A/D converter's typical ± 10-V full-scale input, an operational amplifier may be the best choice. If the system involves a number of sources, each transducer might be provided with a local amplifier so that the low-level signals are amplified before being transferred.

Data-Acquisition Components

If the analog data must be transmitted over any distance, differences in ground potential between the signal source and final location can add noise in the interface design. In order to separate common-mode interference from the signal to be recorded or processed, devices designed for this purpose, such as instrumentation amplifiers, may be used. An instrumentation amplifier is characterized by good common-mode-rejection capability, a high input impedance, low drift, adjustable gain, and greater cost than operational amplifiers. They range from monolithic ICs to potted modules, and larger rack-mounted modules with manual scaling and null adjustments. When a very high common-mode voltage is present or the need for extremely-low common-mode leakage current exists (as in many medical-electronics applications), an isolation amplifier is required. Isolation amplifiers may use optical or transformer isolation.

Analog function circuits are special-purpose circuits that are used for a variety of signal conditioning operations on signals which are in analog form.[1] When their accuracy is adequate, they can relieve the microprocessor of time-consuming software and computations. Among the typical operations performed are multiplication, division, powers, roots, nonlinear functions such as for linearizing transducers, rms measurements, computing vector sums, integration and differentiation, and current-to-voltage or voltage-to-current conversion.[2] Many of these operations can be purchased in available devices as multiplier/dividers, log/antilog amplifiers, and others.

When data from a number of independent signal sources must be processed by the same microcomputer or communications channel, a multiplexer is used to channel the input signals into the A/D converter.

Multiplexers are also used in reverse, as when a converter must distribute analog information to many different channels. The multiplexer is fed by a D/A converter which continually refreshes the output channels with new information.

In many systems, the analog signal varies during the time that the converter takes to digitize an input signal. The changes in this signal level during the conversion process can result in errors since the conversion period can be completed some time after the conversion command. The final value never represents the data at the instant when the conversion command is transmitted. Sample-hold circuits are used to make an acquisition of the varying analog signal and to hold this signal for the duration of the conversion process. Sample-hold circuits are common in multichannel distribution systems where they allow each channel to receive and hold the signal level.

In order to get the data in digital form as rapidly and as accurately as possible, we must use an analog/digital (A/D) converter, which might be a shaft encoder, a small module with digital outputs, or a high-resolution, high-speed panel instrument. These devices, which range from IC chips to rack-mounted instruments, convert analog input data, usually voltage, into an equivalent digital form. The characteristics of A/D converters include absolute and relative accuracy, linearity, monotonicity, resolution, conversion speed, and stability. A choice of input ranges, output codes, and other features are available.[3] The successive-approximation technique is popular for a large number of applications, with the most popular alternatives being the counter-comparator types, and dual-ramp approaches. The dual-ramp has been widely-used in digital voltmeters. (A typical data acquisition system is shown in Figure 5.2.)

D/A converters convert a digital format into an equivalent analog representation. The basic converter consists of a circuit of weighted resistance values or ratios, each controlled by a particular level or weight of digital input data, which develops the output voltage or current in accordance with the digital input code. A special class of D/A converter exists which have the capability of handling variable reference sources. These devices are the multiplying DACs.[4] Their output value is the product of the number represented by the digital input code and the analog reference voltage, which may vary from full scale to zero, and in some cases, to negative values.

Conversion techniques are examined in more detail in Chapter 6.

Component Selection Criteria

In the past decade, data-acquisition hardware has changed radically due to advances in semiconductors, and prices have come down too; what have not changed, however, are the fundamental system problems confronting the

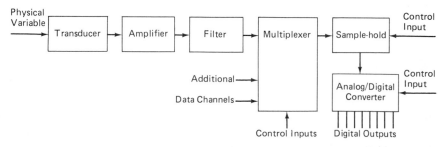

Fig. 5.2. Typical data acquisition system.

designer. Signals may be obscured by noise, rfi, ground loops, power-line pickup, and transients coupled into signal lines from machinery. Separating the signals from these effects becomes a matter for concern.

Data-acquisition systems may be separated into two basic categories: (1) those suited to favorable environments like laboratories and (2) those required for hostile environments such as factories, vehicles, and military installations. The latter group includes industrial process control systems where temperature information may be gathered by sensors on tanks, boilers, vats, or pipelines that may be spread over miles of facilities. That data may then be sent to a central processor to provide real-time process control. The digital control of steel mills, automated chemical production, and machine tools is carried out in this kind of hostile environment. The vulnerability of the data signals leads to the requirement for isolation and other techniques.

At the other end of the spectrum—laboratory applications, such as test systems for gathering information on gas chromatographs, mass spectrometers, and other sophisticated instruments—the designer's problems are concerned with the performing of sensitive measurements under favorable conditions rather than with the problem of protecting the integrity of collected data under hostile conditions.

Systems in hostile environments might require components for wide temperatures, shielding, common-mode noise reduction, conversion at an early stage, redundant circuits for critical measurements, and preprocessing of the digital data to test its reliability. Laboratory systems, on the other hand, will have narrower temperature ranges and less ambient noise. But the higher accuracies require sensitive devices, and a major effort may be necessary for the required signal/noise ratios.

The choice of configuration and components in data-acquisition design depends on consideration of a number of factors:

1. Resolution and accuracy required in final format.
2. Number of analog sensors to be monitored.
3. Sampling rate desired.
4. Signal-conditioning requirement due to environment and accuracy.
5. Cost trade-offs.

Some of the choices for a basic data-acquisition configuration include:

1. Single-channel techniques.
   A. Direct conversion.
   B. Preamplification and direct conversion.
   C. Sample-hold and conversion.
   D. Preamplification, sample-hold, and conversion.

    E. Preamplification, signal-conditioning, and direct conversion.

    F. Preamplification, signal-conditioning, sample-hold, and conversion.

2. Multichannel techniques.

    A. Multiplexing the outputs of single-channel converters.

    B. Multiplexing the outputs of sample-holds.

    C. Multiplexing the inputs of sample-holds.

    D. Multiplexing low-level data.

    E. More than one tier of multiplexers.

Signal-conditioning may include:

1. Radiometric conversion techniques.

2. Wide-dynamic-range techniques.

    A. High-resolution conversion.

    B. Range biasing.

    C. Automatic-gain switching.

    D. Logarithmic compression.

3. Noise-reduction techniques.

    A. Analog filtering.

    B. Integrating converters.

    C. Digital data processing.

We shall consider these techniques later, but first we will examine some of the components used in these data-acquisition system configurations.

INSTRUMENTATION AND ISOLATION AMPLIFIERS

In many data-acquisition systems, it is necessary to retrieve millivolts of analog data from volts of common-mode interference. It may be necessary to galvanically isolate the amplifier's input from its output and the power source in order to protect the amplifier from high voltage or to protect the object being measured (perhaps a hospital patient) from leakage current.

Instrumentation amplifiers are the components for achieving these objectives. They include the special subclass of isolation amplifiers. Instrumentation amplifiers may contain operational amplifiers, but they are distinguished from op-amps in that they are committed devices with a definite set of input-output relationships in a fixed configuration.[5] They are designed for a high common-mode rejection ratio (CMRR), low noise and drift, moderate bandwidth, and a limited gain range—usually 1 to 1000, programmed by a fixed resistor.

The common-mode rejection ratio is the ratio of the common-mode voltage to the common-mode error referred to the input, and it is generally expressed in dBs:

$$CMRR = 20 \log_{10} \left[\frac{V_{cm}}{e_{cm}} \right]$$

Where V_{cm} is the common-mode voltage and e_{cm} is the common-mode error referred to the input. CMRR is an important parameter of differential amplifiers. An idea differential amplifier would respond to voltage differences between its input terminals without regard to the voltage level common to both inputs. In practice, however, there is a variation in the balance of the differential amplifier due to the common-mode voltage, which results in an output even when the differential input is zero.

Instrumentation amplifiers generally use high-precision feedback networks. Their drift, linearity, and noise-rejection capability make them useful for extracting and amplifying low-level signals in the presence of high common-mode noise voltages. They are commonly used as transducer amplifiers for thermocouples, strain-gauge bridges, and biological probes.[6] As preamplifiers, they can be used for extracting small differential signals superimposed on large common-mode voltages.

Figure 5.3 shows a simple subtractor which uses one operational amplifier. It has the problem of poor source unbalance characteristics, with its low input impedance since CMRR depends on resistance matching. When a FET-input amplifier is used with very large values of resistance, noise and bandwidth problems can occur.

The usual configuration of the instrumentation amplifier does not use gain-setting resistors or other components connected to the input terminals, thereby degrading the input impedance. The high impedance inputs can maintain the high common-mode rejection characteristic even with moderate source impedances.

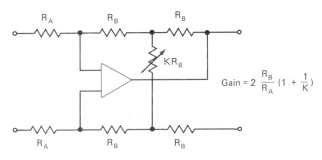

$$\text{Gain} = 2 \frac{R_B}{R_A} \left(1 + \frac{1}{K} \right)$$

Fig. 5.3. Subtractor instrumentation amplifier.

The buffered subtractor shown in Figure 5.4 does not have this problem, bu it uses two additional op-amps. Bipolar op-amps are adequate, but FET-inputs should be used with inputs having a high source impedance. Matched input-followers can provide low drift and keep high CMRR, when the main amplifier's drift is low and the resistances are well-matched.

The requirements for the resistance match for CMRR are reduced, and the bandwidth is improved for high-gain applications by using a buffered subtractor-with-gain (Figure 5.5). The first stage has unity gain for the common-mode signal, thus increasing the overall CMRR by the differential gain of the first stage. Separate followers-with-gain would not result in this improvement, since they would amplify differential and common-mode signals equally. Matched amplifiers can help CMRR and drift-stability.

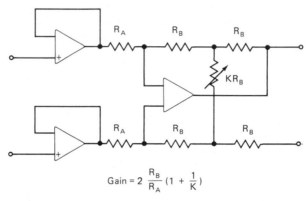

$$\text{Gain} = 2\,\frac{R_B}{R_A}\left(1 + \frac{1}{K}\right)$$

Fig. 5.4. Buffered subtractor instrumentation amplifier.

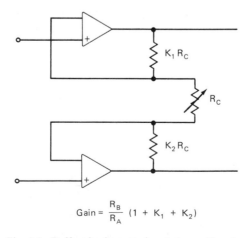

$$\text{Gain} = \frac{R_B}{R_A}\left(1 + K_1 + K_2\right)$$

Fig. 5.5. Buffered subtractor input stage with gain.

The differential current-feedback amplifier uses high-impedance sense and reference input terminals. Resistance in series with either of those terminals, unless matched, will cause common-mode errors. The ability to match the transistors and current-sources, due to the close spacing on the IC chip, makes this approach feasible in low-cost ICs. These commonly-used circuit design approaches use only one resistor which is adjusted to control the gain. Most commercially-available types have feedback sense and reference terminals for lead compensation, current-output sensing, and adjustable offset reference voltage.[7]

Instrumentation Amplifier Applications

In data-acquistion systems, instrumentation amplifiers are used for preamplification and for adapting the input signal range to the range of the A/D converter. Because instrumentation amplifiers respond only to the difference between two voltages, they can be used in both balanced and unbalanced systems. In balanced systems, the output of the signal source appears on two lines, both having equal source resistances and output voltages in relation to ground or the common-mode level (see Figure 5.6).

An unbalanced system does not use symmetry in the configuration. A major application of instrumentation amplifiers is in eliminating the effects of ground-potential differences in these single-ended systems (as shown in Figure 5.7).

Since instrumentation amplifiers can measure voltage differences at any level within their range, they are useful in measuring currents. Typically, they measure and amplify the voltage appearing across a low-resistance shunt (as shown in Figure 5.8).

When the reference terminal is available, it can be used to bias out dc voltages, such as contact potentials; or it can be used to bias relay or comparator trip points. The reference terminal may be driven by an operational

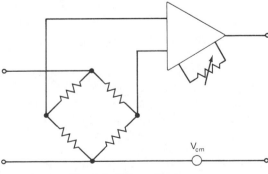

Fig. 5.6. Balanced system.

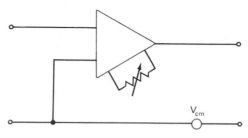

Fig. 5.7. Unbalanced system.

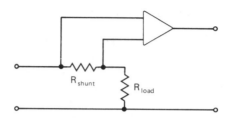

Fig. 5.8. Current measurement with an instrumentation amplifier.

amplifier with either constant or variable voltage, or if the amplifier has high input impedance at the reference terminal, it can be driven by a voltage divider or potentiometer. In applications, the sense and reference terminals are connected to the specific points at which the output is to be maintained. The circuit will then ignore any voltage drops in the output signal or ground lines.

An error analysis can be used to find the sources of errors. An example for a bridge circuit is given in Table 5.1.

Isolation Amplifiers

Isolation amplifiers are used in those applications that require an actual galvanic isolation of the amplifier's input circuit from the output and the power supply. Typical applications include:

1. High common-mode voltages between input and output.
2. Medical-electronics equipment.[8]
3. Two-wire inputs with no ground return for bias currents.
4. Situations where high CMRR is required, with a large source unbalance.

The two most common approaches for obtaining isolation are transformer and optical coupling. Optical coupling is quite effective for isolation,

Table 5.1 Bridge Circuit Errors

OPERATING CONDITIONS	INSTRUMENTATION AMPLIFIER SPECIFICATIONS	ERROR SOURCE	CALCULATION	VALUE	%F.S. (5V)
$E_{IN} = \pm 5mV$	E_{OS} Drift $11mV/°C$ (G=1000) at output	Gain Drift (=5° to 45°C)	$0.01\%/°C \times \Delta T \times E_{OUT}$	$\pm\ 10mV$	0.2%
	Gain Drift $= \pm0.01\%$ (G=1000)	Offset Drift (+5° to 45°C)	$11mV/°C \times \Delta T$	$\pm\ 220mV$	4.4%
$E_{OUT} = \pm 5V$	$I_B = 20nA$	Total Drift Error		$\overline{230mV}$	$\overline{4.6\%}$
$E_{CM} = +5V$					
	$Z_d = 300M\Omega$	Linearity Error	$0.01\%@10V$	$\pm\ 10mV$	0.2%
$\Delta T = \pm 20°C$	$Z_{CM} = 1000M\Omega$	Common-Mode Error	$E_{CM} \times A_D/CMRR$	$\pm\ 50mV$	1.0%
$T_A = +25°C$ (ambient)	CMRR $(A_D/A_{CM}) = 10^5$				
$R_L = 10k\Omega$	Gain = 1000	Output Loading Error	$(R_o/R_L) \times E_{OUT}$	$\underline{5mV}$	0.1%
$R_{BRIDGE} = 500\Omega$	Nonlinearity $= \pm0.01\%$	Total Error at 25°C		$\pm\ 65mV$	1.3%
	$R_o = 10\Omega$	Total Error (+5°C to +45°C)		$\pm 295mV$	5.9%

since it uses a portion of the electromagnetic spectrum that completely eliminates voltage, current, and magnetic flux for its energy transmission. (The components and technique are shown in Figure 5.9.)

Typical isolation amplifiers employing transformer coupling offer total galvanic isolation, a low capacitance of < 10pF between input and output ground circuits, a CMRR of 115dB at 60Hz, and common-mode voltage ratings to 5kV. Capable of transmitting millivolt signals with unity or adjustable gain, these devices are used for medical applications such as where an ECG waveform is the input in order to isolate patients from ground-fault currents.[9]

Like the instrumentation amplifiers, these amplifiers use committed gain circuits with internal feedback networks and can operate from dc to 2kHz. They are designed in two parts: (1) an isolated amplifier section and (2) an output section. (See Figure 5.10) The amplifier section includes a fixed-gain op-amp, a modulator and a dc-regulator enclosed in a floating guard-shield. The output section contains the demodulator, filter, and power-supply oscillator circuit, operating from a single supply. Operating power is transformer-coupled into the shielded input circuits, and it is capacitively or magnetically coupled to the output demodulator circuit. A typical ECG application in a medical-electronics data-acquisition system is shown in Figure 5.11.

Filtering

After the amplifier in the data-acquistion system, it may be necessary to use a lowpass filter. Filtering is used for two reasons: (1) to limit the bandwidth of the signal to less than half the sampling frequency in order to eliminate distortion frequency due to folding and (2) to reduce man-made or electrically generated noise in the system. Man-made noise usually has some regular

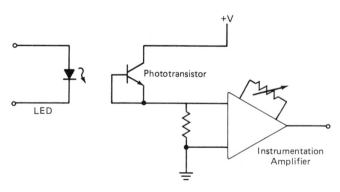

Fig. 5.9. Optical coupled isolation amplifier.

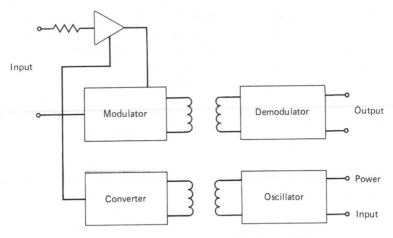

Fig. 5.10. Transformer coupled isolation amplifier.

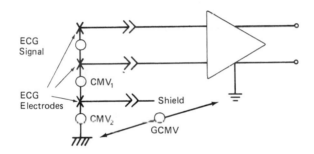

Fig. 5.11. ECG amplifier.

characteristics such as periodicity and regular shape and can be eliminated by some specific technique such as a notch filter. Thermal, or Johnson noise, is random noise with a noise power proportional to the bandwidth. It is minimized by restricting the bandwidth to the minimum required to pass the necessary signals.

No filter is perfect for eliminating noise or all undesirable frequency components. The choice of a filter is a compromise. Ideal filters have flat response, infinite cutoff attenuation, and linear phase response. In practice, one has the choice of a cutoff frequency, and an attenuation rate and phase response based on the number of poles and filter characteristic. The effect of overshoot and nonuniform phase delay must also be considered.

Active filters are popular due to a number of advantages they have over passive filters. They can eliminate inductors, with associated saturation and temperature stability problems. The response of an active filter can be set by temperature-stable capacitors and resistors. They overcome the problems of insertion loss and loading effects by the use of operational amplifiers.

A typical active filter is shown in Figure 5.12. It is manufactured with thick-film hybrid technology. It uses the state-variable active filter principle to implement a second-order transfer function. Three operational amplifiers are used for the second-order function, while a fourth uncommitted op-amp may be used as a gain-stage, summing amplifier, buffer amplifier, or to add another real pole. Two-pole lowpass, bandpass, and highpass output functions are available simultaneously from three different outputs. Notch and allpass functions are available by combining these outputs in the uncommitted op-amp. To realize higher order filters, several devices can be cascaded. Q-range is 0.1 to 1,000 and resonant frequency range is 0.001 Hz to 200 kHz. Frequency stability is 0.1%/°C. Frequency tuning is done by two external resistors and Q-tuning by a third external resistor. For resonant frequencies below 50 Hz, two external capacitors are added.

By proper selection of the external components, any of the popular filter types such as Butterworth, Bessel, Chebyshev, or Elliptic may be designed.[10]

MULTIPLEXERS

When more than one channel requires analog-to-digital conversion, it is necessary to use time-division multiplexing in order to connect the analog inputs to a single converter, or to provide a converter for each input and then combine the converter outputs by digital multiplexing.

Analog Multiplexers

Analog multiplexer circuits allow the timesharing of analog-to-digital converters between a number of analog information channels. An analog multiplexer consists of a group of switches arranged with inputs connected to the individual analog channels and outputs connected in common (as shown in Figure 5.13). The switches may be addressed by a digital input code. MOS-FET switches are generally used and can be connected directly to an output load if its impedance is high enough, or to an output buffer amplifier which provides a high impedance to the switches. Using a bipolar transistor follower-amplifier as a buffer, an input impedance of 10^9 ohms may be achieved resulting in a negligible transfer error switch resistance of typically 2K ohms.[11] As shown in Figure 5.14, the MOS-FET multiplexer has reversed biased diodes which protect the input channels from being damaged by overvoltage signals. The input channels are protected for up to 20 V beyond the supplies and can be increased by adding series resistors (R_i) to each channel. This input resistor limits the current flowing through the protection diodes to 10 mA.

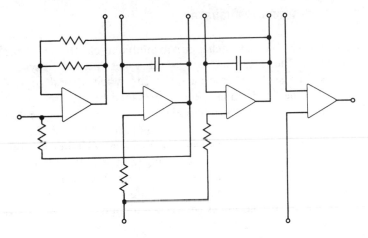

Fig. 5.12. Typical active filter IC.

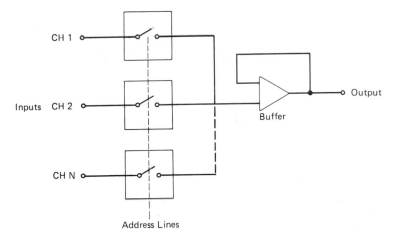

Fig. 5.13. Analog multiplexer.

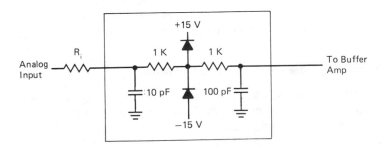

Fig. 5.14. MOS-FET multiplexer equivalent circuit.

Many alternative analog switches are available in electromechanical and solid-state forms. Electromechanical switch types include relays, stepper switches, cross-bar switches, mercury-wetted switches, and dry-reed relay switches. The best switching speed is provided by reed relays (about 1 ms). The mechanical switches provide high dc isolation resistance, low contact resistance, and the capacity to handle voltages up to 1KV, and they are usually inexpensive. Multiplexers using mechanical switches are suited to low-speed applications as well as those having high resolution requirements. They interface well with the slower A/D converters, like the integrating dual-slope types. Mechanical switches have a finite life, however, usually expressed in number of operations. A reed relay might have a life of 10^9 operations, which would allow a 3-year life at 10 operations/second.

Solid-state switch devices are capable of operation at 30 ns, and they have a life which exceeds most equipment requirements. Field-effect transistors (FETs) are used in most multiplexers. They have superseded bipolar transistors which can introduce large voltage offsets when used as switches.

The circuit arrangment in a multiplexer usually ensures that the gate voltage of a conducting junction-FET tracks the drain-source voltage to maintain $V_{GS} = 0$. Thus, the on resistance of a switch is constant and is not a function of the signal level being multiplexed. This is not true of MOS-FET multiplexers, where the insulated gate is driven to a fixed potential in the on condition. V_{GS} and the on resistance may vary with the level of the applied signal. A typical p-channel device may have $R_{ON} = 200\Omega + 10$ V, and $R_{ON} = 1000\Omega$ at -10 V.

FET devices have a leakage from drain to source in the off state and a leakage from gate or substrate to drain and source in both the on and off states. Gate leakage in MOS devices is small compared to other sources of leakage. When the device has a Zener-diode-protected gate, an additional leakage path exists between the gate and source.

Enhancement-mode MOS-FETs have the advantage that the switch turns off when power is removed from the MUX. Junction-FET multiplexers always turn on with the power off.

A more recent development, the CMOS—complementary MOS—switch has the advantage of being able to multiplex voltages up to and including the supply voltages. A $\pm$ 10-V signal can be handled with a $\pm$ 10-V supply.

Trade-off Considerations for the Designer

Analog multiplexing has been the favored technique for achieving lowest system cost. The decreasing cost of A/D converters and the availability of low-cost, digital integrated circuits specifically designed for multiplexing provides an alternative with advantages for some applications. A decision on the technique to use for a given system will hinge on trade-offs between the following factors:

1. *Resolution*. The cost of A/D converters rises steeply as the resolution increases due to the cost of precision elements. At the 8-bit level, the per-channel cost of an analog multiplexer may be a considerable proportion of the cost of a converter. At resolutions above 12 bits, the reverse is true, and analog multiplexing tends to be more economical.[12]

2. *Number of channels*. This controls the size of the multiplexer required and the amount of wiring and interconnections. Digital multiplexing onto a common data bus reduces wiring to a minimum in many cases. Analog multiplexing is suited for 8 to 256 channels; beyond this number, the technique is unwieldy and analog errors become difficult to minimize. Analog and digital multiplexing are often combined in very large systems.

3. *Speed of measurement, or throughput*. High-speed A/D converters can add a considerable cost to the system. If analog multiplexing demands a high-speed converter to achieve the desired sample rate, a slower converter for each channel with digital multiplexing can be less costly.

4. *Signal level and conditioning*. Wide dynamic ranges between channels can be difficult with analog multiplexing. Signals less than 1V generally require differential low-level analog multiplexing which is expensive, with programmable-gain amplifiers after the MUX operation. The alternative of fixed-gain converters on each channel, with signal-conditioning designed for the channel requirement, with digital multiplexing may be more efficient.

5. *Physical location of measurement points*. Analog multiplexing is suited for making measurements at distances up to a few hundred feet from the converter, since analog lines may suffer from losses, transmission-line reflections, and interference. Lines may range from twisted wirepairs to multiconductor shielded cable, depending on signal levels, distance, and noise environments. Digital multiplexing is operable to thousands of miles, with the proper transmission equipment, for digital transmission systems can offer the powerful noise-rejection characteristics that are required for long-distance transmission.

Digital Multiplexing

For systems with small numbers of channels, medium-scale integrated digital multiplexers are available in TTL and MOS logic families. The 74151 is a typical example.[13] Eight of these integrated circuits can be used to multiplex eight A/D converters of 8-bit resolution onto a common data bus.

This digital multiplexing example offers little advantages in wiring economy, but it is lowest in cost, and the high switching speed allows operation at sampling rates much faster than analog multiplexers. The A/D converters are required only to keep up with the channel sample rate, and not with the commutating rate. When large numbers of A/D converters are multiplexed, the data-bus technique shown in Figure 5.15 reduces system interconnections. This alone may in many cases justify multiple A/D con-

Analog Inputs

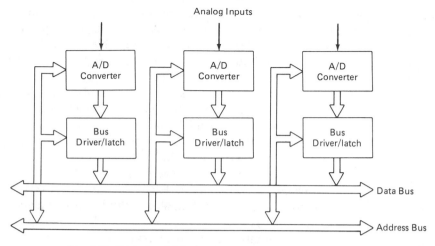

Fig. 5.15. Digital multiplexing into the microcomputer bus system.

verters. Data can be bussed onto the lines in bit-parallel or bit-serial format, as many converters have both serial and parallel outputs. A variety of devices can be used to drive the bus, from open collector and tristate TTL gates to line drivers and optoelectronic isolators. Channel-selection decoders can be built from 1-of-16 decoders to the required size. This technique also allows additional reliability in that a failure of one A/D does not affect the other channels. An important requirement is that the multiplexer operate without introducing unacceptable errors at the sample-rate speed. For a digital MUX system, one can determine the speed from propagation delays and the time required to charge the bus capacitance.

Analog multiplexers can be more difficult to characterize. Their speed is a function not only of internal parameters but also external parameters such as channel source impedance, stray capacitance and the number of channels, and the circuit layout. The user must be aware of the limiting parameters in the system to judge their effect on performance. These parameters are detailed in succeeding sections.

The nonideal transmission and open-circuit characteristics of analog multiplexers can introduce static and dynamic errors into the signal path. These errors include leakage through switches, coupling of control signals into the analog path, and interactions with sources and following amplifiers. Moreover, the circuit layout can compound these effects.

Since analog multiplexers may be connected directly to sources which may have little overload capacity or poor settling after overloads, the switches should have a break-before-make action to prevent the possibility of shorting channels together. It may be necessary to avoid shorted channels when power is removed and an a channels-off with power-down characteristic is desirable. In addition to the channel-addressing lines, which are normally binary-coded, it is useful to have inhibit or enable lines to turn all switches off regardless of the channel being addressed. This simplifies the external logic necessary to cascade multiplexers and can also be useful in certain modes of channel addressing. Another requirement for both analog and digital multiplexers is the tolerance of line transients and overload conditions, and the ability to absorb the transient energy and recover without damage.

High-Level Multiplexers

High-level multiplexers are designed to operate with input signals greater than 1V. The most common type uses a bank of switches connected to a common output bus (as shown in Figure 5.16). The bus output can be buffered by a noninverting amplifier, as shown. The configuration is simple, and with an output amplifier, it offers a high input impedance. Depending on the switching device, this multiplexer can operate over a wide variation of input voltage. With solid-state switches, the input-voltage excursion is limited to about ± 20V. Most multiplexers are designed for the standard analog range of ± 10V, but some that use high-threshold switches must be used for only a ± 5V range.[14]

For switching up to several hundred volts with solid-state speed, the inverting current-switch MUX can be used (see Figure 5.17). Since switching takes place at the summing junction, with the protective diodes to ground, the switches are not subjected to the high voltages. This MUX has a high immunity to transient voltages and has a constant but low input resistance while conducting. It assumes a safe state when power is removed. Each channel can be adjusted for gain. This multiplexer is rugged and suited to industrial system control. Interfacing with ± 100V analog computers has been popular with this type in the past.

Two modifications are possible. First, the diodes can be replaced by FETs driven in a complementary mode to the transmission switch. This will ensure

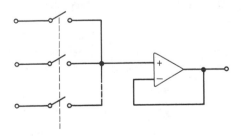

Fig. 5.16. High-level multiplexer.

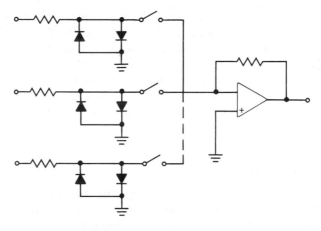

Fig. 5.17. Inverting current switch multiplexer.

that the input resistor is terminated in a real or virtual ground; thus, the input resistance is almost constant regardless of the channel selected (see Figure 5.18). This can avoid settling problems at the transducer during switching due to a change in loading. As a second modification, the input resistor can be removed to allow the multiplexing of current-output transducers (as shown in Figure 5.19). When current-output switching is used, the transfer accuracy is relatively unaffected by variations in line and connection resistance.

Lower-Level Multiplexers

The multiplexing of voltages in the millivolt range, up to 1V, requires more sophisticated multiplexers. Low-level interference and thermal effects can be great, so lines are run in pairs, and differential techniques are commonly used to remove interference which is present as a common-mode signal. When high common-mode voltages are present, guarding techniques are used along with three-wire multiplexing of shielded input pairs.

A two-wire differential MUX may be constructed with pairs of switches

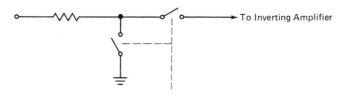

Fig. 5.18. Constant impedance multiplexer.

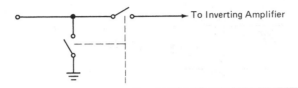

To Inverting Amplifier

Fig. 5.19. Current multiplexer.

(as shown in Figure 5.20). The output amplifier is usually an instrument amplifier with a high common-mode rejection. This rejection can only be achieved if the input lines are identical, so twisted pairs for cabling and matching the parameters of the channels and switches are required. Integrated circuits and dual-FET switches can allow the matching required. Switch leakages and thermal EMFs may introduce errors in the low-level inputs, and drift is a greater problem.

In order to reduce the effects of unbalance in the input cables, shielded pairs can be used with the shield driven by the common-mode voltage, either by the source or a mid-position tap in the data amplifier or between the input terminals. This shielding, or guarding, is common in high-resolution data-acquisition systems.

Another low-level multiplexer that is useful against common-mode interference is the flying-capacitor multiplexer. This is a two-wire sample-hold type (as shown in Figure 5.21). Switches X and X' are turned on with Y and Y' off to acquire the input signal. When the capacitor is fully charged, all switches are momentarily turned off; then Y and Y' are turned on to transfer the signal to the output amplifier. No common-mode voltage is transferred across the switches, and the output amplifier may be single-ended and noninverting. This is effective in eliminating common-mode voltages, but if normal-mode interference is present as well, better rejection of both normal-

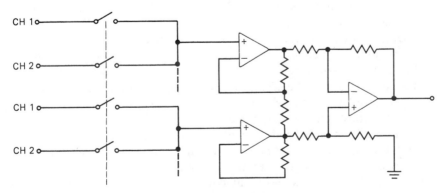

CH 1

CH 2

CH 1

CH 2

Fig. 5.20. Differential multiplexer.

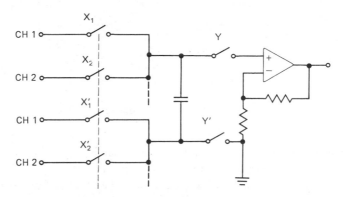

Fig. 5.21. Flying-capacitor multiplexer.

mode and common-mode can be obtained with a straight multiplexer and a floating-input integrating converter. An integrating converter used with the flying-capacitor multiplexer will integrate a sample of the input rather than the complete input, and the sample will include variations from normal-mode interference.

Error Reduction

Multiplexing will introduce both static (dc) and dynamic errors into the system. When these errors are large in relation to the resolution of the measurement, they produce undesirable variations in performance. Static voltage errors are due to switch leakage and offsets in output buffer amplifiers. Gain errors are due to switch-on resistance, source resistance, amplifier input resistance, and amplifier-gain nonlinearity. Dynamic errors come from charge injection of the switch control voltages, settling times of the bus and input sources, circuit time constants, crosstalk between channels, and output-amplifier settling. Dynamic errors are also affected by the multiplexer system layout.

Other errors can be due to the characteristics of the multiplexer components; for example, reed relays may generate thermal EMFs of up to $40\mu V/°C$.[15] The errors found in high-level multiplexers can also occur in low-level multiplexers, but the effects are more serious because of the smaller signal amplitudes. Low-level multiplexers are always differential or two-wire, so the converter sees only the difference in the errors of two identical channels. Leakage, gain, and crosstalk effects can be greatly reduced, provided that matching is maintained. The magnitudes of most settling errors are decreased, although their duration remains the same.

When multiplexers must be operated in conditions causing high common-mode interference, two-wire differential and guarded or flying-capacitor multiplexers are used. If considerable normal-mode interference also exists, further steps are required. The common techniques include filtering, digital averaging, and the use of integrating converters. These are briefly considered below.

The use of lowpass filters in the channel inputs of the multiplexer is one method of reducing normal-mode interference. Filter characteristics can be tailored for the particular channel. Filters can increase the settling time, but this effect is usually small. It is possible to place the filter after the multiplexer, but then each channel will have to charge the filter, greatly increasing the settling time. In differential systems, the filters should have balanced impedance in both inputs or be connected differentially so as to reduce the common-mode effects.

When passive filtering of each channel is not practical, an integrating A/D converter can provide high normal-mode rejection.[16] This rejection is obtained with a conversion time that is usually shorter than the settling time of a filter that would be required to provide the same rejection. Rejections of normal-mode interference to 70dB can be obtained with an integrating converter, many of which are designed for floating guarded-inputs.[17]

In computer systems where processing time and memory are available, software can be used to reduce the effects of interference, if the converter can track the variations in input signal produced by interference. Multiple samples may be taken for each channel and the results summed and averaged. The signal-to-noise ratio will improve as the square-root of the number of samples, provided that the sampling and interference frequencies are not correlated.

SAMPLE-HOLD DEVICES

The sample-hold is a device with a signal input, an output, and a control input. It has two operating modes: sample or track. In the track mode, it acquires the input signal and tracks it until commanded to hold, at which time it retains the value of the input signal at the time the control mode changed. Sample-holds are also known as "track-holds" if they spend a large portion of time in the sample mode, tracking the input.[18] Sample-holds normally have unity gain and are noninverting. The control inputs are usually TTL-compatible. Logic 1 is usually the "sample" command and logic 0 the "hold" command.

A sample-hold in its basic form consists of a switch and a capacitor. When the switch is closed, the unit is in the sampling or tracking mode and will follow the changing input signal. When the switch is opened, the unit is in the hold mode and retains a voltage on the capacitor for a period of time, depending on capacitor size and leakage resistance. Practical sample-hold circuits may also use input and output buffer amplifiers along with sophisticated switching techniques. The output buffer amplifier should be a low input current FET amplifier in order to have a small effect on leakage of the capacitor. The electronic switch used should also have a low leakage.

Sample-hold devices are widely used in data-acquisition systems, like the one shown in Figure 5.1. The sample-hold maintains the input to the A/D converter constant during the conversion interval, while the multiplexer is seeking the next channel. As the conversion is completed, the sample-hold samples the new input, and the cycle is repeated. This is called synchronous sampling because the sample-hold operates in a synchronous mode with the other system elements. If the input signals vary at different rates, a programmed access scheme is necessary, so the signals with the most information are sampled more often. In the asynchronous mode, a number of sample-holds are used to acquire and store the data at rates suited to each individual channel. They are then either sampled by analog multiplexers, or the signals can be converted asynchronously and then multiplexed digitally after digital signal processing.

Sample-hold circuits are used with both A/D converters and D/A converters. With A/D converters, they shorten the aperture time for the converter by sampling the input signal and then holding this value until the conversion is completed. With D/A converters, they are used to remove transients which appear at the outputs as the converters change from one analog level to another.

Sample-Hold Characteristics

The Sample-hold device has some characteristics which need to be understood. An ideal sample and hold, or "zero-order hold" as it is also called, takes a sample in zero time and then holds the value of the sample indefinitely with perfect accuracy. In practical devices, a sample is taken in a time period which is short compared to the holding time. During the holding time, there is some change in the output which may affect the system accuracy. The effect on a continuous analog input signal can be determined by finding the transfer function of the sample-hold. By use of the impulse response of the device and the Laplace transform method, the transfer function is found for the ideal sample-hold:[19]

$$G(j\omega) = \frac{1 - e^{-j\omega T}}{j\omega} = \frac{2\pi}{\omega_s} \frac{\sin \pi \, \omega/\omega_s}{\pi \, \omega/\omega_s} \, e^{-j\pi(\omega/\omega_s)}$$

where T is the sampling period and ω_s is the sampling frequency. The magnitude and phase of this function are plotted in Figure 5.22, which shows that the sample-hold acts like a lowpass filter with a cutoff frequency of approximately $f_s/2$ and a phase delay of $T/2$, or on during half of the sampling period.

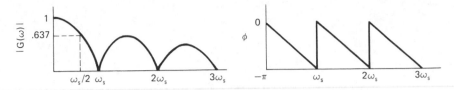

Fig. 5.22. Sample-hold transfer function.

Sample-Hold Circuits

The type of storage element used for sample-holds divides them into two classes. The conventional type employs a capacitor for storage, and several variations of this design will be discussed shortly. The other type uses an A/D converter and a register for storage, and outputs via a D/A converter. It is more complex and costly, but it has the advantage of an arbitrary hold time. Some techniques of achieving this approach will be discussed later.

An open-loop follower circuit is shown in Figure 5.23. As the switch is closed, the capacitor charges exponentially to the input voltage, and the amplifier's output follows the capacitor voltage. As the switch is opened, the charge and voltage level remain on the capacitor. The capacitor's acquisition time depends on the series resistance and the current available. Once the charge is complete to the desired accuracy, the switch can be opened, even though the amplifier may not have settled. This will not affect the final output value or the settling time greatly, since the amplifier's input stage should not draw any appreciable current (the switch is typically a FET and the amplifier has a FET-input). This circuit has a disadvantage, though, in that the capacitor loads the input source which may either oscillate or lack the current to charge the capacitor fast enough. The circuit shown in Figure 5.24 can be modified to include a follower to isolate the source. Many commercial devices use this scheme.[20] For faster charging at close to a linear slew rate, a diode bridge may be used (as shown in Figure 5.24). The current sources are then switched on in order to charge the capacitor. If the bridge and current sources are balanced, current flow into the capacitor stops when the capacitor voltage is equal to the input voltage.

The circuits discussed thus far have the advantage of fast acquisition and

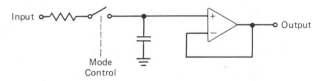

Fig. 5.23. Basic open-loop follower sample-hold.

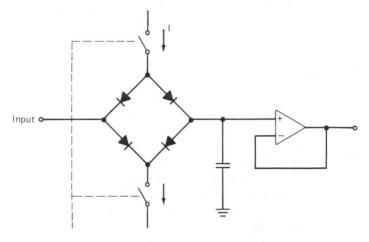

Fig. 5.24. Current source sample-hold.

settling time, but they are open-loop devices. If low-frequency tracking accuracy is more critical than speed, the cascaded amplifier configuration will be less satisfactory than a single amplifier configuration that provides isolation. This is accomplished by closing the loop around the capacitor, and using a high loop gain for tracking accuracy. Figure 5.25 shows a circuit where the input follower amplifier is replaced by a high-gain difference amplifier. As the switch is closed, the output represented by the charge on the capacitor is forced to track the input as a function of the gain and the current-driving capability of the input amplifier. The common-mode and offset errors in the output follower are compensated by the charge on the capacitor.

In Figure 5.26, a current amplifier is used with an integrator, thereby permitting the switch to operate at ground potential and easing the leakage problem.

In both circuits, the acquisition time and settling time are the same, since the charge is controlled by the output, as well as the input. If the basic feedback circuit of Figure 5.25 is switched into hold before the output has settled

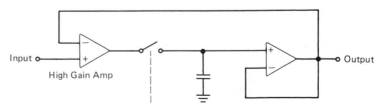

Fig. 5.25. Low-frequency sample-hold with feedback.

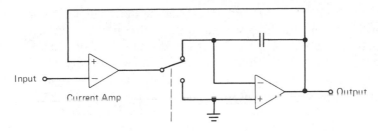

Fig. 5.26. Low-frequency sample-hold with integrator feedback.

at the input value, the sample can be in error. Since the loop is open during the hold, it must reestablish the input when returned to the sample mode even if the input has not changed. This can result in a step or spike when the input amplifier has a high voltage gain.

Sample-Hold Specifications

In the ideal sample-hold, tracking is error-free, acquisition occurs instantaneously with zero settling times, and hold time is infinite with zero leakage. Commercial units are usually specified in the ways in which they depart from the ideal.[21] Here are some of the common parameters:

1. *Acquisition Time.* This is the time from when the sample command is given to the point when the output enters and remains within a specified band around the input value. At the end of the acquisition time, the output is tracking the input.

2. *Aperture Time.* This is the time between the hold command and the point at which the sampling switch is completely open. It is also called "turn-off time."

3. *Aperture Uncertainty Time.* This is the variation in the aperture time, that is, the difference between the maximum and minimum aperture times.

4. *Decay Rate.* This is the change in output voltage with time in the hold mode.

5. *Feedthrough.* This is the amount of input signal appearing at the output when the unit is in the hold mode. Feedthrough varies with signal frequency and is sometimes expressed as an attenuation in dBs.

6. *Settling Time.* This is the time from the command transition until the output has settled within a specified error-band around the final value.

Applications

In data-acquisition systems, sample-holds are used either to hold fast signals during conversion or to store multiplexer outputs while the signal is being converted and the multiplexer is seeking the next channel. In analog data-reduction, sample-holds are used to determine peaks or valleys, establish amplitudes, and allow computations involving signals obtained at different times. In some data-distribution systems, sample-holds are used for holding the converted data between updates. Fast sample-holds can also be used to acquire and measure short pulses of arbitrary occurance and width. For data distribution, 0.01% sample-holds may cost less than large numbers of D/A converters having comparable accuracy.[22] In a typical system, a fast D/A converter can update a number of sample-holds at the required speeds and accuracy levels for the individual channels. Sample-holds may be used to smooth D/A outputs in systems that may be sensitive to spikes by sampling the outputs after the settling time is over.

There are also sample-hold applications in hybrid computing and data-reduction systems. For example, a peak-follower is composed of a sample-hold and a comparator circuit. (An example is shown in Figure 5.27.) Balancing the unknown input voltage against some form of internally-produced reference, the comparator circuit responds to the polarity of the inequality between input and reference. The sample-hold output is biased by a few millivolts of hysteresis signal to avoid ambiguity problems during step inputs, and reduce false triggering from noise. When the input is greater than the S/H output, the comparator's positive output forces the S/H to a track mode. When the input becomes less than the S/H output, the comparator moves the S/H to the hold state until the input once again becomes greater than the output. To reset the circuit, the control input is switched into *sample,* and a low level is applied at the input.

Digital storage can provide a long hold duration with no droop. Other benefits are no sample-hold offset, no feedthrough, and no dielectric leakage effects. Disadvantages are increased cost and complexity, longer acquisition times, and the possible need for presampling (as shown in the counting sample-hold in Figure 5.28). This sample-hold uses a D/A converter, an up-down counter, a comparator clock, and logic gates. The initial acquisition

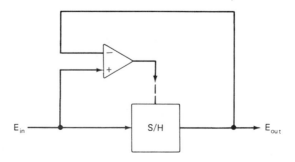

Fig. 5.27. Peak-follower with sample-hold.

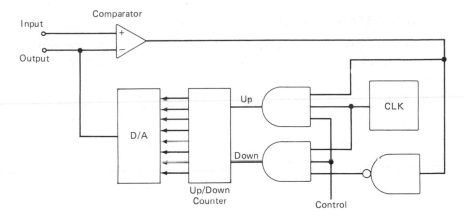

Fig. 5.28. Counting sample-hold.

time can be very long, since the clock period (t_s) depends on the LSB settling time of the D/A converter, while the number of counts depends on the resolution. For a full-scale step, the acquisition time is approximately $(2^n - 1) \, t_s$.[23] Smaller, slower changes are followed rapidly. The system can also be converted into a peak-follower by disabling the up-count function. The range of input signal levels and polarity will determine the choice of D/A converter. A BCD counter and BCD DAC can be used with a display for a maximum peak DVM.

Figure 5.29 shows another approach, using an A/D converter and a D/A converter. When averaging is desired, an integrating type A/D converter is used. The acquisition time is approximately equal to the sum of the A/D converter's conversion time and the D/A settling time. If the D/A output of a successive-approximations A/D is used, a separate D/A converter is not required and the acquisition time is equal to the conversion rate.

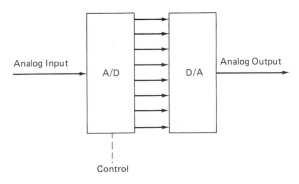

Fig. 5.29. Digital sample-hold.

SINGLE-CHANNEL SYSTEMS

The simplest data-acquisition system is a single A/D converter, performing repetitive conversions at a free-running rate. It has an analog signal input and its outputs are a digital coded word with an overrange indication, polarity information if necessary, and a status output to indicate when the output is valid. A well-known example of this system is a digital panel meter, which consists of an A/D converter and a numeric display. In many applications, the purpose of digitizing is to obtain the numerical display and to use the DPM as a meter rather than as a system component. Some DPMs allow connection to the A/D output for transmission or digital processing.

Direct conversion is useful if the data must be transmitted through noisy environments. This can be illustrated for the case of an 8-bit converter with 1/256 resolution and a 10V signal. Consider the bits that may be lost if the peak-to-peak noise level induced in the analog signal is greater than 40mV or 10V/256. Standard TTL noise immunity is 1.2V or 2.0–0.8V compared to the 40mV analog noise immunity.

Since most converters designed for system applications are in most cases single-ended in reference to signal ground and have normalized analog input ranges of the order of 5 or 10 V (single-ended or bipolar), one should scale signal inputs up or down to the converter input level in order to allow the fullest-possible use of the converter's resolution. This is shown in the circuit of Figure 5.30. When the signals are of a reasonable magnitude (perhaps already preamplified) or when they are the outputs of an analog power device, the scaling might be accomplished with operational amplifiers in a single-ended or differential configuration. If the signals are small, or have a large common-mode component, a differential instrumentation amplifier might be used. The amplifier characteristics will depend on the gain required, signal levels, and possible cost trade-offs. If the input signals must be

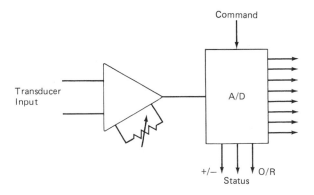

Fig. 5.30. Single-channel system with scaling.

galvanically isolated from the system, a optical- or transformer-coupled isolation amplifier can be used to break the conductive signal paths. This isolation is essential in many medical-instrument applications.[24] It is also used when large common-mode spikes are possible for applications requiring intrinsic safety, and for applications in which the source is at a high potential.

Successive-Approximations Systems

A successive-approximations type of converter can operate at greater accuracies and higher speeds, overcoming the problems mentioned above, by using a sample-hold device at its input. (See Figure 5.31) Between conversions, the sample-hold acquires the input signal. Just before conversion takes place, it is in hold, where it remains throughout the conversion. If the S/H responds quickly and accurately enough, the converter will convert the changes from the preceding sample accurately, at a speed up to the conversion rate. In practical sample-holds, however, there is acquisition time, tracking delay, and aperture time. If the aperture time and tracking delay compensate one another, or are unimportant if they are consistent, the principal source of error will be the aperture uncertainty. The relation between the aperture uncertainty and maximum rate of voltage change for maintaining the resolution in an n-bit system is given by[25]

$$dV/dt \bigg|_{max} = 2^{-n} V_{F.S.}/t_{A.U.}$$

thus for an 8-bit system with

$$f_{sample} = 100KHz, V_{F.S.} = 10V, t_{A.U.} = 5ns$$

$$dV/dt \bigg|_{max} = 5mV/5ns = 1.0 V/\mu s$$

This number is also limited by the slew rate of the sample-hold.

The successive-approximations converter, with a constant input applied by the S/H, will deliver an accurate representation of the beginning input at the end of each conversion period. Errors that are functions of time will be due to the sample-hold, including the acquistion errors discussed above, plus any droop during the conversion interval, linearity, offsets, and transient errors. Since sample-holds usually operate at unity gain, (the errors are referred to full-scale which should be the same as the converter's full scale range) any scaling or preamplification should occur before the sample-hold.[26]

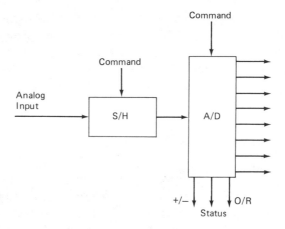

Fig. 5.31. Single-channel system with sample-hold.

Sample-hold devices can be used with other types of converters. They are sometimes used to establish the timing of the signals being sampled, independently of the time required by a device to complete a conversion. Their utility is most evident when the conversion time is variable, as in the counter types of converters.

Signal Conditioning

Signal conditioning may include a variety of possibilities. The scaling of input gains to match the input signal to the converter's full-scale range is the most common example. One can also include a dc offset to bias odd ranges, such as 2.5 to 7 V, to levels more compatible with standard converters (as shown in Figure 5.32). Linearizing of data from thermocouples and bridges can be performed by analog techniques, using piece-wise-linear approximations with diodes or smooth series-approximations using IC multipliers. It can also be done digitally after conversion, using a ROM to store the func-

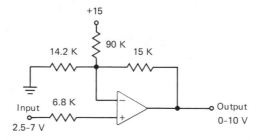

Fig. 5.32. Range conversion.

tion.[27] Analog differentiation might be used to measure the rate at which an input varies. Integration could be used to obtain the total flow from a rate of flow. Sums and differences might be used to reduce the number of data inputs for data-reduction purposes. Analog multipliers can be used to compute power by squaring the voltage or current signals, or multiplying them together as shown in Figure 5.33. Analog dividers could be used to compute the ratios, or the logarithms of ratios, or square roots. These devices can compute ratios over wide dynamic ranges as found in gas flow computations. Comparators may be used to make decisions based on signal levels when an input exceeds a threshold or is within a window. Logarithmic modules can be used for range compression to permit the conversion of signals having greater resolutions than the converter resolution.[28] Active filters are useful in order to minimize the effects of noise and unwanted high-frequency components of the input signal. In many system designs, all data-processing may not need to be digital. Analog circuits may perform processing or data-reduction effectively and economically. They should be considered as an alternative way of reducing the number of transmission channels, the software complexity, and noise.

MULTIPLE-CHANNEL SYSTEMS

In multichannel conversion systems, parts of the acquisition chain, are usually shared by two or more input sources. The sharing may occur in a number of ways, depending on the desired specifications of the system. Large systems might combine several different types of multiplexing and perhaps even cascaded tiers of the same type.

The most conventional way to digitize data from many analog channels is to use a time-sharing process, where the input of a single A/D converter is multiplexed in sequence among the various analog sources. Data-acquisition systems of this type are available in boards, modules, integrated circuits, and systems.

System Packages

A typical data-acquisition system board might be capable of a 110 KHz throughput rate with 12-bit resolution. In this system, a sample-hold is used

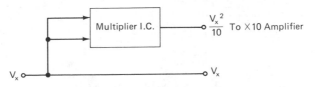

Fig. 5.33. Analog multiplication.

with a high-speed, hybrid 12-bit A/D converter, and a monolithic analog multiplexer. (The basic configuration is shown in Figure 5.34.) The sample-hold might have a 1 μs acquisition time while the A/D converter does a conversion every 8 μs.

Most of the module types utilize hybrid technology. A typical module data-acquisition system may have eight differential input channels and 16 single-ended input channels for 12-bit data-acquisition in a 72-pin package.[29] Acquisition and conversion time combined are 20 μs giving a throughput rate of 50 KHz. The 12-bit binary data can be transferred out in three 4-bit bytes, by the three-state data bus drivers. Output coding is straight binary in unipolar operation and offset binary in bipolar operation.

The circuit shown in Figure 5.35 includes a multiplexer, programmable-gain instrumentation amplifier, sample-hold circuit complete with hold capacitor, 10-V buffered reference, and a 12-bit A/D converter with three-state outputs along with digital logic.

The instrumentation amplifier is programmed with a resister for gains of 1 to 1000. This feature is useful in low-level applications involving transducers, strain-gauges, and thermocouples. The module uses a small hermetic package. Models may be available in three temperature ranges: 0 to +70, −25 to +85, and −55 to +125 degrees Celsius. High reliability versions of each model may also be available. Power requirements are ±15V dc and +5V dc.

We now consider a single-chip, 16-channel, 8-bit data-acquisition system. Monolithic CMOS technology allows a 16-channel multiplexer, 8-bit successive approximation A/D converter, and microprocessor-compatible con-

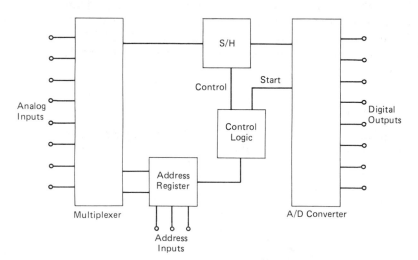

Fig. 5.34. Data acquisition system board.

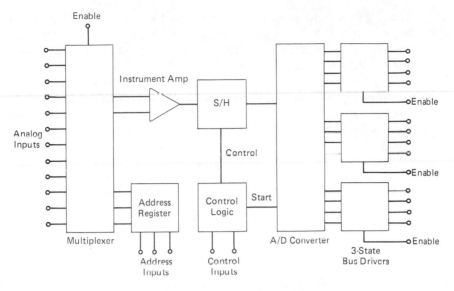

Fig. 5.35. Data-acquisition module.

trol logic to be fabricated on a single chip and contained in a dual-in-line package.

This system has low power consumption and a minimum of adjustments with no full-scale or zero adjustments required. Latched and decoded address inputs and latched TTL three-state outputs allow simple interfacing to microprocessors.

The input multiplexer allows random access to any one of 16 single-ended analog input channels and provides the necessary logic for additional channel expansion. Connection of the multiplexer output to the converter input is by external connections, thus permitting signal conditioning such as linearization and the use of a sample-hold.

The 8-bit A/D converter uses a 256R ladder network, a successive approximation register, and a chopper-stabilizer comparator for the successive approximation conversion. Use of the 256R ladder network allows monotonicity while the chopper-stabilizer comparator makes the converter resistant to thermal effects and long-term drift. In the ratiometric conversion, the converter expresses the analog value being measured as a percentage of the reference input. Speed, flexibility, and performance over a temperature range of -25 to $+85°C$, along with low cost, make chips like this a practical answer to many data-acquisition needs.

For the most efficient use of time, the multiplexer seeks the next channel to be converted, while the sample-hold, in the hold mode, has its output converted. When the conversion is complete, the status line from the converter forces the sample-hold to return to sample and acquire the next channel. When the acquisition time is complete, immediately, or on command, the sample-hold is switched to hold, conversion begins, and the multiplexer switches to the next channel.

This system is slower than other configurations. In systems where the channels may be diverse rather than identical, the multiplexer could be switching sequentially or in a random selection mode. In some cases, manual operation, for checkout purposes may be desired. With the random-access mode, it is desirable that those channels with more intelligence be accessed more frequently. In addition to sharing the converter and the sample-hold, expensive instrumentation-amplifiers can be conserved. But with the decreasing cost of instrumentation amplifiers along with the disadvantages of low speeds and the effort involved in the successful transmission and multiplexing of low-level data, there is likely to be a decreasing use of this approach.

Low-level multiplexing often uses programmable-gain amplifiers, or automatic range-switching preamps, which allow the use of converters having medium resolutions with range-switching to obtain additional significant bits. For example, a 12-bit converter, and 32 steps of adjustable gain, could provide 17-bit resolution, if the resolution is actually present in the signal and if the system can operate on it without degradation.[30]

More than one tier of multiplexers may be required if there are about 64 or more channels to be multiplexed. But then the problems of stray capacitance and capacitive unbalances are increased by the capacitance of the off channels on the conducting channel. When there are n channels, the capacitance is $(n - 1)C$ plus the stray capacitance. It is possible to reduce this capacitance by using two tiers of multiplexers. For a 64-channel system with 8 channels per switch, the capacitance is reduced to 14C from 63C.[31]

Parallel Conversion Systems

Parallel conversion is becoming practicable. The cost of A-D converters has dropped radically during the past decade, and it is possible to assemble a multichannel conversion system with one converter for every analog source almost as economically as the conventional analog multiplexed system. (Figure 5.36 shows the basic configuration.)

There are several advantages to this conversion approach, which is used for resolver/synchro conversions beyond the 10-bit level.[32] First, slower converters can be used to obtain a given throughput rate; or the converters may run at top speed, providing a greater flow of data into the interface. For a constant data rate, the reduced conversion speed and the fact that each converter is looking at continuous data rather than changing from one level to another, may allow the sample-holds to be eliminated. Second, the parallel-

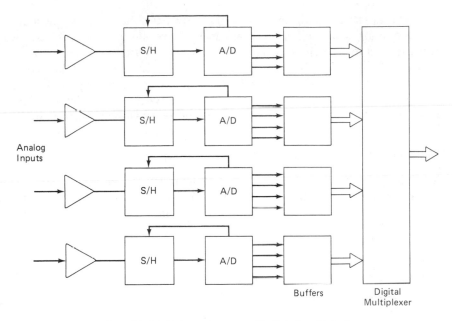

Fig. 5.36. Multichannel system with digital multiplexing.

conversion approach may provide a further advantage when applied to industrial data-acquisition systems, where many strain-gauges, thermo-couples, thermistors, or other sensors are strung over a large area. By digitizing the analog signals at the source and transmitting serial digital data back to the data center, a considerable immunity to line-frequency pickup and ground-loop interference can be achieved. The digital signals may be transformer- or optically-coupled for complete electrical isolation. Also, the use of low-impedance digital driver and receiving circuits can drastically reduce vulnerability to noise. Moreover, by digitizing sensor signals at their source, logical operations can be performed on the digitized data before it is fed into the microcomputer. Processing is then streamlined, and test problems are minimized. Preprocessing circuits or microprocessors can access data from slow thermocouple sensors less frequently, while reading data from faster more critical sources at greater speeds. The digital subsystem may make its own decision as to when particular data should be fed into the main microcomputer. When certain signal sources remain constant or are within a narrow range for long periods and then later change rapidly during the physical process, it may be useful to ignore the data until those changes occur.

A great deal of flexibility and versatility may be gained by transferring the interface process from analog multiplexing to digital multiplexing. Decision circuits may exercise judgement on when and what data to feed to the main microcomputer, and this in general can improve the overall interface. In some applications, such as when data is being transmitted from a space vehicle to earth, the transmission channel is crowded, and the sort of data compression described is essential to make certain that the items of data that get through are those having the highest priorities, by virtue of their intelligence, rather than the data which contain only additional redundant information.

Multiple Sample-Holds

Moving back from the interface towards the more conventional system in which the number of shared elements is maximized, we consider the case of a shared A-D converter, with a multiplexer at its input, switching among the outputs of a number of sample-holds (as shown in Figure 5.37). This configuration is used where the sample-holds must be updated rapidly, or even simultaneously, and then read out in some sequence. It is usually a high-speed system in which items of data indicating the state of the system must do so at the same approximate time. Multiplexing may be sequential, or by some random addressing method. The sample-holds must be relatively free from droop in order to avoid accumulating excessive errors while waiting for readout, which may be longer than in the case of a converter-per-channel cir-

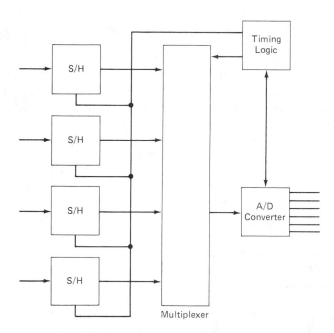

Fig. 5.37. Simultaneous multichannel system.

cuit. Increased throughput can be obtained by using additional converters if desired. Typical applications that use this approach include wind-tunnel measurements, seismographic experiments, or the testing of radar or fire-control systems. Usually, the event is a one-time phenomenon, where the information is required at a critical time during the event, for example, when a ground shock or air blast hits the test specimen.

PLANTWIDE TECHNIQUES

Computer control equipment has evolved to the configuration shown in Figure 5.38. A single computer performs supervisory control and process monitoring. The computer monitors the process by reading analog and digital data from the field via the input/output equipment. It may change an analog controller set-point in order to perform supervisory control by sending either incremental or analog signals to the controller. Analog signals, such as flows or levels, are used by both the computer and the analog panel instrumentation. The control console consists of CRT displays, input keyboards, and typewriters. Most peripheral equipment used with such a minicomputer is connected to the I/O channel by interface circuitry. This hardware performs functions related to the operation of both the channel and the peripheral device, such as address detection, decoding, timing, and error detection/correction.

This single computer configuration is used in many installations today, and it has had a large influence on the technical and human aspects of computer control. Considerable effort has been put into the development of process control software for a single computer configuration and the development and marketing of analog control instrumentation.[33] Also, plant

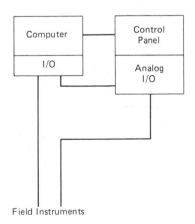

Fig. 5.38. Plantwide data-acquisition configuration.

personnel have been conditioned to think that a single large control panel is required for the computer system.

The installed cost including materials and labor of wiring and cabling has been increasing, while the installed cost of digital systems has been decreasing. As a result, remote multiplexing has evolved because it can reduce a large amount of the wiring necessary in a process plant.

Remote Multiplexing Systems

Remote multiplexing takes on a configuration like that shown in Figure 5.39. The remote multiplexers are located throughout the plant. Analog and digital signals are sent to the nearest remote multiplexer.

A-D converter circuits in the remote multiplexer convert the signal to a digital word, usually 16 bits long. The control unit signals the remote multiplexer when it needs to request the unit to send a particular block of words or a group of blocks. The remote multiplexer then responds by sending the data requested to the control unit. The control unit scans the data to ensure that the transmission is complete. As the data are received, they are sent to the central computer. Data may also be displayed on the operator console, depending on the request of the control room operator. If either operator or the computer requests an item or word of data, the control unit interrupts the sequential scan and retrieves the required data from the remote multiplexer.

Remote multiplexing is also employed in plants where there is no control

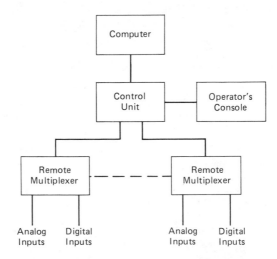

Fig. 5.39. Remote multiplexing configuration.

computer, but the reduction of field wiring is still achieved. In some plants, only analog signals are remote multiplexed. Then, a less sophisticated multiplexer that sends analog signals is used.

Remote multiplexing is mainly used for process monitoring but not for process control. The reliability of remote multiplexing is high enough so that it can be employed for control signals as well. This can be accomplished with an expanded loop configuration (similar to Figure 5.39) which is sometimes called total multiplexing.

This system allows both analog and digital signals to flow either to or from the control room and the remote multiplexer. In a flow-control loop, a flow transmitter could provide analog signals to the remove multiplexer. The remote multiplexer converts the analog signals (usually 4-20 milliamps) to digital words with an analog-to-digital converter and transmits them to the control unit. The control unit may convert the digital data back to a 4-20 mA analog signal for an analog instrument, such as a flow controller. In this example, the flow controller may be a standard analog controller. The flow transmitter sends a 4-20 mA signal and the controller receives a 4-20 mA signal.

The remote multiplexing equipment available today transmits data at a rate which updates each analog value once a second. In most petrochemical applications, values which are updated every second are, for most purposes, the same as continuous signals.

Even though the use of electronic instrumentation technology is increasing rapidly, many plants still employ pneumatic instrumentation, which are thought to be safer in hazardous locations.[34]

Pneumatic Interfacing

Many of these pneumatic systems use computers. There are two basic methods of interfacing the pneumatic instruments to the computer.

One system is to use P/I (pneumatic-to-current) and I/P (current-to-pneumatic) converters. In this system, the output of the converters is continuous.

The other system replaces the P/I converters with a pneumatic multiplexer/converter. This can be accomplished with either a host or remote multiplexing configuration. A typical pneumatic multiplexer will handle six pressure inputs per second. Each pneumatic input of 3 to 15 psi, is converted into an analog dc voltage. The computer controls the pneumatic multiplexer as it switches from one input to the next. Still another approach uses a separate control device that accepts the analog signal from the pneumatic multiplexer and controls the stepping. This reduces the software in the computer. The cost of one pneumatic multiplexer is much less than the cost of individual P/I converters.[35]

Digital-Data Communications

Digital-data communications is growing and has a major influence on modern plant control. This section considers the fundamentals of digital-data communications, with emphasis on the areas applicable to remote multiplexing and computer communications networks.

A facility which allows signals to be sent from one place to another is considered to be a communications channel. Telephone lines, coaxial cables, and microwave links are all examples of communications channels. Voice channels use a bandwidth of 1000 to 3000 Hz, depending on fidelity. Commercial television requires band-widths of 6 MHz. The bandwidth required for digital transmission is a function of the data rate.

Digital data can be transmitted as modulated signals. At the receiver, the signals are demodulated into digital format. The transformation of digital to modulated signals and the transformation from modulated to digital signals is performed by a modulator-demodulator, usually referred to as a modem.

Computers, teletypes, and CRT terminals are devices that can use digital communications. Communications over distances of several feet do not require modems; digital logic signals can be sent directly over short distances.

Modem channels can be divided into three types: (1) simplex, (2) half-duplex, and (3) full-duplex. Data is only sent in one direction on a simplex channel. This type of channel can be used by a receive-only (RO) teletype. A half-duplex channel allows data to travel in both directions, but in only one direction at any instant. Data can travel in both directions at the same time with a full-duplex channel.

A modem may use a particular type of modulation as well as a particular communications protocol. The protocol sets the sequence in which the data is to be transmitted, the structure of the message, the method of synchronization for the transmitter and receiver, and the error-checking procedure. Examples of protocols are IBM's Binary Synchronous Communications (BISYNC), DEC's Digital Communications Message Protocol (DDCMP), and IMB's Synchronous Data Line Control (SDLC). The use of communications protocols has simplified many of the problems of data transfer between digital devices.

Data communications can be either asynchronous or synchronous. Asynchronous data usually occurs in short bursts while synchronous data transfers are suited for long streams. Asynchronous messages are preceded by a start signal, which synchronizes the transmitting and receiving circuitry. Synchronous data usually contain a special bit pattern for synchronization. The pattern is defined by the protocol.

Error-Checking

Communications channels may be sensitive to intermittent noise and signal failures; thus one would like to determine if the transmitted message is received without errors. This may be important in process control where undetected bits could cause erroneous control. One technique requires the receiving station to retransmit the received message back to the transmitting device. The message must, then, be transmitted twice, with transmission rates up to 1 million bits per second. This can be done for most applications.[36]

There are other methods of error-checking that allow the receiving unit to determine if the message was received correctly. The simplest method involves adding an extra bit, called a parity bit, to each block of data in the message. This bit may be set so that the total number of ones in the block is always odd. This is called odd parity. One may also use even parity where the number of ones in the block is always even. However, parity checks do not provide sufficient security for control, and for that reason other methods are normally used.

Three other methods of error-checking are (1) vertical redundancy checking (VRC), (2) longitudinal redundancy checking (LRC), and (3) cyclic redundancy checking (CRC).[37] A combination of these checks may be used, depending on the protocol. A message may contain several blocks of data. VRC adds a parity bit to each block of data. LRC adds an additional block to the message. Each bit in this check block is obtained by performing an EXCLUSIVE OR on corresponding bits in the other blocks in the message. The receiving device calculates the contents of the check block from the data received. If the check block received is the same as the one calculated, then the message has been received correctly. An example of VRC and LRC is shown below:[38]

	Bit 0	Bit 1	Bit 2	Bit 3	VRC Bit
Block 0	0	0	1	0	1
Block 1	0	1	0	0	1
Block 2	0	1	1	0	0
Block 3	1	0	1	1	1
Block 4	1	1	0	0	0
LRC Check Block	0	1	1	1	1

In CRC, a polynomial is calculated from the data stream. This polynomial is divided by a constant polynomial and the remainder is used as the check block.

Distributed Processing

The first processing control computers were used for process monitoring only.[39] Closed-loop control then became popular, and plant optimization uses followed. The computer became larger and larger as the number of functions increased. This paralleled the growth of large mainframes in the data processing industry. Recently, there has been a trend away from the use of large, single, central processing units towards the use of several smaller processors. The processors may be located in close proximity to one another and connected together in a network. This approach is known as distributed processing. The processors are not usually dedicated to any single function, but are assigned tasks to perform by one processor which operates the network.

One advantage of distributed processing is the division of labor, as the remote units off-load the processor for enhanced performance of the total system. Time response may be increased by less overhead in the system and by the execution of functions, such as scanning in remote units without waiting for the availability of the central computer.

Distributed processing systems have a modularity which is difficult to achieve in a centralized system. As sections of a plant are automated, remote units can be added. Thus, there is no need to initially install a system large enough for all anticipated expansions. (There is still, however, the need to design the system so that any planned expansion can be accomplished.) Distributed processing can also improve system reliability. The remote units may allow operation independent of the central computer for a limited time; thus, a short outage in the central computer or communications may be tolerated. Also, it may be possible for the central computer to maintain control for a limited loss of remote units.

Multiprocessing

With multiprocessing, two or more processors are interconnected to form a multiprocessor, which operates on the computing requirements of the application. Multiprocessors have been used in industrial applications primarily to improve system reliability, although there are other advantages as well. A shared file may provide the means of communication between several processors. Requests from one processor to the others are posted in the shared file. A scheduling program periodically checks to determine if a request is waiting; if one is, the request is scheduled according to the operating system.

One serial device which both processors cannot use at the same time is a disk file. This contention problem is solved by circuits or another microprocessor which might be part of the file I/O. Some of the sensors for the process may be connected to several process I/O subsystems and the rest to only one. The shared sensors can be those which are critical to the process. If one of the processors becomes inoperable, the other processor still has access to the data in order to maintain control.

Another method of connecting processors is a connection through I/O channels. The transfer of information will be accomplished by using the data rate of the slower processor.

Multiprocessor systems may use a number of operating modes. The processors can cooperate in solving a problem which requires more computing speed than a single processor provides; each processor can control a portion of the process. The necessary coordination may be effected through the interconnection.

Duplexed Operation

A common mode of operation in industrial control is duplexed operation, which is used to increase the reliability of the system.[40] A primary processor performs the control task. If a failure occurs, a backup processor takes over. The primary processor is then taken off-line, repaired, and returned to service without interrupting control of the process. Duplexed processors provide twice the computing capacity, since either processor may control the process. In addition, this excess power can often be used for other optional tasks.

To guarantee higher reliability, the entire system should be examined for the consequences of each possible failure. Also, software for the duplexed processors must be designed to achieve the higher potential reliability of the duplicated hardware.

Duplexed operation allows the selection of two processors to take advantage of special characteristics. For example, one may be designed to perform fast floating point calculations which would be its function during normal operation of the system.

In order for the backup processor to keep up to date, it must have access to the current process status information. With a shared-file interconnection, the information is maintained in the shared file. With channel-to-channel connections, the primary processor periodically posts the process status information into the memory of the backup computer. If posting is done frequently enough, switching from the primary to the backup computer results in only a small control deviation.

In utilizing duplexed processors, one must consider when the backup processor should be activated to take over. One could have the primary processor set a timer in the backup unit on a periodic basis, Then, failure to set the timer causes the backup to assume control and disable the primary unit. The timer is called a "watchdog timer."[41]

Distributed Control

The increased use of computer networks in data processing, along with the increased popularity of remote multiplexing, has resulted in the wider use of distributed control in the process control industry. Distributed control differs from distributed processing in that it also makes use of remote multiplexing. The processors communicate with field-located multiplexers and each processor is usually dedicated to performing the same task in an on-line environment. We can now consider computer networks, as applied to distributed control systems.

There are two basic techniques of distributed control: (1) the loop approach and (2) the unit approach. The loop approach uses satellite microprocessors to perform a fixed number of functions. For example, a microprocessor might perform a function such as square root extraction. Thus, a single microprocessor could perform a single function in a number of different loops. Normally, a microprocessor is dedicated to a single loop, so a single failure will cause the loss of only one loop. The unit approach, on the other hand, has a separate control system for each unit in the plant with a microprocessor assigned to each unit. As an example, a microprocessor might be assigned to the control of a distillation column. Some advantages of distributed control can be obtained by either approach, but others can only be realized using the unit approach. A major advantage of distributed control is the reduction in field wiring. Since the microprocessor's I/O equipment is located in the field, wires must be run for only a short distance. This provides a savings in installation and since the runs are shorter, there are fewer problems from interference on the low-level signals.

There is no need for a large control panel with distributed control; the operator can run the plant from a CRT terminal, and with no control panel, a large amount of instrumentation is eliminated and the control room is much smaller. However, some feel that the control panel is required for the operators to properly run the plant. During a plant upset, more operators can operate simultaneously using a control panel. The CRT method allows the operator to access more information and perform more control functions in a shorter period of time than with a control panel. Also, enough CRT consoles can be used in the system so that a sufficient number of operators can operate the plant during a plant upset. If desired, a panel board can be used in conjunction with a distributed control system.

The reliability and maintainability of a system is improved with distributed control. The cost of microprocessor hardware is so low that processors in a unit configuration can be backed up with a spare (duplexed processing) so that the processor failure will have no effect on the operation of the plant. Since microprocessors are built on a single printed circuit board, the system is easily repaired; it is normally a matter of replacing one board.

The unit approach is inherently modular. Computer control can be added to the units in the plant one at a time, without disrupting control of those units already on computer control. This is attractive to a plant that has been operating without computer control.

The most likely unit for computer control can be established after a study. The unit may be the plant bottleneck, a large energy user, or the part of the process which is difficult to operate.

Computer Networks

Computer networks are an extension of the distributed processing concept. The difference between a distributed processing system and a computer network is a matter of degree. Computer networks consist of two or more computer systems which are separate. The distance may be a number of feet within a plant or miles between separate facilities connected by common-carrier lines.

Computer networks can be organized in a number of ways, for such computers are loosely coupled and are capable of stand-alone operation. For instance, network configurations may be master-slave, hierarchial, or peer-connected. The configuration determines how control responsibilities are to be assigned among the processing units.

In the simplest master-slave network, a host processor is connected by one line to a satellite processor. The communication line between the processors is referred to as a link. A link may be any communications channel, such as coaxial cable or telephone line. Each device in the network is sometimes referred to as a node. A master-slave network with multiple slaves is also referred to as a multipoint or multidrop configuration.[42]

In a master-slave network, a single processor has control and determines which slave computer shall operate on a task; communications between slave computers is under control of the master. After it is assigned a task, the slave proceeds asynchronously with respect to the master until completion of the task, or until it requires services from the master. The master-slave configuration is used primarily to provide load-sharing.

Hierarchial networks use a multilevel master-slave configuration. Various levels in the hierarchy have assigned responsibilities for certain functions. The highest level in the hierarchy makes all major decisions, and the lower levels have the responsibilities for specific operations.

A three-tier hierarchical system is shown in Figure 5.40. This configuration might be a computer control system for two plants. The top tier is a large data processing computer. Two supervisory minicomputers, one in each plant, are shown in the middle tier. The bottom tier uses microprocessors, for direct digital control.

The master-slave and hierarchial networks use a top-down control philosophy. The peer-connected configuration uses mutually cooperating computers in which there is no defined master or slave relationship of one system over the other. This peer network requires that the operating system of each computer be aware of the other computers in the network and that a

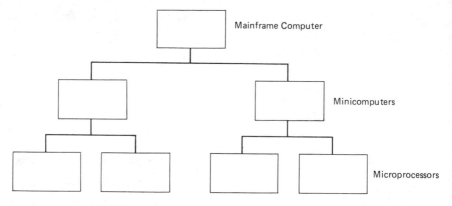

Fig. 5.40. Three-tier hierarchical network configuration.

scheduling program provide the task distribution.[43] As a job is passed to a computer in the network, the originating computer moves to a new task. A computer which is busy passes the task on to an available computer which executes the task. The time response in peer networks is difficult to predict, since one computer does not know the workload of another and there is no master which can impose tasks.

Peer networks provide access to specialized facilities not available on the originating computer, and the processors share the computing load for a more efficient use of the total facility.

There are also a number of physical connections for a network. Figure 5.41 illustrates the star configuration. Here, the host processor is the center of the system and each satellite processor communicates with the host; communication between satellite processors is carried out through the host. This

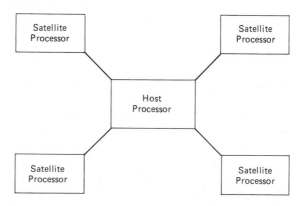

Fig. 5.41. Star network configuration.

configuration is also known as a radial or centralized configuration. It clearly lends itself to control by the host. Yet since more than one satellite can talk to the host at the same time, the host may be burdened with supervising data flow between satellites.

A multidrop configuration (as shown in Figure 5.42) is also called the data bus, data highway or Multipoint configuration. Here, the host controls the flow of data between any two nodes, while any satellite can communicate with the host or any other satellite at any one time.

The loop configuration (shown in Figure 5.43) is used in remote multiplexing; this is also called a ring configuration. If a single link breaks, the nodes can still communicate. The loop may begin and end at a loop controller, which is a computer that controls the communications. Messages between computers in the loop are handled as a string of words containing information on the originator and addressee. When a computer recognizes a message addressed to it, it accepts the message. Loops can be difficult to control and the way that messages are sent past the computers requires higher data rates.

In the point-to-point network, all processors have a direct access to every other processor (see Figure 5.44). For n processors, n(n − 1)/2 interconnections are required. With three processors, three communication links are re-

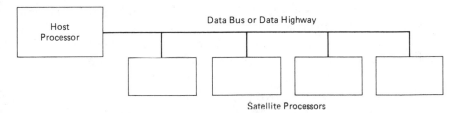

Fig. 5.42. Multidrop network configuration.

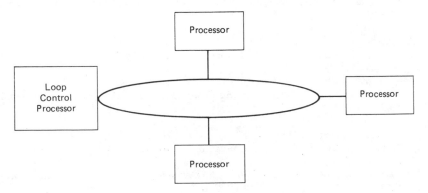

Fig. 5.43. Loop network configuration.

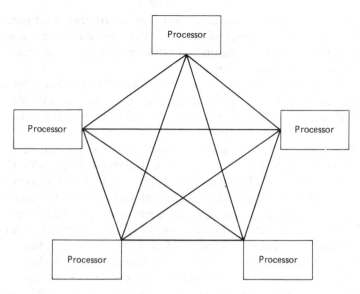

Fig. 5.44. Point-to-point network configuration.

quired. For example for five processors the number of links is 10; for 10 processors the number of links is 45.[44] The number of links quickly becomes excessive. Yet the advantages of this configuration are faster response or lower grade communications lines. Moreover, the alternate paths allow messages to still be forwarded if some of the links are interrupted.

REFERENCES

1. Sheingold, D. H., ed., *Nonlinear Circuits Handbook,* Norwood, Analog Devices, 1978.
2. Ibid.
3. Sheingold, D. H., ed., *Analog-Digital Conversion Handbook,* Norwood, Analog Devices, 1978.
4. Ibid.
5. Ibid.
6. Webster, J. G. and Johnson, B., *Medicine and Clinical Engineering,* Englewood Cliffs: Prentice-Hall, 1977.
7. Sheingold, D. H., ed., *Analog-Digital Conversion Handbook.*
8. Spooner, R. B., ed., *Hospital Instrumentation Care and Servicing,* Pittsburg, CA: ISA, 1977.
9. Ibid.
10. Mitra, S. K., Synthesizing Active Filters, *IEEE Spectrum,* January 1969.
11. Sheingold, D. H., *Analog-Digital Conversion Handbook.*
12. Ibid.
13. Texas Instruments, *The TTL Data Book for Design Engineers,* Dallas: Texas Instruments, 1978.
14. Sheingold, D. H., *Analog-Digital Conversion Handbook.*

15. Ibid.
16. Analog Devices, *Data Acquisition Products Catalog,* Norwood, MA: Analog Devices, 1978.
17. Sheingold, D. H., *Analog-Digital Conversion Handbook.*
18. Ibid.
19. Kuo, B. C., *Automatic Control Systems,* Englewood Cliffs: Prentice-Hall, 1962.
20. Sheingold, D. H., *Analog-Digital Conversion Handbook.*
21. Ibid.
22. Ibid.
23. Ibid.
24. Spooner, R. B.
25. Sheingold, D. II., *Analog Digital Conversion Handbook.*
26. Ibid.
27. Hordeski, M. F., Process Controls are Evolving Fast, *Electronic Design,* November 22, 1977.
28. Sheingold, D. H., *Nonlinear Circuits Handbook.*
29. Datel Systems, *Miniature Modular Data Acquisition System,* Canton, MA: Datel Systems, 1976.
30. Sheingold, D. H., *Analog-Digital Conversion Handbook.*
31. Ibid.
32. Ibid.
33. Jenkins, D. W., *Centralized vs. Computer Control: What are the Trade-offs?,* ISA Conference, Niagara Falls, October, 1977.
34. Hordeski, M. F., When should you use pneumatics, when electronics, *Instruments and Control Systems,* November 1976.
35. Skrokov, M. R., *Mini- and Microcomputer Control in Industrial Processes,* New York: Van Nostrand Reinhold, 1980.
36. Ibid.
37. Ibid.
38. Ibid.
39. Ibid.
40. Ibid.
41. Kraft, G. D., and Toy, W. N., *Microprogrammed Control and Reliable Design of Small Computers,* Englewood Cliffs: Prentice-Hall, 1981.
42. Skrokov, M. R.
43. Harrison, T. J., ed., *Minicomputers in Industrial Control,* Pittsburg, CA: ISA, 1978.
44. Ibid.

EXERCISES

1. List the properties and applications for some typical instrumentation amplifier circuits.
2. How is the sense terminal of an instrumentation amplifier used?
3. Describe some isolation techniques used in isolation amplifier modules.
4. In general, the objective of amplifier selection is to choose the least expensive device that will meet the physical, electrical, and environmental requirements for the application. Does this mean that a "general purpose" amplifier will be the best choice in applications where the desired performance requirements can be met? Where is this not possible?
5. The difficulties in single-channel, low-level circuitry are compounded by the addi-

tion of low-level multiplexing of such channels. Discuss the use of shields and shield grounds in a low-level multiplexing system.

6. Discuss the trade-offs between using digital multiplexing before transmission or remote A/D conversion and serial transmission.

7. Discuss the use of sample-holds in data-acquisition. In what ways may they be used to improve performance?

8. What is an error-budget analysis? Discuss its importance in analyzing the error problem and applying error reduction to the most-important sources of error.

9. What circuit resistances control the gain or transfer accuracy in a data-acquisition system? How can these resistances be minimized?

6. Data Conversion

DIGITAL CODES

Analog-to-Digital (A/D) converters translate analog measurements—which are a characteristic of most phenomena in the real world—to digital or binary codes for use in data processing, transmission, and control systems. D/A (digital-to-analog) converters are used in transforming data or the results of computations back to analog variables for control, display, or analog processing.

The analog variables, whatever their origin, are usually converted into voltages or currents. These quantities appear as continuous ac measurements or, perhaps, as a modulated ac waveform or some combination. Some examples would be outputs of thermocouples, ac strain gauges, and synchros and resolvers. Most of the analog variables that will be discussed in this chapter are changing dc voltages or currents. They can be either scaled from a direct measurement, or subjected to demodulation or filtering; the voltages and currents are scaled to ranges compatible with the converter input range. (The way and means of preprocessing are discussed in Chapter 5.)

Synchro-to-digital and digital-to-synchro converters are sometimes used in control applications. These are discussed at the end of this chapter.

Digital numbers are represented by the presence or absence of fixed voltage levels occurring at the outputs of logic gates, or applied to their inputs. These digital numbers are binary, and each bit or unit of information has one of two possible states. The states are off, false, or 0 and on, true, or 1. Words, which are groups of bits representing digital quantities, may appear in parallel simultaneously on a group of lines, or in series on a time sequence over a single line.

In a binary code, the first bit is called the most significant bit or MSB. The last bit is called the least significant bit or LSB. The resolution of the converter is determined by the number of bits. The coding used is the set of coefficients representing a fractional part of full scale. The MSB is always positioned on the left and the LSB on the right of the digital code.

Natural Binary

The most common digital code is natural binary. In a natural binary code of n bits, the MSB has a weight of $\frac{1}{2}$: (2^{-1}), the second bit has a weight of $\frac{1}{4}$: (2^{-2}), and so on to the LSB which has a weight of 2^{-n}. The value of the binary number represented is obtained by adding up the weights of the non-zero bits. A 4-bit representation is shown in Table 6.1, with the binary weights and the equivalent numbers shown as both decimal and binary fractions.

Table 6.2 shows the bit weights in binary for numbers having up to 16 bits, the range for the majority of control applications (for larger numbers of bits, you would continue to divide by 2).

The weight assigned to the LSB is the resolution. The dB column is the logarithm (base 10) of the ratio of the LSB value to unity multiplied by 20. Each successive power of 2 represents a change of 6.02dB (20 $\log_{10} 2$) or approximately 6dB/octave. In the A/D conversion process, a basic quantization uncertainty of $\pm \frac{1}{2}$ LSB exists in addition to the conversion errors existing in the converter. To reduce quantization uncertainty, one increases the number of bits. There are statistical interpolation techniques that can be performed in processing, or in filtering following conversion, that will fill in missing analog values for rapidly-varying signals, but they will do nothing to indicate the variations within $\pm \frac{1}{2}$ LSB for an apparently-constant digital number. Since it is usually easier to determine the location of a transition than to determine a mid-range value, errors and settings of A/D converters are defined in terms of the analog values when transitions occur in relation to the ideal transition values.[1] Both D/A and A/D converters have (1) offset errors, since the first transition may not occur at exactly $+\frac{1}{2}$ LSB; (2) scale-factor or gain errors, since the difference between the values at which the first transition and the last transition occur are not always equal to full scale $-$ 2LSB; and (3) linearity error, since the differences between transition values are not all equal or uniform in changing. If the differential linearity

Table 6.1 Natural Binary Code

| | | DIGITAL CODE | | | |
| | BINARY | MSB | BIT 2 | BIT 3 | BIT 4 |
DECIMAL FRACTION	FRACTION	($\times 1/2$)	($\times 1/4$)	($\times 1/8$)	($\times 1/16$)
0	0.0000	0	0	0	0
$1/16 = 2^{-4}$ (LSB)	0.0001	0	0	0	1
2/16 = 1/8	0.0010	0	0	1	0
3/16 = 1/8 + 1/16	0.0011	0	0	1	1
4/16 = 1/4	0.0100	0	1	0	0
5/16 = 1/4 + 1/16	0.0101	0	1	0	1

Table 6.2 Binary Weights

BIT	2^{-n}	$1/2^n$ (Fraction)	d B	$1/2^n$ (decimal)	%	ppm
FS*	2^0	1	0	1.0	100	1,000,000
MSB	2^{-1}	1/2	-6	0.5	50.	500,000
2	2^{-2}	1/4	-12	0.25	25	250,000
3	2^{-3}	1/8	-18.1	0.125	12.5	125.000
4	2^{-4}	1/16	-24.1	0.0625	6.2	62,500
5	2^{-5}	1/32	-30.1	0.03125	3.1	31,250
6	2^{-6}	1/64	-36.1	0.015625	1.6	15,625
7	2^{-7}	1/128	-42.1	0.007812	0.8	7,812
8	2^{-8}	1/256	-48.2	0.003906	0.4	3,906
9	2^{-9}	1/512	-54.2	0.001953	0.2	1,953
10	2^{-10}	1/1,024	-60.2	0.0009766	0.1	977
11	2^{-11}	1/2,048	-66.2	0.00048828	0.05	488
12	2^{-12}	1/4,096	-72.2	0.00024414	0.024	244
13	2^{-13}	1/8,192	-78.3	0.00012207	0.012	122
14	2^{-14}	1/16,384	-84.3	0.000061035	0.006	61
15	2^{-15}	1/32,768	-90.3	0.0000305176	0.003	31
16	2^{-16}	1/65,536	-96.3	0.0000152588	0.0015	15

*Full Scale

error is large, it is possible for codes to be missed. Some important factors are the choice of full scale, the LSB magnitude, and the transition points. Many converters use a full scale of 10 or 10.24V. For 10V, the bit values are expressed as negative powers of 2, multiplied by 10. For 10.24V, the LSB is expressed in rounded numbers (multiples or submultiples of 10mV).

Binary is the most common code but there are several other popular codes used in systems, depending on the signal range and polarity, conversion technique, special characteristics, and origin or destination of information.

Binary-Coded Decimal

Binary-coded decimal (BCD) is a code in which each decimal digit is represented by a group of 4 binary-coded digits. The LSB of the most significant group, (sometimes called a quad), has a weight of 0.1; the LSB of the next group has a weight of 0.01; and the LSB of the next group has a weight of 0.001. Each group or quad has 10 levels with weights 0 to 9, while group values in excess of 9 are not allowed. (The BCD codes for the numbers between 0 and 0.10 are shown in Table 6.3.)

A/D converters using BCD code are found in digital voltmeters. Each quad's output is decoded to drive a numeric display digit. BCD is somewhat wasteful, in that each BCD quad has only 10/16 the resolution of the com-

Table 6.3 BCD Code

DECIMAL FRACTION	MSQ ($\times 1/10$) $\times 8 \times 4 \times 2 \times 1$				2ND MSQ ($\times 1/100$) $\times 8 \times 4 \times 2 \times 1$			
0.00 = 0.00 + 0.00	0	0	0	0	0	0	0	0
0.01 = 0.00 + 0.01	0	0	0	0	0	0	0	1
0.02 = 0.00 + 0.02	0	0	0	0	0	0	1	0
0.03 = 0.00 + 0.03	0	0	0	0	0	0	1	1
0.04 = 0.00 + 0.04	0	0	0	0	0	1	0	0
0.05 = 0.00 + 0.05	0	0	0	0	0	1	0	1
0.06 = 0.00 + 0.06	0	0	0	0	0	1	1	0
0.07 = 0.00 + 0.07	0	0	0	0	0	1	1	1
0.08 = 0.00 + 0.08	0	0	0	0	1	0	0	0
0.09 = 0.00 + 0.09	0	0	0	0	1	0	0	1
0.10 = 0.10 + 0.00	0	0	0	1	0	0	0	0

parable binary quad. The relative resolution of the two codes is shown below:

BITS	LEAST SIGNIFICANT BIT		BITS NEEDED FOR THE
	BINARY	BCD	SAME RESOLUTION AS BCD
4	0.062	0.1	4
8	0.0039	0.01	7
12	0.00024	0.001	10
16	0.000015	0.0001	14

Some BCD A/D converters have an additional bit with a weight equal to full scale in a position even more significant than the MSB.[2] This additional bit provides a 100% overrange capability. Additional significant bits could provide 300% (2 bits) and 700% (3 bits) overrange capability or extend the range of the BCD full scale. The overrange bit is common in digital voltmeters in order to indicate that nominal full scale has been exceeded and that the reading may be in error. Overrange bits are used with other codes, as well. These bits are used as flags when an overrange input would give an ambiguous reading, or where an overrange input indicates out-of-tolerance system behavior.

The 2–4–3–1 BCD code is still in use; in it, the bit in the MSB position in each quad has a weight of 2 instead of the 8 for BCD. It is used at the digital output of some digital voltmeters. The relative weights in such a quad are illustrated on page 239.

	2 (× 2)	4 (× 4)	2 (× 2)	1 (× 1)
0.0	0	0	0	0
0.1 = 0.1	0	0	0	1
0.2 = 0.2	0	0	1	0
0.3 = 0.1 + 0.2	0	0	1	1
0.4 = 0.4	0	1	0	0
0.5 = 0.1 + 0.4	0	1	0	1

Gray or Cyclic Binary

The Gray code is a binary code in which the bit position does not signify a numerical weighting; each code corresponds to a unique portion of the analog range. A comparison of the Gray code with natural binary is shown below:

DECIMAL FRACTION	GRAY CODE				BINARY CODE			
0	0	0	0	0	0	0	0	0
1/16	0	0	0	1	0	0	0	1
2/16	0	0	1	1	0	0	1	0
3/16	0	0	1	0	0	0	1	1
4/16	0	1	1	0	0	1	0	0

In the Gray code, as the number value changes, the transitions from one code to the next require only one bit change at a time. (The bits that change are underlined above.) The conversion from binary to Gray code takes place as follows: when the binary MSB is zero, the Gray code MSB will be zero. Then, from MSB to LSB each change produces a "1," each nonchange a "0." Figure 6.1 shows a circuit in which binary to Gray code conversion may be achieved. The conversion from Gray code to binary is the reverse of the conversion from binary to Gray code: the binary MSB will be the same as the Gray code MSB. Then, from MSB to LSB, if the next bit is 1, the next binary bit is the complement of the previous binary bit. A mechanization of Gray code-to-binary conversion appears in Figure 6.2.

The Gray code is used in shaft encoders because the change of only 1 bit for each transition eliminates false codes that could occur with natural binary; in the Gray code encoder, (see Figure 6.3), there is only a single bit change at each transition. If the edge of a shaded area is out of line, the coding will be in error by a small fraction of the LSB. In a binary encoder, many bits change at once at some transitions.

The shaft encoder is a simultaneous converter: all bits appear at once and can be read in parallel at any one time. There is an equivalent form of

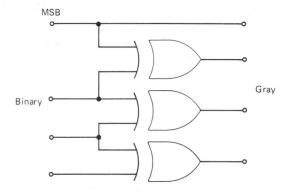

Fig. 6.1. Binary-to-gray code conversion logic.

simultaneous A/D converter having a Gray code output.[3] It uses a chain of biased comparators and the outputs provide a quantized indication of the analog input level. All comparators above are 0 and all comparators below are 1. Logic gates are used to obtain the parallel Gray code output. Such converters are fast, being capable of 10 million conversions per second. But they require a number of comparisons that is a geometric function of the required resolution, as well as large numbers of logic gates.

A variation of this technique is the cyclical converter, which also uses the gray code.[4] It uses fewer comparators, but it requires more time for a conversion. The use of the Gray code in fast converters has the same rationale as for the shaft encoder. Any Gray code output value that is latched into a register will be within ± 1 LSB of the correct value, even if latching occurs as a bit is switching. With binary, where many bits can switch at a transition, it is possible to latch in mid-transition and lock in a false code.

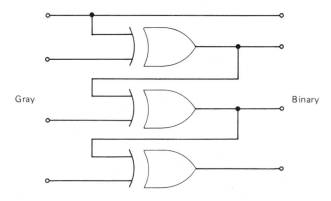

Fig. 6.2. Gray-to-binary code conversion logic.

Fig. 6.3. This small linear shaft encoder uses the Gray code for its 8-bit parallel output word. (*Courtesy Siltran Digital.*)

Complementary Codes

The actual mechanization of some converters may require codes, such as natural binary or BCD, in which bits are represented by their complements. These codes are known as complementary codes. In a 4-bit complementary-binary converter, 0 may be represented by 1111, half-scale (MSB) by 0111, and full scale (less 1 LSB) by 0000. This can be obtained from the $\overline{Q}$ outputs of a register IC in which Q is the normal output. In a similar manner, for each quad of a BCD converter, complementary BDC is obtained by representing all bits by their complements; thus, O is represented by 1111, and 9 is represented by 0110. The equivalents for 1 through 4 in complementary binary and complementary BCD (with an overrange bit) are shown below:

DECIMAL	NUMBER	NATURAL BINARY	COMPLEMENTARY BINARY	BCD	COMPLEMENTARY BCD
0 BIN.	DEC.	0000	1111	00000	11111
1, 1/16,	1/10	0001	1110	00001	11110
2, 2/16,	2/10	0010	1101	00010	11101
3, 3/16,	3/10	0011	1100	00011	11100
4, 4/16,	4/10	0100	1011	00100	11011

When a natural binary input is applied to a D/A converter coded to respond to complementary binary, the output is in reverse order. A zero output for all 1's input results. The complementary codes thus far have involved complementing all bits. These complementary codes have nothing to do with representation of the analog polarity, a matter that is considered next.

Polarity

The conversion relationships mentioned so far have been unipolar. These codes represent numbers, which in turn represent the magnitudes of the analog variables, without regard to their polarity. Gray code is an exception to this rule. Since it is not quantitatively weighted, it can represent any arbitrary range of magnitudes of either polarity. A unipolar A/D converter responds to analog signals of one polarity and a unipolar D/A converter produces analog signals also of one polarity. The signal polarity is determined by the converter reference.

The conversion of bipolar analog signals into a digital code requires sign information in the form of one extra bit called the sign bit. This bit doubles the analog range and halves the resolution. In some, the sign bit is obtained by interpreting the existing MSB; then the analog range is still doubled, but the resolution is twice as coarse. A 10-bit converter's resolution is 1/1024, with a + 10V range, if we use a bipolar code of 11 bits, the resolution is 1/2048 and range is ± 10V. When the sign digit doubles both the range and the number of levels, the LSB's ratio to full scale in either polarity is $2^{-(n-1)}$, not 2^{-n}.

The most common binary codes for bipolar conversion are: sign-magnitude (magnitude plus sign), offset binary, two's complement, and one's complement. (Each of these codes in 4 bits (3 bits plus sign) are represented in Table 6.4.)

Table 6.4 Bipolar Codes

DECIMAL NUMBER	DECIMAL FRACTION POSITIVE REFERENCE	NEGATIVE REFERENCE	SIGN + MAGNITUDE	TWO'S COMPLEMENT	OFFSET BINARY	ONE'S COMPLEMENT
+ 7	+ 7/8	− 7/8	0 1 1 1	0 1 1 1	1 1 1 1	0 1 1 1
+ 6	+ 6/8	− 6/8	0 1 1 0	0 1 1 0	1 1 1 0	0 1 1 0
+ 5	+ 5/8	− 5/8	0 1 0 1	0 1 0 1	1 1 0 1	0 1 0 1
+ 4	+ 4/8	− 4/8	0 1 0 0	0 1 0 0	1 1 0 0	0 1 0 0
+ 3	+ 3/8	− 3/8	0 0 1 1	0 0 1 1	1 0 1 1	0 0 1 1
+ 2	+ 2/8	− 2/8	0 0 1 0	0 0 1 0	1 0 1 0	0 0 1 0
+ 1	+ 1/8	− 1/8	0 0 0 1	0 0 0 1	1 0 0 1	0 0 0 1
0	0+	0−	0 0 0 0	0 0 0 0	1 0 0 0	0 0 0 0
0	0−	0+	1 0 0 0	(0 0 0 0)	(1 0 0 0)	1 1 1 1
− 1	− 1/8	+ 1/8	1 0 0 1	1 1 1 1	0 1 1 1	1 1 1 0
− 2	− 2/8	+ 2/8	1 0 1 0	1 1 1 0	0 1 1 0	1 1 0 1
− 3	− 3/8	+ 3/8	1 0 1 1	1 1 0 1	0 1 0 1	1 1 0 0
− 4	− 4/8	+ 4/8	1 1 0 0	1 1 0 0	0 1 0 0	1 0 1 1
− 5	− 5/8	+ 5/8	1 1 0 1	1 0 1 1	0 0 1 1	1 0 1 0
− 6	− 6/8	+ 6/8	1 1 1 0	1 0 1 0	0 0 1 0	1 0 0 1
− 7	− 7/8	+ 7/8	1 1 1 1	1 0 0 1	0 0 0 1	1 0 0 0
− 8	− 8/8	+ 8/8		(1 0 0 0)	(0 0 0 0)	

The analog signal now has a choice of polarity, but we must define the relationship between the code and the polarity of the signal. Positive reference indicates that the analog signal increases positively as the digit number increases. Negative reference indicates that the analog signal decreases towards negative full scale as the digital number increases.

Code Implementation

Sign-magnitude is a straightforward way of expressing signed analog quantities. With this, one determines the code for the particular magnitude and adds the polarity bit. It is used in D/A converters that operate near zero, where the application calls for a smooth and linear transition from a small positive voltage to a small negative voltage. It is the only code in which the three magnitude bits do not have a major transition such as all 1's to all 0's, at the zero. Crossover Sign-magnitude BCD is used in almost all bipolar digital voltmeter designs.[5]

Sign-magnitude has several disadvantages compared to other codes. For example, other codes are readily usable for computations with less translation. One potential problem is the two codes for zero. This makes sign-magnitude harder to interface digitally, since it requires either software or additional hardware. Moreover, the circuits for sign-magnitude conversion tend to be more complicated and costly than for some of the other codes.

The two's complement code used in conversion consists of a binary code for positive magnitudes with a 0 sign bit and the two's complement of each positive number to represent its negative equivalent. The two's complement is formed by complementing the number and adding one LSB. For instance, the two's complement of 3/8 (binary 0011) is the complement plus the LSB; 1100 + 0001 = 1101. Two's complement is easy to work with since it may be thought of as a set of negative numbers. Thus, addition can be used instead of subtraction. To subtract 3/8 from 4/8, one adds 4/8 to − 3/8, or 0100 to 1101. The result is 0001, neglecting the extra carry, or 1/8.

In comparing the two's complement code and the offset binary code, it can be seen that the only difference between them is that the MSB of one is replaced by its complement in the other. Since both a bit and its complement are available from most flip-flops, an offset-binary-coded converter can be used for two's complement by using the complement of the MSB at the output of an A/D converter or at the output of a D/A converter's input register.

Offset binary is the easiest code to implement with converter circuits. The offset binary code for three bits plus sign is the same as natural binary for four bits, except that zero is at negative full scale. The LSB is 1/16 of the total bipolar range, and the MSB is on at zero. An offset binary 3-bits-plus sign converter can be made from a 4-bit D/A converter with a 0-to-10V full-scale range. We double the scale factor to 20V and offset the zero by half of the full range to $-10V$. For an A/D converter, we reduce the input by half, and increment a bias of half the range. Offset binary is more compatible with microcomputer inputs and outputs since it is easily changed to the more common two's complement (by complementing the MSB). It also has a single unambiguous code for zero.

The principal disadvantage of offset binary is the bit transition which occurs at 0 when bits may change, from 0111 to 1000. The difference in speeds between circuits turning on and off can lead to large spikes and to linearity problems since linearity errors are likely to occur at major transitions because the transition is a difference between two large numbers. Zero errors can be greater than sign magnitude, since the zero level is usually obtained by taking the difference between the MSB ($\frac{1}{2}$ full scale) and a bias ($\frac{1}{2}$ full scale), usually two large numbers. Two's complement has the same disadvantages as offset binary, since the conversion process is the same.

The one's complement code is a technique of representing negative numbers. The one's complement is obtained by complementing all bits. For example, the one's complement of 3/8 (0011) is 1100. A number is subtracted by adding its one's complement, while the extra carry that is disregarded in the two's complement code causes one LSB to be added to the total in the end-around carry. Subtracting 3/8 from 4/8 we get 0100 + 1100 = 0001 (or 1/8). The one's complement is formed by complementing each positive value so as to obtain its corresponding negative value, including zero, which is represented by two codes, 0000 and 1111. Along with the ambiguous zero, one other disadvantage is that it is not as readily implemented as is two's complement in converter circuits. If not converted to two's complement before a D/A conversion (by adding one LSB when the MSB is 1, indicating a negative value), then one may perform a two's complement conversion and add the analog value of one LSB, if the MSB is 1. Adding the analog value may be done resistively dividing the digital MSB level down to the LSB's analog value and summing this signal.

In sign-magnitude and one's-complement A/D converters, the ambiguous zero must be considered. In some converters, one of the codes is forbidden; DVM's read $+0$ only. In other cases, the $\pm\frac{1}{2}$ LSB zero region is divided into two regions, 0 to $+\frac{1}{2}$ LSB, and 0 to $-\frac{1}{2}$ LSB, one which produces one code, the other the other code.

DIGITAL-TO-ANALOG CONVERTERS

The basic D/A converter circuit consists of a reference, a set of binary-weighted precision resistors, and switches (as shown in Figure 6.4.) In this circuit, an operational amplifier holds one end of all the resistors at zero volts. The switches are operated by digital logic. Each switch that is closed adds a binary-weighted increment of current E_{ref}/R_j through the summing

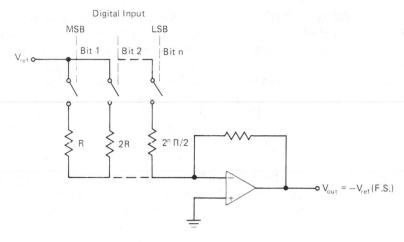

Fig. 6.4. Basic D/A converter.

bus at the amplifier's negative input. The output voltage is proportional to the total current, which is a function of the value of the binary number. In an application which requires 12-bit D/A conversion, the range of resistance values needed would be 4,096:1, or up to 40MΩ for the LSB. If the resistors are manufactured in thin- or thick-film, or integrated circuits, this range is not practical.[6] If discrete resistors are used, cost, size, tracking, and inventory become a problem.

Resistance Ladders

The resistance ladder provides a way to reduce the resistance range. One uses a limited number of repeated values, with attenuation. One approach (as shown in Figure 6.5) uses a binary resistance quad, consisting of the four

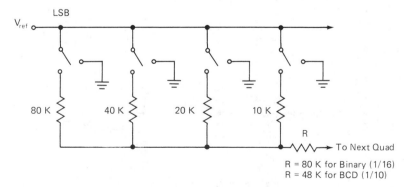

Fig. 6.5. Quad resistance ladder.

values 2R, 4R, 8R, and 16R for each group of 4 bits, with an attenuation of 16:1 for the second quad and 256:1 for the third quad. The proper quad weights for BCD conversion can be achieved with an attenuation between quads of 10:1.

The R-2R ladder allows a greater reduction of resistance values, and it is a convenient and popular form. (See Figure 6.6, which shows its use with an inverting operational amplifier.)[7] If all bits but the MSB are off—therefore grounded—the output is $(-R/2R)V_{ref}$. If all bits except Bit 2 are off, it can be seen that the output voltage will be $\frac{1}{2}(-R/2R)V_{ref} = \frac{1}{4}V_{ref}$: The lumped resistance of the LSB circuit to the left of Bit 2 is 2R. The equivalent circuit looking back from the MSB towards Bit 2 is $V_{ref}/2$, and the series resistance is 2R. The grounded MSB series resistance, 2R, has no influence since the amplifier is at ground. The output voltage is therefore $-V_{ref}/4$. The same reasoning can be used to show that the nth bit produces an output increment equal to $2^{-n}V_{ref}$.

The R − 2R network may be used to give an unattenuated noninverting output by connecting the output to a high-impedance load, such as the input of the follower amplifier shown in Figure 6.7. Following the same reasoning described earlier, the MSB output is $\frac{1}{2}V_{ref}$ (2R − 2R divider). Since the entire network may be considered as an equivalent generator having an output voltage NV_{ref} (where N is the fractional digital input) and an internal resistance R, the output may be scaled accurately by connecting precision resistors to ground. Because of symmetry and duality qualities, the R − 2R network is also used in other configurations.[8] Figure 6.7 shows an example in which the input and output leads are interchanged from the configuration shown in Figure 6.6, for use as a current-switching circuit.

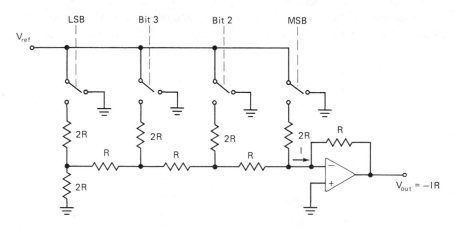

Fig. 6.6. R-2R resistance ladder.

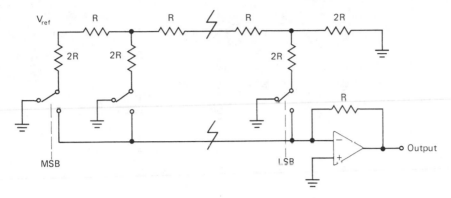

Fig. 6.7. Inverted R-2R ladder for current switching.

Ladder Switches

A variety of voltage and current switches are used in converters. Voltage switches are used like that shown in Figure 6.6. There, switching takes place between the reference and ground in order to maintain a constant impedance. Since they can be used with reference voltages of either polarity, they also find use in 4-quadrant multiplying DACs.

Current switches steer the current between an amplifier summing point and ground. They are capable of higher speeds than voltage switches since the reference current is not interrupted. The major voltage change appears at the output, but not across the switches. (A simplified form of current switch is shown in Figure 6.8.) In this circuit, the switching transistors tend to isolate the weighting resistors from the output line and attenuators.

In the switching circuit shown in Figure 6.8, consider the Q_1 base-emitter voltage. If it is equal to that of Q_R, the voltage across 2R will be equal to V_R. The current through the resistor will be $\frac{1}{2}V_R/R$, and assuming negligible current through the diode and a high B, this same current will flow through to the collector circuit (at the output). Thus, the cathode of the diode will be above the anode. If the base is at 1.4V, and with 0.6V diode conduction, an anode voltage of 2V, which is the minimum for TTL logic, is sufficient. If the anode of D_1 is now switched to 0.8V or less, Q_1 is cut off, since D_1 now assumes its current, clamping the emitter of Q_1 at or below the base and eliminating Q_1's contribution to the output amplifier. Since the current is not interrupted, the voltage change is small and the switching time is short, settling to within 1 LSB typically within a few hundred nanoseconds. Now if Q_1 and Q_R are matched for V_{BE} and have equal currents through their emitters, the voltage across 2R will track V_R with temperature, making the MSB current almost independent of temperature, except for B effects. The other bits

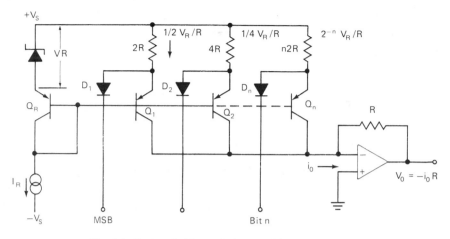

Fig. 6.8. Basic switching technique used in D/A converters.

operate in the same manner, except the switching transistors are matched to the reference at the binary-weighted currents.

The switches and resistors are usually grouped as quads, with repeated 2R, 4R, 8R, 16R resistance values and an 8:1 maximum range for bit currents.[9] The less significant bit currents are attenuated in the output line (as shown in Figure 6.9). With the quad structure, there are only four different current values, which eases current-matching. The attentuation allows the tolerances on the resistor values and transistor tracking in the less significant quads to

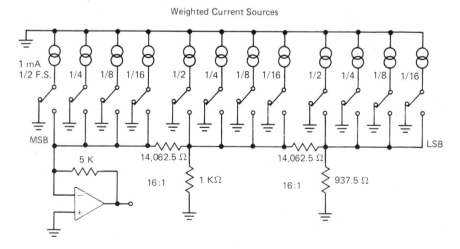

Fig. 6.9. 12-bit current switching D/A converter.

be relaxed. In the monolithic quads, the switching transistors have emitter areas with a power-to-two relationship in order to maintain a constant current density and equal tracking of V_{BE} and B. The reference transistor, on the same chip, is usually identical to one of the switching transistors.

Reference Configurations

The most common reference is the temperature-compensated zener diode.[10] It is often used with operational amplifiers for operating-point stabilization or transducing to current. (Some typical reference circuits are shown in Figure 6.10.)

In bipolar current-switching D/A conversion with offset binary or two's complement codes, an offset current equal and opposite to the MSB current is added to the converter output. This can be done with a resistor and a

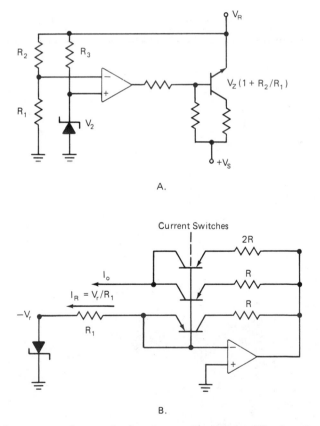

Fig. 6.10. D/A converter reference circuits: *A*. operating point stabilization; *B*. voltage-to-current conversion.

separate offset reference, but usually, it is derived from the converter's basic reference voltage in order to minimize drift with temperature. The gain of the output inverting amplifier is doubled in order to double the output range, which changes from 0–10V to ± 10V. Figure 6.11 shows a current-switching converter connected for a bipolar output. Since the amplifier is connected for sign inversion, the conversion relationship is negative reference, + F.S. for all 0's − F.S. for all 1's. For noninverting applications, the same values of offset voltage and resistance are used, but the value of the output voltage scale-factor depends on the load of the parallel combination of the internal and offset resistances, as well as the external load.

Bipolar D/A converters with voltage switches and R-2R ladder networks and offset binary or 2's complement coding may use the network terminals that are normally grounded for unipolar operation, (one side of the switches and the LSB termination) and use the reference signal in the opposite polarity. If the LSB termination remains grounded, the output will be symmetrical. For sign-magnitude conversion, the converter's current output can be inverted. Circuitry, controlled by the MSB, determines if the output amplifier's input is direct or through the current inverter. (One technique is shown in Figure 6.12.)

The basic parallel-input D/A converter circuits discussed above have the common property that the analog output continually follows the state of the logic inputs. If the conversion circuit is preceded by a register, the converter will respond only when the inputs are gated into it. This property is useful in data distribution, in which data are continually appearing, but it is desirable that a D/A converter respond at certain times and then hold the analog output constant until the next update. The D/A converter with buffer storage acts as a sample-hold with digital input and analog output with an infinite hold time. The register is controlled by a strobe signal, which causes the converter to update. The rate at which the strobe may update is determined by two factors: (1) the settling time of the converter and (2) the response time of

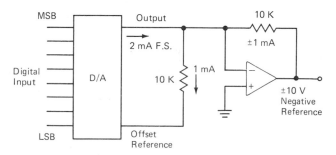

Fig. 6.11. Bipolar current-switching D/A converter connected for offset binary or 2's complement codes.

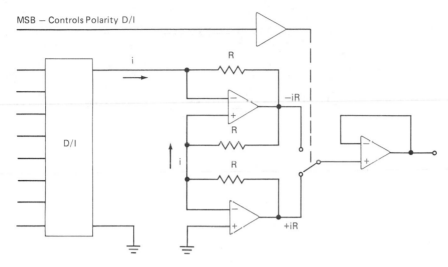

Fig. 6.12. Sign-magnitude bipolar D/A converter.

the logic. Usually, the settling time of the analog portion of the D/A converter is an order of magnitude slower than the response time of TTL circuits. The speed of the digital portion of a D/A converter is of some importance when the spikes caused by unequal turn-on and turn-off times are critical in the application. The digital inputs to a D/A converter come from logic circuits, which exhibit unequal turn-on and turn-off times.

The inputs to A/D converters are usually in the form of voltages. The outputs from D/A converters are often voltages at low impedance from an operational amplifier; however, many converter types provide an output current instead of a voltage. The basic conversion process may result in a current output that is fast, linear, and free from offsets. An operational amplifier may be used to convert that current to voltage, but as a result of design trade-offs the amplifier may tend to limit converter performance.

Voltage and Current Outputs

Converters that use current outputs or voltage outputs directly from resistive ladders can be considered as voltage generators with series resistance or current generators with parallel resistance. They can be used with operational amplifiers in either an inverting or noninverting mode (as shown in Figure 6.13). Some types use internal feedback resistors for output voltage scaling which track the ladder resistors in order to minimize temperature variations.[11] The gain-determining feedback resistances (R_1, R_2) do not track the converter's internal resistors, only one another.

The inverting current-output connection is preferred for a number of

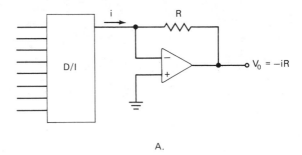

A.

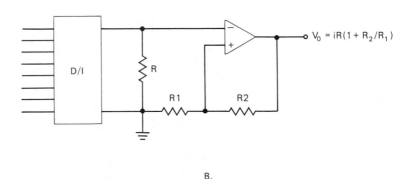

B.

Fig. 6.13. Current-to-voltage conversion: *A.* inverting mode; *B.* noninverting mode.

reasons. For instance, the internal impedance of the D/I converter is usually high, and the loop gain will be close to unity, essentially independent of the feedback resistance and minimizing the amplifier errors, such as voltage drift. The output swing of the converter at the amplifier's negative input terminal will be negligible, minimizing loading of the current output, voltage-dependent nonlinearity, and variations of internal impedance with temperature. Common-mode rejection is not a consideration, since there is no common-mode swing.

The conversion relationship of D/I converters is usually positive reference. As the current flowing out of the converter increases, the value represented by the digital code increases. It does not depend on the actual polarity of the converter's reference. If current flowing towards the converter increases as the number represented by the digital code increases, the relationship is negative reference.

Through an understanding of some of the basic design principles of converters, users of converters can gain a better insight into the devices they are using, which may result in some ideas or principles that will help them in their future designs.

Design Considerations

Many designers feel that a high-precision D/A converter is the most difficult section to design of any device using it, including an A/D converter. The added design elements and physical layout involved in using a D/A converter in an A/D converter can also be a difficult task. The increased difficulty in building A/D converters with high speeds and accuracy, even with a well-designed D/A converter block, can be large, and these difficulties increase rapidly with the resolution. Eight-bit D/A converters are relatively easy to design and manufacture, since the accuracy requirement is of the order of 0.2%. Ten-bit converters are more difficult to design, since the requirement is 0.05%. As one reaches 12 bits of resolution (0.0125%), the design and manufacturing becomes critical.

Figure 6.4 (see page 245) shows the basic current-weighting D/A converter.[12] This may be the simplest approach to performing the digital-to-voltage conversion. A set of binary-weighted currents flows through a 5KΩ feedback resistor, producing an analog output voltage proportional to the sum of the currents that are allowed on by the switches. While this approach seems simple, there are problems in manufacturing a converter of this type. The difficult problems are the switching speed and resistor temperature matching. In a 12-bit converter using a 10KΩ resistor for the most significant bit, the least-significant-bit resistor is 40.96MΩ This range of resistance cannot be obtained from a consistent film, so the resistance temperature coefficients cannot even be approximately matched.[13]

The switching speed of a current switch depends upon the current available to charge the stray capacitance. As an example, let the LSB current be 0.5 µA and let the stray capacitance be 10pF; then the settling time for the LSB is 200µs. If all currents could be of the order of 1mA, the conversion time for all bits would be uniformly shortened. (Figure 6.14 shows a way in

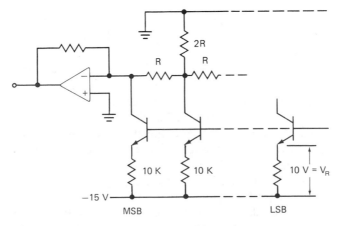

Fig. 6.14. R-2R D/A converter with equal current sources.

which this is commonly accomplished. Here, the NPN current sources are all made equal to 1mA.)

ANALOG-TO-DIGITAL CONVERTER CIRCUITS

There are a number of circuits for A/D converters. A limited number of these designs are available in small, modular form, which are designed for incorporation into equipment or systems. The most popular of these are:

1. Successive-approximation.
2. Integration: single, dual, and triple ramp (slope).
3. V/f types.
4. Counter comparator.
5. Parallel.

Each type has different characteristics which make it useful for a specific application.

Successive-Approximation

The successive-approximation A/D converter has been widely used for interfacing with computers because of high resolution to 16 bits and high speed to 1 MHz. Conversion time is fixed and independent of the magnitude of the input voltage. Conversion is independent of the results of previous conversions, since the internal circuits are cleared at the start of a new conversion.

The technique consists of comparing an unknown input against a precisely-generated internal voltage at the output of a D/A converter.[14] The input of the D/A converter is the digital output number of the A/D converter. The conversion process is similar to a weighing process with a set of n binary weights.

When the conversion command is applied, the converter has been cleared and the D/A converter's MSB output ($\frac{1}{2}$ full scale) is compared with the input. If the input is greater than the MSB, it remains on and the next bit is tested. If the input is less than the MSB, it is turned off, and the next bit is tested. If the second bit doesn't have enough weight to exceed the input, it is left on and the third bit is tested. If the second bit exceeds the input, it is turned off and the third bit is tested. The process continues until the last bit has been tested. When the process is completed, the status line changes to indicate a valid conversion. The output register now holds the digital code corresponding to the input signal. (Figure 6.15 is a block diagram of a successive-approximation A/D converter.)

As explained in the preceding paragraph, the basic idea of successive-approximation is simple. A more detailed explanation follows. As the logic

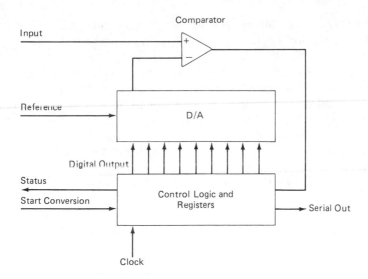

Fig. 6.15. Successive-approximation A/D converter.

signal is applied to the command terminal, the D/A switches are set to their off state, except for the most significant bit, which is set to logic 1. This turns on the corresponding D/A switch to apply the analog equivalent of the MSB to the comparator. Simultaneously, an internal clock is released from the inhibit state and allowed to run. Until the first clock-pulse arrives, the MSB is compared with the analog voltage. Upon the arrival of the first clock pulse, the MSB has been tested and shown to be either heavy or light. If the analog input voltage is less than the MSB weight, the MSB is switched off at the first edge of the clock pulse; if the analog input is greater than the MSB, the 1 will remain in the register. The clock pulse also turns on the second bit. During the second pulse, the sum of the first result and the second bit is compared with the analog input voltage. The comparator, when gated by the next clock pulse, causes the register to either accept or reject that bit. Succeeding clock pulses cause all the bits, in order of decreasing significance, to be tried, until the LSB is accepted or rejected.

During the conversion time, the output of a status flip-flop indicates when a conversion is taking place.

The data from the parallel output lines of a successive-approximation converter are not valid until the end of conversion. In some applications, it may be desired to output the data serially.[15] In this case, one must accept the data only as each bit becomes valid, after each bit-decision is made. Serial data can also be obtained at a later time if they are loaded into a shift register which may then be interrogated. Serial data cannot be taken from the comparator output, unless it is bistable, since ambiguous levels with the comparator in the linear range may cause errors if the internal/flip-flop and external shift register have different thresholds. This can result in errors as large as $\frac{1}{2}$ full scale.

The input cannot change during conversion, for if it were to change during the conversion, the output would no longer represent the analog input. It is usual to employ a sample-hold device ahead of the converter so as to retain the input value that was present at the time before the conversion started. The status output of the converter can be used to release the sample-hold from the hold mode at the end of the conversion. The sample-hold may not be needed, however, if the signal varies slowly enough and is noise-free enough such that significant changes will not be expected during the conversion interval.

The accuracy, linearity, and speed of the successive-approximation converter are affected by the characteristics of the D/A converter, its reference, and the comparator. The settling time of the D/A converter and the response time of the comparator are usually much slower than the switching times of the digital elements. The differential nonlinearity of the D/A converter is reflected in the differential nonlinearity of the resulting A/D converter. Also, if the D/A converter is non-monotonic, one or more codes can be missing from the A/D converter's output range. Bipolar inputs are handled by using a D/A converter with bipolar output and the correct input scaling.

Integration Types

The integration family of converters is quite popular. These converters perform an indirect conversion, by first converting to a function of time, then converting the time function to a digital quantity by using a counter. The dual-ramp type is used in digital voltmeters and other applications in which a relatively long time may be taken for conversions. This allows some benefits of noise reduction via signal averaging.

In the dual-ramp (or slope) type the input signal is applied to an integrator and a counter is started, counting the clock pulses.[16] After a predetermined number of counts fixes the period of time, T, a reference voltage with an opposite polarity is applied to the integrator. At this time, the charge on the integrating capacitor is proportional to the average value of the input over the period T. The integral of the reference is an opposite slope ramp with a slope V_R/RC. Now, the counter starts counting from zero. When the integrator output is zero, the counter is stopped and the analog circuit reset. Since the charge is proportional to $V_{IN}T$ and the charge lost is proportional to $V_R \Delta t$, then the number of counts relative to the full period is proportional to $\Delta t/T$, or V_{IN}/V_R. The output of the binary counter is therefore a binary representation of the input voltage. When the input is attenuated and offset by half of the reference voltage, the output is an offset binary representation of a bipolar input. (Figure 6.16 shows a dual-ramp A/D converter for bipolar signals with an offset-binary output.)

The dual-slope integrator has a number of advantages. For instance, accuracy is independent of the capacitor value and clock frequency, since they affect both the up and down ramps by the same amount. Differential linearity is good because the analog function is free of discontinuities, and the codes are generated by the clock and counter so all codes can inherently exist. Resolution is not limited by differential nonlinearity. The integration technique provides rejection frequency noise and averaging during sampling.

The fixed averaging period also allows normal-mode rejection at frequencies that are integral multiples of $1/T$.[17] Normal-mode noise consists of the unwanted signals that appear on the input line, even without common-mode error. If a low-frequency or dc quantity is converted in the presence of high-frequency ripple, a successive-approximation A/D converter, even if used with a sample-hold, converts the instantaneous values of signal-plus-noise. An integrator will attenuate the high frequencies, producing smoothing, and if combined with a fixed averaging period, nulls those frequencies that have whole numbers of cycles during the averaging period.

The throughput rate of dual-slope converters is limited to less than $1/2T$ conversions per second.[18] The sample time, T, will be determined by the fundamental frequency to be rejected. If one wishes to reject 60HZ noise and its harmonics, the minimum integrating time is 16–2/3 ms and the maximum number of conversions is less than 30/second.

Dual-slope converters have adequate speed for transducers such as thermocouples. They are the predominant type used in digital voltmeters. Since

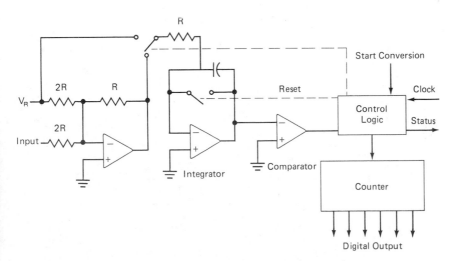

Fig. 6.16. Dual-ramp A/D converter.

many DVM's use sign-magnitude BCD coding, the bipolar operation requires polarity sensing and switching.

The other conversion circuits in this class include the single-and triple-ramp types. The single-ramp converter uses a reference voltage of opposite polarity to the signal which is integrated while the counter tracks clock pulses until the integrator output is equal to the signal input. At this time, called Δt, the output of the integrator is $V_R \, \Delta t / RC$. The number of counts is proportional to the ratio of the input to the reference. This circuit has the disadvantage that its accuracy depends on the capacitor and the clock frequency. The multiple-ramp types provide increased compensation.

In the V/f converter, a frequency is generated in proportion to the input signal; a counter measures the frequency and provides a digital output which is proportional to the input signal.

Counter Comparator Conversion

The counter-comparator A/D converter (as shown in Figure 6.17) is analogous to the single-ramp type, except that it is independent of a time scale. The analog input is compared with the output of a D/A converter and the digital input of the D/A is driven by a counter. At the start of a conversion, the counter begins the count, which continues until the D/A output exceeds the input value. Now, conversion stops and the converter is ready for the next conversion once the counter has been read and cleared. The number of counts is held in an output register. For bipolar input signals, a bipolar D/A converter is used and the count is offset binary starting from negative full scale.

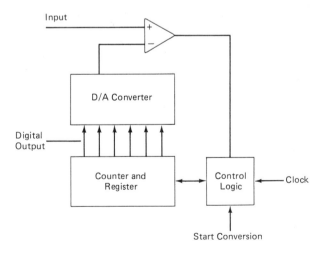

Fig. 6.17. Counter-comparator A/D converter.

This circuit has the disadvantage of limited speed for a given resolution, since the conversion time for a full-scale change is equal to the maximum number of counts divided by the clock frequency. If the clock frequency is 10MHz, the maximum throughput rate for 10-bit resolution (1,024 counts) is less than 10KHz or $100\mu s$ per conversion.

A variation of this circuit uses an up-down counter.[19] When the output of the D/A converter is less than the analog input, the counter counts up. When the D/A output is greater than the analog input, the counter counts down. When the analog input is constant, the counter hunts between the two adjacent bit values. This converter can follow 1 LSB changes at the clock rate, but it requires the full count for full-scale changes. It tries to convert continuously, which may be a disadvantage in a fast data-acquisition system, since it can give a conversion complete signal only during the clock period following a change in state of the comparator which occurs at irregular times.

A buffer storage register can be used to store the previous count, while the counter is seeking the next value. By stopping the count after a completed conversion, this converter may be used as a sample-hold with a long hold time and no droop.

If the up or the down count is disabled, the circuit acts as a valley peak follower, counting only when the input exceeds the previous extreme value.

Parallel Conversion

A parallel 3-bit converter with Gray code output is shown in Figure 6.18. It has $2^n - 1$ comparators, biased 1 LSB apart and starting with $+\frac{1}{2}$ LSB. For zero input, all comparators are off. When the input increases, the number of comparators in the on state increases. For any given bit position for the code, those comparator outputs that should give a logic 1 for a given input level are connected to the first NOR gate, and those that should be zero are connected to the next NOR gate, thus generating the correct code. Natural binary can be implemented in the same way. In this approach, conversion occurs in parallel, with the speed limited only by the switching times of the comparators and logic gates. When the input changes, the output changes as a function of the switching times. This is the fastest approach to conversion, but the number of elements increases geometrically with the resolution. A 4-bit converter uses 15 comparators and seven 8-input gates. A 5-bit circuit requires 31 comparators and nine 16-input gates.

The combining of parallel conversion for small numbers of bits with successive-approximation for several bits at a time gives better resolution than the parallel circuit, with less complexity and improved speed over the successive-approximations circuit.[20]

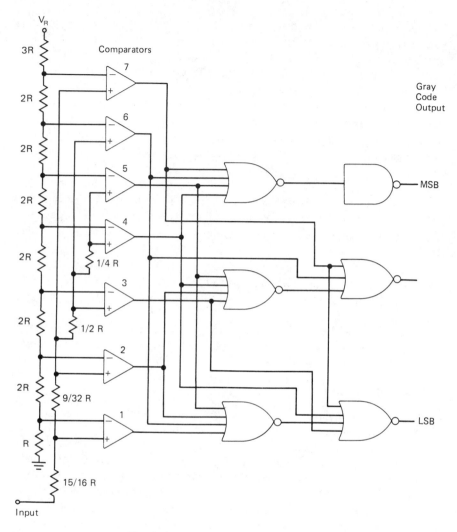

Fig. 6.18. Three-bit parallel A/D converter.

Applications

Converters designed for system applications usually receive external commands to convert or hold. For low-frequency signals, the converter may be an integrating type, which is inherently a lowpass filter. It is capable of averaging out high-frequency noise and nulling those frequencies harmonically-related to the integrating period. The integrating period can be made equal to the period of the line frequency, since a major portion of interference occurs at this frequency and its harmonics. If the converter must respond to individual samples of input, the maximum rate of change of the average input, the full-scale voltage, and the conversion time (TC), have the following relationship for binary conversion:

$$\left. \frac{dV}{dt} \right|_{max} = 2^{-n} V_{FS} \Big/ T_C$$

If individual samples are not important but instead large numbers of samples are to be used (essentially a stationary process), the only requirement is that the signal be sampled at least twice each cycle for the highest frequency of interest.

The dual-slope integrating A/D converter spends about 1/3 of its sampling period performing an integration and the remainder of the time counting out the average value over the integrating period and resetting for the next sample. The dual-slope type will always read the average value, which results in a sample of the input waveform over the integrating window or period. Although it is slow, the integrating A/D converter is useful for measurements of temperature and other slowly-varying voltages, especially in the presence of noise.

The successive-approximation device is capable of high resolution and high speed, at a reasonable cost. If T_C, using a successive-approximation converter, is 10μs, the maximum allowable dV/dt is 500V/s. The successive-approximation converter weakness is that at higher rates of change, it generates linearity errors since it cannot tolerate changes during weighting. The converted value is somewhere between the values at the beginning and the end of conversion, and the time uncertainty can approach the conversion interval. When the signal is slow enough, noise with rates-of-change that are large can cause errors that may not be averaged. However, an external sample-hold can be used to greatly improve matters in this situation.

CONVERTER APPLICATION

In this section, we seek to help the designer in choosing a converter by providing relevant questions in making the choice, formulating the definitions of specifications, and deciding upon the features of selection and evaluation. We now go to some considerations on what must be done to make the system perform as expected.

Defining the Design

A key factor in choosing the right device is to completely define the design objectives. Consider all known objectives and try to anticipate the unknowns. Include such factors as signal and noise levels, desired accuracy, throughput rate, characteristics of the interfaces, environmental conditions, and size and system budgetary limitations that may force performance compromises or a different approach to the system.

Some general considerations for the control system include the following:

1. An accurate description of input and output signal range, source or load impedances, type of digital code, logic level, and logic polarity.
2. Data throughput rate.
3. Interface specifications.
4. System error budget allowed for each functional block.
5. Environmental conditions.
6. Supply voltage, recalibration interval and other operating requirements.
7. Special environmental conditions: RF fields, shock, and vibration.

In addition to these general considerations, there are specific requirements to consider for the blocks in the system.

The following are some specific considerations for D/A converters:

1. Resolution: how many bits of the incoming data word must be converted? What analog accuracy and linearity are required?
2. What digital codes and logic levels are required?
3. What are the output signal requirements: current or voltage, full-scale range. Voltage-output D/A converters are more convenient to use. Current-output D/A converters are used in applications where high speed is more important than a voltage output, such as A/D circuits with comparators.
4. What type of reference is required: fixed, internal or external, variable, multiplying? How many quadrants are needed for multiplying?
5. Speed requirements: what is the shortest time between data changes? After a change in the input, how long can the system wait for the output signal to settle for a full-scale change?
6. Switching transients: how can they be filtered?
7. Temperature range, including internal temperature rises: over how much of this range can the converter perform within specifications without readjustment?
8. Power-supply sensitivity: is it adequate to hold errors within limits?

The process of selecting an A/D converter system is similar to that required for D/A converters. Some of the following considerations are analogous to those for D/As, while others are unique.

1. What is the analog input range and resolution of the signal to be measured?

2. What are the requirements for linearity error, relative accuracy, and stability of calibration?
3. Must the various sources of error be minimized as the ambient temperature changes? Are missed codes tolerable?
4. What is the time allowed for a complete conversion?
5. Type of reference is to be used: fixed, adjustable or variable?
6. What type of power supply should be used for the system?
7. What is the character of the input signal noise level sampled: filtered, rapidly-varying, or slowly-varying? Are conversion circuits acceptable for preprocessing? Integrating types are best for noisy input signals at slow rates, while successive-approximation is best for sampled or filtered inputs at rates to 1MHz. Counter-comparator types provide low cost but are slow and noise-susceptible.

When a system is assembled, in which one A/D converter is time-shared among input channels by a multiplexer and sample-hold, their contribution to system errors must be considered. These devices have been discussed in Chapter 5 and they are also considered here because of their relevance to the converter selection process. Multiplexer considerations include:

1. Number and type of input channels needed: single-ended or differential, high or low-level, dynamic range.
2. Type of hierarchy used for a large amount of channels; addressing scheme.
3. Settling time when switching from one channel to another; maximum switching rate.
4. Allowable crosstalk error between channels; frequencies involved.
5. Errors due to leakage current through the source resistance.
6. Multiplexer transfer errors due to the voltage divider formed by the on-resistance of the multiplexer and the input resistance of the sample-hold.
7. Channel-switching rate: fixed or flexible, continuous or interruptible, capable of stopping on one channel during test purposes.
8. Source damage when the power is off; MOS–FET multiplexer switches open when power is removed. J–FET multiplexer switches can conduct when power is removed. Thus, it is possible to interconnect and damage active signal sources.

Sample-Hold considerations may include:

1. Input signal range.
2. Slewing rate of the signal; multiplexer's channel-switching rate; sample-hold acquisition time.

3. Accuracy, gain, linearity, and offset errors.
4. Aperture delay; jitter.

The delay component of aperture time may be correctable, since switching can be advanced in time to compensate. The uncertainty or jitter cannot be compensated. A random jitter of 5 ns applied to a signal slewing at $1V/\mu s$ results in an uncertainty of 5 mV. In systems with a constant sampling rate, using data that are not correlated to the sampling rate, the aperature delay is not important, but jitter can modulate the sampling rate. Other considerations when selecting a sample-hold are as follow:

1. Amount of droop allowable in hold.
2. The effects of time, temperature, and power supply variations.
3. Offset errors due to the sample-hold's input bias current through the multiplex switch and sources.

Converter Specifications

It is essential to have an understanding of what the manufacturer means by the "specifications." It should not be assumed that manufacturers mean the same thing when they publish the same numbers defining a parameter for a specific product. Product information must be interpreted in terms meaningful to the user's requirements, which requires a knowledge of how the terms are defined.

The specifications of typical D/A and A/D converters may not mean what the user thinks they mean. It is important to consider their implications. The following should prove useful:[21]

Absolute Accuracy. As the converter's full-scale range is adjusted, it will be set with respect to the reference voltage, which can be traced to some recognized voltage standard. The absolute accuracy error is the tolerance of the full-scale point referred to this absolute voltage standard.

Acquisition Time. The acquisition time of a sample-hold circuit is the time it takes to acquire the input signal to within the stated accuracy. It may include the settling time of the output amplifier. Since it is possible for the signal to be acquired and the circuit switched to hold before the output is settled, one should be sure of what it is meant by this term, since the output may not be meaningful until it is settled.

Common-Mode Range. The common-mode rejection usually varies with the magnitude of the input signal swing, which is determined by the sum of the common-mode and the differential voltages. Common-mode range is the range of input voltage over which the specified common-mode rejection is maintained. When the common-mode signal is $\pm 5V$ and the differential signal is $\pm 5V$, the common-mode range is $\pm 10V$.

Common-Mode Rejection. This is the ability to reject the effects of voltages applied to both input terminals simultaneously. It is usually expressed either as a ratio (CMRR = 10^5) or as $20 \log_{10}$.

Droop. A drifting of the output at an approximately constant rate. It may be caused by the leakage of current out of a storage capacitor.

Feed Through. The fraction of the input signal that appears at the output in the hold or off mode, caused primarily by capacitance across the switch. It can be measured by applying a full-scale sinusoidal input at a fixed frequency and observing the output.

Offset. For a zero input, the extent to which the output deviates from zero, usually a function of time and temperature.

Monotonicity. The ability to include all code numbers in actual operation.

Nonlinearity. The amount by which the plot of output vs input deviates from a straight line.

Settling Time. The time required for the input to attain a final value within a specified fraction of full scale, usually $\pm \frac{1}{2}$ LSB.

Slew Rate. The maximum rate at which the output voltage can change. Slew rate is usually an indication of settling time.

When considering the problem of determining converter performance requirements, it is useful to divide the converter specifications into three groups: (1) those that determine accuracy under optimum conditions, (2) those that are time dependent, and (3) those that are affected by the environment.

The first group includes resolution, relative accuracy, differential linearity, noise, quantization uncertainty, and monotoncity.

Time-dependent specifications include the conversion time, bandwidth, and settling time. Environment-related specifications include the gain or scale-factor, temperature coefficients, and operating temperature range.

Designing with Fixed Specifications

A relaxation of the specifications of the first type can be done through the use of signal conditioners. The specific form of signal-conditioning must be based on knowledge of the input signals and the information to be extracted from them, for unwanted signal components can be extracted from the input signals. The remaining signal is scaled to equal the input range of the A/D converter. A differential instrumentation amplifier may be used to reject common-mode signals, bias out the dc offsets, and scale the input (as shown in Figure 6.19).

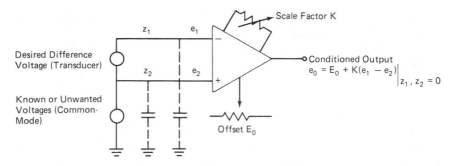

Fig. 6.19. Differential amplifier used as signal conditioner.

Logarithmic compression can be used in applications which require a wide dynamic signal range. If the system is capable of tolerating a constant fractional error of 1% or less, a logarithmic amplifier for data compression can be used (as shown in Figure 6.20).[22] The logarithmic amplifier allows the encoding of signals that would ordinarily require a 20-bit conversion to cover the dynamic range to be done with a 12-bit converter. Modest accuracy in a fixed ratio is substituted for extreme accuracy over the entire full-scale range; for many applications this is acceptable, and the data can be handled easily because it is to be processed digitally.

Another common signal-conditioning device is the filter. Lowpass filters can extract carrier, signal, and noise components above the signal frequencies. These components will appear as noise if the converter cannot follow them, so A/D converters often contain follower circuits for impedance buffering. With a minimum of external wiring, these can be connected as active lowpass filters (as shown in Figure 6.21).

A relaxation of specifications can be achieved by adding a sample-hold amplifier (as shown in Figure 6.22). The use of a sample-hold amplifier can increase the system throughput rate and increase the highest-frequency signal that can be encoded within the converter resolution. System throughput rate, without the sample-hold, is determined mainly by the multiplexer's settling time and the A/D conversion time.

Multiplexer settling time is the time required for the analog signal to settle

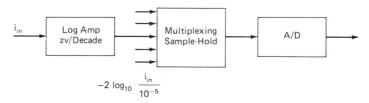

Fig. 6.20. Logarithmic range compression.

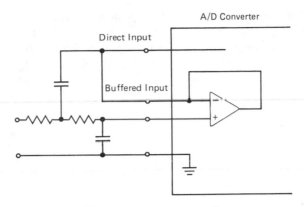

Fig. 6.21. A/D input amplifier connected as lowpass filter.

to within its error budget, as measured at the input to the converter. In a 12-bit system, with a $\pm 10V$ range, the multiplexer units typically settle within $1\mu s$ and a typical conversion time might be $20\mu s$.

A sample-hold can be used to hold the last channel's signal level for conversion, while the next channel is selected and settles. Sample-hold amplifiers with acquisition times of less than $5\mu s$ to within 0.01% are available, so the throughput time can be reduced to approach the conversion time. Pairs of sample-holds and A/D converters may be used for alternate conversions to increase the throughput rate further.

A relaxation of the class of errors due to environment-related specifications can be achieved by allotting one multiplexer channel to carry a ground-level signal and another to carry a precision reference-voltage level that is close to full-scale. Data from these channels is used by the microprocessor to correct gain and offset variations common to all the channels. These might be generated in the sample-hold, A/D converter, or wiring.

System Considerations

Upon selecting the appropriate converter system, the user should be aware that the analysis involved is usually not by itself sufficient to ensure proper

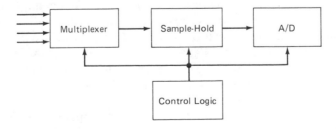

Fig. 6.22. Data-acquisition system with sample-hold.

system performance. The system designer must consider the physical inter-connections, grounding, power supplies, protection circuitry, and the other details that constitute good engineering practice. To evaluate the perform-ance trade-offs, an error budget is useful. Three classes of errors can be con-sidered: (1) those due to the nonideal nature of components (2) the physical interconnections, and (3) the interaction of components. The first class of er-rors is determined from the specifications of the components. The second type results from the parasitic interactions that are a function of the inter-connections: grounding and shielding methods and contact resistance. The third group results from interactions between components in the system. These interactions can be predicted from analysis of the specifications of the devices, or how they are designed. An example of this type of error might be the offsets created by series impedances in the signal path from signal sources or multiplexer-switch impedances. The bias and leakage currents of the stages following these impedances will also be affected. Another example might be the disturbances caused at the source, as the multiplexer switches to its terminal.

The error budget can be used as a tool for establishing the trade-offs for the performance requirements of the system. The error budget can be used for predicting the overall expected error. A worst-case summation, a root-sum-of-the-squares summation, or other combinations may be used.

The popularity of modular converters requires that we consider some ele-ments of their design. Many types are programmable; this allows the user to select one of several voltage ranges by choosing the appropriate jumper con-nection. In addition, many modules permit modifications by the connection of external resistors.[23] The gain and offset temperature coefficients of these devices are achieved by a close tracking with temperature of the key resistors within the module. Even if low ppm/°C resistors are used externally, the overall gain and offset performance vs. temperature can be degraded.

Noise

In the design of a converter module, care should be taken to separate the analog and digital signal lines. This should also be followed in the layout of the board on which the converter is to be mounted. Digital lines should not run parallel in close proximity with runs of analog signal lines. When these lines cross, they should do so at right angles. Care should also be taken with low-level high-gain points, such as the comparator input on A/D converters and the summing junction of the output amplifier in D/A converters. Runs to these points should be short and not create loops. Grounded guard runs can be used to reduce interference.

Converter modules and most data-acquisition components have a number of ground terminals that are not connected together in the module.[24] These grounds may be referred to as the logic power return, analog common, analog power return, analog signal ground, or analog sense. These grounds should be tied together at one point, usually at the system power-supply ground. Ideally, a single solid ground is desirable. But current flows through the ground wires and through tracks of the circuit cards, and since these paths have some resistance and inductance, hundreds of millivolts may be generated between the system ground point and the ground terminal of the module. To help alleviate this problem, separate returns are used to minimize the current flow from sensitive points to the system ground point. Thus, supply currents do not flow in the same return path with analog signals, and logic return currents are not summed with the return current from a precision zener diode. The connections between the system ground point and the ground terminals should be as short as possible and should have the lowest possible impedance. The module's supply terminals should be capacitively decoupled as close to the module as possible.

A capacitor with a good frequency response should be used. A 15μF solid tantalum capacitor is usually recommended. The analog supplies are by-passed to the analog power return terminal and the logic power terminal is bypassed to logic power return.

When gain and offset adjustments are required, the potentiometers should be mounted with short leads in a position that will be accessible.

A converter should not be located near a transformer or fan motor. Using shielding to protect against interference is expensive and not always successful. D/A converters should be located near their loads. This may require longer cable runs for the digital signals; however, the overall reduction in noise can justify the expense. A/D converters should be located as near the signal source as possible. One can also use a differential amplifier to receive the signal at the end of a long run before entering the A/D converter. Unshielded analog signals should never be run near either digital or power lines.

In order to reduce common-mode errors, a differential amplifier may be used to eliminate ground-potential differences (as was shown in Figure 6.19). The signal source may be a remote transducer; the differential amplifier should be located at the A/D converter. The common-mode signal is the potential difference between the ground signal at the converter and the ground signal at the transducer, plus any common-mode noise produced at the transducer and voltages developed by the unbalanced impedances of the two lines. When the signal source is the output of the D/A converter, the differential amplifier is located near the load. The common-mode signal will be a function of the differences in ground potential at the two locations.

The amount of dc common-mode offset that is rejected will depend on the CMRR of the amplifier. Bias currents flowing through the signal source leads may cause offsets if either the bias currents or the source impedances are unbalanced, although CMRR specifications may include a specified amount of source unbalance. The specifications may also indicate an upper frequency for which CMRR is valid, usually 50–100Hz. At higher frequencies, unbalanced conditions in series resistance, shunt capacitance, and the amplifier's internal unbalances reduce the common-mode rejection by producing a quadrature normal-mode signal. This error can be reduced by the use of a shield, as shown in Figure 6.23. In the circuit shown in this figure, no part of the common-mode signal appears across the line capacitors since the shield is driven by the common-mode source. The shield also provides some electrostatic shielding in order to limit coupling to other lines in close proximity.

It is important that the shield be connected only at one point to the common-mode source signal and that the shields be continuous, through all connectors. The shield carries the common-mode signal, so it should be insulated in order to prevent it from shorting to other shields or ground. A return path must exist for the bias and leakage currents of the differential amplifier unless it has transformer or optically coupled inputs.

In the foregoing discussion, we have examined the system aspects of applying converters. Considering the different types of converters on the market and the complex manner in which converter specifications may relate to a system application, selecting the best converter for an application is not always a simple task. To make the most appropriate choice, we have considered a number of issues: the objectives of the conversion process and how they relate to the converter's specifications; how the system may be configured to relax the performance requirements; how the other system components limit and degrade converter performance; and trade-offs in the system error budget.

SYNCHRO CONVERSION

Synchros and resolvers are angle sensing transformer devices with two or more windings that are brought out separately to appropriate sets of terminals. They are treated in this separate section because of the nature of the

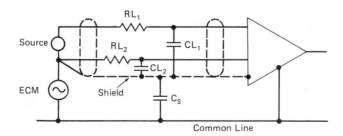

Fig. 6.23. High-frequency common-mode rejection using a shield.

ac input and output signals of this class of transducers. The advantages of synchros and resolvers in various configurations are (1) improved accuracies, (2) increased reliability due to fewer moving parts, and (3) low driving torque required. With these things considered, the cost differential between a mechanical transducer arrangement and synchro or resolver unit may be negligible.

This section will consider some circuit techniques used for synchro/resolver data manipulation. It does not attempt to present a survey of every kind of circuit in use; instead, it reflects a selective concentration on what seems to be the most important and effective techniques.

We will start with the following review of the technology. Synchro-to-digital conversion is accomplished by four different classes of circuitry, each of which is subject to wide variations:[25]

1. Single-RC phase-shift.
2. Double-RC phase-shift.
3. Real-time trignometric function-generator.
4. Ratio-bounded harmonic-oscillator.

Let us consider each of them, recognizing that examples of each type are subject to wide variation.

Single-RC Phase-Shift

The single-RC phase-shift synchro-to-digital converter shown in Figure 6.24 operates by comparing the zero-crossing times of the reference wave and the

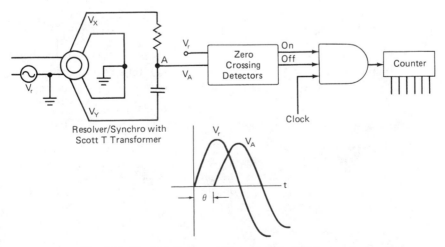

Fig. 6.24. Single R-C phase-shift synchro-to-digital converter.

phase-shifted sine-to-cosine (resolver-format) wave.[26] It may be shown that, if $\omega RC = 1$ (where $\omega = 2\pi$ times the reference carrier frequency) then the phase shift between the voltage from A to ground and the reference wave is equal to $(\theta - \alpha)$. If α (the time-phase error caused by rotor-to-stator phase lead) is small compared to θ, the time interval between the zero crossings of V_A and V is a measure of θ. A counter totals the number of digital clock pulses during the time interval and the clock frequency is scaled to make the count read directly in a digital coded angle.

The main advantage of the single-RC S/D converter is its simplicity. The disadvantages of this approach include the following:

1. The difficulty of maintaining $\omega RC = 1$ due to the instability of the capacitor with the time and temperature variations.
2. The difficulty of maintaining $\omega RC = 1$ due to variations in the carrier frequency. (These can be eliminated by generating the carrier in the converter by dividing down from the clock frequency.)
3. The difficulty of maintaining negligible time-phase error (α) at all times in the reference wave. (Some relief may be obtained by compensating the reference input, with a lag network, but α varies with temperature, θ, and excitation, as well as from device to device.)
4. Significant errors due to noise quadrature components in V_X, V_Y and harmonics in V_X, V_Y.
5. Errors due to the fact that only one conversion is made per cycle.
6. The circuit works at only one carrier frequency.

This list confines the single-RC phase-shift converter to relatively low accuracy applications.

Double-RC Phase-Shift

The double-RC phase-shift synchro-to-digital converter shown in Figure 6.25 eliminates at least two of the error sources that limit the performance of the single-RC circuit. In this approach, V_A and V_B have equal but opposite

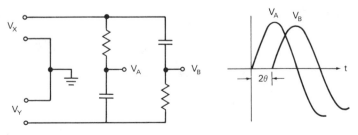

Fig. 6.25. Double-RC phase-shift configuration.

phase shifts with respect to V_{re}. By measuring the time interval between the zero crossings of V_A and V_B and then using it to gate a clock pulse into a counter, it allows the count to be scaled directly in degrees of θ at one-half the clock frequency used in the single-RC design. The disadvantages of this approach are similar to those of the single-RC approach, but with these exceptions:

1. The time-phase error (α) in V_{re} is no longer a factor.
2. The reference carrier frequency is not required to be as stable as before, but it is still an error factor and must be internally generated, even for moderate accuracy.
3. There is some improvement in RC stability, due to the ability of the capacitors to track each other for temperature variations.

An added difficulty in the double-RC approach is a 180° effect that causes the same reading at θ and $\theta \pm 180°$. This requires added circuitry to prevent false readings.

The other error factors remain the same. The double-RC phase-shift S/D converter can be made to perform with a worst-case error limit of 10 minutes.

Real-Time Trignometric-Function-Generator

The real-time trignometric-function-generator approach of Figure 6.26 has many forms.[27]

In this general discussion, the resolver signals, V_X and V_Y, are applied to trignometric function generators, which may be either tangent bridges or sine/cosine nonlinear multipliers. By manipulating the generator outputs in accordance with trignometric identities, an analog voltage proportional to the difference between θ and the function-generator setting ϕ is developed. The integral of this voltage is digitized and this digital value is fed back (as ϕ) to drive ($\theta - \phi$) to null; then ϕ equals the shaft angle θ. This circuit has the following advantages over the preceding approaches:

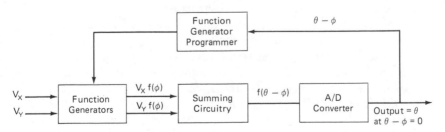

Fig. 6.26. Real-time trignometric-function-generator S/D converter.

1. A real-time, continuous measurement of θ is made, so there is no stale data.
2. The ratio technique is an advantage in maintaining accuracy.
3. It is independent of the carrier frequency and will work over several decades of frequency, without design changes.
4. It is possible to reject the quadrature components.
5. It is possible to reject most noise components.
6. It can reject most harmonic distortion, since it is responsive only to the differential harmonics between V_X and V_Y,
7. It is relatively independent of the reference time-phase error, α.
8. There is no 180° problem.

The implementation of this approach has been more expensive than either of the earlier schemes, but modular techniques and integrated circuit technology have erased most cost differences. This can achieve accuracies better than ± 2 seconds.

Ratio-Bounded Harmonic-Oscillation

We will now consider an approach that has some of these advantages but generally achieves a better price-performance ratio when its disadvantage can be accepted. The ratio-bounded harmonic-oscillator circuit of Figure 6.27 uses a pair of integrators which are cascaded with a unity-gain inverter, into a closed loop circuit with positive feedback, such that they will oscillate at their RC time constants.[28] The oscillation frequency does not have any special relationship to the reference carrier frequency, except that it is usually higher for faster conversions.

First, the integrators are set with initial conditions, by scaling their output voltages in the ratio V_X/V_Y; the voltages are obtained by sampling V_X and V_Y. The loop will oscillate, and the ratio of the interval between the zero crossing of the signal in a positive direction to the natural period of oscillation is proportional to θ. This ratio is digitized by counting clock pulses. The advantages of this approach are:

1. Lower costs than for the function-generator circuit.
2. Independence from noise, harmonics, and quadrature components, provided they are equally present in V_X and V_Y.
3. Independence from carrier frequency. It is a broad-band approach.
4. Independence from the two RC time constants, provided that the ratio of the oscillator frequency to the counter frequency does not change.
5. The accuracy of the ratio technique in which the initial conditions are set to be the V_X/V_Y ratio.
6. Independence from reference time-phase error, α.
7. No 180° problem.

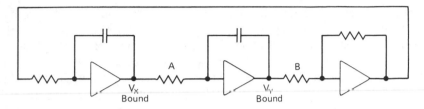

Fig. 6.27. Harmonic-oscillator S/D converter.

This circuit has one significant disadvantage for some applications: it is not a real-time measurement, but a periodic technique, like the phase-shift converters and suffers from stale data errors.

Tracking Converters

The tracking converter in Figure 6.28 is a functional diagram of a 14-bit synchro-to-digital tracking converter.[29] Three-wire synchro-angle data are sent to a Scott-T transformer, isolated from ground, and then translated into two signals, one of which whose amplitude is proportional to the sine of θ and the other whose amplitude is proportional to the cosine of θ. These amplitudes are the carrier amplitudes at the reference frequency. The cosine wave is $\cos\theta \cos\omega t$; the carrier term, $\cos\omega t$, is removed in the demodulator. The quadrant selector circuit selects the quadrant in which θ lies and also sets the polarities of the sine θ and cos θ signals for computations. The outputs of the quadrant selector are then sent to the sine and cosine multipliers.

The multipliers are digital-programmed resistive networks.[30] The transfer functions of these networks are determined by a digital input which switches

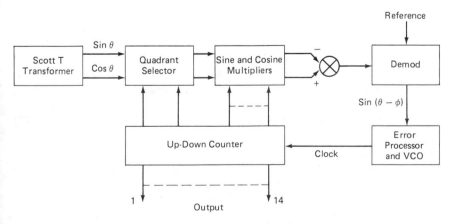

Fig. 6.28. Tracking S/D converter.

in the resistors such that the instantaneous value of the output is the product of the instantaneous value of the analog input and the sine or cosine of the digital encoded angle ϕ. When the instantaneous value of the analog input to the sine multiplier is $\cos \theta$, and the digital encoded word sent to the sine multiplier is ϕ, then the output is $\cos \theta \sin \phi$. Thus the outputs from the multipliers are:

Sine multiplier: $\cos \theta \sin \phi$.
Cosine multiplier: $\sin \theta \cos \phi$.

These outputs are sent to a subtractor; thus, the input to the demodulator is:

$$\sin \theta \cos \phi - \cos \theta \sin \phi = \sin (\theta - \phi)$$

This identity indicates that the output represents a carrier-frequency sine wave with an amplitude proportional to sine of the difference between θ and ϕ. The demodulator has access to the reference voltage which has been isolated from the reference source and scaled by the reference isolation transformer. The output of the demodulator is an analog dc level, proportional to: $\sin (\theta - \phi)$. This is the sine of the error between the angular position of the synchro and the digital encoded angle, ϕ, which is the output of the counter. For small errors, $\sin$ (error) $\cong$ (error). This analog error signal is then fed to the error processor and VCO block.

This circuit block consists of an analog integrator output (the time-integral of the error) which controls the frequency of a voltage-controlled oscillator (VCO). The VCO produces clock pulses that are counted by an up-down counter. The sense of the error (ϕ too high or ϕ too low) is determined from the polarity of ($\theta - \phi$). This is used to generate the counter control signal, which determines if the counter is up or down. It is normal practice to add a small amount of hysteresis into the reaction of the error-processor.[31]

The two most significant bits of the angle ϕ, which are stored in the up-down counter, control the quadrant selection and the remaining 12 bits are fed in parallel to the inputs of both multipliers. The up-down counter acts as an incremental integrator. Therefore, the tracking converter acts as a closed loop servomechanism (continuously attempting to null the error to zero) with two lags, since there are two integrators in series. This is then a Type II servo loop, which has advantages over Type I or Type 0.

The tracking converter described in this section is a high-performance device and the logical choice for many applications. However, there are other methods of digitizing the data represented by the angle θ.[32] Two of them are considered here. Both use the fact that the angle θ can be determined from the carrier-envelope amplitudes of the two resolver-format inputs at a selected instant of time during the carrier cycle—if they are measured simultaneously. If the reference input is $V_{re} = = K_1 \cos (\omega t)$, after corrections for rotor-stator phase shift, the two resolver inputs are:

$$V_X = K_2 \sin \theta \cos (\omega t)$$
$$V_Y = K_3 \cos \theta \cos (\omega t)$$

Then simultaneous samples of V_X and V_Y will yield as much information on $\sin \theta$ and $\cos \theta$ as will continuous observation. The only essential requirement is that we must measure the envelope amplitudes at the same instant in time. The ideal time for measurement is at the peak of the carrier wave (either positive or negative) when the carrier amplitude is largest; then the carrier waves (V_X and V_Y) will produce the largest signals with respect to noise, drift, quadrature, and other error sources. The optimum time is obtained from the reference signal after correcting for synchro time-phase shift by phase-shifting the signal by 90°; at that point its zero-crossing is at the correct time and then will clip to a pulse of the desired width, with a trailing edge that occurs at the peak of the phase-corrected reference wave. Thus, sampling converters contain circuits that will generate a control pulse at the peak of the reference wave, and sample and hold V_X and V_Y. This produces dc levels proportional to $\cos \theta$ and $\sin \theta$.

Successive-Approximation Sampling

The successive-approximation sampling synchro-to-digital converter is shown in Figure 6.29. This is one of the two types of sampling S/D converters to be discussed. (Note that part of the circuit is similar to the quadrant-selector and sine/cosine multiplier section of Figure 6.28, which was analyzed earlier.) The only differences are:

1. The signals from the sampler are sampled sine and cosine dc levels, rather than continuous modulated carriers.
2. The cirucit that stores the digital angle output is a sequentially addressed register, instead of an up-down counter.
3. The error processor performs a simpler function.

The error processor has two elements: (1) a comparator to sense the polarity of the input signal, $\sin (\theta - \phi)$, and (2) a clockpulse generator.

The entire conversion process can be done quickly. Modern high-speed converters are fast enough so that hundreds of complete conversions can be done in a single carrier period.[33] This fact becomes important when multiplexed systems are considered. In spite of the high conversion speed, the successive-approximation converter can suffer from stale data errors,

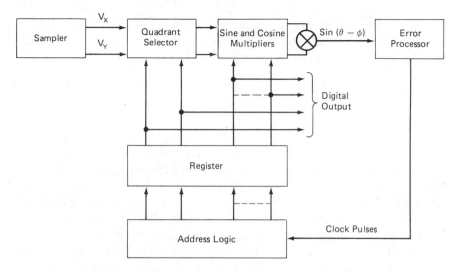

Fig. 6.29. Successive-approximation S/D converter.

from using data sampled once per carrier period. When θ is changing, a periodic velocity error results. This error is close to zero immediately after each new sample and increases to a maximum given by:

$$\frac{\text{Velocity}}{\text{Error}} = \frac{\text{Velocity (degrees/second)}}{\text{carrier frequency}}$$
$$\text{(degrees)} \qquad \text{(Hertz)}$$

This equation holds for a constant velocity between samples.

Harmonic-Oscillator Sampling

The sampling harmonic-oscillator S/D converter is illustrated in Figure 6.30. The sampling technique is somewhat different from that used in the sampling successive-approximation converter. The resolver-format input signals are first sent to phase-sensitive demodulators, with dc output levels:

$$V_X = K \sin \theta$$
$$V_Y = K \cos \theta$$

Where K is a constant and θ is the shaft angle to be digitized. It is the dc levels that are sampled at the proper time in order to set the initial conditions

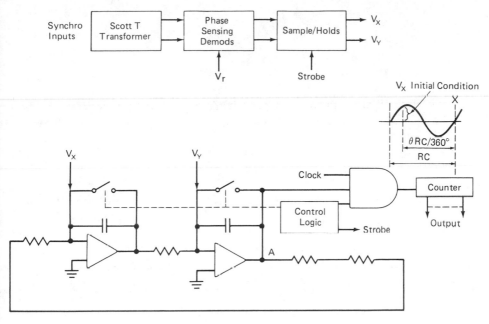

Fig. 6.30. Sampling harmonic-oscillator S/D converter.

of the integrators in a harmonic-oscillator converter. The rest of the circuit
has two major sections:[34]

1. A two-integrator and inverter chain, in a positive-feed-back loop. This
   loop, under the command of the control logic, will oscillate at a frequency determined by the integrator time constants.
2. A clock-pulse generator counter circuit that is on when the oscillator is
   on and off at the positive-going zero-crossing of the voltage at the second integrator.

Initially, the loop is prevented from oscillating by the control logic, which
also applies the sampled dc levels, V_X and V_Y, as initial conditions to the two
integrators. As the integrators stabilize at the initial conditions, the oscillation begins, and simultaneously clock pulses are sent to the counter. When
the positive-going zero-crossing (point X) is reached, the counting stops.

At this point, the total stored in the counter is the digitized value of θ, the
shaft angle, provided that the clock frequency has the correct relationship to
the integrator time constants.

At point X, the positive zero-crossing that stops the counting process, the
following relationships/hold:

$$\sin\left(\frac{t}{RC} - \frac{2\pi\theta}{360°}\right) = 0$$

$$\text{or} \quad \frac{t}{RC} - \frac{2\pi\theta}{360°}$$

If the clock rate is proportional so that some convenient number of pulses like 3600 are produced in $2\pi RC$ seconds, then the count at point X will be:

$$\frac{3600}{360}(\theta)$$

The total stored in the counter represents the angle 0 to a resolution of 0.1°. (1 part in 3600) Any desired resolution can be obtained within the stability and accuracy limits of the system.

Although it is easy to stabilize the frequency of a clock generator, it is not as easy to stabilize the RC time constants of the integrators, and it is the ratio of the clock frequency to the integrator time constants that determines the accuracy and resolution without considering the other error sources.

In the many harmonic-oscillator designs, a phase-locked-loop is used to force the clock frequency to track the drift in the integrator time-constant which compensates for other error sources, as well.[35] The overall accuracy of this type of conversion can be made better than most conventional designs. Typical worst case static error for this design is ±6 minutes.

Either of the two sampling S/D converters described above may be shared by a number of synchros or resolvers. Thus, more than one shaft angle can be digitized by the same converter circuitry, with a saving of equipment and power-supply energy. Reliability is also increased due to the reduction in component count. Some additional circuitry is required to perform the

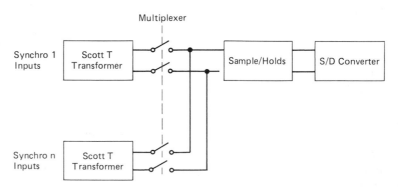

Fig. 6.31. Multiplexed sampling S/D converter system.

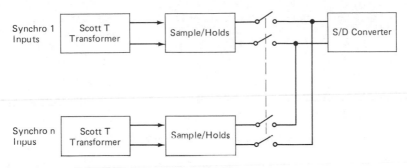

Fig. 6.32. Simultaneous sample-hold S/D converter system.

multiplexing, while some systems require a separate set of sample-hold circuits for each input.

In Figure 6.31, a pair of sample-holds are switched from input to input, sampling each and holding the value during conversion, which takes less than one carrier cycle. The sampling is done at the peak of the carrier cycle. The only added hardware is the multiplexer module and one input isolation module for the synchro or resolver per input.

The disadvantage of successive-peak sampling is that it compounds the stale data error problem by making each successive reading one carrier period later than the preceding one. In multiplexing n inputs, the possible skew error between readings of the first and the nth channels as well as between two successive readings of any channel is n times the possible skew error of a one converter per channel system.[36]

In systems with high velocity inputs, a better approach is the simultaneous sample-hold technique shown in Figure 6.32. In this circuit, each input has its own pair of sample-holds and all samples are taken at the carrier peak.

REFERENCES

1. Sheingold, D. H., ed., *Analog-Digital Conversion Handbook,* Norwood, CA: Analog Devices, 1978.
2. Ibid.
3. Ibid.
4. Ibid.
5. Ibid.
6. Ibid.
7. Kershaw, J. D., *Digital Electronics,* North Scituate, MA: Duxbury, 1976.
8. Sheingold, D. H.
9. Ibid.
10. Ibid.
11. Ibid.
12. Kershaw, J. D.
13. Sheingold, D. H.

14. Hordeski, M. F., Balancing Microprocessor-Interface Tradeoffs, *Digital Design,* April 1977.
15. Ibid.
16. Ibid.
17. Sheingold, D. H.
18. Ibid.
19. Ibid.
20. Ibid.
21. Ibid.
22. Sheingold, D. H., ed., *Nonlinear Circuits Handbook,* Norwood, CA: Analog Devices, 1978.
23. Analog Devices, *Data Acquisition Products Catalog,* Norwood, CA: Analog Devices, 1978.
24. Ibid.
25. Schmitt, H., *Electronic Analog/Digital Conversions,* New York: Van Nostrand Reinhold, 1979.
26. Ibid.
27. Ibid.
28. Ibid.
29. Ibid.
30. ILC Data Device, *Synchro Conversion Handbook,* Bohemia, Long Island, NY: ILC Data Device, 1974.
31. Ibid.
32. Ibid.
33. Ibid.
34. Ibid.
35. Ibid.
36. Ibid.

EXERCISES

1. What is meant by logic that is defined as negative true? Why should one define logic in terms of "positive true"?

2. If the speed of an A/D converter is limited by the settling time of the input buffer-follower, how can one increase the throughput rate?

3. Discuss some ways of avoiding errors when external resistors are connected to the converter. Why is it helpful to understand resistor tracking in actual applications?

4. In what circumstances is it more economical to choose either a "general-purpose" converter, which will meet the needs of a large number of system designs, or to go through an optimum selection process for each individual application? Discuss your answer.

5. Discuss some techniques of relaxing converter specifications, based on the availability and cost of added devices, compared to the cost of alternatives. Discuss any additional problems envisioned.

6. How should one treat terminals that are used to determine the signal voltage range in a converter involving analog signals in order to protect the low resolution levels? How should one treat runs that carry logic signals?

7. Describe the internal operation of a successive-approximation converter if complementary logic is necessary—as is typical of some D/A converters.

8. Consider the techniques for synchro/resolver-to-digital conversion. What are the advantages and disadvantages of each method in a low-cost microprocessor control system?

9. For the sampling harmonic-oscillator of Figure 6.30, develop the proof of the relationship between θ and the stored count. Assume that the voltage at point A has the following relationship for the initial conditions:

$$V_A = \sin\left(\omega_L t - \frac{2\pi\theta}{360°}\right)$$

Where $\omega L = 2\pi f L$

fL = the natural oscillation frequency of the loop,

t = time in seconds.

θ = the input shaft angle in degrees.

Let the integrator time constants be equal and the inverter gain be unity.

7. Interfacing The Microprocessor

MEMORY INTERFACING

After the processing of the microcomputer is complete, the next step is to communicate with the peripherals. Information must be gathered and processed; then, the information may be displayed and sent to control the other devices. This chapter will consider input/output techniques. Basic input and output interfacing will be described for both serial input-output and parallel input/output. The basic concepts of interfacing will be discussed followed by a consideration of the chips which implement the interface functions. Scheduling techniques for sequencing the input/output devices will also be considered, as will polling, interrupts, and direct memory access.

Bus Systems

As we have said, an 8-bit microprocessor has eight pins for the movement of data into and out of the chip, generally to and from one of the registers. The eight wires are called the data bus, and information can usually flow in both directions along the bus at different times. The bidirectional data bus is used in most microprocessors because it reduces the number of pins in the package.

An 8-bit microprocessor also has a set of 16 pins to carry the binary numbers called addresses. These pins are called the address bus. The address bus carries information out from the microprocessor to ROMs, RAMs, or I/O chips. Signals on the address bus are used to select a certain memory or I/O chip and to select a particular location inside that chip.

There is a group of assorted signals that enter and leave the microprocessor. Some carry the control signals between the microprocessor and the ROMs, RAMs, and I/O chips. These signals are grouped together as the control bus. (The microprocessor bus system is shown in Figure 7.1.)

The control logic operates the sequence of operations within the microprocessor. It controls the various cycles and data transfers through the internal bus system. The control logic also provides external signals to let other modules know the status of the microprocessor at any particular time. For example, during a fetch-cycle, the microprocessor generates a status

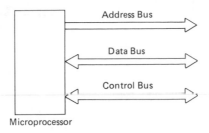

Fig. 7.1. Microprocessor bus system.

signal to request an instruction from memory. During an execute cycle, the microprocessor may be in a memory-read, memory-write, or an input/output status. The bidirectional bus buffers are controlled by the status request. When the microprocessor is requesting data from the external environment, the bidirectional bus is placed in an input mode. When it sends data to the external environment, the bus buffers are placed in the output mode, and the information is placed on the data bus.

The external modules connected to the microprocessor detect the status condition generated by the microprocessor. Communication is achieved by conforming to the status request and the direction of information flow on the data bus.

When only one external data bus is available in a microprocessor, it must be used alternately for data, addresseses, and instructions. A double-bus system uses one bus for data and instructions and another for addresses. Control information may or may not have a special bus. In a double-bus system, data and addresses can be transferred back and forth simultaneously in the same cycle without waiting for the sequential use of a common bus. A multiple-bus requires a larger number of pins in the IC microprocessor package.

The bus buffers that control the direction of information flow are usually constructed with tri-state gates (as shown in Figure 7.2). The control input of each tri-state buffer controls its output. When the control input is enabled, the output of the gate is equal to its input value. When the control input is disabled, the output of the buffer may be disabled regardless of the input condition. By controlling the selection lines S_1 and S_2, the data bus lines are placed in an input or output status. These two selection lines can also be used to inform external modules of the status condition in which the data bus is at a particular time.

Memory Addresses

The memory section of a computer contains storage units, which usually consist of semiconductor cells. (Chapter 2 describes these.) The storage units

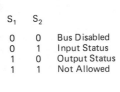

S_1	S_2	
0	0	Bus Disabled
0	1	Input Status
1	0	Output Status
1	1	Not Allowed

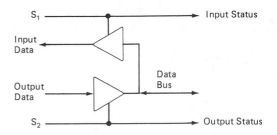

Fig. 7.2. Using tri-state gates for the bidirectional data bus.

are coded in binary numbers, with two stable states to represent the zeros and the ones. The memory may be organized into bytes, which are groups of 8 bits or words; these words may have the same bit length as the data registers, data buses, or arithmetic logic unit. A byte consists of 8 bits, but a word may be 4 to 64 bits in length. The memory is arranged sequentially into bytes or words, each of which has a unique address. Keep in mind, though, that the address of a word in memory is not to be confused with its contents—a memory location could contain any value.

Think of the address as a binary number that can run from 0 to 65,535 for most 8-bit microprocessors. Then A_{15} is the left-most bit, it represents a weight of 32,768. A_0 is the least significant bit, it represents a weight of 1. But binary numbers, when they are 16 bits long, are difficult to work with and are impossible to remember. It's also clumsy to think of the addresses in decimal form, because it takes a good amount of work to convert back and forth between the decimal number and the pattern for 16 bits. Yet it is usually necessary to work with the bit patterns with microcomputers since you may be designing your own mix of peripherals: ROMs, RAMs, and I/O chips, and all of these may have addresses peculiar to your application. So to understand how to wire up the address lines, and how to debug the system, it helps to be able to work comfortably with 16-bit addresses.

The scheme that one usually uses to work with the addresses is the hexadecimal form normally called hex. Hex codes are numbers in a number system having the base 16, hence the derivation of the word "hexadecimal." The 16 bits are broken up into four groups of four bits with a code, consisting of a letter or number to represent each group. An address that is 16 bits long then is given as four of these number codes: for example FA84 or 05BC.

There is, however one reason for using decimal numbers: to verify that we have enough room in a memory chip, but there is a way to do this in hex and avoid converting to decimal.

A Memory Map

Visualize a map of the memory (see Figure 7.3). Let the memory space be 65,536 locations and divide it up into 256 rows of 256 locations each. A 1K

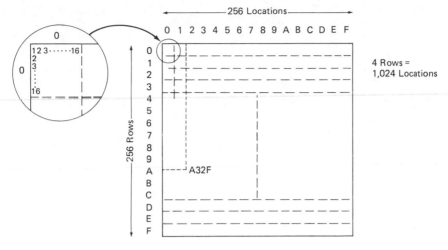

Fig. 7.3. Memory map.

memory of 1,024 locations is four rows on the map, while a 4K memory of 4,096 locations is 16 rows. Using hex addresses, the form of the map can indicate how close we are to the end of a block of memory.

The map can be marked on the left side with the hex digits O to F. These will correspond to the left-most digit of the address. Between each pair of digits there are 16 rows. These rows are numbered by the second digit. The map is also marked with the digits 0 to F along the top edge. These correspond to the third digit. Between each pair of these digits there are also 16 locations, and these are numbered by the fourth digit.

Using this technique, we can move around the map with the addresses and find the locations of block boundaries. For example, to stay within a 1K memory (1,024 locations), you must stay within four rows of the map.

Let us consider that we are wiring up a ROM so that its addresses go from 0C00 to 0FFF hex. The first two hex digits indicate a row of the memory map. Here, the ROM occupies rows 0C, 0D, 0E and 0F. The numbers in the first row go from 0C00 to 0CFF; and the others go similarly, such that the fourth row goes from 0F00 to 0FFF. Since each row contains 256 locations, the ROM must have 1,024 locations. (This is shown in Figure 7.4.)

To address one location from the other 1,023, you need 10 bits of address, since it takes 10 bits to give that information ($2^{10} = 1,024$). Of the 16 address bits, the lower 10 to the right should be wired to the ROM's internal address lines. When this ROM chip is selected, these ten lines will indicate what location you want access to.

ROM and RAM Selection

To select the ROM chip, the remaining address lines must be wired to the ROM's chip select inputs. ROMs generally have four chip-select inputs,

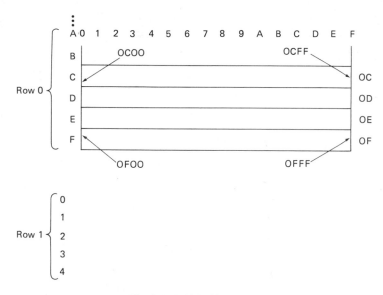

Fig. 7.4. ROM address map.

which means that some external AND gates may be required.[1] It depends on how many different devices—ROMs, RAMs, and I/O chips—you are trying to distinguish. With only four chips to control, then you need only two bits to distinguish among them 00, 01, 10, 11. You can take advantage of this by choosing the addresses in the ROMs and RAMs and using the ten least significant address bits for the locations in the ROM. For address bits A0 to A9, you would use bits A10 and A11 to distinguish among the chips: in this case, a ROM, a RAM, and two I/O chips. You would assign addresses so that bits A11 and A10 will be 00 for the RAM, 01 for one I/O chip, 10 for the other I/O chip, and 11 for the ROM. (See Figure 7.5.) When A11 and A10 are both 1's, then we have the ROM selected. The address of the starting location in the ROM is then 0000 1100 0000 0000. Converting each set of four bits to hex, we get OCOO. The ROM has 1,024 locations, so the ad-

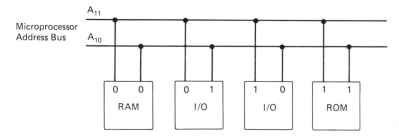

Fig. 7.5. Chip selection interface.

dresses in the ROM will go to OFFF, which is 0000 1111 1111 1111. The ten least significant bits have gone from 0's to 1's, in order to cover the 1,024 locations.

Some chip select inputs respond to 0 volts and remain unactivated at +5 volts. These are called active low inputs and designated by a bar over the pin call out such as $\overline{CS1}$. Those which are active high respond to +5 volts are called out without the bar.

In addressing other chips, we must not cause the address bits A11 through A0 to take on values in the range that would activate the ROM. If the combinations used for A11 and A10 are not used for any other device, then we cannot accidentally address the ROM. Bits A15, A14, A13, and A12 don't matter in this case because we have used just A11 and A10 to differentiate these four chips.

Since the first four bits of the address (which is the first hex digit) do not matter, the microprocessor may address one of the chips with any of 16 different first digits and it will still work the same.

ROM and RAM Addressing

We have decided that the ROM will run from 0C00 to OFFF; but the first hex digit doesn't matter, so the microprocessor could address it as 1C00 to 1FFF, or 2C00 to 2FFF. It turns out to be convenient, though, to have the microprocessor know that while the RAM is in the range from 0000 to 0100, the ROM may be in the range from 0C00 to OFFF or in the range from FC00 to FFFF.

Why should the RAM start at 0000? The programs in the ROM are always referring to data stored in the RAM, and these programs must include addresses for the data in the RAM. We would like to keep these addresses as short as possible in order to save ROM memory space. Microprocessors like the 6800 have short instructions that can save this space, if one arranges the RAM data in the first 256 locations of memory or starting at 0000.[2] Then, with these instructions, one needs only 8 bits of address stored with the instruction rather than 16.

When should the ROM start at FC00? When an interrupt occurs we want the microprocessor to stop what it's doing and begin immediately another operation. Instructions in the ROM to do this operation will begin at some other location in the ROM and the microprocessor knows where this is. In the 6800, when an interrupt occurs, the microprocessor always uses locations FFF8 and FFF9 to get the 16-bit address to tell it where to begin executing the interrupt operation. We store, in locations FFF8 and FFF9, the address of the start of the new operation, and we want to store that address in the ROM, along with the program.

But if the ROM runs from 0C00 to OFFF how can FFF8 and FFF9 be in the

ROM? Since the first digit doesn't matter because of the way the ROM is wired, the microprocessor can fetch FFF8 and FFF9 and it will get what is stored in 0FF8 and 0FF9.

We can only do this when we have extra address space.

Assume that we need only 1,288 locations: 1,024 for the ROM, 256 for the RAM and the 8 for the I/O chips. Figure 7.6 shows how we would wire up the ROM and RAM to the address bus. We leave the highest four bits of the address bus unconnected; bits A11 and A10 are the chip selects. The RAM uses A7–A0 and the ROM A9–A0.

The basic principle to remember is that the address bus is used to select a location within a component. To perform this function, two selections must be performed:

1. The device must be selected.
2. The location within the device must be selected.

Two basic techniques are used to perform the addressing function. A variety of internal decoding techniques are implemented on the devices themselves both for the chip select and for the location. From the point of view of the address bus connections, these two techniques are linear selection and decoded addressing.

Linear Selection

The linear selection technique which we have discussed uses a line of the address bus to select a component. If a system requires a 4K memory, it implies that 12 bits of the address be reserved for this function ($2^{12} = 4K$). The other 4 bits can be used as chip selects. One bit can be allocated to selecting ROM or RAM memory. In most cases, the RAM requirements are smaller than the ROM requirements. The 12 bits allocated for word selection will also pro-

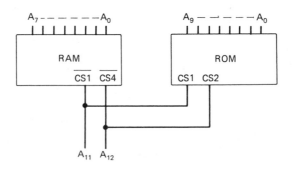

Fig. 7.6. RAM and ROM address connections.

vide the addressing for the RAM, when it is selected. This leaves a maximum of three bits available. Excluding one of the codes, such as 000, for memory selection; 7 combinations of these 3 bits can be used to address the I/O devices. Any of the 12 address bits are reused to select locations within the devices.

The limitation of this technique is the number of addressable devices, but the technique is frequently used for small systems. In a small system that requires only a small amount of memory and few I/O chips, no address decoders are required. Bits 15, 14, 13, and others of the address field are directly connected to the chip-select pin of the component. This minimizes the chip count.

If the system should ever expand, then rewiring and reprogramming are necessary as well as the addition of address decoders. Medium-sized systems can use decoding so that additional memory can be conveniently added later. This requires initially a larger number of components than is necessary for expansion later.

Another disadvantage of linear selection is a fragmenting of the address space. Each time an address line is used, the addressing space is divided by two. This results in discrete address blocks in the addressing space. The waste of memory space, however, is usually not objectionable, since it is assumed that the system does not require the full 2^{16} locations. But, since these blocks are discrete, programming may be more difficult because of the caution that must be used in addressing the various blocks. This is illustrated by the following example.

Let us allocate bit 13 to RAM selection and bit 12 to ROM selection. Then, the possible ROM addressing will be from decimal 2048 to 4095 and RAM addressing will be from decimal 4096 to 6143. If bit 14 is used to select another device, the next address will start at decimal 8192. The regions or blocks from 0 to 2047 and 6144 to 8191 are not used. They are gaps or discontinuities in the memory space which must be considered when working with the program.

Decoded Addressing

In decoded addressing, the lines are connected to a decoder which then linearly selects the components. An 8205 decoder appears in Figure 7.7.[3] It accepts three inputs and selects one of eight possible outputs. The 8205 has been widely used in 8080 systems. In Figure 7.8, it can select an 8708 ROM or a pair of 8111 RAM's which provide 8-bit words.

When a large address space is used, the required decoders become complex, although this approach is used for many minicomputers. The complexity of using the required decoders and the number of chips involved are a disadvantage with low-cost microprocessors.

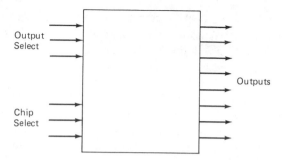

Fig. 7.7. 3-to-8 decoder chip.

Several alternatives can be used. One technique is to perform a partial decoding such as a 3-bit decoding with an 8205 and combine this with linear addressing for the other devices. Another approach uses components which are equipped with multiple chip-selects or enables. A single chip-select minimizes the number of pins on the component. Multiple chip-selects provide the address decoding within the component. If three chip-selects are provided, three lines from the address bus are directly connected to these pins. Provided that all chips connected to the system decode a different combination, then the necessity of external decoding disappears. The disadvantage is that the increased number of pins results in higher costs for the component. In the 6800 system, each device has three chip-selects or more, and a medium-sized system may be built without any decoders. For small and medium-sized systems, this approach is advantageous. Many peripheral interface chips, as well as some memories, now use multiple chip-select inputs.[4]

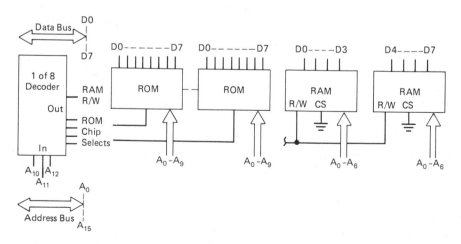

Fig. 7.8. Typical ROM-RAM memory interface.

Some memories, however, may become large and involve a large number of chips, so low chip cost may be essential. This is achieved by the smallest number of pins. Thus, single chip-selects are implemented on most general-purpose memories.

Several choices may be exercised when selecting memory. The most inexpensive memory chip minimizes the number of pins. In an 8-bit system, if 4-bit memory chips are used then two chips must be connected in parallel (as shown in Figure 7.8.) If 8-bit memory chips are used, the number of pins on the package is greater, thus resulting in a higher cost per bit, but the interconnect system is simple and the number of chips are smaller.

When there are extra chip-select inputs left over, they are connected to + 5 volts if active-high and to 0 volts if active-low. These chip select inputs are then always activated.

A RAM, in contrast to a ROM, can be both read and written into. There is an output from the microprocessor, the read/write signal (R/W) which is connected to the RAM. It is also connected to the I/O chips, since in general they may be used for both input and output without rewiring.

You may wonder why all standard memories use separate data input/output pins while microprocessors have a bidirectional data bus. The answer is that memories are standard components not intended solely for microprocessor applications. Larger computers may not always use a bidirectional data bus. Those that are equipped with separate data-in and data-out buses require separate input and output connections. The 2 pins are simply connected together for microprocessor transceivers.

Memory Unit Operation

The main memory in a computer system occupies a central position through which information passes to and from peripheral units and the CPU. A large computer system may have several CPUs and several I/O processors communicating with the memory through a bus system. The rate at which information is transferred between the various units and main memory is limited by the transfer capabilities of the memory itself and the memory bus. The transfer rate is sometimes called the memory band-width and measured in words or bits per second. The functional organization of the memory may consist of the array of cells for storing the information, an address register, and a buffer register. The data and address busses may be controlled by a memory controller. In smaller systems, the controller may only initiate a read or write signal; whereas in sophisticated systems, the memory control logic may permit the processors to operate at maximum speed with minimal interference among themselves.

A memory module may be defined as a memory array, together with an address register and a buffer register. A single module is used in small systems for economy. In large systems where speed may be of some importance, one finds it convenient to use multiple modules.

Consider a memory unit organized in four modules. Each module has its own address register and buffer register. The two most significant bits of the address distinguish between the four modules. It is the memory controller which routes the address from the bus to a specified module and transfers the data to and from a specified module and the data bus. The system is more expensive but provides higher speeds than a single-module system. The modular system allows one module to be accessed while other modules may be reading or writing a word. Each module can honor memory requests independent of the state of other modules. If an I/O processor and the CPU request data from different modules, both may be serviced as soon as the bus is available without having to wait for a memory access from an other module. Another advantage of modular memory is that it allows the use of interleaving. In an interleaved memory, consecutive addresses are in different modules. In a two-module system, all the even addresses would be in one module and all odd addresses in the other. By staggering the memory access, one reduces the effective memory cycle time by half. If instructions and operands are placed in two different modules, the instruction fetch and the reading of the operand may be interleaved. The initiation of the fetch can then occur while the operand for the previous instruction is read from another memory module.

In a multiple-bus structure, any memory module may send or receive information from several processors operating concurrently. This type of connection sometimes is called an electronic crossbar switch. The switch-points determine the path from each processor to each memory module. Each switch-point has control logic to set the path between processor and memory module. The switch-point logic examines the word on the bus to determine the particular module being addressed and establishes a linkage directing the word to the proper module. The operation of each module is independent of the operation of the other memory modules, and memory cycles may occur simultaneously within all four modules.

Some applications may require a search of items stored in memory. For example, a number may be searched in a file in order to determine a previous status. The usual way to perform such a search is to store all items so that they can be addressed in sequence. The search procedure is the strategy for choosing a sequence of addresses, reading the content of the memory at each address, and comparing the data read with the item being searched until a match occurs. Search algorithms have been developed which minimize the number of accesses while searching for an item in a random access memory. The time required to find an item stored in memory can be reduced if the stored data can be identified by the content of the data rather than by the address.

A memory accessed by content is called an associative memory or content addressable memory (CAM). This type of memory is accessed simultaneously in parallel on the basis of the data content rather than by the address or location. As a word is written in an associative memory, no address is given. The memory finds an unused location to store the word. As a word is read from an associative memory, the content or part of the word, is specified. The memory then locates all words which match the specified content. Searches may be done on an entire word or on a field within a word. Associative memory is more expensive than random access memory since each cell must contain storage as well as the logic for matching the content. Associative memories are normally used in applications where the search time is critical.

Auxiliary Memory Units

A small microcomputer with a limited application may be able to fulfill its task without the need of additional storage capacity. However, most computers run more efficiently if they are supplied with additional storage beyond the capacity of the main memory. Most computers accumulate and continue to accumulate large amounts of information. Not all the accumulated information is needed by the processor at the same time. Therefore, it is more economical to use lower cost storage devices to serve as a backup for storing the information that is not currently in use. The memory which communicates directly with the CPU is called the main memory. The devices that are used to provide the backup storage are called auxiliary memory. Auxiliary memory devices may include magnetic disks and tapes. Programs and data currently in use by the processor reside in main memory, while the other information is stored in auxiliary memory and then transferred to the main memory on a demand basis.

The total memory capacity of a computer may be visualized as a hierarchy of components that goes from the slow, but high-capacity auxiliary devices to the faster main memory. The cost per bit of storage is proportional to the memory's level in the hierarchy, for it would be expensive to maintain programs and data in the main memory during the time when they are not required by the processor. A memory management system can be used to distribute programs and data to the various levels in the hierarchy according to their expected usage. The memory management system can provide a more efficient method of transfers between levels; this tends to maximize the utilization of all components.

Common mass or auxiliary memory devices used in computer systems are magnetic disks and tape. Other memory components used infrequently, are core memories, plated wire, and laser memories. Although the physical properties of these storage devices are quite different, their system properties can be characterized by a few parameters. The important characteristics are access time, transfer rate, capacity, and cost. The average time required to reach a location in memory is called the access time. In electromechanical devices such as disks and tapes, the access time is made up of the seek time required to position the read-write head and the transfer time to transfer data to or from the device. The seek time is usually much longer than the transfer time.

Auxiliary storage is normally organized in records or blocks. A record is a specified number of characters or words. Reading or writing is done on entire records. The transfer rate is the number of characters or words that the device can transfer per second, after the head is positioned at the beginning of a record.

Magnetic Disk Units

Magnetic drums and disks are similar in operation. Both use high-speed rotating surfaces coated with a magnetic recording medium. The recording surface rotates at uniform speed and is not started or stopped during access operations. Bits are recorded as magnetic spots on the surface as it passes the write-head, and bits are detected by a change in magnetic field produced by recorded spots on the surface as it passes through the read-head. The amount of surface available on a disk is greater than in a drum of equal physical size; thus, more information can be stored on a disk than on a drum. As a result disks have replaced drums.

A disk unit is an electromechanical assembly, containing a flat disk coated with magnetic material. Both sides of the disk may be used, and several disks can be stacked on a spindle. The disks rotate together at high speed. The bits are stored on the magnetized surface in spots along concentric circles called tracks. The tracks are divided into sectors. One sector is usually the minimum quantity of information which can be transferred. The division of a disk into tracks and sectors is shown in Figure 7.9.[5] Some units use a single read-write head for each disk. In this unit, address bits are used to move the head to the specified track position before a read or write. In other systems, separate read-write heads are used for each track on each disk. The address bits then select a particular track with a decoder circuit. This unit is more expensive and is used in large systems. (See Figure 7.10)

Timing tracks are used to synchronize the bits and recognize the sectors. A disk is addressed by bits that specify the disk number, disk surface, sector number, and the track. As the read-write heads are positioned on the specified track, the system waits until the rotating disk reaches the specified sector under the head. Information transfer then starts once the beginning of a sector is reached. Some units have multiple heads for the simultaneous transfer of bits from several tracks.

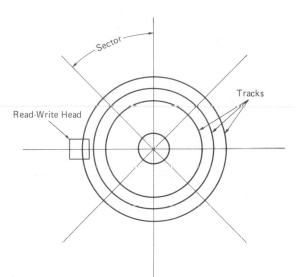

Fig. 7.9. Magnetic disk memory configuration.

Fig. 7.10. A large magnetic disk memory system with removable disks. (*Courtesy Intel Corporation.*)

A track near the circumference is longer than a track near the center of the disk. If bits are recorded with equal density, some tracks will contain more bits than others. In order to make all the records in a sector of equal length, a variable recording density may be used with a higher density on tracks near the center than on tracks near the circumference.

In some units, the disks are permanently attached to an assembly and are not meant to be removed by the user. Another type of unit called a "disk-pack" allows the disk to be removed easily. A more recent type of disk storage is the flexible or floppy disk that replaces the rigid disk. The flexible disk is made of plastic coated with a magnetic recording medium and is about the size of a 45-rpm record. The floppy disk may be inserted and removed as easily as a tape cartridge, and it is popular in microprocessor-based systems. (See Figure 7.11)

Magnetic Tape Units

A magnetic tape transport consists of the electrical and mechanical components for the control of a magnetic tape. The tape is a strip of plastic coated with a magnetic recording medium. Bits are recorded as magnetic spots on the tape along several tracks. Normally 7 or 9 bits are recorded simultaneously to form characters along with a parity bit. The read-write heads are mounted one to each track such that data is recorded or read as a sequence of characters. Magnetic-tape units may be stopped and moved forward or in reverse, but they do not start or stop fast enough between the individual characters. Thus, information is recorded in blocks called records. Gaps or unrecorded sections are inserted between the records where the tape can be stopped. The tape starts in a gap and attains a constant speed by the time it reaches a record. Each record has identification bits at the beginning and end. In reading the bits at the beginning, the tape control can identify the

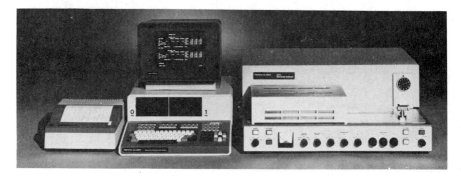

Fig. 7.11. This elemental analyzer system uses a floppy disk memory for its microprocessor. (*Courtesy Perkin-Elmer Corporation.*)

record. In reading the bits at the end of the record, the control can recognize the beginning of a gap.

The mass memories frequently used with microprocessors have been the cassette tape and the flexible or floppy disk, especially the mini- or microfloppy disks. But cassette tape is the lowest cost mass memory available. With a standard audio tape recorder, a number of programs can be stored on a standard cassette. One disadvantage is that the tape recorder must usually be operated manually. Also, it is slow and may be unreliable. It is best suited for storing programs in very small systems. Reliability may be insufficient for some needs in an industrial situation. A standard BASIC interpreter may require 30 seconds of winding time.[6]

The interface required to connect a tape recorder is simple. The connection may be through the microphone input and from the audio output using a simple buffer interface.

The most popular mass memory for microprocessors is the floppy disk or the minifloppy. The floppy disk is a soft magnetic disk that is accessed by a movable head. The disk is divided into sectors which resemble slices and tracks of concentric rings. The typical size of a data block in a sector is 128 words. A floppy typically supplies 110K bytes at 125K bits-per-second.

The drive mechanism requires a disk controller in order to be interfaced to the microprocessor system. These controllers are available on chips or boards from a variety of sources. Many systems use two disks. One reason for this is that floppy disks are typically used for files. If files are to be sorted, or merged, one must have access to two files simultaneously. Also, a dual-disk drive is only a little more expensive than a single drive, and it uses the same controller.

PARALLEL INPUT/OUTPUT TECHNIQUES

Connecting an input/output device to the system usually requires an interface. The device may also require a device-controller, and using a device connected to the microcomputer system normally requires some form of scheduling strategy.

The input/output device interface may range from a few registers or gates, to several boards. To simplify the interfacing, a number of general-purpose interface chips are available, which will be described in this section. The actual interfacing techniques for the most common input/output devices will also be considered.

Controllers are usually required for devices having complex time-dependent mechanical operation. The controller may incorporate a processor which receives instructions and also executes them. It implements the control sequence required by the I/O device and might advance a mechanical linkage, perhaps using a stepping motor in a specified number of steps.

These device controllers can range from simple circuits to complex boards. Device controllers are available in LSI chips for the most common I/O devices.

Three major types of devices can be considered: (1) input devices, (2) output devices, and (3) mass or bulk-memory devices. A common input device in microprocessor systems is a hexadecimal keyboard with 16-keys such as the one used in pocket calculators.

The most common output devices are displays, such as light-emitting diodes (LEDs) and liquid-crystal displays (LCDs). These 7-segment displays allow the display of digits from 0 through 9 and the letters A through F; they thus display each of the 16 hexadecimal digits. These are the cheapest display devices and have been used in digital watches, pocket calculators, and other low-cost applications. Each LED or LCD displays one hexadecimal digit.

Another common output device is a printer, of which one of the most common has been the standard teletype (TTY). Many other output devices are available, and the microprocessor system may be connected to any external mechanism such as relays to stepper-motors.

Larger computers have traditionally used memory-type instructions and I/O-type instructions.[7] This distinction, however, is almost obsolete in microprocessor systems.

I/O Mapping Techniques

Memory-mapped I/O is the use of memory-type instructions to access the I/O devices. A memory-mapped system allows the processor to use the same instructions for memory transfers as it does for input/output transfers. An I/O port is treated as a memory location. The advantage with this is that the same instructions that are used for reading and writing memory may be used to input and output data. The traditional computer usually had many more memory instructions than I/O instructions. In a memory-mapped I/O computer, arithmetic can be performed directly on an input or output circuit or register without having to transfer the contents in and out of temporary intermediate registers. One disadvantage, though, is that for each I/O port used in this way there is one less location available for memory. If all memory locations are needed as memory, memory-mapped I/O cannot be used. Also, instructions that operate on the memory may require three bytes to address the location of the port; whereas some I/O instructions may need only one byte to specify a port. Memory-mapped I/O instructions can also take longer to execute than I/O instructions because of the extra bytes. However, this problem can be solved by using short addressing modes.

In an I/O-mapped input/output system, the processor uses control signals to indicate that the present cycle is for input or output and not for memory. Fewer address lines are used to select the input/output ports, since the system normally needs fewer input/output ports than memory locations. One advantage to I/O-mapped input/output is that since separate I/O instructions are used, they can be distinguished from a memory-reference instruction for ease in programming. Also, with the shorter addressing, less hardware is required for decoding, and instructions are shorter and usually faster. The disadvantages are the loss of processing power and the two control pins that must be used for I/O read and I/O write. This technique is not used with most microprocessors, but the 8080 is an exception to this rule.

Figure 7.12 shows a memory-mapped input/output system in which a control signal determines if the address bits are for memory or I/O.

A basic parallel interface uses latches and bus drivers. The latches are used to hold signals from the microprocessor for as long as the external device requires them. Also, there must be a selection mechanism and read/write control for the registers or ports. Figure 7.13 shows that a simple I/O port requires the following: an input latch to hold external information until the system can read it, an output latch to hold data from the system until required, and bus buffers to receive and drive the data bus. There should also be an internal status register to indicate if there is data to be read, or if the data is to be output. although these ports can be built as shown in Figure 7.14 from SSI devices, other components are available in lower cost, higher integration packages.

Programmable Input/Output Devices

These programmable parallel LSI input/output devices can perform the following functions: address decoding, data input/output buffering,

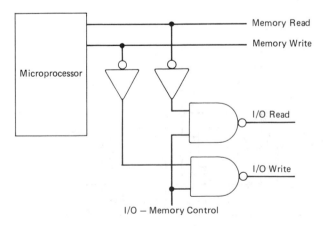

Fig. 7.12. Memory-mapped I/O configuration.

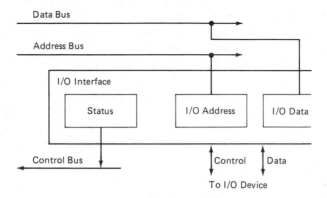

Fig. 7.13. I/O port requirements.

multiplexing, generating status signals for handshaking, and other control functions.

The selection of the input/output interface chips for addressing purposes is accomplished exactly in the same way as for memory which has been described. The selection of registers within the chips is done using the address bus, in the same way as addressing a memory location. For a chip with up to eight internal registers, three pins will normally be provided for inter-

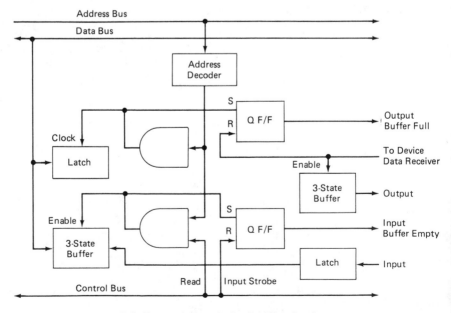

Fig. 7.14. Typical strobed I/O bidirectional port.

nal register selection. These signals are internally decoded to select one of the registers, which are connected to the address bus. An internal address decoder will select the internal registers to be read or written into. The registers may be an input latch, output latch, direction register, or status register. Three address bits in addition to the chip select are used.

There are three basic general-purpose I/O interfaces.

1. The nonprogrammable hardware interface performs the basic bus-interface functions and includes some interrupt-request control logic. It operates as a parallel I/O port.

2. The hardware programmable interface includes the decoding logic, addressable parallel I/O ports, and interrupt-control logic. External wiring determines the address, data direction, and width of each port and controls the operations.

3. The general-purpose interface that we are discussing is software-programmable. The software determines how the interface is structured and operates from the contents of a control register, loaded by the program. The interface also includes another control register, the data-direction register, which allows the function of individual I/O lines to be selected by software.

The programmable input/output interface chip or parallel input/output chip is not an industry standard. No standard has been established for these devices. The manufacturers may use other names for these devices, such as PIA, PPI, and PDC. PIO is used here to designate this general class of programmable input/output devices. One should be aware, though, of the differences that will be found in the manufacturers' literature.

A PIO is a programmable interface device which provides the basic input and output interface for parallel data. In order to connect an input or output device to a microprocessor data bus, it is necessary to provide latches for input and latches for outputs. The input latches will keep the data valid long enough for the microprocessor to read the data. It also isolates the signals from the bus. The output latches will hold the output data long enough for the output device to use it. For example, data presented on a typical bus is valid for less than 500 nanoseconds. This is not long enough for most input/output devices to make use of it. The status of these registers must also be available to affect handshaking communications. Before reading the contents of an input buffer or register, the microprocessor must be sure that the contents are valid. A status bit is supplied, or an interrupt is sent to the microprocessor. This denotes if the output buffer is full or empty so that the microprocessor can determine if it can output the next word. It may also be required for the output devices to determine if they can use the contents of the buffer or register.

The general-purpose parallel I/O interface thus requires at least one input register, one output register, status bits, and some interrupt control. Eight lines are usually not sufficient for most applications; the typical applications require 16 to 24 I/O lines. The general-purpose interface chip, therefore, provides several channels. The channel, which is also called a port, is an 8-bit connection which can be used as inputs or as outputs.

The PIO uses the data-direction register. With this register, it is possible, on a bit-by-bit basis, to define a port as having bits that are configured as inputs and outputs in any combination—each bit of the data-direction register specifies if the corresponding bit of the PIO port will be an input or an output. A zero in the data-direction register specifies an input, while a one specifies an output. The PIO also has one or more command registers which may specify the configuration of the ports and the operation of control logic. The PIO multiplexes its connection to the microprocessor data bus into 2 or more 8-bit-ports. The maximum is 3, including the control lines for the I/O device, with a 40-pin package. (A typical PIO appears in Figure 7.15.) This device has two ports, each with its own direction register and a status or mode register to indicate the status of each port.[8]

We have been considering standard PIO devices. The main differences between the PIO and the usual standard interfaces is that the PIO is programmable and contained on a single chip. The control logic is program-

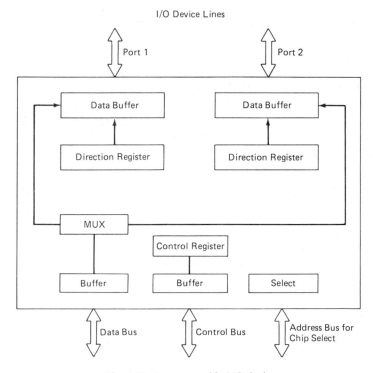

Fig. 7.15. Programmable I/O device.

mable for each port. Thus, the user can specify which line will be used for handshaking, the direction in which it will be used, and perhaps its function. The control logic can also specify when a device signal will trigger interrupts.

Each data line or group of data lines for a port is programmable as to direction and may be defined as an input. This is almost never done in a traditional hardware interface, and this feature makes the PIO a general-purpose interface device that can be used in almost any situation, since it is possible to connect any combination of input and output lines to the same PIO or group of PIOs. One can build an interface with PIOs, which can interface to almost any system or device.

Three types of registers are used in a PIO interface: (1) the data registers, (2) the direction registers, and (3) the control registers. The data registers accumulate the data for inputs or outputs on each of the I/O lines. The direction registers configure the lines as an input or an output. Zero is normally used for an input and one for an output. (This is done for safety; when the system is initialized, the contents of all the registers are normally reset to zero. During system startup, spurious signals might be generated. Thus, if any signals are present on the I/O lines, the lines would be configured as input to the microprocessor rather than as outputs to devices.) The control register stores the command bits issued by the microprocessor for the port. For each port, the microprocessor will specify if interrupts are to be generated and which control signals will be used by the port. Whenever a data buffer is full or empty, a status bit in a control register is set or reset. To use the PIO, the microprocessor executes two basic operations:

1. It leads the control registers to specify the mode in which the control signals will operate.
2. It loads the direction registers to specify the direction in which the lines of the ports will be used.

This is done for every port in the interface. A data transfer will then be performed by a transfer instruction, such as a MOV instruction in the case of the 8080. But two problems remain: (1) how the data is to be transmitted to the internal PIO registers and (2) how the registers are to be selected. The data transmitted by the microprocessor appears on the data bus, while the data to be loaded in the various PIO registers is placed on the data bus and a register select is performed. This is accomplished by providing an address on the address bus. At least one bit must be used to select the chip and allow the selection of eight possible registers.

So the microprocessor selects one of the PIO internal registers with the appropriate pattern on the address bus and then supplies the eight data bits to be transferred into one of these registers via the data bus. The multiplexer in the PIO gates the 8-bit data to the register. Our PIO is now ready to be used.

The microprocessor must provide the signal for selecting the data buffer register and generate the read signal on the control bus. For a write operation, it will supply a write signal on the control bus. To read the status from the PIO, the contents of the control register are read. After the PIO has been configured (its control and direction registers loaded) no changes are necessary, and the microprocessor communicates with the data buffers with a single instruction.

It is predicted that the power of PIOs will increase with more programmed functions. LSI evolution is towards more integration thus supplying more functions per chip. Future PIOs will be equipped with processors in order to provide them with local processing capabilities. This trend is already occurring with some of the newer 16-bit microprocessors that use input/output processors, such as the 8086.

Let's consider now, how to use a typical PIO interface chip. Assume that we desire to connect three L.E.D. display digits. We might use three I/O chips, one for each digit. There are a number of different kinds of chips one may use for this purpose and whichever one is chosen, it will have certain characteristics that set it apart from other chips.

Using the 6800 Interface Chip

The PIO chips for use with the 6800 are 6820 peripheral interface adapters, or PIA's.[9] Each 6820 PIA is a double I/O chip with two sets of eight lines (as shown in Figure 7.16). In the case of three digits, we need one-and-a-half

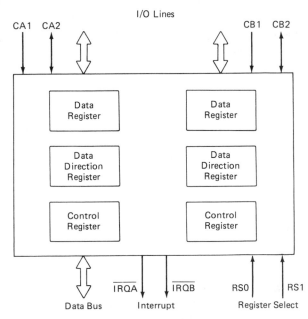

Fig. 7.16. 6820 PIA.

PIAs to service the display, even though the other half is not used, which is typical with microcircuits.

Each PIA has two data registers—or peripheral registers as they are called. One is used for each set of input/output lines. There are also two other registers used with each peripheral register, which results in a total of six for each PIA.

The PIA has a data direction register to control the directions of the input/output lines. One data direction register has eight bits, one for each input/output line.

The control register format is shown in Figure 7.17. Bit 7 indicates a transition of the CA1 input and it is used as an interrupt flag. Bit 6 monitors the CA2 input. Bits 5, 4 and 3 establish the eight different modes of the device and the function of the CA2 pin. Bit 2 indicates if the direction register or data register is to be selected. Bits 1 and 0 are the interrupt enable/disable control bits.

The PIA has 6 registers and only two register select (RS) pins. The data and data direction registers in each port share the same address. They differ by the value of bit 2 of the control register, which can be a source of programming errors. The following table indicates how the registers are selected by use of the RS1 and RS0 pins and the state of the internal bit 2 of the control register.

RS1	RS0	CRA BIT 2	CRB BIT 2	REGISTER
0	0	0	—	Data Direction A
0	0	1	—	Data Buffer A
0	1	—	—	Control A
1	0	—	0	Data Direction B
1	0	—	1	Data Buffer B
1	1	—	—	Control B

Since the PIA cannot drive a heavily loaded data bus, it is sometimes necessary to buffer the data bus to this chip. (This can be done as shown in Figure 7.18.) The 6800 microcomputer (see Figure 7.19) uses three PIAs for 60 I/O lines which are buffered.

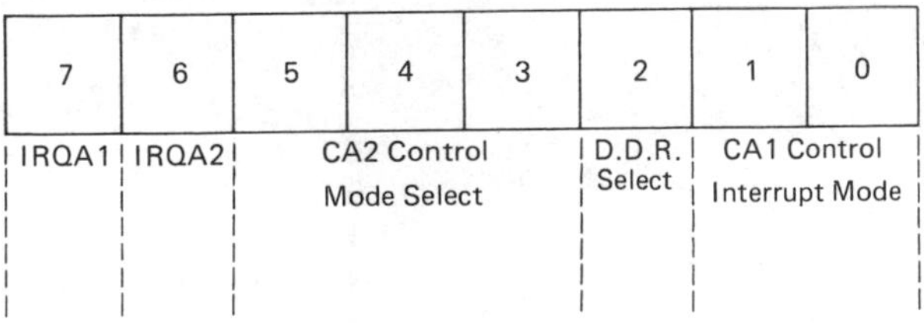

7	6	5	4	3	2	1	0
IRQA1	IRQA2	CA2 Control Mode Select			D.D.R. Select	CA1 Control Interrupt Mode	

Fig. 7.17. 6820 control register.

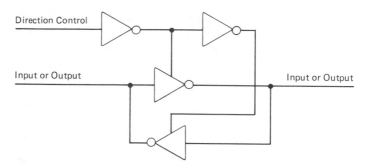

Fig. 7.18. Bidirectional buffer.

SERIAL INTERFACE

Some I/O devices accept the data over a single signal wire and a ground wire in bit-serial format. Usually seven bits representing the digits are sent one bit at a time, in synchronism with a clock signal that the device provides.

A serial I/O port consists of two single-bit serial-data busses linked to the serial-input and serial-output lines of a shift register which is usually 16 bits

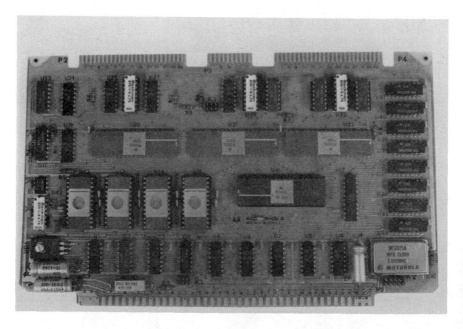

Fig. 7.19. This 6800 microcomputer includes power reset circuitry, RAM, ROM, and three PIAs. (*Courtesy Siltran Digital.*)

long. The shift register is loaded or read via parallel input and output lines and shifted one bit at a time under software control. The serial I/O port is often used as a simple asynchronous serial-data communications interface for a teleprinter. The shift register performs parallel-to-serial and serial-to-parallel code conversions under program control.

UART Chips

Microprocessor manufacturers commonly provide special I/O chips for this task such as a UART (Universal Asynchronous Receiver Transmitter). The UART converts the serial input into a parallel output and may simultaneously convert a parallel input to serial output. These asynchronous devices are normally used for low-to medium-speed applications. The main function of the UART is serial/parallel conversion (as shown in Figure 7.20). On the left of the UART, a digital signal appears as a sequence of 0's and 1's. The device output appears on the right of the UART. This output is supplied on eight parallel bits. One question, however, arises: how does the UART know that there are three zeroes or ones in succession rather than one of them? The answer is that it uses the timing supplied by an external clock, which is always supplied from the outside. The clock must be synchronized with the serial signal. One pulse of the clock (a half-period) will identify the presence and duration of a bit. Three successive clock pulses then identify three zeroes or ones in sequence in the input signal. With the two input signals, the receiver portion of the UART can assemble an 8-bit word and output it on its 8-bit port to the data bus. The UART will also accept an 8-bit input signal from the microprocessor data bus and serialize it onto an output line, using the clock supplied by the external device. The receiver and the transmitter sections are independent (as shown in Figure 7.21).

UARTs were among the first LSI chips to be standardized, so most UARTs are essentially identical. Some manufacturers have added features or merged several devices into one in order to adapt them to their microprocessor.[10] Except for speeds, the characteristics are essentially the

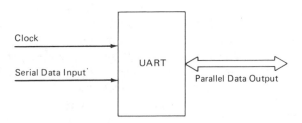

Fig. 7.20. UART receiver operation.

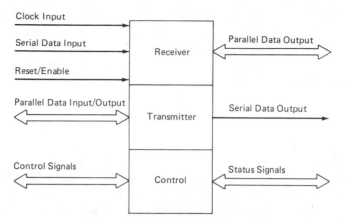

Clock Input

Serial Data Input

Reset/Enable

Receiver

Parallel Data Output

Parallel Data Input/Output

Transmitter

Serial Data Output

Control Signals

Control

Status Signals

Fig. 7.21. UART functions.

same. These standard UARTs have three sections: (1) a receiver, (2) a transmitter, and (3) a control section (as shown in Figure 7.21). The receiver takes the serial input and clock and supplies a parallel 8-bit output as we have discussed. The transmitter section receives an 8-bit parallel input along with a clock and supplies a serial output. The control section receives the control signals from the microprocessor and implements the required operations. It also supplies the status and control outputs to the microprocessor.

The UART can also provide a number of standard functions. It can manage the start and stop bits and verify the correct transmission of data, using parity. In an 8-bit serial transmission, each 8-bit character may be framed by a start bit and two stop bits. The UART can then strip the characters from its start and stop bits and retain only the 8-bit data. During transmission, it adds the required start and stop bits to the output data stream.

Parity is an extra bit which is used to verify the correct transmission of the data, by adding an extra bit to a 7-bit code in order to detect when a bit may have changed. The number of 1's in the 7-bit word is counted. If this number is odd, and we are using even parity, the parity bit is 1. If the parity were odd, the parity bit would be 0. Thus, with even parity, the total number of 1's contained in an 8-bit word is even. If any of the eight bits change during transmission, a parity detecting circuit will detect this. This scheme detects single-bit errors. More sophisticated techniques are used for detecting multiple-bit errors. The single-bit scheme, however, solves most of the problems normally encountered in transmission, and it is the one most often used. The UART can implement parity detection or generation if required, using the appropriate control word; it can implement odd or even parity.

The length of a word handled by the UART may be 5, 6, 7, or 8 bits. Stop bits may be 1, 2, or $1\frac{1}{2}$ for a 5-bit code.

Using the 6800 UART

In the case of the 6800, the UART chip is called an Asynchronous Communications Interface Adapter, or ACIA.[11] The ACIA operates by placing the 8-bit byte into a shift register. Then the bits are shifted one bit at a time each time the register is shifted. The shifting is done in synchronism with a clock, which can come from the device or one that is generated locally.

The ACIA also has a data register to accept the 8-bit byte from the microprocessor data bus and store it until the shift register is ready for it. This tends to smooth out the transmission rate of the bits. While the shift register is shifting, the data register can accept the next eight bits. When the shift register finishes, the movement of data from the data register to the shift register is done by the chip to keep the bits flowing in an uninterrupted manner.

The ACIA has other registers, which use the data bus to and from the microprocessor. To save pins, the commands are given to the chip by transmitting control bits into a register in the ACIA.

Since the ACIA receives and transmits on separate wires, it has two shift registers, each of which has its own data register. One is used for receiving and the other one for sending (as shown in Figure 7.22).

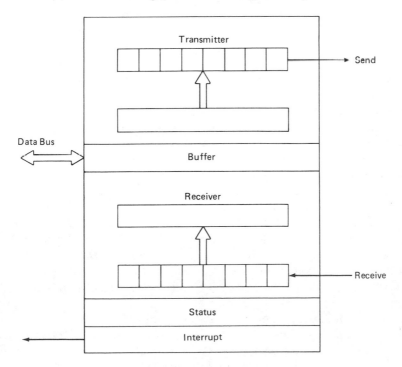

Fig. 7.22. ACIA functions.

There is also the control register and a status register, which holds information about the status of the transmissions and is then read by the microprocessor. There is also an interrupt signal with which the chip may interrupt the microprocessor; an external source may use this signal when it wants to send data to the ACIA to be sent on to the microprocessor.

When the microprocessor reads the status register, it does so by selecting the chip and setting the register select lines into the chip. It is usually looking for either a message that the transmit-data register is empty and needs another byte from the microprocessor or that the receive register is full and has a byte that the microprocessor can read. The messages are bits in the status register. The rightmost bit (bit 0) is labeled receive-data register full, while bit 1 is labeled transmit-data register empty.

In the case where the microprocessor has to send three bytes of information to the ACIA, it would send the first byte, then keep checking the status register until the transmit-data register empty bit becomes a 1, indicating that the first byte has been transferred to the transmit-shift register and that the second byte can now be sent to the transmit-data register.

If the I/O device is slow, we might program a loop that continually reads the status register in the ACIA until it comes back with the empty message.

If there is another register in the I/O device, the transfer may be done in a short time. Two other signals called "request to send" from the ACIA to the device and "clear to send" from the device to the ACIA are provided for improved communications. The ACIA monitors these signals and will not attempt to send bits unless it knows that the device on the other end is ready.

The ACIA chip also checks for certain error conditions. If the data being received has a parity bit with each byte, the ACIA can check if one of the bits in the byte was lost. The ACIA can also add parity bits to outgoing bytes as well as check incoming bytes. The sum can be even or odd parity, and the number of bits per byte can be selected to be seven or eight.

Along with the byte that the ACIA transmits or expects to receive come either one or two stop bits. These are at the end of the byte and are included according to the device standards. Some devices require one stop bit, while others need two. This is selected by the bits sent to the control register.

The bits in the control register are also used for enabling or disenabling interrupts from the ACIA to the microprocessor when the transmit-data register empty condition occurs and for the operation of the request-to-send signal to the device on the other end. One may also set the ACIA chip to expect a data bit, when receiving, every time a clock pulse arrives from the other device, every 16 clock pulses, or every 64 pulses. The control register bits can also initiate a master reset, clearing all the registers. To select the ACIA, two chip-select inputs are used. To select one of the four registers inside the ACIA, there is a register-select line, which distinguishes the registers into two groups of two: (1) a high selects the transmit-receive data registers and (2) a low selects the control-status registers. Selecting the register out of the pair is done with the read/write line which selects the read-only or the write-only register.

USART Chips

The Intel 8241 USART is both a UART as well as a USRT (Universal Synchronous Receiver Transmitter).[12] Thus, it can be used in either an asynchronous or synchronous mode. In most designs, the system will be either synchronous or asynchronous. (The organization of the 8251 device appears in Figure 7.23.) The functional blocks shown in the figure are the transmitter section, the receiver section, and the control section. The data bus buffer communicates with the other sections. The connections to the microprocessor are on the left side. The connections to the peripherals are on the right side. There are two signals per I/O function: (1) a data line and (2) a clock signal. There is also a synchronization line for the synchronous mode. In 8251 is selected by the CS signal gated at the bottom. When CS is 1, the 8251 device is selected. It can receive four commands from the microprocessor, which appear below:

C/D	RD	WR	CS	Operation or Mode
0	0	1	0	8251 to Data Bus (Read)
0	1	0	0	Data Bus to 8251 (Write)
1	0	1	0	Status to Data Bus (Read)
1	1	0	0	Data Bus to Control (Write)
—	—	—	1	Data Bus to Buffer

These commands read or write the data bus buffer, read the status, or write a control word into the control section.

A typical application of the 8251 in the asynchronous mode appears in Figure 7.24. In this system, the UART reads serial information from a keyboard and sends display information to a CRT. A baud rate generator is used to supply the clock pulses. The slowest mode of operation is normally 110 baud (where a baud is a bit-per-second). Most CRT controllers use a baud-rate generator, where the rate may be selected from 110 baud to 9,600 baud. The main applications for the UART mode are for communications with devices such as a teletype, a printer, or modem connected to a telephone line.

In the synchronous mode, the device might be connected to a modem for communications with another computer. Synchronous transmission is characterized by the transmission of blocks of data at high speeds. In the asynchronous mode, 8251 operates up to 9.6K bauds, whereas in the synchronous mode, it operates up to 56K bauds.

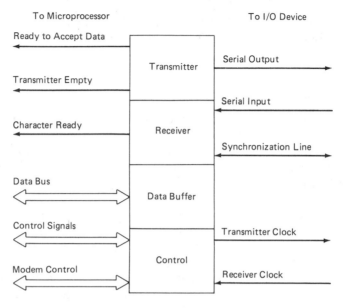

Fig. 7.23. 8251 USART.

INTERFACE SCHEDULING TECHNIQUES

As the input/output device is connected to the system using the interface, a communication procedure must be established between the I/O device and the microprocessor. Three basic scheduling techniques are used for controlling input/output devices. These three techniques are considered in this section. The three basic ways to control and synchronize data transfers are:

1. Polled or programmed I/O.
2. Interrupt-controlled I/O.
3. Direct-memory-access I/O.

The one which is used depends on three factors:

1. The rate at which that the data must be transmitted.
2. The maximum time delay between the I/O device signal to transmit or receive and the actual data transfer.
3. The feasibility of interleaving input/output with other operations.

Polled or Programmed I/O

Polled or programmed I/O is the simplest technique. With this procedure, I/O devices are connected to the system bus; they may also have to be con-

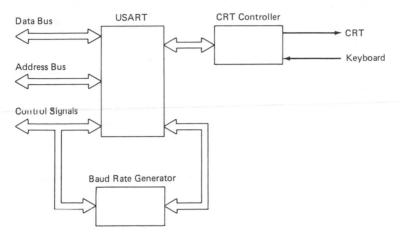

Fig. 7.24. USART CRT control.

nected to some control lines. The principle, though, is to implement a procedure for determining the next input/output device that requires service. The polling technique is a synchronous technique. The microprocessor periodically asks each device connected to the data bus if it requires service. Each device answers with a yes or no. When a no is received, the microprocessor proceeds to the next device and asks it. The microprocessor thus calls each I/O device successively in order to determine if service is required. In actual practice, a status flag is tested on the device or its interface. If the test is true, action is initiated. This is usually the transfer of a word or block of data to or from the device.

The software used to implement the polling algorithm is sometimes called a polling loop. The process of asking the device and receiving information in return is called handshaking. The communications protocol between one device and the next one on a link normally uses some form of handshaking. Before transmitting information to the device, a status bit is checked to test if the device is ready to accept data. Before reading a word from a device, a status bit is checked to test if the word is complete. (The concept structure of a polling loop appears in Figure 7.25.)

Using program-controlled I/O, the input/output instructions are used to initiate and control the transfer of the data. Two basic types of information control data. Message data are transmitted between the microcomputer and the I/O device. The control data synchronizes the I/O device with the program execution before the message data is transmitted. The input control data are the device-status words, and the output control data are the device-command words.

The status words describe what the I/O device is doing. Each status bit in-

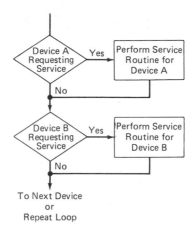

Fig. 7.25. Basic polling technique.

dicates a certain condition, such as message data ready for transmission, device busy, or transmission error.

The command words control the device operation. A command bit may function to stop a motor or change the transmission rate.

The I/O program instructions may be organized in several ways. For example, a unique instruction might be provided for each type of I/O data transfer. This might take four instructions:

1. Read the input message data.
2. Write the output message data.
3. Send the output command word.
4. Accept the input status word.

One might also use two I/O instructions—one for input and one for output—to transfer the message and control data. Two device addresses can be used to differentiate between the message and control-data transmissions. These could be READ DATA for the message data or status word and WRITE DATA for either the message data or command word.

Another technique uses memory data transfer instructions to communicate with the I/O devices. Here, a block of unused memory addresses serves as device addresses. This memory-mapped I/O approach shrinks the available memory-address area, but it may reduce program-storage requirements and execution times in some cases. The memory instructions would be LOAD DATA (input message data or status word), and STORE DATA (output message data or command word). Message and control data are usually sent or received through a working register. Some microprocessors have special-purpose registers for the control data, or use a status register. With a status register, the conditional branch instructions can check the status register's individual bits directly.

The control data can synchronize the data transfer with the following steps:

1. The command word is written to the device.
2. The status word is read from the device.
3. The appropriate status bits are tested to check if the message data can be transferred to the device.
4. If the device is not ready for the transfer, the first two steps are repeated until it is.
5. The message data is read or rewritten. This step resets the status of the device.

When the data transfer originates from the I/O device itself, the device indicates its need to transfer data by setting the correct status bits.

In the basic program, the status check is repeated continuously until the device is ready. This loop effectively stalls the program execution and can thereby use too much processing time. To avoid this, one can interleave the status check with other microprocessor operations (as shown in Figure 7.26).

In a microcomputer system that communicates with several I/O devices, periodic status checks must be made on each device. But these checks or pollings can result in considerable time lags between the time a device indicates that it's ready to transfer the data and the actual transfer. In some systems,

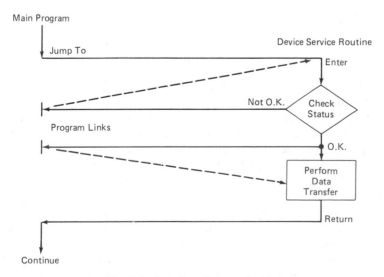

Fig. 7.26. Interleaved status checking.

however, the time spent checking device status can be reduced by using a common test line, which signals when a device requires attention. The microprocessor periodically checks the status of this line without having to poll individual devices until one of them signals for service. The advantages of polling are:

1. It requires minimal hardware for the interface; usually no special lines are required.
2. It is synchronous with program execution. One can predict when a device will be interrogated and how long it will take to service it. No events can occur that would tend to disrupt the scheduled polling sequence. By contrast, the other two techniques—interrupts and DMA—are asynchronous.

The main disadvantage of polling is the software overhead. Each time that a polling loop is entered, all the devices are checked. In general, most of them will not require service. Yet to guarantee that each device is checked within a specified period, the entire loop is executed, even though this may be needless. This waste of processor time may require the use of one of the other techniques. Nevertheless, when this use of microprocessor time is not objectionable, polling is the simplest technique to use, for the predictability of the order in which devices are polled is a major programming advantage.

Polling is normally advised for all programs that do not require an interrupt-driven design. If a complex interrupt structure is needed in the system, another design approach should be considered before implementation.

Interrupt-controlled I/O

When the polling technique does not provide a fast enough response, or uses too much microprocessor time, interrupts can be considered. In the interrupt-driven scheme, the devices have the initiative for requesting service. An extra line is used as an interrupt line which is connected to the MPU, and each of the devices is connected to this line. Every one of the devices wishing to get service has the option of using this line to request service. A device that requests service generates an interrupt pulse or level on this line. The microprocessor then detects the presence of interrupts on the line and manages them.

The microprocessor must accept the interrupt, identify it, and service it. Accepting this interrupt is implemented with an internal mask bit called an interrupt mask, interrupt-inhibit, or interrupt-enable. This bit is normally stored in the flag or status register. After an interrupt is accepted, the microprocessor must determine which device originated the interrupt. Also, several devices might generate interrupts simultaneously. For this reason, when multiple devices are connected to the same interrupt line, priorities must be assigned. (This problem will be considered shortly.) Once the interrupt has been accepted and the device identified, the service requested by the device must be performed. The microprocessor will suspend the program that it was executing and branch to an interrupt handling routine or handler. When the required branching address is available, the interrupt is presented to the microprocessor; it is called a vectored interrupt. Execution of the interrupt handler is similar to what happens in a polling system. Upon the termination of the handler, the program which has been suspended by the interrupt is installed again. This requires several instructions.

Usually when an interrupt-controlled I/O device is ready to transfer data, it may break into the main program. The simplest interrupt system has a single I/O device connected to a single interrupt-request line. A signal on this line causes the microcomputer to jump from the main program to a location in program memory called the interrupt-trap address. This happens provided that:

1. The current instruction is executed.
2. The current contents of the program counter are stored in the stack.
3. The program counter is loaded with the proper program memory address.

Since only one I/O device can generate interrupts, its service routine for the data transfer is loaded into memory starting at the interrupt-trap address (as shown in Figure 7.27). After completion of the routine, the previously stored contents of the program counter provide the return address back to the main program. Interrupts are inhibited before the service routine starts, to prevent multiple interruptions by the same interrupt-request. In some systems, the instruction for the jump back to the main program also re-enables the interrupts. The interrupts are inhibited by setting a mask bit in the microprocessor, which is most often a part of the microprocessor's status register and may be set or reset by the program. The mask bit may be used to prevent the interruption of certain sections of a program that must be executed before the next input/output operations occur.

Indirect-addressing links allow the service program to be located at an arbitrary position in the program memory. If the interrupt-trap address is in a read/write memory, one may change the program entry point while the main program is going so as to vary the response of the system to the interrupt.

The service interrupt and a jump to a subroutine both cause the contents of the program counter to be saved and then restored in order to allow the return to the main program. The service program can modify the main program execution if it uses and modifies any registers of the microprocessor.

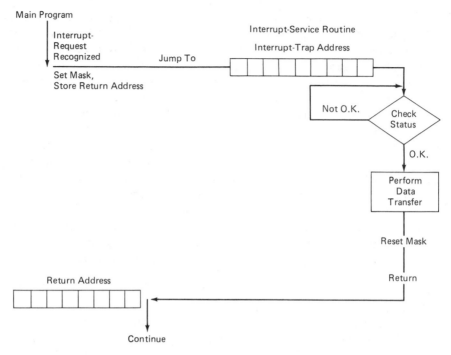

Fig. 7.27. Interrupt-controlled input/output.

The program must save and restore the contents of these registers so that they will be the same after the interrupt.

The more registers used this way, the longer the interrupt-response time. More rapid response is achieved by microcomputers designed to facilitate interrupts. Some have two sets of internal registers. The main program uses one set while the service program uses the other set. Other microcomputers use locations in data memory to replace some of the internal registers.[13] A pointer inside the register defines the memory locations. The system will store and modify the contents of the pointer before executing the service program; thus it uses a workspace that differs from that used by the main program. After the service program is complete, the pointer register is restored.

The input/output operation may be required to occur at a particular instant or period within an interval. The operation of the I/O device and the execution of the program controlling the data transfer must then be synchronized in real time. To synchronize the I/O device with the program, one can connect an external pulse generator to the interrupt-request line. The program is interrupted periodically at a known time space between the interrupts. The microprocessor then counts the interrupt requests and controls the data flow. This real-time clock may be a high-frequency crystal oscillator feeding into a chain of frequency dividers. Programmable clock chips, which allow software to control the interrupt rate can also be used.[14]

An example of a real-time application is an on-line data-acquisition system using a microprocessor-controlled multichannel analog-to-digital converter. The flow shown in Figure 7.28 illustrates the program operation during data collection. Device-status and command words for the A/D converter and clock might be as shown on top of page 322.

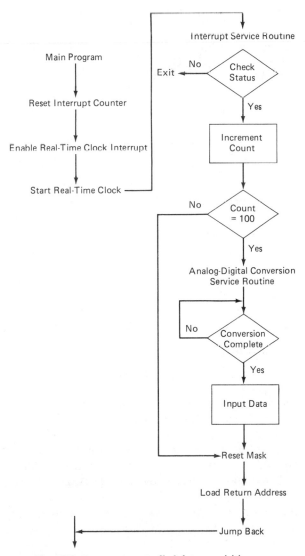

Fig. 7.28. Interrupt-controlled data acquisition.

A/D CONVERTER—

Device Status Word
CONVERSION COMPLETE   Bit 1

Device Command Word
CHANNEL NUMBER   Bits 1–4
START CONVERSION   Bit 5

REAL–TIME CLOCK—

Device Status Word
INTERRUPT STATUS BIT   Bit 1

Device Command Word
ENABLE INTERRUPT LOGIC   Bit 1
START CLOCK   Bit 2

The simplest interrupt-servicing procedure thus considered only applies when a single device is generating interrupts. Many systems may have more than one source and more than one type of interrupt. The three main types of interrupts are as follows:

1. External interrupts generated from one or more devices.
2. Internal interrupts generated by the microcomputer system to indicate certain conditions or errors such as power failure, system malfunctions, or transmission errors.
3. Simulated interrupts generated by software for use in program debugging or interrupt testing.

The different sources of interrupts may have different service requirements. Some may require immediate attention, while others will wait until the task underway is completed. The interrupt procedure must then:

1. Differentiate between these various sources.
2. Determine the order in which interrupts are serviced when more than one occurs at the same time.
3. Save and restore the contents of registers in order to assure that the program will continue following multiple interrupts.

Some systems use several interrupt-request lines, each with its own interrupt-trap address. If one source of interrupt is assigned to each line, the system can differentiate between internal, external, and simulated interrupts.

When several I/O devices use the same interrupt-request line, the interrupt can be recognized either by polling with software, or by vectored interrupts using hardware.[15]

In polling, as we have seen, the interrupt causes a jump to the service program using the interrupt-trap address. The service program checks the status word of each I/O device in order to determine which one caused the interrupt. (Figure 7.29 shows the flow of a interrupt-service program for two I/O devices.) The interrupt status bit indicates if a device has generated an interrupt request. This bit is checked for each device. The device status word is read into the status register of the microprocessor. If the bit is set, a jump is then made to the service program.

In a vectored-interrupt system, the microprocessor recognizes the interrupting device, since each I/O device is assigned a unique interrupt address. This address is then used to generate an interrupt-trap address for the device. The trap addresses are usually located sequentially in program memory to form the interrupt vector. Each location contains the starting address of a device-service program. The contents of the interrupt vector are loaded into the program counter, and program control is transferred to the correct device-service program.

Instead of transmitting an address, some vectored systems use an I/O device to transmit a single-byte instruction to the microprocessor after the request has been acknowledged. The interrupt-control logic loads the instruction code into the instruction register. Normal operation continues after this instruction is executed. Vectoring is achieved by a single-byte jump

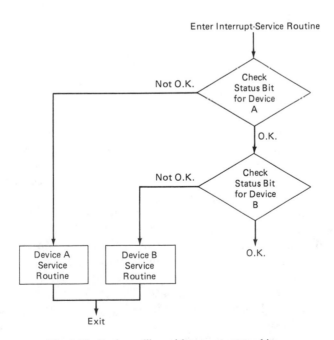

Fig. 7.29. Device polling with separate status bits.

instruction that derives the jump address from a part of the instruction code.[16] A unique jump address is defined for each I/O device in the system.

In systems with several sources of interrupt, one or more interrupt requests may occur during the servicing of an earlier request. In simple systems, the interrupt-mask bit is set when the first request is recognized. Subsequent requests are placed in a queue, waiting until the service of the first interrupt is complete before they are recognized and serviced. The order in which the queued interrupts are recognized determines the time delay before service. This order, or priority, is dictated either by software or by hardware with software priority. After recognizing an interrupt request, the service program can poll the devices in an order which determines the interrupt priority of each device. The devices polled first are serviced first.

In systems with hardware priority, interrupt-control logic sends an external signal to the request logic in each of the I/O devices. The signal, which reflects the state of the interrupt-mask bit, is passed to each device in turn. If the mask is set, this signal prevents all devices from generating interrupt requests. If the mask is reset and a device has no interrupt request pending, the signal passes on to the next device. At a device waiting for interrupt service, the interrupt logic in the device generates the interrupt request and prevents the signal from passing on. When more than one device requires interrupt service, the device receiving the control signal first is serviced first.

Both software and hardware priority schemes, however, are slow to respond to a high-priority interrupt when it occurs during the servicing of a low-priority interrupt. Software control priority can be used with individual interrupt-mask bits for each interrupt-request line or each I/O device. By setting and resetting the individual mask bits under program control, the interrupt priorities may be changed during program execution.

Some microprocessors have one interrupt-request line with software-controlled mask bits and another that is permanently enabled.[17] The nonmaskable interrupt-request line has the highest priority, and it is used when service is required immediately, for example, after a power failure is detected.

In some vectored systems, the priorities are defined and controlled by the microprocessor. After an interrupt request occurs, it is transmitted to the microprocessor and the address is compared with a multibit interrupt-enabling mask. If the address is equal or less than the mask, the request is recognized. The mask is then forced to one less than the address, and servicing begins. If the address is greater than the mask, the request is queued. In this scheme, only interrupts from a device with an address lower than that of the device being serviced are recognized. Therefore, the lower the address, the higher the priority (as shown in Figure 7.30). The interrupts are nested for rapid service of high-priority interrupts even if they occur when a low-priority interrupt is being serviced.

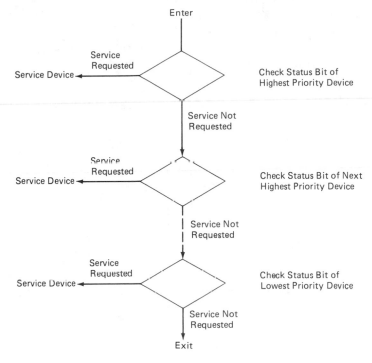

Fig. 7.30. Software priority interrupt system.

Direct-Memory-Access I/O

Some I/O devices must transfer large amounts of data too quickly to be controlled by a microprocessor. In this case, information can be transferred directly between the device and the memory of the microprocessor system using direct-memory-access (DMA). The transfer is controlled by a DMA controller, a dedicated circuit or chip that can operate independently of the microprocessor. In a DMA data transfer, the DMA controller takes over the control of the microprocessor memory in one of several ways. For example, an external control line can stop the microprocessor after the current instruction is completed (as shown in Figure 7.31). The microprocessor memory-control signals are disabled, and the DMA controller initiates the data transfer. After the DMA transfer is completed, the controller resets the halt line and the microprocessor resumes execution of the next memory-access instruction.

Cycle stealing uses external control lines to initiate a pause in a microprocessor operation by suspending instruction execution within the instruction cycle. The microprocessor clock is halted and its memory control lines are disabled. The controller takes over and steals several machine cycles

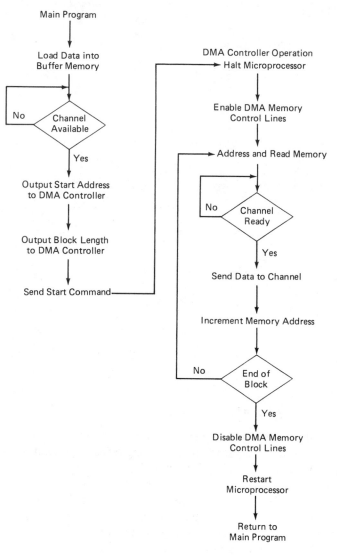

Fig. 7.31. DMA control.

for the data transfer. After the transfer, the control lines are reset, the clock restarts and the microprocessor continues executing the instruction. In effect, the instruction execution is delayed by the DMA.

Microprocessors using dynamic memory may restrict the number of machine cycles that may be stolen so that status is not lost. Input or output of a long block of data may require several separate DMA operations. Another alternative is memory sharing; here, the microprocessor accesses the memory only at certain times during the machine cycle. This leaves the memory available for other devices at the other times. By synchronizing the DMA controller operation with the processor clock, the DMA data can be transferred within the machine cycle. This interleaved DMA reduces the delay of the microprocessor. (A DMA controller is shown in Figure 7.32.)

INTERFACE SCHEDULING CHIPS

We have seen that supplying an input or output facility requires, at the minimum, a latch. In most cases, it is economical to provide bidirectional facilities using an I/O interface chip like a PIO, which was described earlier in this chapter. In a typical system design, we connect PIOs or UARTs to the microprocessor busses; this involves connecting the devices to the data bus and the address bus for the chip and register selects as explained earlier.

In the previous section of this chapter, we examined the essential opera-

Fig. 7.32. This DMA controller module can achieve data rates of up to 500K bytes per second. (*Courtesy Rockwell International.*)

tion of the three input/output scheduling techniques. We will now review the various interface devices and then consider the appropriateness of each one for the required input/output facilities.

Three kinds of chips can be distinguished: (1) the PIO types of interface chip, (2) device-controller chips, and (3) scheduling chips. Two different classes of chips have been introduced for the scheduling of input/output processing: (1) the priority-interrupt controllers (PIC) and (2) the direct-memory-access controllers (DMAC).

It has been shown how interrupts are used to obtain a faster response time from the microprocessor system when it is required to service I/O devices. Two problems have been discussed.

1. Simultaneous interrupts may occur which requires using a priority scheme.
2. The availability of a single interrupt line in most microprocessors imposes the requirement of identifying the device which requested the interrupt. This interrupt-identification problem will be considered next.

With the limitation on the number of pins on the chip package, it has been noted that most microprocessors usually have one or two interrupt lines. But this is not sufficient to dedicate an interrupt line for every device, so several devices are connected to the same interrupt line. When an interrupt signal is sent to the microprocessor, it is necessary to determine which device caused the interrupt in order to execute the correct interrupt service routine. Several methods are used.

The software method uses a polling program to interrogate, in turn, each of the devices connected to the interrupt line in order to determine which is requesting the interrupt. The simplest form of this method uses the polling routine to read an interrupt status bit on each device to determine which one caused the interrupt. If a particular device did, the routine can then branch to the appropriate interrupt-handler if required. In addition, identifying the device which caused the interrupt can be assisted by external hardware.

A method which is software-driven, with the help of additional hardware, uses a daisy-chain to identify the device. (This is shown in Figure 7.33.) After preserving the registers, the microprocessor generates an interrupt-acknowledge (ACK) which is gated to device A. If device A generated the interrupt, it places its identification number on the data bus, where it is read by the microprocessor. If it did not generate the interrupt, it will propagate the acknowledge signal to device B. Device B will then take up the same procedure. The physical arrangement of devices is called a daisy-chain. This method can be implemented by most PIOs.

The hardware methods are more efficient. The software schemes are simple in terms of the connections required, but they require appreciable time

Interrupts (1 to N Lines)

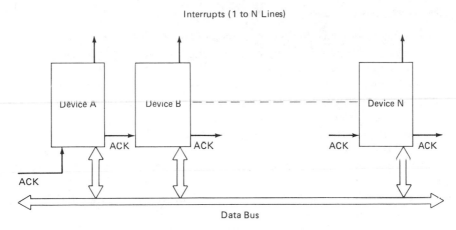

Fig. 7.33. Daisy-chain polling technique.

from the processor, increasing the overhead for responding to an interrupt. The hardware schemes make it the responsibility of a hardware device to automatically supply the address of the correct interrupt handling routine. This is called the automatic interrupt-vectoring technique.

One of the fastest methods is the vectored-interrupt. Here, it is the responsibility of the I/O controller to supply the interrupt and to identify the device causing the interrupt, or even the branching address for the interrupt-handling routine. If the controller only supplies the identity of the device, it is usually the software's task to look it up in a table containing the branching address for each device. This allows simpler hardware, but one does not achieve the best possible performance. The highest performance is obtained when the microprocessor receives an interrupt and the direct branching address. It may then branch to the required location in memory and start servicing the device. The priority-interrupt controllers (PIC chips) allow this.

Another problem that is encountered is to determine which I/O device should be granted service in the event of simultaneous interrupts; one must implement a priority scheme. In the simplest form, one assigns a fixed priority number to each device. Priority level 0 is, by convention, the highest priority; 1 is next, and so on to the lowest device. Typically, level 0 would be for a power-failure-restart, level 1 for a CRT device, and level 2 possibly left vacant for the addition of a second CRT. Level 3 might be a disk memory. Level 5 could be a printer. Level 6 might be a teletype, and level 7 for external control switches, while in this example level 4 is reserved for a second disk unit. These priorities can be enforced in hardware or in software.

Software enforcement of priorities has been described. The routine for checking the status of the devices checks the device with the highest priority first. Enforcing priorities in hardware is also possible.

Masking Techniques

One technique which offers an improvement to the fixed-priority scheme has become common in managing interrupts. This is the masking facility. Most hardware interrupt-handlers supply a masking register. (This will be explained using the basic interrupt-management logic shown in Figure 7.34, which does not include priority-encoding or the vectoring facility.)

The circuit shown in Figure 7.34 manages eight interrupts, which are on the right of the diagram. The mask register appears at the bottom. When the contents of a bit of the mask are 0, it blocks the propagation of the interrupt signal. The interrupt level is then masked. The presence of a 1 in the mask register allows the interrupt to propagate towards the left. When all interrupt lines are used, or allowed, the mask register contains all 1's. If interrupt line 2 is not allowed, then bit 2 of the mask register is set to 0. The interrupt levels which are not masked out will set a bit in the interrupt register. The contents of this register can be read out of the circuit via the data bus. It will be shown shortly how this register allows the implementation of the software-priority

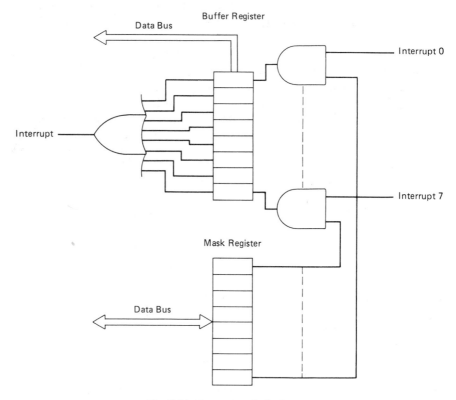

Fig. 7.34. Interrupt-priority logic.

decoding. An EXCLUSIVE OR of the lines of this register provides the final interrupt signal shown on the left of the circuit. This interrupt request line is connected to the microprocessor interrupt line.

In normal operation, the mask register is loaded by the programmer with the correct bit pattern to enable the selected interrupt lines. If all interrupt lines are used, the mask register will contain all 1's. When one or more interrupts are requested, they propagate to the left of the circuit when an interrupt request results. The microprocessor then reads the contents of the interrupt register and finds 1's in every bit position where a device has requested service.

Where several devices may request service simultaneously, you would then implement a priority scheme. For instance, assume that interrupt 0 is the highest priority, interrupt 1 next, and so on to the lowest priority device. The microprocessor tests bit 0 of the interrupt register, then bit 1, and so on until it finds a 1. When it finds a 1, the corresponding interrupt line is serviced. Thus, the highest level of interrupt is serviced first. After this interrupt is serviced, the microprocessor reads the contents of the interrupt register. If INT is still true, it will service any other waiting interrupts. This is a software implementation of a priority-interrupt scheme.

Priority-Interrupt Controllers

Priorities do not have to be fixed, and some PICs allow the user to modify the priorities by using software. But managing priorities which vary dynamically may be a complex software problem that requires careful analysis. This problem is more easily accomplished using a PIC. These priority-interrupt controllers provide a mask which allows the programmer to mask selectively any interrupt level. (The basic logic is the same as shown in Figure 7.34. It does not show the address-vectoring, only the generation of the level vector.) PICs typically accept 8 interrupt levels, which are shown on the right of Figure 7.34. Each one will set a bit in the interrupt register. The mask register allows the programmer to mask-out interrupt levels selectively. Typically, the unused interrupt levels are masked, but it is also possible to mask levels at certain times in the program. The AND gate allows the propagation of unmasked interrupts.

The level of the interrupt of highest priority is converted to a 3-bit word code by an 8-to-3 encoder. The level of the interrupts is compared to the contents of the 3-bit priority register which is set by the user. It prevents interruptions by any interrupt of level higher than a priority. This is a global masking process for interrupts of a level higher than n. A comparator in the PIC chip determines if the levels of the interrupt is acceptable. If it is, it then generates a final interrupt request.

Some PICs directly supply a branching address. This is accomplished with a RAM of 16-bit registers in the PIC. The 3-bit level vector then selects the contents of one of the registers. The contents of the register are then placed on the microprocessor data or address bus. This allows a branch to the desired address. (A complete PIC is shown in Figure 7.35.)

We will now consider the operation of some actual priority-interrupt controller chips. The structure of the Intel 8259 appears in Figure 7.36. It provides interrupt-management including priorities, interrupt mask, and automatic vectoring. It is implemented in an NMOS 28-pin package. The chip can be cascaded with up to eight other PICs so as to manage 64 separate interrupt levels.[18] Let us consider the 8080 interrupt-management system.

In response to an interrupt signal, the 8080 accepts the interrupt and returns an interrupt-acknowledge signal. Next, the microprocessor waits for the instruction to appear on the data bus. The instruction is then transmitted into the instruction register of the control unit where it can be decoded. External logic must supply the instruction.

The 8259 can place the instruction on the data bus and provide automatic vectoring. The programmer, however, is still required to preserve the data which existed prior to the interrupt. The 8259 also has an interrupt mask and a priority facility in which the priority level is loaded into a register and compared using an on-chip comparator.

The 6800 microprocessor uses an external bit in the mask register, which can be set by the programmer.[19] The 6800 saves its register automatically and branches to a reserved memory location. This provides a faster response to interrupts but does not lend itself easily to automatic vectoring.

The interrupt signal forces a bit to be checked in one of the control

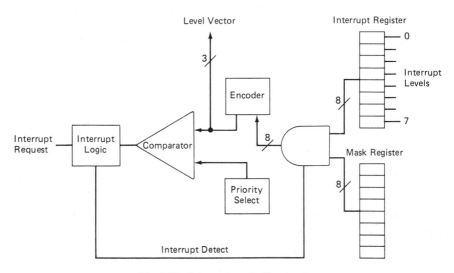

Fig. 7.35. Interrupt-controller structure.

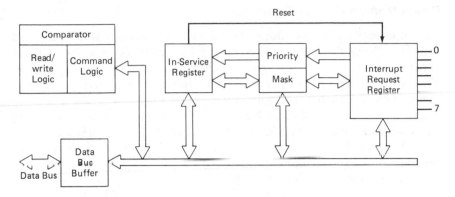

Fig. 7.36. The Intel 8259 interrupt controller.

registers; if the bit is set, an input to the register is stored. If the bit is not set, or after this input to memory is made, a bit check is made of the other register which produces an output if the bit is set and produces a return from the interrupt if it is not set.

The polling approach tends to be the lowest cost method for identifying interrupts, but in some applications it may be too slow. In these cases, hardware is added to the interface in order to use a priority encoder for interrupts. The output of the encoder can then be used as an address to transfer control to the correct routine. When the interrupt occurs, there will be a branch to the address that has been stored at FFF8 and FFF9. A software routine would then be necessary to determine which interrupt handler should be activated.

The 6800 PIC manages eight interrupt levels, and to provide automatic vectoring, it monitors the address bus. When the PIC detects FFF8 and FFF9, it assumes control of the data bus, and instead of letting the memory supply the contents of FFF8–FFF9, it is the PIC which supplies the branching address.

The 6800 PIC has eight 16-bit registers.[20] Depending on the interrupt level which is activated, it provides the correct branching address for that level. Thus, the PIC substitutes the correct 16-bit address for one of eight interrupt levels, instead of the 16-bit address which was contained in the memory at FFF8–FFF9.

The 6800 PIC is incompatible with the 8080 PIC. The benifits are similar, however, except that the 6800 automatically preserves the registers; in the 8080, this must be accomplished by a short software routine, if required. In some cases, it is not necessary to store all of the machine registers. Then, the 8080 would have a performance advantage. Since the 8080 has more internal registers than the 6800, saving all the internal registers all the time would be inefficient.

Direct-Memory-Access Controllers

Interrupts may not be fast enough for some devices which require fast word transfers. When the interrupt is received, the microprocessor suspends the program which is in execution and switches to another routine. It then usually transfers one word by software. Due to the instructions that are executed before the word is actually transferred, a large number of microseconds may elapse. This can be too slow for devices such as floppy disks or CRT display terminals which must be refreshed. To speed up the process, one can implement directly in hardware the software process which has been identified as the bottleneck. This is the essence of the DMA technique.

The direct-memory-access controller (DMA or DMAC) is a block-transfer processor. This device implements automatically, at hardware speed, the process which would normally be executed by a program in the microprocessor. (The principle of DMAC operation appears in Figure 7.37) Instead of sending an interrupt to the microprocessor, the I/O devices send the interrupt to the DMAC. The DMAC then suspends the microprocessor by putting it in a HOLD mode. It then takes over the operation of the system and transfers the words between the memory and the I/O device.

The DMAC complexity can be compared with the complexity of the microprocessor. It is the most expensive interrupt system, and it is used only when the block-transfer speed of the microprocessor is not sufficient. It provides the high-speed word or block transfers between device and memory. DMA is typically used for faster I/O devices such as CRTs. It can add significantly to the system's cost and complexity and thus is normally not used in the smaller microprocessor systems.

Several techniques are used which allow a peripheral to communicate directly with the memory. The processor can be halted by the DMAC or suspended, or the DMAC may steal a memory cycle from the microprocessor, or a combination of these techniques may be used.

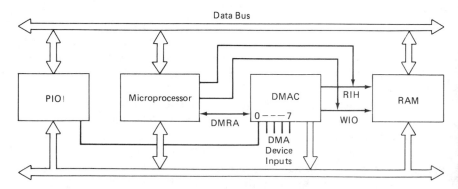

Fig. 7.37. DMA controller application.

The operation of a DMAC will be discussed using the DMAC as shown in Figure 7.37.[21] The following sequence of operations is performed:

1. The PIO requests service from the DMAC.
2. The DMAC forwards the request to the microprocessor using the DMRA line.
3. The microprocessor finishes the instruction it was executing and returns an acknowledge signal using the DMRA bidirectional line to the DMAC. The MPU microprocessor has now entered a WAIT state and places the data and address busses in a high-impedance or floating state.
4. The DMAC forwards an acknowledge signal to the PIO stating that the transfer may proceed.
5. The DMAC loads the transfer address on the address bus. The DMAC has eight 16-bit registers which are used for the beginning address of the transfer to the memory. The DMAC also has other registers, such as a counter register to specify how many words are to be transferred. The contents of these registers must be preloaded by the program prior to their use.
6. The DMAC supplies a read or write signal on RIH or WIO.
7. The I/O device through the PIO can now input or output the data.
8. Upon each transfer of a word, the DMAC increments an internal address register and updates its word counter.

This block transfer operation will continue until one of the following conditions occur:

1. The I/O block transfer stops the DMA request.
2. The word counter reaches zero. This signals the end of the block of words and the DMA transfer is stopped.
3. The lower half of the internal DMAC address register goes from 11111111 to value 00000000. This is due to the paged organization of the memory. When one crosses a page boundary, (any multiple of 256), the page register must be incremented and the DMA transfer interrupted.
4. An interrupt at level zero occurs. This level normally corresponds to a power failure on most systems. A few milliseconds of processing time are still available to preserve some of the system state. Normally, this time is used to preserve the contents of the internal microprocessor registers and then to shut down the system in an orderly manner. The DMA transfer, as well as other I/O operations, is stopped, and a branch to a power failure routine is used for the shutdown. Preserving the contents of the internal microprocessor registers naturally is

reasonable. A memory that is battery-assisted may be used so that the RAM contents are held for the full duration of the power failure.

5. The DMAC receives a request at a higher priority level. Let the highest priority level be 0 and the lowest 7. If we were honoring a request at level 3, any request on levels 0, 1, or 2 would result in a suspension of DMA. The highest priority level would be honored. When the block at the high priority level is completely transferred, the transfer for the lower level would then resume.

Other manufacturers have their own version of a DMAC for their system. Intel has the 8257 which requires an external latch in order to preserve the eight address bits.[22] A typical configuration of the 8257 appears in Figure 7.38. Four DMA levels are shown for controlling four different disk units with each one connected to its own DMA level.

The operational structure of the 6800 DMAC is shown in Figure 7.39. This is a cycle-stealing DMA controller.

Peripheral Controllers and Utility Chips

Another category of interface chips are the direct peripheral controllers. Traditionally, these controllers required one or more boards of logic in order to connect it to any type of processor. Since about 1976, however, it has

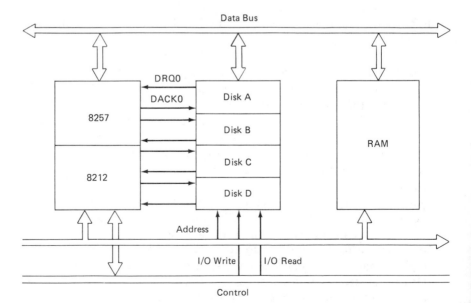

Fig. 7.38. 8757 DMA configuration.

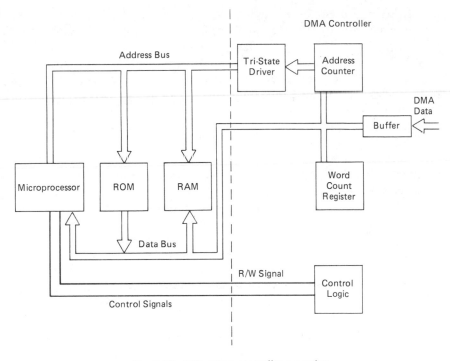

Fig. 7.39. 6800 DMA controller operation.

become possible to implement complete interfaces using simplified controller chips for most devices that are connected to the microprocessor system. There are controllers for keyboards, printers, disks, cassettes, and CRTs. It is likely that there will be single-chip interfaces available for each type of peripheral that is likely to be interfaced to a microprocessor. Typically, the controller chip is interfaced directly to one or several PIOs or a UART. (The system aspects of peripheral control and controller chips are considered in the applications section concluding this chapter.)

A number of utility chips are available which supply hardware facilities that used to require additional external components and software. One utility chip used for scheduling is the programmable-interval timer (PIT).[23] The PIT has several independent counters that can operate in input or output modes. In the output mode, one can measure the duration of external pulses. A counter register is loaded with the desired value in micro or milliseconds. Then, a status bit can be set, or an interrupt generated when the counter reaches zero; thus, a signal is generated as the desired period of time has elapsed. The 8253 PIT has three 16–bit independent counters counting in binary or BCD with six programmable modes of operation. In some applications, it is necessary to measure the elapsed time for input or output scheduling. Using microprocessor looping techniques is a time-consuming task; thus, the availability of this component frees the microprocessor for other tasks.

A PIT is usually required in all real time operations. In a real time system using interrupts, software counters cannot provide the accuracy timing. An internal counter could be interrupted by external events, resulting in erroneous time measurements.

An external PIT entails adding an extra chip to the system. Some microcomputer chips implement a PIT directly on the chip. In the future, it is most likely that the PIT will be implemented on the same chip as the CPU. In some microprocessor families, a PIT is often included on one of the other I/O chips such as a PIO or a UART.

Components are also available as a combination of PIO, UART, microprocessor, and other components such as interval timers. The TMS5501 has a PIO with an 8-bit input port, an 8-bit output port, plus an asynchronous serial line, two interrupts and five programmable interval timers. It interfaces directly to the 8080 without the 8228. This component is a combination of a PIO, UART, and PIT (programmable-interval timer). The 8741 microcomputer is similarly a combination of processor and interface functions.[24]

BUS STRUCTURE AND STANDARDS

We have examined schemes and hardware for handling input/output devices. Now we will consider in more detail the combinations of communications lines that tie the microcomputer system together: the bus structure. One has little control over the basic structure of a microcomputer system, but the bus lines that the system elements use to communicate with one another can help one determine how the external input/output devices will interface with the microcomputer.

Bus Structures and Interface Techniques

The most fundamental bus structure links each device in the system to the processor using unique signal lines. The structure is simple in function but expensive because of the many connections required. Most microprocessor systems use some form of multiplexed bus structure.

Two types of multiplexed bus structures are based on the shared bus concept: (1) daisy-chain and (2) party-line. In the daisy-chain structure, the information passes through each system element until it arrives at the correct device; each device acts as both a source and acceptor on the bus. (See Figure 7.33 on page 329 for an example of daisy-chain polling.)

In the party-line structure, each device is linked to a single bus through tristate buffers. The bus may be unidirectional, but more often a bidirectional bus is used so that the information can pass among the various sources and acceptors.

Most microcomputers use a bidirectional party-line structure for the main data bus, but the number and structure of the busses may differ. A single, all purpose bidirectional structure was common in the first microprocessors, which had fewer external pins. Often, some used a bus which was 4 bits wide, while the instruction codes and addresses were split into 4-bit segments. This approach made it harder to demultiplex the proper information. As the number of pin connections increased, microprocessors first used a single 8-bit-wide bus and then two separate busses: a unidirectional bus for addresses and a bidirectional bus for data and instruction codes.

This dual-bus structure with a 12- or 16-bit address bus and an 8-bit data bus is now standard for 8-bit microprocessors. A variety of bus structures are used in the 16-bit microprocessors. Some use a single, 16-bit-wide shared data/address bus, while others have separate 16-bit buses for data and addresses. Most systems communicate with the I/O devices using the bidirectional data bus. If the system has several microprocessors, each may have one or more separate I/O busses. Both serial and parallel I/O busses are used. Almost all microcomputer systems use one bus for both memory and I/O device addresses.

When the information is supplied to the bus from more than one source, bus-driver circuits must be used to select and control the outputs from each source so that they won't interfere with each other. The bus drivers will do the following:

1. Ensure that each of the sources connected to the bus are compatible.
2. Control the connection and disconnection of the various sources from the bus.
3. Multiplex the information onto the bus.

A tri-state bus transceiver (bus receiver and a driver) is normally used to link the I/O device line to the bus.

Another major interface is between the microprocessor and the memory. The interface between the microprocessor bus and memory performs three basic functions:

1. Ensures the bus and the memory are compatible.
2. Generates the memory address.
3. Interacts with the bus-control signals to synchronize data transfer to and from the memory with the operation of the bus.

The interface is as complex as the type of memory and the structure of the bus system require. Memory interfaces range from general-purpose interface chips to special-purpose, user-designed interfaces.

The memory chips are now standardized by the organization of the memory arrays into 4-bit or 8-bit words and functionally by the external connections.[25] Because the maximum number of external pin connections per chip was more limited in the early single-bus microprocessor systems, complex bus multiplexing and demultiplexing logic was required for the memory interface.

In a microcomputer system with separate data and address busses, a general-purpose memory chip may be used that includes the interface logic to decode the address-bus lines and generate a chip-select signal. Special-purpose memory interfaces can also be designed. The interface is relatively simple in a multiple-bus microcomputer without much multiplexing.

Systems that use large memory facilities are often better designed using a special-purpose interface. One cannot avoid this approach when the technology or structure of the memory array is fundamentally incompatible with that of the bus system.

An I/O-bus interface design is more complicated. Most I/O devices operate in real time and demand joint, asynchronous control of the data flow through the interface. Many of these I/O devices are electromechanical and cannot provide the speed of response to keep up with the rest of the microprocessor system.

A special-purpose bus interface may use one or more integrated circuits to link the microprocessor to a particular I/O device. In addition to the basic bus-interface circuits, the interface may contain circuits for specific functions peculiar to the I/O device. A keyboard interface would require matrix encoding and perhaps parity-generating functions. A line-printer interface would require message formatting, character storage and print-head control and timing functions. A communications interface could require serial-to-parallel/parallel-to-serial conversion, parity generation, message formatting, and modem-control.

The intelligent bus-interface concept reduces some of the development costs required with special-purpose interfaces. The intelligent interface as shown in Figure 7.40 consists of a microprocessor system specially designed with a limited instruction set to emphasize I/O control and interface operations instead of the usual general-purpose instructions.[26] The microprocessor system has a bus that is compatible with the host microprocessor system and extensive I/O facilities along with on-chip data and program memories. The system can be programmed to perform the interface functions required by the particular I/O device.

Bus standards define the way two subsystems are to interface. An electrical interface standard when properly implemented can assure that products designed by different groups can work together in a system.

16-Bit Microprocessor Bus Characteristics

We will now discuss some of the characteristics of some actual microprocessor bus structures in conjunction with their 16-bit processor units. At

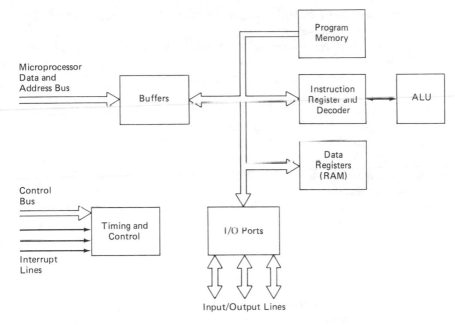

Fig. 7.40. Intelligent interface.

least one of these (the Intel Multibus) is being implemented as an IEEE standard.[27]

The Multibus is the bus structure for interfacing Intel's 8080/85/86 products. It supports a one-megabyte address space. The 8289 bus arbiter controls accesses by multiple processors. The control lines use a master-slave concept: a master processor takes control of the bus; then the slave device, I/O or memory, acts upon the command provided by the master. An asynchronous handshaking protocol allows units of different speeds to use the bus.

The system also may include intelligent slaves, which cannot control the bus, but add more processing power onto the bus. Multiple masters may be connected in a daisy-chain priority or a parallel priority. The coordination features for a 8086 multiprocessor environment include:

1. A bus arbiter, which decides which device may use the bus during the next cycle.
2. A bus-lock signal for blocking interrupts and requests by other processors.
3. Synchronization to an external event using a WAIT instruction and the input signal.
4. Two bidirectional request/grant lines, which are used to share the local

bus between host and other processors using a handshake sequence: request, grant, and release.
5. A bus controller to produce system bus signals compatible with Multibus.
6. A semaphore for locking devices and processes.

Two multimicroprocessor techniques are used in the Z8000.[28] The first technique uses a FIFO buffer communication module, which runs each processor as a separate system and passes messages through buffers to achieve system communications. Here, the processors are loosely coupled, and high-speed resource sharing is not possible.

The second technique uses two signals in a daisy-chain global priority. A processor examines the bus for a busy condition. If the bus is not busy, the processor places a request into the chain. The result is reported with a flag. The time required to operate this mechanism rules out high-speed communications. Multimicroprocessor operation with the Z8000 bus uses the following features:

1. Special multimicroprocessor control and output instructions.
2. Signals for bus request, bus acknowledge, multimicro-in, multimicro-out, and segment traps.
3. Bus arbitration mechanisms.
4. Asynchronous Z-bus to Z-bus communications using a FIO.
5. A semaphore to synchronize software processes.

In the 68000 system, each processor uses a local bus with local memory and peripherals.[29] A global bus connects the local busses together using bus arbitration modules. This is not a true multiprocessing system, but a connected group of microcomputer systems. An access involving the global bus takes longer than a local access. Access from the global bus to a local bus is obtained by a DMA operation. With the priority on the global bus fixed, a processor with low priority may never get a global transaction started or completed. Multimicroprocessor operation uses the following features:

1. The bus arbitration modules.
2. Signals for bus request, bus grant, and bus grant-acknowledge for arbitration.

The extended bus arbitration used by the Versabus may be powerful, but the master/slave protocol can produce bottlenecks as the number of processors increases.

We will now consider the external bus standards that enable one to link a microcomputer to peripherals and communications equipment. These standard bus interfaces fall into two major categories: (1) serial interfaces that transmit data a bit at a time and (2) parallel interfaces that send data in groups of bits.

The serial standards tend to be more general than the parallel standards, since they do not specify the number of bits in a word. The parallel interface standards specify a fixed word size, and words having nonstandard lengths may need to be treated in a special way. The major advantage of parallel transmission, however, is the higher throughput.

Serial Standards: RS–232 and RS–449

The most popular serial interface standard has been the RS–232C interface for terminals and data communications equipment.[30] The RS stands for recommended standard; the C indicates that this is the third version of the standard. This standard defines 20 distinct signals (as shown in Table 7.1.)

Table 7.1 RS–232C Signals

AB	Signal Ground
CE	Ring Indicator
CD	Data Terminal Ready
CC	Data Set Ready
BA	Transmitted Data
BB	Received Data
DA	Transmitter Signal Element Timing (Data Terminal Source)
DB	Transmitter Signal Element Timing (Data Communications Source)
DD	Receiver Signal Element Timing
CA	Request to Send
CB	Clear to Send
CF	Received Line Signal Detector
CG	Signal Quality Detector
CH	Data Signal Rate Selector (Data Terminal Source)
CI	Data Signal Rate Selector (Data Communications Source)
SBA	Secondary Transmitted Data
SBB	Secondary Received Data
SCA	Secondary Request to Send
SCB	Secondary Clear to Send
SCF	Secondary Received Line Signal Detector

The RS–232 standard was originally intended to interface terminals and communications gear. Some devices do not use all the signals, so not all RS–232 devices will operate together without modifications. The standard defines 13 different combinations of the 20 signals. The simplest interface for a send/receive terminal requires three signals: signal ground (AB), transmitted data (BA), and received data (BB). The device at the other end of the cable might require a clear-to-send (CB) signal before it will transmit the data.

Data terminals that conform to the RS–232C standard use a 25-pin male connector that mates with a corresponding female connector.

The RS-232C standard was developed to interconnect terminals and modems. But when the standard is used to interconnect other kinds of equipment such as microcomputers, the modems used to interconnect RS-232 devices may have the wrong connectors. As a result, a null modem, which is a pair of identical connectors with some wiring changes, may be required. The transmitted-data pins are wired to the received-data pins between the connector. Other pairs of control signals may be wired to assure the proper operating conditions. A terminal that must recognize the clear-to-send (CB) may also produce a request-to-send (CA) signal. Wiring the two pins together assures that the terminal will operate with equipment that may not produce a clear-to-send signal.

The RS–232C standard does not specify the shape or spacing of the pins on the connector. A terminal could use any connector that has 25 pins and still conform to the standard. However, most devices use the same connector as Bell modems use.

The RS–232 standard was originally developed to give computers and terminals a reliable link to telephone company modems. The standard has withstood the test of time and can be considered as one of the most successful in the industry.

But the RS–232C has some serious drawbacks. Its electrical specifications are not defined for the present logic technology. Most contemporary logic uses a single 5-volt supply while RS–232 uses two equal voltages of opposite polarity in the 5- to 25-volt range. To resolve the incompatibility, the Electronic Industries Association (EIA) has introduced two newer standards, RS–422 and RS–423, which use TTL voltage levels. These standards differ in only the electrical characteristics of the interface signals; the functions remain essentially the same.

The RS–232 standard has another disadvantage in some applications: its speed is limited to about 20,000 bits a second. A new standard called RS–449 accommodates data rates as high as 2 megabits a second.[31] It also differs from RS–232 in other ways as well. For example, it introduces a few more signals (as shown in Table 7.2).

It also uses two connectors: (1) a 37-pin unit for the most frequently used signals and (2) a 9-pin unit for a secondary channel. A single 37-pin connector is used in most applications. The RS–449 is intended to replace the RS–232C. In the meantime, new equipment conforming to the RS–449 standard will require an adapter to mate to RS–232 devices. Some applications may require cables with 36-, 9-, and 25-pin connectors to interconnect newer and older equipment. The RS–449 standard adapter requires resistors for the logic conversion.

A serial interface trades efficiency for generality since any number of bits may be transmitted in any order, and the data may be transmitted synchronously or asynchronously. The major reason for using the RS–232 is the wide range of equipment available with this interface. Most microcomputers

Table 7.2 RS-449 Signals

SG	Signal Ground
SC	Send Common
RC	Receive Common
IS	Terminal in Service
IC	Incoming Call
TR	Terminal Ready
DM	Data Mode
SD	Send Data
RD	Receive Data
TT	Terminal Timing
ST	Send Timing
RT	Receive Timing
RS	Request to Send
CS	Clear to Send
RR	Receiver Ready
SQ	Signal Quality
NS	New Signal
SF	Select Frequency
SR	Signaling Rate Selector
SI	Signaling Rate Indicator
SSD	Secondary Send Data
SRD	Secondary Receive Data
SRS	Secondary Request to Send
SCS	Secondary Clear to Send
SRR	Secondary Receiver Ready
LL	Local Loopback
RL	Remote Loopback
TM	Test Mode
SS	Select Standby
SB	Standby Indicator

contain an RS-232 compatible I/O port and almost all data terminals have RS-232 interfaces. They are common for many cassette tape drives, PROM programmers, and other low-speed peripherals. If compatibility is a consideration and if the flexibility to change subsystems and components without system redesign is important, the RS-232 is the best choice.

Parallel Standards

The low throughput of serial transmission may be overcome by transmitting the data bits in parallel. The most widely-used parallel standard is the General Purpose Interface Bus (GPIB), also known as the Hewlett-Packard Interface Bus (HP-IB), IEEE-488 Bus (IEEE Standard 488-1975), or ANSI bus (ANSI MC1-1975).[32] The standard was originally developed by Hewlett-Packard for interfacing programmable electronic test equipment; it was later adopted by the IEEE and the American National Standards Institute.

The standard has wide acceptance in the test-equipment industry. There are many IEEE–488 bus-compatible devices, including computer peripherals. The IEEE-488 bus supports data transfer rates as high as 1 megabyte and most microcomputer peripherals. Some personal computers use a 488 bus to interface with floppy disks.

The IEEE-488 bus uses a 24-pin-wide cable for the 16 signals: eight parallel data lines and eight control lines (as shown in Figure 7.41). Devices that interface to the bus always use a male plug. The bus cables have both male and female plugs at each end to allow multiple devices to be connected in a daisy chain. As many as 15 devices may share the bus. Devices may talk, transmit data, listen, receive data, and/or control the bus. Devices can be separated by 20 meters, but for maximum speeds cable lengths should be limited to one meter for each device. Every device on the bus is assigned a control address, and a listener can respond only to messages addressed to it. A control device can cause a talker to send data to a desired listener by issuing the correct address. Thus, peripheral devices can transfer data among themselves without involving a host computer.

The IEEE–488 bus has a number of advantages over a serial interface like RS-232. For instance, it is more efficient, since the data is transferred eight bits at a time. It is also compatible with almost all microcomputers. The IEEE-488 bus also has a greater channel capacity. A single IEEE–488 channel can accommodate as many as 14 peripherals. Thus, the bus is useful in those systems where the peripheral configurations may vary widely. A word processing system, for instance, that includes an IEEE–488 bus interface could handle operator terminals, printers, floppies and cassettes—all on a single channel. Yet in spite of the advantages, designers have been slow to adopt the IEEE–488 bus due to the apparent complexity of the IEEE–488 control sequences. These sequential control patterns can sometimes be difficult to increment, and the availability of the one-chip universal asyn-

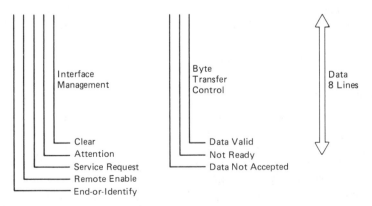

Fig. 7.41. IEEE-488 bus.

chronous receiver-transmitters (UART) interfaces makes adoption of the RS–232 serial interfaces much easier.

Now, however, there are products that facilitate use of the IEEE bus. These single-chip, general purpose interface ICs are nearly all the circuits a user needs to build a microprocessor-controlled interface to the IEEE bus. The only additional components needed are the bidirectional buffers.

There are also single-card IEEE–488 bus interfaces that link directly to the microcomputer bus.[33] This relieves the microcomputer from some of the detailed transactions required to transfer blocks of data.

APPLICATION

We have shown in the previous sections how the various interface techniques are used. Assembling a system for a given application requires that two additional essential tasks need be done specifically for the application: (1) interfacing and (2) programming. Most interfaces required to connect standard input output devices are available in chip or board form and can be connected to the system, as will be discussed below.

Assembling a Small System

We can use a standard microprocessor such as the 4-bit 4040 to build progressively more complex systems, while the basic architecture of the system will remain constant. Additional functions are obtained by connecting more hardware modules. The assembly of any of these systems using other standard microprocessors such as the 6800, 6500, or 8086 would be similar. For example, let us start with a basic input device with hexadecimal input and LED output; then we will consider a system paper-tape and cassette controllers. Finally, we will discuss systems for industrial monitoring and control.

For our basic input/output device, only four chips are required (as shown in Figure 7.42): the 4040 microprocessor and a clock chip—the 4201. The 4002 RAM provides the read/write-I/O capabilities. A 4308 ROM-I/O chip provides the program storage and I/O capabilities.[34] In most designs, it is desirable to reduce the number of components so that we may use chips which incorporate both memory and I/O facilities when available. In a larger system, where expansion capability would be essential, the memory and I/O chips would be separate. These two chips, the 4002 and the 4308, allow both memory and I/O facilities. Each has 16 lines of I/O. (The use of these lines will be discussed shortly.) Our basic I/O controller provides input facilities through the keyboard and display facilities through a 4-digit display. It will also communicate with an external microcomputer using a 16-bit bus. The program is contained in the 4308 ROM. A scratch pad area

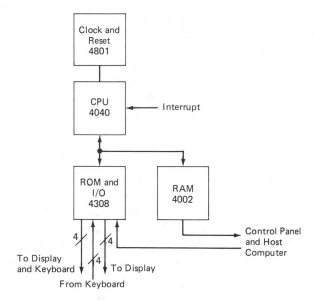

Fig. 7.42. Basic control system.

for storing temporary data and for intermediate computations is contained in the 4002.

In the input/output functions provided by the 4308, four pins are used to connect the columns of a 16-key keyboard. The scanning technique is used. Four pins collect the data from the four keyboard rows; four other pins connect the LED display. Three lines would be used for seven-segment LEDs, while the remaining four bits would be used for a control panel or communicating with the host computer. Communication to this computer uses 16 lines from the 4002.

The preceding example is the simplest interface application. It is analogous to a calculator with communication lines. We can use this basic system to build more complex interfaces, by adding more chips to the system to achieve the desired functions.

We will now consider a paper-tape controller. The tape controller reads seven or eight bits of ASCII coded data from the tape and punch data with the punching mechanism. It also has a front test panel which uses eight lines for communication. Four lines are used to give commands to the mechanism, while four sense lines are used for the switch and status indications. The required functions are obtained by adding two more chips to the basic system. (A block diagram of the system is shown in Figure 7.43.) We can add a 4308 ROM for the additional program storage required by this application. For the 16 lines of I/O, a 4211 GP I/O chip is added. This is a general-purpose interface chip with 16 lines that are individually programmable for

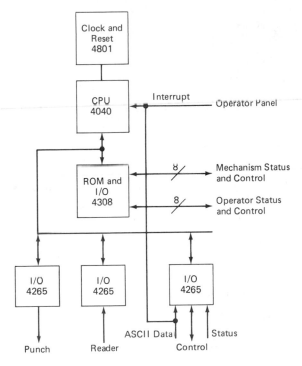

Fig. 7.43. Paper-tape controller.

direction.[35] If more program storage had not been necessary, we could have used another 4211 instead of the 4308.

The 4308 ROM uses eight lines to interface with the mechanism and eight lines to the operator's panel. The data transfer uses an 8-bit bidirectional bus which is in the ASCII format. Communication with the host computer can be accomplished by using a second 4308 ROM. The control logic required to interface to the reader-punch mechanism has been accomplished with six chips (again, see Figure 7.43). We next consider a more complex system.

A cassette controller can be implemented using one more additional chip than in the previous example. Another 4211 GP I/O is used for the 16 control lines for the tape mechanism. Data to the tape drive is serial, although it can be converted from serial to parallel 4-bit format by a UART. (The structure of the system appears in Figure 7.44.) Data from the tape cassette uses a 4308. A 4265 GP I/O is used for the 16 lines required by the mechanism.[36] The remaining lines of the 4308 are used to provide control functions for data transmission and the interface to the control panel. The data accumulated by this controller can be transmitted to a host computer with a 16-bit bidirectional data bus (which appears on the bottom of the diagram). The 4308 ROM, the 4002 RAM, and the second 4211 GP I/O are used for

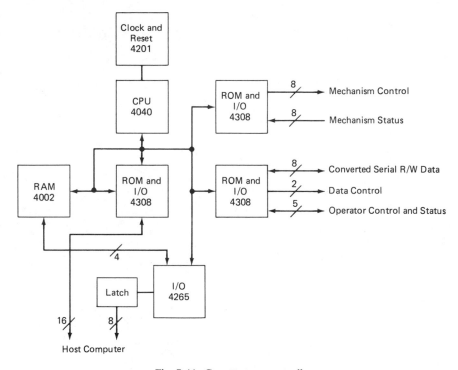

Fig. 7.44. Cassette tape controller.

this interface. If a longer program should be required, the storage would be provided by more ROM or more 4308 chips. One can keep adding functions by adding the required chips as long as the basic microprocessor used is fast enough to provide the required response time for the application algorithms. If the 4040 should prove to be too slow, however, it can be replaced by a faster microprocessor, such as an 8-or 16-bit chip.

The conclusion to be drawn from these examples is that there is essentially no hardware design in assembling these basic controller boards. Functions are achieved by connecting the required chips to the system as long as the processing speed is sufficient. We have not considered, however, the additional complexity of the required software; this problem is discussed later.

Analog Input and Output

One additional facility required in many industrial systems is analog input and output. To provide analog input/output functions, a DAC is used for digital-to-analog conversion and one or more ADCs are used for analog-to-digital conversion. Conversion techniques have been described earlier (see Chapter 6). Our basic 4040 system is shown in Figure 7.45, configured to

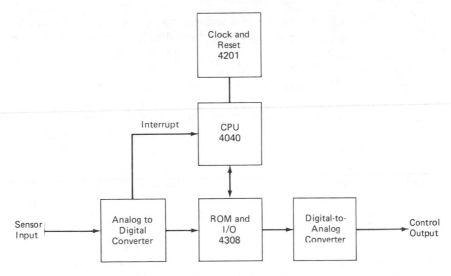

Fig. 7.45. Basic industrial control system.

provide these facilities. An 8-bit ADC is used to convert the analog signal into a digital 8-bit value, while one or more DACs are connected to the system to convert the digital output into an analog signal for the control device.

In an actual application, the ADC may be interfaced to the external analog signals through a multiplexer and one or more sample and hold circuits in order to freeze the information for the ADC. The multiplexer will connect a number of analog signals to one analog-to-digital converter, provided that the conversion speed is sufficient. The analog multiplexer may be used to reduce the component count.

Adding the analog facilities to our basic system requires a number of additional chips connected into the standard microprocessor architecture. Other functions which may be required in an application are provided by connecting the required interface to the same basic microprocessor system. The architecture of the system is essentially fixed.

When a microprocessor has access to a large number of samples over a period of time, the input can be filtered to eliminate spurious indications and to obtain a more precise result. This filtering can be done in software. If a digital multimeter sampled 10,000 times every second, the simplest filtering technique is averaging 10,000 measurements which are added together and then divided by 10,000. The result is the filtered or averaged voltage. Any unreasonable values would be averaged out, and the resulting measurement would have a higher precision in this programmable filter.

In many systems, it is necessary to provide an interface for analog devices such as transducers for pressure, temperature, or other variables. The output of the transducer can be a voltage or current which may or may not require amplification for interfacing. The output is converted into a digital word to be used by the microprocessor.

In the past, analog-to-digital conversion involved a large number of components compared to the few necessary for the microprocessor system. ADCs are now available on single chips at low cost. Some chips have tri-state drivers and buffers to interface directly to the microprocessor data bus.

A number of modules and boards are available which interface directly to the microprocessor systems.[37] These allow the microprocessor system to be coupled to an analog-to-digital and digital-to-analog multichannel conversion system.

The primary concern when designing an interface to link the data acquisition components with the microprocessor revolves around the data transmission. Since most transducer outputs are analog signals, one must decide whether to remotely convert these outputs to digital form and transmit them using digital techniques, or to transmit the outputs in analog form and then convert them at the CPU. One must also decide whether to make the conversion hardware or software-oriented. Moreover, one may also strive for a minimum of hardware connections and a minimum of software memory locations. The design will depend on the type of transducers the system incorporates.[38] We will now discuss a few examples. In each case, the design path will depend on the microprocessor the system uses. We will consider 6800 systems, but the techniques also apply to other microprocessors.

Analog transducers may output either voltages in the 1 to 5, 2 to 10, 5 to 25 or ± 10V ranges or currents in the 1 to 5, 4 to 20 or 10 to 50 mA ranges. Digital transducers fall into two basic groups: (1) those that incorporate a sensing unit as part of an oscillator circuit and determine the frequency of that circuit as a function of the measured quantity and (2) those that detect the position of a primary sensor and convert that quantity into a coded digital word.

Interfacing Analog and Digital Transducers

We will consider interfacing analog transducers of the voltage-output type and the coded type of digital transducer or encoder using several 6800 system configurations to show how the interface can achieve minimum hardware or minimum software in the system. In all cases, we will also try to maintain a minimum of wiring, connections, and memory. The 6800 uses the 6820 PIA to interface with I/O equipment. The control bus channels the data flow in the PIA's data bus, while the address bus lets the 6800 read or write into the PIA's registers, which are divided into two independent sections, with a control data and address register. There are a number of ways this interface may be done, and several of the most obvious methods follow.

In the successive-approximation converter, each bit is compared with the analog input voltage and the bit is left on by the register if it is less than this voltage, but turned off if greater. If the register is part of the microprocessor, then it is only necessary to have a comparator and digital-to-analog converter to implement this conversion (as shown in Figure 7.46).[39] The comparison operation is repeated for each bit-related position in the register until a close approximation of the input voltage is completed. The successive-approximation method is fast and it does not require a large amount of hardware. This method, however, tends to be sensitive to temperature and voltage drifts. Therefore, it is normally used only when high-speed conversions are required.

The dual-ramp method uses an integrating technique to cancel out many of the drift problems which occur with successive-approximation. The two ramps occur from a ramp time when the input voltage is integrated for a fixed number of clock periods; the input voltage to the integrator is then switched to a reference voltage and the ramp time required for the integrator to decrease to the level of the original input voltage is counted. Then the ramp times are compared to allow the calculation of the unknown transducer voltage. The interface and converter hardware for a dual ramp are shown in Figure 7.47.

The actual comparison and calculation are done in the microprocessor using the instructions shown in Table 7.3.[40]

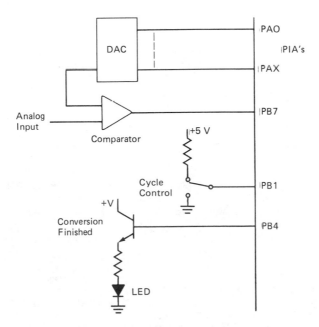

Fig. 7.46. Successive-approximation conversion interface.

Table 7.3 Dual Ramp Converter Program

```
 1. NAM  DWA10
 2. OPT  MEM
 3. *
 4. *
 5. *
 6. *
 7. *
 8. **
 9. *
10. *12 BIT DR
11. *
12. **
13. *
14. *
15. *
16. *
17. *
18. *
19. *
20. *
21. *
22. *
23. *
24. *
25. ORG $0
26. TEST RMB 2                   FINAL 12 BIT ANSWER MEMORY LOCATIONS
27. *
28. ORG $4004
29. PIA1AD RMB 1
30. PIA1AC RMB 1
31. PIA1BD RMB 1                 B SIDE, DATA REGISTER
32. PIA1BC RMB 1                 B SIDE, CONTROL REGISTER
33. *
34. ORG $OAOO                    BEGINNING ADDRESS
35. *
36. *
37. CLR PIA1AC
38. CLR PIA1BC
39. LDA A + $7C
40. STA A PIA1BD                 SET PIA TO HAVE 3 INPUTS AND
                                 5 OUTPUTS
41. LDA A + $04                  SET BIT 3 OF PIA CONTROL REGISTER
42. STA A PIA1BC
43. *
44. *
45. *
46. LDA A + $04
47. STA A PIA1BD                 RAMP CONTROL HIGH
48. START LDA A PIA1BD           COMPARATOR TEST TO INSURE THAT RAMP
                                 IS LOW
49. BMI START                    STARTS CONVERSION
```

Table 7.3 (*cont.*)

```
50. RSTART LDA A + $14
51. STA A PIA1BD          CONVERSION READY—RAMP CONTROL HIGH
52. *
53. *
54. *                      **CYCLE TEST**
55. CYCLE LDA PIA1BD
56. AND A + $02
57. BEQ CYCLE
58. LDX + $2000           INITIALIZATION FOR RAMP
                          UP TIMING
59. *
60. CLR PIA1BD            RESET OVERRANGE—CONVERSION
                          COMPLETED
61. *
62. COMP LDA A PIA1BD
63. BPL COMP
64. *
65. *
66. *                     **RAMP UP TIMING CYCLE**
67. RAMPUP LDA B + $04
68. DEX
69. BNE RAMPUP
70. *
71. *                     **RAMP DOWN TIMING CYCLE**
72. *
73. *
74. RAMPDN STA B PIA1BD   RC HIGH
75. INX
76. CPX + 0000            DUMMY STATEMENT FOR TIME DELAY
77. LDA A PIA1BD          COMPARATOR TEST
78. BMI RAMPDN
79. *
80. *
81. *
82. STX TEXT
83. LDA A TEST            512 COUNT SUBTRACTION
84. SUB A + $02
85. STA A TEST
86. SUB A + $10           OVERRANGE TEST
87. BCS RSTART
88. LDA A + $1C           SET CONVERSION FINISHED—OVERRANGE
89. STA A PIA1BD          AND SET RAMP CONTROL HIGH
90. BRA CYCLE
91. MON
```

The interface connections are programmed using lines 16 to 22. Lines 25 and 26 are used to hold the final answer, $0000 and $0001. $0000 will contain the four most significant bits and the remainder is stored in $0001. Lines 37 to 42 of the program are the instructions to initialize the input and output

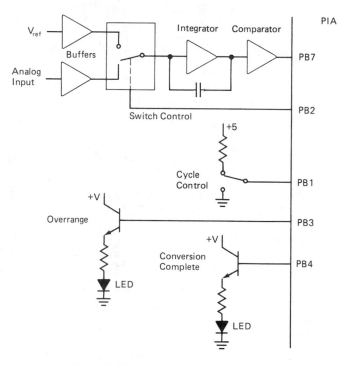

Fig. 7.47. Dual-ramp conversion interface.

ports of the PIA. The ramp control is set and the comparator tested using lines 46 to 49. This ensures that the comparator output is below the reference voltage level at the beginning of conversion. Then a conversion finished flag is set and the microprocessor enters a loop (as shown in the flow diagram of Figure 7.48).

This loop uses the PBI cycle input from the PIA, and it resets the conversion finished flag when the ramp control goes low to start a new cycle.

The index register is loaded with the contents of $2000 which is then decremented to provide the ramp-up timing. As the ramp crosses the threshold level, the comparator output is switched causing the microprocessor to enter the ramp-up cycle of lines 67 to 69. The index register is decremented until empty. Next, the ramp control switches to high and the index register is incremented (lines 74 and 75). A dummy statement equalizes the count for the ramp periods. Then, as the ramp-down period ends, the contents of the index register are stored in locations $0000 and $0001 (line 82). The offset counts are obtained by subtracting $01 from the result stored in $0000. An overrange test then checks the contents of location TEST for a value greater than 4095. If the test is true, the conversion is finished and the ramp control bits are high; if the test is false, the microprocessor branches to

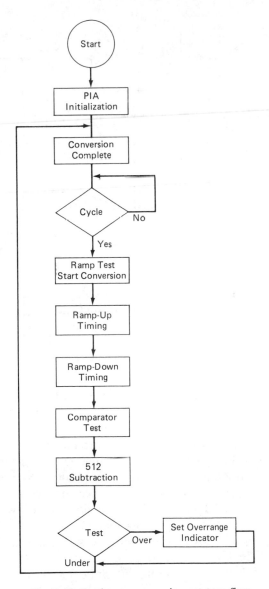

Fig. 7.48. Dual-ramp conversion program flow.

line 50. The status of the cycle input is checked before beginning another conversion cycle.

We will now examine a dual-ramp converter connected in a $3\frac{1}{2}$ digit interface configuration for operating a digital display. (The interface is shown in Figure 7.49.) This circuit requires some additional hardware compared to the

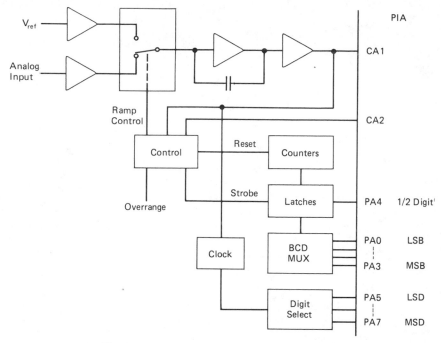

Fig. 7.49. 3½ digit dual-ramp conversion interface.

binary converter shown in Figure 7.47. The increase in hardware reduces the software required for the microprocessor; hence, this configuration needs fewer instructions (as shown in Table 7.4).[41]

If this system used less hardware, then the binary-to-BCD conversion routine required would almost triple the number of instructions shown. Lines 18 to 25 set the input and output ports. Lines 36 to 39 are used to simulate the main program of the microprocessor, while the conversion routine starts at line 42. First, the display update is set low, and the data enters the latches shown in the interface diagram.

The microprocessor stack is stored with a WAIT FOR INTERRUPT instruction until the comparator output forces CA1 to interrupt. The microprocessor is then vectored to line 50 for demultiplexing the BCD input data.

The least significant digit (LSD) is selected by the pointer. When a low condition appears on the PA5 line, the BCD data is stored at location $0100. The pointer is then moved, and as the PA6 line goes low the data is placed in the next location, which is $0101. The most significant digit data is placed in $0102 when its line goes low and the half digit is moved to $0103 after all BCD input data is placed in memory. The display update is then returned to high to signal the microprocessor to return from the interrupt routine back to the main program which requested the data.

Table 7.4 Dual-Ramp Program for Display

```
 1. NAM DWA4
 2. OPT OT
 3. *
 4. **
 5. *                    3½ DIGIT DUAL—RAMP DISPLAY CONVERT
 6. *
 7. **
 8. *
 9. ORG $0010
10. POINTR RMB 1               DIGIT SELECT POINTER
11. *
12. *
13. ORG $400A
14. PIA1AD RMB 1
15. PIA1AC RMB 1
16. *
17. *
18. *                    **PIA1AD CONFIGURATION**
19. **
20. *PA7*PA6*PA5*PA4*PA3*PA2*PA1*PAO*
21. **
22. *MSD        LSD        *½D*        MSB        LSB*
23. **
24. *        DIGIT SELECT        *        *        BCD        *
25. **
26. *
27. *                    RESULTS STORED IN LOCATIONS 0100–0103
28. *                         LSD = 0100        ½ DIGIT = 0103
29. *
30. ORG $0900
31. CLI
32. CLR PIA1AC               PIA ASSEMBLY
33. CLR PIA1AD
34. LDA A  +$3C
35. STA A PIA1AC
36. LDS  +$0020
37. *
38. *
39. NOP                     MAIN PROGRAM SIMULATION
40. JSR CONVRT
41. END NOP
42. BRA END
43. *
44. *
45. CONVRT LDA A  +$35          A/D CONVERSION SUBROUTINE
46. LDA B PIA1AD            DUMMY READ OF PIA DATA REGISTER
47. STA A PIA1AC
48. WAI
49. RTS
50. *
51. *
```

(*continued*)

Table 7.4 (cont.)

```
52. *
53. *
54. BEGIN LDA A  + $20        BEGINNING OF INTERRUPT PROGRAM
55. STA A POINTR
56. LDX  + $0100
57. NEXT LDA A PIA1AD
58. TAB
59. AND A POINTR
60. BNE NEXT
61. ROL POINTR
62. AND B  + $0F
63. STA B O,X
64. INX
65. BCC NEXT
66. LDA A PIA1AD
67. AND A  + $10
68. LSR A
69. LSR A
70. LSR A
71. LSR A
72. STA A O,X
73. LDA A  + $3C
74. STA A PIA1AC
75. RTI
76. *
77. *
78. *
79. MON
```

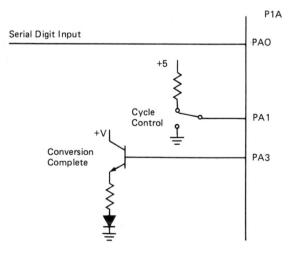

Fig. 7.50. Digital transducer input interface.

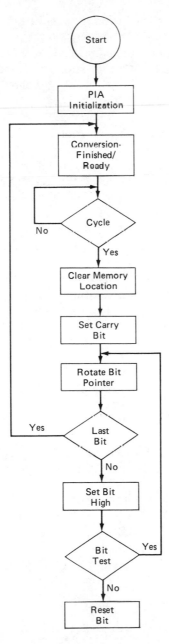

Fig. 7.51. Digital transducer program flow.

Digital transducers or encoders can simplify the system interface. For minimum software, one can connect each of the parallel outputs of a digital transducer to a corresponding PA line in a PIA.[42] Unclocked, the transducer outputs present a word, which the microprocessor may sample at almost any desired rate. Even for a relatively long sampling period, only the least significant bits will change during the measurement of most parameters. This configuration uses the software to define the connections as inputs. The sampling rate is under main program control.

To achieve minimum hardware usage in an interface for a digital transducer, one can use a software-oriented interface (see Figure 7.50).[43] A digital transducer with a serial output requires two connections: (1) a PAO and (2) a ground to interface with the PIA. The flow diagram in Figure 7.51 shows one way to simulate the serial-to-parallel register that this interface requires. One defines PAO and cycle control PA1 as inputs, and PA3 as an output to control the conversion-finished LED. But one can eliminate the PA3 output by making the conversion a subroutine of a larger control program. A cycle loop causes the microprocessor to wait until PA1 switches to high, and then it clears a memory location to use as a pointer which tracks bit processing. The routine rotates the carry bit and resets the conversion-finished line. It uses a conditional branch to determine when all bits have been tested. Then the program sets the carry bit to signify that all bits have been checked. It uses another branch for bit testing and pointer control and prepares the bits for the microprocessor.

In applications where switches are used to control the inputs to the microprocessor as shown in the examples above, it may be desirable to have a delay in the program in order to allow for switch bounce.[44] A mechanical switch can cause on and off transients for as long as 40 milliseconds. A sequence like the following can be used to ensure that the processor does not sample this input until the transients have settled.

```
           LDX  #5000    : Load index register, 3 cycles
    LOOP   DEX           : Decrement index register, 4 cycles
           BNE  LOOP     : Branch to LOOP, 4 cycles
```

The loop uses 5000*8 + 3 cycles or about 40 milliseconds at a 1 MHz clock rate. The time required to process the switch input also adds to this time.

REFERENCES

1. Intel, *Component Data Catalog,* Santa Clara: Intel, 1981.
2. Hordeski, M. F., *Microprocessor Cookbook,* Blue Ridge Summit, CA: Tab, 1979.
3. Intel.
4. Ibid.

5. McGlynn, D. R., *Microprocessors,* New York: Wiley, 1976.
6. Zaks, R., *Microprocessors,* Berkeley: Sybex, 1980.
7. Ibid.
8. Motorola, *M6800 Microprocessor Applications Manual,* Phoenix: Motorola, 1975.
9. Ibid.
10. Ibid.
11. Ibid.
12. Intel.
13. Hordeski.
14. Intel.
15. Hordeski.
16. Ibid.
17. Ibid.
18. Intel.
19. Hordeski.
20. Motorola.
21. Zaks.
22. Intel.
23. Ibid.
24. Ibid.
25. Ibid.
26. Intel, *The 8086 Family User's Manual,* Santa Clara: Intel, 1980.
27. Ibid.
28. Zilog, *Z8000 User's Guide,* Cupertino, CA: Zilog, 1980.
29. Motorola, *M68000 Microprocessor User's Manual,* Austin: Motorola, 1980.
30. Electronics Industries Association, *RS-232C Bus Standard,* Washington: Electronics Industries Association 1974.
31. EIA, *RS-449 Bus Standard,* Washington: Electronics Industries Association 1978.
32. IEEE, *IEEE Standard 488-1978,* New York: IEEE, 1978.
33. Schwartz, I., STD-Bus Roundup, *Electronic Products,* May 1980.
34. Intel.
35. Ibid.
36. Ibid.
37. Schwartz.
38. Hordeski, M. F., Balancing Microprocessor-Interface Tradeoffs, *Digital Design,* April 1977.
39. Ibid.
40. Ibid.
41. Ibid.
42. Ibid.
43. Ibid.
44. Hordeski, M. F., *Microprocessor Cookbook.*

EXERCISES

1. Discuss the trade-offs of the technique, and present an example of, linear selection used for chip addressing.
2. Design the priority logic and encoder for an interrupt system with eight interrupt sources.
3. What is the major advantage of a priority-interrupt over a nonpriority system? How is it possible to have a priority-interrupt without a mask register?

4. What are the programming steps needed in order to check when a source interrupts the microcomputer while it is still being serviced by a previous interrupt request from the same source?

5. A microcomputer is without any priority interrupt hardware. The interrupt request results in storing the return address in memory location A and branching to location B. Discuss how a priority is established by software.

6. A routine for a peripheral device consists of a variable number of command words. Design a control word format such that the processor knows when there are more command words in its routine.

7. A peripheral processor responds to one of three CPU instructions by placing a word in a specified memory location that corresponds to the instruction requested. Diagram a method such that the CPU will know that the word in that location is the one that the instruction requested.

8. Formulate a command word to be used when the I/O device controls a cassette tape. The word should specify the number of blocks to be read or written on tape, the address of the first block, and the number of characters in each block.

9. Discuss how a vectored-interrupt system can use nested-interrupts so that high-priority interrupts can be rapidly serviced if they occur during a lower priority interrupt.

10. Draw a program flow diagram for a software interrupt-priority scheme in which the microcomputer program polls the I/O devices in a preset order to determine which will be serviced first. Discuss the advantages and disadvantages of this technique.

11. Discuss some of the problems one may encounter with multiple interrupts. Outline some ways to save and restore the contents of registers for each of the 16 different interrupt lines in a system.

12. A typical 6800 polling routine follows:

```
            POLL PIA ON INTERRUPT AND SERVICE
POLL        LDA A $2005     : load accumulator
            BPL POL2        : branch to POL2
            •               : input character handling
            •               : input character handling
POL2        LDA A $2007     : load accumulator
            BPL POL3        : branch to POL3
            •               : output character handling
            •               : output character handling
POL3        RTI             : return from interrupt
```

Draw a flow diagram for this routine.

13. Draw an interface for a parallel output digital encoder to the 6800 microprocessor. Draw the program flow diagram for this interface.

14. Discuss the two basic ways to control the rate of information flow in a computer system.

15. Direct-memory-access data transfers may be controlled by the main program using program-controlled I/O. Diagram how a microcomputer's program would initiate the DMA operation to allow a block of data to be transferred from the microcomputer to an I/O device.

16. Discuss how a real-time clock can be used to synchronize I/O operations with periodic interrupts in this example. Use an ac line frequency clock to generate interrupts to allow a microcomputer to sample and digitize analog signals from two input channels. Develop device status and command words to control the process.

17. Diagram a possible procedure and character sequence for the communication between a processor and a remote terminal. The processor inquires if the terminal is operative. The terminal responds with *yes* or *no*. If the response is *yes,* the processor sends a block of text.

18. The address of a terminal connected to a data communication processor consists of two letters of the alphabet or a letter followed by one of the 10 numerals. How many different addresses can be used with this format?

19. The longitudinal redundancy check (LRC) character is calculated by an EX-CLUSIVE–OR of the longitudinal or vertical bits of a block. Prove that the total bits in a column including the LRC bit has even parity.

20. Every standard has its flaws, since no standard is satisfactory to all. Standards also inhibit flexibility and that can be deemed to be a flaw, as well. Discuss the implications of these statements regarding the bus standards discussed in this chapter.

21. An intelligent interface is a single-chip microcomputer with a limited instruction set designed to control I/O operations. List some required instructions for intelligent interfaces for keyboards, magnetic-tape cassette drives, and printers.

22. Among the required components and functions for assembling a system, differences arise as a function of the microprocessor chosen. Discuss how the characteristics of, and differences between, microprocessors might affect the techniques and components for interfacing a system.

8. Control System Design Elements

MOTORS AND MOTOR CONTROLS

In this chapter we consider some of the techniques used to provide the control function in an industrial system application. We will start with a general discussion of motors and motor controls.

Although motor control is commonly thought of as speed control, many other useful motor control functions such as switching, direction control, or programming can also be performed by semiconductor devices. Speed control is most easily accomplished on motors whose speed is a function of power input. This is generally true of dc or universal brush-type motors. In most types of ac motors, however, the speed control must be accomplished by varying the frequency. A variable frequency drive can be used with a variable frequency trigger. In some cases, though, the control range may be limited because of the fall off in torque as the frequency is reduced.

Speed Control

Speed control by variation of the average power input to a dc motor can be accomplished by pulse width modulation.[1] This is switching between the "on" state and the "off" state, and controlling the percentage of on-time. In ac systems, this is done by phase control; by controlling the phase relationship between the gate trigger signal of a silicon controlled rectifier (SCR) or similar device and the supply voltage, the percentage of on-time in each cycle is controlled. In a dc circuit, such as an inverter, pulse width modulation may be accomplished by using a constant repetition rate and a variable time delay between the turn-on and the turn-off pulses, which allows an adjustment of the on-time in each cycle. Similar results can be obtained by using a fixed time delay between the on and off pulses and varying the repetition rate. This produces an output with a fixed on-time and a variable off-time.

Since ac power is convenient and since phase control is the most convenient way of regulating this source, phase control is used to control a wide variety of motor types. But most of the motors so controlled were not designed for this type of operation; they are used because they are available or low priced. Often the degree of simplicity of the control circuits is dependent on motor characteristics, and improper motor selection can cause poor circuit operation. Even the best control circuit is only a part of the overall system, and it can be no better than the overall system design.

Most motors have their ratings based on operation at a single speed and depend on this speed for the proper cooling. Attempts to use the motor at a lower speed can cause heating problems.

The presence of odd-order harmonics in a phase-controlled wave form, can produce side effects in induction motors.[2] The speed vs. torque characteristic of a particular induction motor may make it unsuitable for use with a variable voltage control system. Some controls for universal series motors depend on the residual magnetism in their magnetic structures. This is a characteristic that the motor vendor could be trying to minimize.

The use of a proper motor with a phase-control circuit allows versatile applications. In a temperature-compensated control system for a furnace blower, a wide variety of motor sizes and speeds is no longer required. A single motor may be used with the variable requirements in different installations being compensated by means of the control. Where the maximum speed of the motor is set by the control, the need for designing overvoltage capability into the motor is eliminated, thus allowing some savings in the motor design.

One of the drawbacks of motor speed control by variation of the average power input is that as the input power is reduced to reduce the speed, the available torque is also reduced. This disadvantage may be overcome by using a feedback signal to advance the firing angle in proportion to the load on the motor, thus supplying it with a greater amount of power as more torque is required.

In order for the circuit to control the speed of the motor, it must be able to sense the speed of that motor. The way to get this information from brush-type motors is by looking at the back EMF generated by the motor during the time that the controlling SCR is off.[3] In the case of separately excited shunt field wound and permanent magnet field motors, this EMF is directly proportional to speed. In series motors, the field is not energized at this time, and residual magnetism must provide the back EMF used by the circuit. The residual magnetism is a function of the past history of the motor current, so the voltage the circuit sees is not a function of speed alone. Care must also be taken so that brush noise does not interfere with circuit operation.

Relay Control

In addition to controlling or varying the speed of a motor, there are several other control functions which can be done using solid-state control. One of the simplest is the use of a triac as a switch for contactor replacement. When used with a reversing-type split capacitor motor, a pair of triacs can provide a task-responding, reversing motor control, (as shown in Figure 8.1). S1 and S2 can be reed switches, or the triacs can be gated by a number of other methods. The use of a solid-state static switching circuit can also provide a motor over-temperature control which senses the motor winding temperature directly.

The choice of solid-state over electromagnetic relays (EMRs) is often made on the basis of life expectancy. This is due to the limitation on the life of EMRs in high-cycle applications in which the relay must operate at too high a rate. EMRs have life expectancies rated in terms of the number of operations at rated load and the number of operations with no load on the contacts. These expectancies can be 100,000 operations at full load and 10 million operations at no load or low signal.[4]

Contactors for motor control are generally packaged and marketed along with the motors. Actually, they are relays with high contact ratings. Many general-purpose power relays are used for motors starting up to 5 hp in a control system integrated into one package.

More and more motors in all industries are remotely controlled using a logical analysis of contact-closure patterns by computers and programmable controllers. These motors and their relay contactors are really part of the control system.

The simplest manually controlled machine tools use relay control, whereas the most sophisticated tools are numerically controlled by computer (CNC). The trend among users of CNC machine tools is towards central data collection and the down-loading of programs from control and monitoring computers. There are, however, increasing interface problems as once independent unit process control systems are integrated under plant supervisory control systems. Even within a unit control system, there is often an interface box between the electrical and instrumentation equipment,

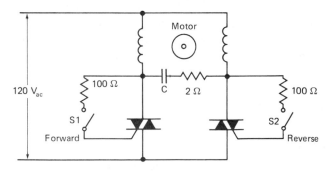

Fig. 8.1. Reversing control.

especially when the motors and the motor contactors control valves and pumps.

In connection with motor control, the increasing use of remote multiplexing systems provides an example of the effect of increasing system sophistication on relay control. A typical application is the relaying for the remote control of a motor operated valve. The valve is opened or closed by a momentary contact closure in a control room, either from a manual pushbutton or from a computer output.

The protective logic for limiting the open or closed movement of the valve is provided by a position-torque switch on the valve. Latching and interlocking of the motor contactor is performed in the motor control center. In a hard-wired system, a ten-conductor cable would be required for the open/close/power indication. Additional two-conductor cables would be needed for both the valve-open and overload annunciators. With a solid-state multiplexing system used to replace the wiring between the field and the control room, the protective and control logic remains basically unchanged, assuring that failure of the remote multiplexing system will not damage the motor or valve or prevent manual operation from the control center. The number of contacts is not reduced; in fact, other relays may be required to increase the power from the multiplexer output in order to drive the motor contactors.[5]

Motor Regulator Systems

We will now consider each of the functional boards of a typical motor regulator.[6] The sequencer module contains the ac buffer circuits and logic circuitry used to operate the drive from a standard operator station. An antiplugging circuit on the sequencer module prevents the plugging or bucking of the motor armature from high currents. The sequencer provides STOP, RUN, JOG and OFF/ON operator functions with unidirectional operation.

The buffer circuits allow the operator control signals to enter the drive system. The ac buffer circuits convert the 115V ac operator signals to logic signals which are then processed by the logic circuits to control the drive references and dc contactor.

The controller module contains speed reference switching circuitry—the ramp circuit, the overload detector circuit, the control loop circuitry for the speed loop, and the current loop. The circuit on the controller module processes the speed reference signals and provides the regulation of the motor armature speed and motor armature current.

The detector module provides detectors, for either speed, armature voltage, or current. With the detector switch, any combination of speed, armature voltage, or armature current may be checked without changing panel wiring. One of the detectors can also be a window detector; to operate within predetermined limits. The outputs of the detectors are relays. Analog signals proportional to the absolute value of speed, armature voltage, and armature current can be available, as well.

The reference module allows for signal following and preset speeds and currents. The signal-follow mode controls speed according to an external signal; the speed range and ratio are adjustable. The preset speeds/currents-mode allows one to recalibrate speed or torque by presetting speeds or currents.

A programmable logic module may provide for the transfer of control from a manual operator station to the control computer. This allows speed references and current limit references, as well as the control functions RUN, STOP, FORWARD/REVERSE and STANDBY STOP MODE, to be controlled from the computer. The programmable logic is a one-bit digital processor capable of performing Boolean algebriac operations on 12 input signals and storing the resultant functions at one of 16 output locations. These 16 output functions are programmed in PROMs which have a capacity of 64 Boolean algebriac operations as well as providing latched functions. The programmable logic is programmed using eight operation codes. Each code entry is a program stop. The logic is static and replaces over 72 relays.

The development of high-performance dc servo motors has been spurred by the need for computer peripherals with increased speed to more fully exploit the productivity of digital computers. The peripherals include not only printers and storage devices such as drum memories and diskettes, but also process controls, NC machine tools, and other production equipment—that is, any application where computer commands must be translated into mechanical motion. A typical application is a servo which drives the capstan of a digital tape drive. The design techniques may require tightly controlled rates of acceleration and deceleration, velocity, and drive reversal.

STEPPING MOTOR CHARACTERISTICS

In considering the characteristics of stepping motors, one must note that such a motor is a transfer device between the electrical information presented by the driver and the mechanical motion delivered to the load. The functioning of the stepping motor system is dependent both upon the load and the driver and both of these must be clearly specified if the performance of a given stepping motor is to be successful. But it is not practical to generate performance data for each driver and load combination, and many systems defy characterization as the load cannot be analyzed readily. The most practical approach is for the designer to understand the general parameters and problems involved, make a reasonable choice of driver and motor, and then test the combination in an actual system. This approach has been more useful than attempts to thoroughly quantify and analyze complex dynamic systems.

Permanent Magnet Motors

A permanent magnet (PM) stepping motor contains a stator with a number of wound poles. Each pole can have a number of teeth for flux distributing. The rotor is cylindrical and toothed. The PM motor uses a permanent magnet in the magnetic circuit. Most PM motors have the permanent magnet in the rotor assembly, and this magnet may be axially charged or radially charged as in the smaller-size motors.[7]

The PM motor operates by the interaction between the rotor magnet biasing flux and the magnetomotive force generated by an applied current in the stator windings. If the pattern of winding energization is fixed, there will be a series of stable equilibrium points generated around the motor. The rotor moves to the nearest of these and remains there when the windings are excited in sequence; the rotor follows the changing points of equilibrium and rotates in response to this changing pattern. The permanent magnet causes a detent torque to be developed in the motor even when stator windings are not excited. This torque is usually only a few percent of the maximum torque.[8]

Variable Reluctance Motors

A variable reluctance (VR) motor uses a stator with a number of wound poles. The rotor is a cylindrical toothed member with teeth that have a relationship to the stator poles. The teeth (if any) are a function of the step angle required. As a current is passed through the windings, a torque is developed such as to turn the rotor to a position of minimum magnetic reluctance. This position is stable in that external torque is required to move the rotor at this position. It is not an absolute position in that there are many stable points in the average motor. As a different set of windings is energized, the minimum reluctance point moves to a different set of poles and rotor teeth, causing the rotor to move to a new position. With the proper energizing sequence, these stable positions will rotate around the stator poles, giving a rotational speed to the rotor. When the energization sequence is fixed, the rotor position is also fixed. The shaft position is stepped by changing the pattern of winding energization.

In the VR motor, the rotor teeth have very little residual magnetism compared to the permanent magnet motor, so there is no force on the rotor in the form of detent torque when the stator is not energized.[9] The VR motor operates in a similar way as an ac electromagnet, in which a magnetic attraction occurs regardless of the direction of the magnetic flux.

There are also linear devices which convert electrical pulse trains, or energization patterns, into motion—each as linear PM or VR stepping motors.[10] Their operation is the same except that the magnetic paths are along a linear axis.

Another approach in stepping motor design uses internal torque amplification with an electrical stepping motor.[11] One can use internal gearing and reduce the step angle with no power gain, or couple a low torque stepper with a linear power amplifier.

Torque and Power Amplification Types

In the torque amplification technique, one uses a stepping motor with a large step angle, along with a gear system integral to the motor. A harmonic drive with a large gear reduction and a flexing mechanical spline may be used. The motor has a small stepping angle of 0.18 to 0.45 degrees and is used where these small step angles are desired.[12]

In the power amplification technique, a small stepping motor is used with a hydraulic amplifier, where the motor drives a control device in the hydraulic motor. If cost of the system and the hydraulic supply can be justified for the application, the power gain can be considerable. Hybrid motors like this can generate several horsepower.

In general, permanent magnet motors compared to VR motors are more efficient, have better damping characteristics, and are available in higher power models. VR motors are simpler in construction, have low rotor inertia, and when lightly loaded, have high speed capability. Table 8.1 is a general summary of stepping motor characteristics.

Table 8.1 Stepping Motor Characteristics

Characteristic	PERMANENT MAGNET (PM)	VARIABLE RELUCTANCE (VR)	HYBRID TYPES Torque Amplified	Power Amplified
Efficiency	High	Low	Low	Med-High
Rotor Inertia	High	Low	Low	Low
Speed	Medium to High	High for limited loads	Low to Medium	High
Damping	Good	Poor	Poor	Good
Power Output	High	Low	Low	Very High
Typical Step Angles	1.8°, 2.5°, 15°, 30°	7.5°, 15°, 30°	0.18°, 0.45°	1.5°, 2.25°

The remainder of the material in this chapter is applicable to permanent magnet stepping motors, in general, although it may be relevant to some VR units.

Dynamic and Static Characteristics

When a stepping motor takes a single step, due to the appropriate excitation of its stator winding, the rotor translates to a new position. The dynamic and static characteristics of such a step are useful to the understanding and the correct application of stepping motors.

The motion of the stepping motor rotor in the single-step mode is similar to that of a torsional pendulum.[13] Excitation is by the stator flux and the rate of increase determines the maximum kinetic energy input to the rotor. The load friction manifests itself as damping, while the system inertia consists of the sum of the rotor and load inertias. The effects of variation in system dynamics on position error can be large. The torque required to accelerate the rotor and load inertia is given by:

$$Ta = (I_{Load} + I_{rotor})\alpha$$

Therefore, one might expect that the torque available for frictional loads would be the difference between the torque shown at the desired frequency on the slow curve and the torque required for inertia acceleration given above. Because the system is accelerating and because there is a torque dip at the resonance point, the actual torque available is less. As the acceleration increases, the available torque becomes significantly less. This is caused by the fact that during acceleration, the rotor-stator lag angle is greater than the angle at steady-state conditions. This additional lag causes a loss of torque.

A digital positioning system may generate motion pulses having a linear velocity ramp so that the last pulse of motion and zero velocity occur simultaneously. Arriving at the final position at too high a speed, or undershooting and wasting time by creeping to this position—which are typical of exponential and linear voltage systems—are eliminated by the careful use of this technique.

The acceleration performance of a stepping motor is a function of driver, load friction, inertia, ramp time, starting frequency, and final frequency. Theoretical models are normally not used to predict the behavior of systems. Trial and error methods tend to be more practical.

Load Requirements

Sometimes stepping motor applications are straightforward—if the load is light and well controlled, the speed requirements low, and the environment constant and agreeable. Here the main concerns of the designer would be the lowest priced motor and driver that could fit in the space allocated. If a heavy load is to be driven as fast as possible because time is valuable, the largest motor and best driver available might be well justified. Many applications lie between these load and speed conditions, and one must make a choice based on a comparative study. The load requirements must be studied to determine the load parameters as well as possible and to consider modifications to the load to optimize the system.

In general, stepping motor systems are more sensitive to inertial loads than to friction loads.[14] So if fast response and quick settling are required, the most favorable load configuration will probably be one that minimizes inertia at the stepping motor.

The friction load is another basic load parameter. Friction and inertia, combined with the required load speed and acceleration, determine the basic requirements for the stepping motor system. Friction determines the power output, while inertia and the speed defines the amount of kinetic energy that must be put into the system on starting and removed on stopping. Although it is not practical to cover all load configurations likely to be encountered, inertial characteristics of some common applications are usually available from the manufacturer.

Power Considerations

Sometimes the required speed and resolution determine the step angle in a motor system, but in others a choice is available, since a gear ratio may be obtained through a timing belt, load screw, or linkage. In these cases, it may be useful to compare motors of different step angles. One approach is to consider shaft speed in RPM. For example, a 200 step/rev (1.8° step) device at 200 steps/sec is moving at 60 RPM. A 24 step/rev (15°/step) motor achieves this speed at 24 steps/sec. In making comparisons involving stepping motor systems with differing step angles and speed-torque characteristics, one can also plot speed in RPM against torque and power output. Power output in watts is calculated from the following:

$$P_{watts} = \text{Speed (steps/sec.)} \times \text{Torque (in.-oz.)} \times .0444 + \text{steps per rev.}$$

For typical step angles, the formulas are:

$$P_{watts} = 2.22 \times 10^{-4} \times \text{Torque (in.-oz)} \times \text{Speed (steps/sec) for 1.8° step angles}$$

$$P_{watts} = 1.84 \times 10^{-3} \times \text{Torque (in.-oz)} \times \text{Speed (steps/sec) for 15° step angles}$$

The power output curves on stepping motors show a broad maximum which arises from the nature of the power output relationships: at very high speeds, zero torque and zero power are delivered; at zero speed, torque is high but the power delivered is zero.[15] If other factors allow it, consideration should be given to operating at the peak of the power output curve in order to obtain the maximum performance from a motor-driver combination.

The operating point selection and motor-driver choice must also take into account the thermal conditions in the motor. High performance drivers generally lead to increased motor dissipation at high speeds. Since the motor thermal lag may be long with a thermal time constant of 20 minutes or more, it is possible to allow high motor dissipation for short periods of time if there is not excessive motor temperature rise. Basically a duty cycle problem, the major criterion is the final temperature rise, considering the effects of ambient temperature, the motor heat-sink, and the operating times. The limitation on the power output of most stepping motors is the temperature rise. Usually, more torque is available at higher than the rated currents if the average motor temperature is held to its rated value.

A good way to determine if a motor will overheat is to measure the temperature rise of the winding by measuring the winding resistance after it has operated at the worst duty cycle for 3 to 4 hours.

STEPPING MOTOR DRIVES

Drive circuit design is an important aspect of the stepping motor system. The overall system performance is heavily dependent upon the drive system, not only in the available power delivered to the load, but also in the efficiency, power dissipation, and cost. The stepping motor drive system as diagrammed in Figure 8.2 accepts a drive signal and converts it to the proper format for driving the motor windings. A power amplifier then drives the current from the windings, and a power return system removes the current from the windings at the termination of the step. As discussed earlier, the motor rotates in response to the changing patterns between the rotor and stator magnetic fields. A state generator is used to create the proper sequence and pattern of states in response to a serial pulse train command.

There are two major sequences which are used to cause the motor to step. One is called the wave drive, in which only one set of stator poles is energized at a time (see Figure 8.3). The other type of sequence energizes both pole sets simultaneously (as shown in Figure 8–4 and is called the two-phase drive. Either of these will cause an N per step motor to step by increments of N, but there is an $N/2$ spatial displacement of the stator and rotor between the two sequences.[16]

Wave Drive

For the wave-drive sequence, the required currents are shown in Figure 8.5. The A_1 current energizes all phase A poles to create a North pole at the stator pole teeth. Current B_1 then generates a North pole at the B-phase pole teeth. The A_2 current generates a South pole at the pole A teeth and B_2 creates a South pole on the B-phase poles. During this sequence, the rotor advances to align the rotor and stator teeth. The logic used to generate these waveforms is shown in Figure 8.6. The logic states can also be placed in memory and used to control a microprocessor.

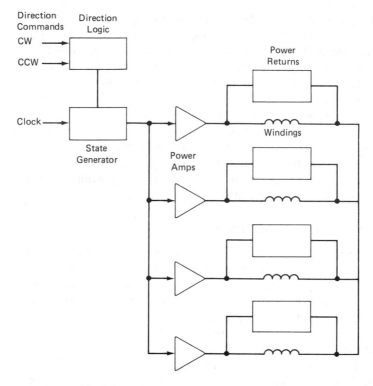

Fig. 8.2. Basic stepping-motor drive system.

Two-Phase Drive

Although the wave drive is a common stepping sequence, it is not the pre-ferred sequence for all two-phase stepping motors. The ampere-turns on the stator poles per watt of input power are 41% higher if both of the phase A and B poles are driven. This can be done by driving the four windings A_1, A_2, B_1, and B_2 two at a time. The torque does not match the increase of 41%. Although the torque per ampere-turn is higher for the wave-drive tooth alignment, there is a net gain in torque-per-watt of about 20% with the two-phase alignment.[17] (The sequence of phase currents is shown in Figure 8.7). The current in A_1 generates a North pole in the A stator poles, while the current in A_2 generates a South pole. The B_1 currents create a North pole in the B stator poles, while B_2 creates South poles. All four combinations of current in the two windings give rise to four motor steps. The pattern repeats every four steps. (The logic required is shown in Figure 8.6). Due to the in-creased performance that can be obtained, the two-phase drive has been more commonly used than the wave drive.

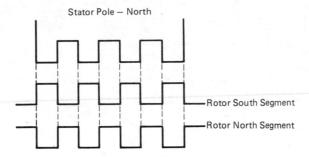

Fig. 8.3. Wave-drive tooth arrangement.

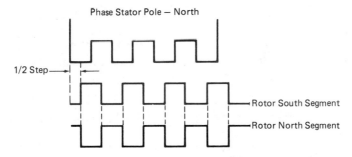

Fig. 8.4. Two-phase tooth arrangement.

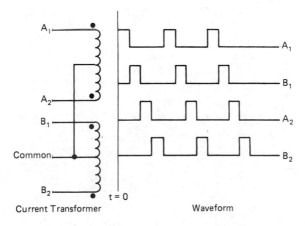

Fig. 8.5. Unipolar wave-drive currents.

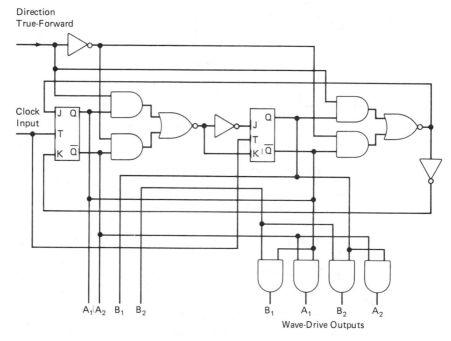

Fig. 8.6. State generator for wave drive or two-phase drive.

Half-Step Drive

If four windings of a stepping motor are energized using the wave drive, and the tooth alignment is like that shown in Figure 8.3, the successive steps will have the spacing of 1.8°. The two-phase drive with the tooth alignment of Figure 8.4 will also have 1.8° steps. If a drive is used that alternates between

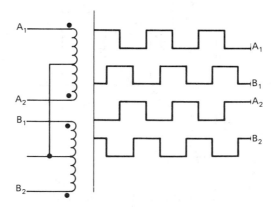

Fig. 8.7. Unipolar two-phase drive currents.

the wave type and two-phase drive as shown in Figure 8.7, then the stepping motor output will be $\frac{1}{2}$ the normal step, or 0.9°.

All three of these drive sequences are used. The two-phase drive is the most widely used since it is more efficient than wave drive. Half-step drive is used in some applications for reducing resonance problems. But the difficulty with half-step drive is that the two types of steps can have somewhat different characteristics due to the different magnetic alignment.[18]

The logic components for a half-step drive are shown in Figure 8.8. The half-step drive can be used with either bipolar or unipolar drivers. For unipolar drivers, A_1, A_2, B_1, and B_2 represent the individual winding drivers. With bipolar drivers, a positive voltage at A_1 drives a positive current into the A-phase winding pair, while a positive voltage at A_2 drives a negative current into the winding pair. This same convention also holds with B_1 and B_2 with respect to the B-phase winding pair.

Synchronous Mode

A major type of operation for stepping motors is the line-operated synchronous mode. Synchronous operation is similar to bipolar drive at a fixed frequency. The driving waveform consists of two sine waves, 90° out of phase. The motor steps when either of the input sinusoids assumes either a

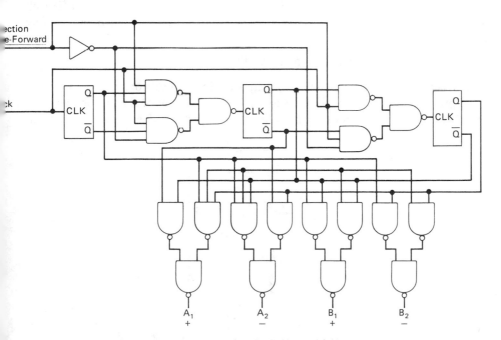

Fig. 8.8. State generator for half-step drive.

positive or a negative maximum. The stepping rate is then 4 times the line frequency. Thus, for an input line frequency of 60 Hz, the motor will take 240 steps/sec. With a 100-step/rev motor, this corresponds to 240/100 rev/sec, or 144 RPM.

The 90° waveform can be generated with an RC network. If three-phase power is available, a Scott T may be used, particularly if a number of motors or high power motors are to be driven. The components in the RC phase-shifting network have some effects on motor performance, and one may have to optimize some parameters by varying the components from their nominal values. For instance, audible noise may be reduced, at the expense of some torque, by adjusting component values. The starting characteristics under inertial load are also affected by variations in the component values.

As is the case with digitally operated stepping motors, synchronous-mode motors have differing starting and running characteristics in the presence of inertial loads.[19] Curves can be used to determine if a proposed operating mode is within the capabilities of a given motor.

A synchronous servo using a stepping motor is shown in Figure 8.9. The synchronous mode requires only a minimum of extra hardware to provide a reversible drive. This mode uses the low synchronous speed of the stepping motor when operated directly from line frequency: 144 RPM for a 100 step/rev or 72 RPM for a 200 step/rev motor at 60 Hz. This low speed and relatively high torque are achieved without a gear box. The motor is well damped for positive starts and stops, and it can be stalled indefinitely without damage.

CONTROL SYSTEM APPLICATION

Microprocessors find many uses in stepping motor controls. The microprocessor can be used with hardwired logic to advance the motor by a step when an output appears from one state generator. The logic sequence can

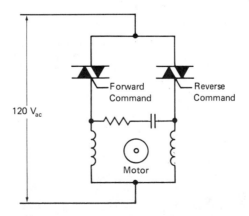

Fig. 8.9. Synchronous-mode servo system.

also be stored in memory, with one bit sent out at a time. A step counter can be used to ensure that the motor goes through the correct number of steps.

Two modes of operation may be used: (1) constant speed operation and (2) automatic acceleration and deceleration. In the constant speed mode, the motor covers the steps at a constant rate. The acceleration-deceleration mode uses progressively decreasing time delays between steps in order to increase the stepping rate.[20] (The general control algorithm is shown in Figure 8.10.)

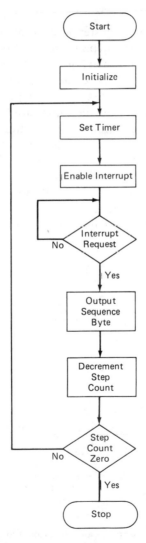

Fig. 8.10. Microprocessor stepping-motor control flow.

The coupling to the load should be compliant, but not sloppy. The attachment of couplings to stepping motors with set screws is satisfactory only for smaller sizes. Larger motors must be pinned or keyed as the discontinuous stepping torque can loosen less than positive fasteners over even short periods of time.

Stepping motors are also used in modes other than digital load positioning. The basic motor operation is the same in all modes. We now consider these modes of operation.

Closed-Loop Systems

In many applications, open-loop stepping motor systems are competitive to closed-loop servos. However, stepping motors are sometimes used as the mover in servo systems (as shown in Figure 8.11). In this system, the stepping motor is used in a digital stepping mode. Thus, the system is limited in resolution to the value represented by one step. This acts as a bang-bang servo where an error signal results in a quantized response. The dead band necessary for stability is represented by the distance between the steps, and the resolution is limited by the step size as seen by the load through gearing. A holding torque is always applied to the load, while almost full torque may be generated by the motor with a shaft position error of less than the deadband. The speed of response is independent of the load characteristics. The load will be driven to null at the same speed regardless of the magnitude of the error. Thus, overshoot problems are easily minimized, since the stepping motor system controls the overshoot.

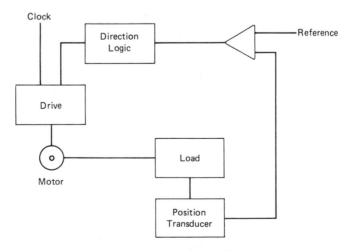

Fig. 8.11. Stepping motor in a closed-loop system.

The stepping motor does not have the brush problems of dc servos and is suited for operation over a wider range of frequencies compared to most two-phase ac servo-motors.

Variable Ratio Systems

The stepping motor with an appropriate driver offers an infinite speed control range, since the lower limit can be as low as desired. The output speed is unaffected by the load up to the torque limit of the motor, and the speed may be programmed or controlled from an external source using either analog or digital signals. This variable speed capability allows two motors to run at identical speeds in remote locations or two motors to run at precise ratios of each other, independent of load. (Figure 8.12 is the block diagram of such a variable ratio system.)

Shaft position encoders are used with stepping motors for improving the acceleration and confirming the motor position. Acceleration improvement can be achieved if the shaft position can be determined accurately as a function of time.[21] It is then possible to control the drive-pulse timing in order to obtain maximum acceleration. The kind of encoder used must allow the determination of direction, such as the class of encoders with quadrature tracks. Overshoots of shaft position could otherwise be interpreted incorrectly by the decoding circuitry. An encoder offers improvement of acceleration that is difficult to obtain in any other way. Step confirmation can be achieved with the encoder.

Digital Control

Over the past years, increasing emphasis has been placed on the control of analog power drives through positioning and tracking commands from digital computers. This is true for industrial processes and for applications such as gun control and tracking antenna systems. The more powerful com-

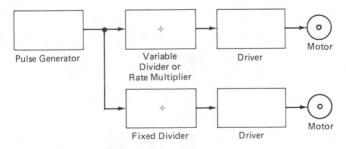

Fig. 8.12. Variable ratio drive.

putational aspects of digital computers have been accompanied by the problem of providing satisfactory dynamic control for inputs in the form of discrete signals. The trend has been toward the development of distributed systems and toward the use of microcomputers as control elements. This trend has resulted in a certain degree of freedom in control system design with a growing number of system designs.

Modern digital controllers have shown extensive versatility in application. They have evolved from a program in a general purpose medium-sized computer, to a minicomputer program, then to a special-purpose hardwired MSI and LSI logic, and finally today toward designs incorporating microcomputers. This evolutionary process has resulted from digital controller designs for a variety of systems. A considerable amount of commonality in hardware configurations and computer programs was used in the earlier designs, and one of those common features in these systems was the basic dynamic characteristics of the power drives. These were usually modeled after the Type 1 servo: a double integration with velocity feedback and velocity and acceleration limiting. Electrohydraulic power drives generally fall into this category and so do most electrical power drives.

The design approach, here, was to make the model of the controlled plants appear to be of the same form from the controller point of view. This was done chiefly with proper selection of velocity loop gains. The design of the digital controller was then optimized for the plant. The result was a controller that was applicable to a broad class of power drives. Early controller hardware used MOS and later CMOS, MSI, and LSI elements. Recently, the design of the controller—or minicontroller as it has been called—has been modified to allow it to be implemented using a microprocessor.

Microprocessor Control

These microprocessor controllers use primarily four types of functional sections or modules, as shown in Figure 8.13: (1) interface module, (2) analog output module, (3) status/test module, and (4) processor module.

Since many of the different types of systems controlled, as a rule, have unique characteristics such as acceleration limits, unique coefficients for difference equations and the solution of polynomials may be required. The values of these coefficients are stored in ROMs. The unique interfacing requirements of a particular plant and master computer are also handled by the interface module to make these signals compatible with the rest of the system.

The analog output module includes the buffer registers and D/A converters for conversion of the digital commands from the controller into analog signals required by the plant. Each of the outputs of these D/A converters is connected to a separate summing amplifier and is summed with the

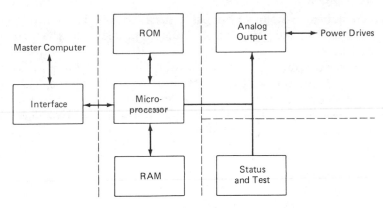

Fig. 8.13. Microprocessor digital control system.

output of the feedback device. Also contained in this module are additional D/As which may be used for monitoring position, velocity, and servo errors.

The status test module is used to generate artificial input orders for use in a test operation. Various commands, such as steps, ramps, and sinusoids are generated from this module. Coefficients for these functions are stored in ROMs.

The processor module contains the arithmetic capability, temporary storage, mode select, and timing and control circuitry. All the control calculations are performed by this module. Use of the microprocesser has resulted in significant space savings through the reallocation of some functions previously performed in other modules.

Sample-Rate Considerations

In many applications, a primary goal is to avoid orders coming from the master computer at an excessively high rate. This is of particular concern in distributed systems where high update rates directly affect bus band-width requirements. Considerations such as this generally limit the desirable sample-rate of these orders to a low value: 20 to 30 samples per second. At this low rate, difficulty may be encountered in maintaining smooth operation of the system. To drive a conventional analog system with 20 samples per second through a digital-to-synchro converter, results in rough, unacceptable operation of power drives leading to premature component deterioration with poor response.

The usual design approach to digital controls of this type is to use sophisticated interface processing. The interface usually involves some form of data extrapolation for digital-to-synchro (or resolver) conversion. The objective is to modify the discrete low sample-rate commands in such a way as to present them to the analog loop as a quasi-continuous signal. The growing use of closed-loop digital control during the past few years has simplified the problem.

If the servo control loop is closed digitally and the digital error signal is operated on, positioning orders on the order of 20 samples per second can yield acceptable performance levels. Position feedback data from a shaft encoder or S/D conversion may require some level adjustments. Signal conditioning of the interface may include level shifting, multiplexing, and buffering.

Position Control

Stepping and servo motors are used in an increasing number of applications which require precise motion to reach a digitally defined position. These applications involve an acceleration to the running speed and a deceleration to the programmed position. Some positioning systems use digital interpolation to generate motion command pulses with a linear velocity ramp for minimum travel time to the desired position. Using this method, the last pulse of motion and zero velocity can be achieved simultaneously. The commands are supplied to either a stepper or servo motor in a closed-loop system to reduce the lag between command and actual positions, which provides faster positioning.

One method of controlling position uses an exponential velocity change for acceleration and deceleration.[22] In a closed-loop system, velocity and position feedback produce the exponential output velocity change for a velocity-step input command.

In a stepping-motor control this can be done using a voltage-controlled oscillator coupled to a pulse generator circuit to supply either an exponential rising or falling voltage for the acceleration or deceleration.

In a servo motor drive, a positioning system with velocity feedback having an exponential characteristic maintains a lag between the commanded and actual positions. The lag distance provides deceleration without overshooting the commanded position. The motion takes longer than necessary, however, since the acceleration is not maintained at its optimum value. In an open-loop system, the effects of aging and temperature on the offsets in the analog circuits cause variations in the speed and the exponential time-constant. If the slowdown is initiated at a fixed distance from the desired final position, the part being positioned can either stop short of its destination or arrive at too high a speed. Provision can be made, though, to permit a low final speed by creeping to reach the commanded position. This consumes excessive time.

An alternative approach for stepping motor control is to generate a linear voltage ramp to the oscillator producing the command pulses. Positioning

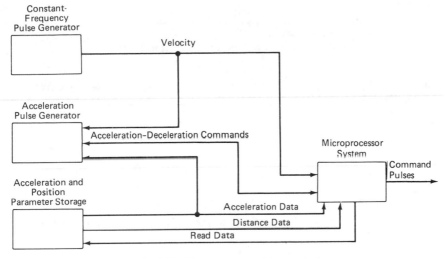

Fig. 8.14. Linear ramp position control.

time is reduced compared to the exponential method, but creeping is still required. The system uses the following components (as shown in Figure 8.14).

1. A constant frequency pulse generator whose output frequency is the desired velocity. Each pulse represents an increment of motion.
2. An acceleration parameter data store to contain the digital number which defines the desired acceleration. The store might be thumb switches, a read-only-memory, or hardwired logic.
3. Storage for programming data which represents the distance of motion required.
4. An acceleration pulse generator to generate a stream of pulses. Each pulse represents a commanded position increment. The frequency of the pulse stream increases linearly when an acceleration signal is present and decreases linearly when a deceleration signal is present.
5. A microprocessor system which monitors the generated motion-command pulses, and determines the acceleration and deceleration phases of the motion and when the programmed distance has been traveled.

REFERENCES

1. Kolk, W. R., Pulse Width Modulation, *Control Engineering,* April 1975.
2. General Electric, *SCR Manual,* Syracuse: General Electric, 1972.
3. Ibid.
4. Kompass, E. J., Relays: The Essential Component in Industrial Control, *Control Engineering,* February 1978.

5. Ibid.
6. Baumgart, G. E., and Jones, D. W., Modular Approach Speeds DC Drive System Build-Up, *Control Engineering,* January 1978.
7. Sigma, *Stepping Motor Handbook,* Braintree, MA: Sigma, 1972.
8. Ibid.
9. Ibid.
10. Baily, S. J., Stepper Torque and Force Moving Up, *Control Engineering,* May 1978.
11. Ibid.
12. Sigma.
13. Ibid.
14. Ibid.
15. Ibid.
16. Ibid.
17. Ibid.
18. Ibid.
19. Ibid.
20. Cutler, H., Linear Velocity Ramp Speeds Stepper and Servo Positioning, *Control Engineering,* May 1977.
21. Ibid.
22. Doherty, D. W. and Wells, E. J., Digital Power Drive Controller Dynamics are Characterized by ROMs, *Control Engineering,* January 1978.

EXERCISES

1. Discuss why the control system designer is often the original specifier of both motors and motor drives. What are some characteristics of drives and drive systems that should be considered in specifications?

2. In the manufacturing industries, general-purpose machine tools are a market for both motors and motor drives. Discuss the use of a standardized drive for some typical applications in this area.

3. Discuss some major methods of controlling motor speed using SCRs. Which of these techniques are also applicable to motor position controls? Give some examples of SCR servo systems which can control other major parameters such as temperature and light.

4. The speed-torque curves of stepping motors with half-step logic using a bipolar drive show that the reduction in resonances is worth the increased logic. Discuss how the system can be arranged to operate on the strong step or full step operation with two pulses per step for improved performance using a microprocessor state generator.

5. For ramp times less than 0.5 seconds, half-step motor drive may deliver more torque than full-step drive. With longer ramp times, full-step drive delivers more torque because of its higher magnetic efficiency. Consider how a microprocessor could be used to provide a dual-ramp control along with any additional components required.

6. What is the most practical way to apply stepping motor systems with regard to changing conditions? Many loads can change during the system life. Is it feasible to handle transient load conditions that occur only infrequently?

9. Microprocessor Application

LOW-COST MICROCOMPUTERS

Applications for microprocessors span the entire range of industrial, commercial, and consumer tasks. (Figure 9.1) In this chapter, we will consider applications in some of these areas.

One of the major applications of the microprocessor is in low-cost general-purpose computers. For under $1000, one may purchase a micro-

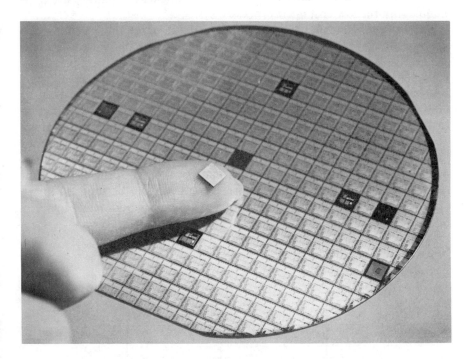

Fig. 9.1. This chip is the "heart" of a microcomputer, which commands an emission control system. It is programmed to receive inputs from engine-mounted sensors. It then analyzes the sensor data and decides what adjustments are to be made in the carburetor in order to maintain the optimum air/fuel mixture for the engine. The 3 in. wafer produces 190 chips. (*Courtesy General Motors Corporation.*)

computer that is able to perform various tasks. Such a low-cost computer is appealing for educational or home use, and there are a number of ways in which this microcomputer may be sold: as components to be assembled, or already assembled as a unit and even preprogrammed for specific applications. The lowest cost microcomputers are those preprogrammed and packaged for a dedicated operation, such as educational toys. A simple system may sell for less than $200, and using a minimum number of parts.

One example of such a system uses the 4040.[1] This configuration is among the simplest that could be assembled, consisting of the CPU, clock, ROM, and one I/O chip. Many different microcomputer chips could be used as a CPU. This simple microcomputer is a dedicated processor. The program to be executed is designed, debugged, and stored in the ROM by the manufacturer. The user enters data through the I/O ports via a data entry device such as pushbuttons or a keyboard. The processor then executes the data input and supplies the appropriate response via the output port. More complex systems use more hardware such as a keyboard and a display. These peripherals are also available as low-cost components so that they are compatible with the low-cost microprocessor system.

For a display, one may use an ordinary television set along with the appropriate interface. Such a low-cost system is illustrated in Figure 9.2; a simple character display for a television monitor is shown in Figure 9.3. Typically, the bit patterns for the characters are stored in a read-only memory. A television set in the United States operates with 525 lines, scanned at a rate of 30 frames per second. This corresponds to 64 microseconds for each picture line. For a display with 64 characters in each line, we must provide one character every microsecond. Shift registers or other recirculating memories are used to allow a character, which is written on the screen, to be continually rewritten or refreshed. The radio frequency section of the display consists of circuits for generating the correct RF signals to be supplied to the television monitor. The bit pattern is used to generate a modulating signal to

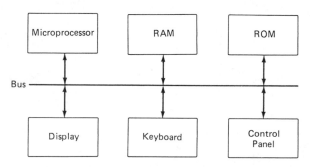

Fig. 9.2. Low-cost microcomputer.

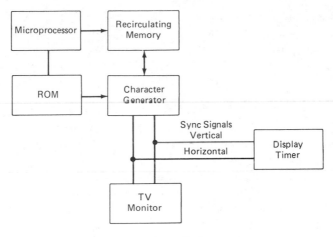

Fig. 9.3. Character display system.

modulate the RF output of an RF signal generator. The display pattern is a series of dots or scanning segments across a picture line.

The arrangement shown in Figure 9.3 is not limited to generating characters: graphics and other images can be generated and displayed by the use of a programmed ROM. For example, a game can be created by providing the means for moving images across the screen by opposing sides. In this case, each player side is provided with a miniaturized joystick. The movement of the joystick corresponds to a vertical and horizontal movement of the player's marker across the screen. In the control unit, the joystick movement is translated into delayed pulses from the horizontal and vertical sync signal generators, and the delayed pulses are applied to a coincidence gate to modulate an RF signal that is applied to the television monitor.

An important input device is a keyboard. A simple numeric keyboard is used for arithmetic or calculator applications, while an alphabetical keyboard is used for word processing applications. In a typical keyboard in a microprocessor system, a scanning keyboard encoder detects the key closures and sends the current digital signal to the microprocessor.

Other peripheral devices may also be used in the system in addition to the TV display and the keyboard. The simplest storage facility is the magnetic tape cassette, which can be used as a low-cost peripheral for the small microcomputer with ordinary audio cassettes for off-line storage.

Consumer Applications

A few of the consumer applications for the small microcomputer are as follows:

1. Educational games and toys.
2. Programmable timing and control systems for appliances or for building heating and cooling.
3. Word processing systems.
4. Information and record storage.

Such applications can be programmed on a general-purpose microcomputer, or dedicated microcomputers can be supplied as parts of consumer products or appliances. A microcomputer can perform certain routine household functions such as menu planning and cooking. Domestic ranges for household cooking feature digital controls, displays, timers, and microprocessor control. Here, a stored program is used to provide information on the cooking time for the various types of food. The program automatically turns burners or ovens on and off. Touch-control panels and displays for such digitally controlled ranges have been developed.

Many of these consumer applications are characterized by large volume and low cost. Hence, this is the area of single-chip microcomputers. These microcomputers are sufficient for simple control functions such as those required by a microwave oven controller. The microprocessor eliminates electro-mechanical or hard-wired logic. It also provides more functions. And it can provide reasonable tests. If the user makes an error in selecting controls, the microprocessor can flash a warning and not execute the command. The F8 microprocessor has been used in color televisions to provide tuning and programming of the set, up to a year ahead. Once a microprocessor is installed in a television set, it is easy to provide a digital clock as well as built-in games, which has been done commercially.

Other examples of microprocessor-equipped goods are washing machines and sewing machines. The Singer Athena 2000, for example, uses a custom microprocessor.

In the office, many of the office machines are microprocessor-equipped. These include word-processing typewriters and copy machines.

Technical Considerations

A number of technical problems were encountered when microprocessors were first put into these goods. Many of the parameters must be stored in a read/write memory. In a washing machine, for example, the microprocessor system must remember the information supplied by the user. In the traditional machine, a rotating switch keeps track of the wash cycle being executed. But the user might disconnect the machine accidently, or there may be a power failure. When this happens, the machine must recover as smoothly as possible. Thus, some amount of nonvolatile storage must be provided in a microprocessor-controlled machine. This can be expensive compared to the cost of the microprocessor alone. Several solutions have been used: EAROM, battery-assisted CMOS memory, and even mechanical devices. On the other hand, digital watches and pocket calculators have solved this cost problem with custom designs. However, for the time being, there is no industrially available general solution, at a low cost which is now on the market. This represents a small obstacle.

Yet because of the new markets open to manufacturers from these applications—which had not existed before pocket calculators—many new products will eventually be introduced. Both standard microprocessors and custom chips may be used. Because of the large quantities involved, it may be reasonable to consider the use of custom chips, which can offer several advantages: they are more immune to direct copying by competition; and they can be better adapted, and therefore cheaper for a given application. A custom design, though, also has its disadvantages: since it is tailored to the application, it will usually be much more difficult to reprogram it for any improvements which might be desirable; and because it is a special-purpose design, its development and debugging may take a long time until it becomes reliable enough. For these reasons, custom chips are a minority. When a market is firmly established, custom designs can be created to cater to it. But, standard microprocessors will still tend to establish all of the market areas. One such market has been electronic games.

Games

The first games shown on television displays were created with standard logic. Low-cost microprocessors allowed the use of a microprocessor system for the development of a variety of games on the monitor screen. Several manufacturers implemented these games and established a new market. Other manufacturers turned to companies for the direct manufacture of those games with game chips. The new custom chips eliminated the prior designs using microprocessor systems, as they accomplished the same function at a lower cost. The widespread use of these games resulted in more product sophistication. Manufacturers now compete not only in cost, but in the complexity and sophistication of their games. Newer complex games are now required which can no longer be created on a single chip; many successful new games use a microprocessor system. Since it is possible to implement a complete microcomputer in one or two chips, and because of the low cost of such microcomputers in quantities, it is likely that games will be supplied as an option for color televisions in the future. This will put a low-cost computer with general-purpose capability in the home. And the availability of a microcomputer in the television means that it can be used for other tasks at no additional cost. It can be used for games, fine-tuning, programmed selection, and data processing, using the screen as a display. Because of the availability of cable TV networks, it may also be connected to a central computer. Much of this is appearing now.

What are the next applications for microprocessors? Any device costing several hundred dollars or more is a likely candidate, since the extra cost involved in adding a microprocessor/microcomputer to the product is small compared to the total price. And if the functions or the intelligence introduced by the microcomputer are valuable, it will be a success.

LOW-COST CONTROLS

Many applications for industrial microprocessors essentially are the replacement of minicomputers or complex hard-wired logic by low-cost microprocessors (Figure 9.4). The essential goal of microprocessors, however, has not been to reduce the hardware price but to provide new functions making control more simple, more powerful, and more intelligent with the same cost. Microprocessors have introduced software into a hardware world, making it possible to use standardized products over a longer period of time. This results in lower costs.

Industrial Control Considerations

Many industrial applications use analog inputs and outputs. The resulting system is the equivalent of an analog controller with a number of control loops. A control loop is the implementation of an algorithm which will regulate an output as a function of one or more inputs. Most applications are characterized by costly sensors and control mechanisms. The cost of the sensors required for input and the cost of the control devices required for output

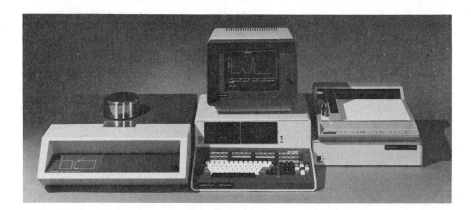

Fig. 9.4. This thermal analyzer system is possible with today's low-cost microprocessors. (*Courtesy Perkin-Elmer Corporation.*)

is such that the cost of the microprocessor system may be small compared to the cost of these devices. In view of the overall cost of the process control facility, the low cost of the microprocessor system itself is not the major advantage. But there is one strong advantage: the availability of software where hardware was used before. Programmed logic can now provide a flexibility for many applications that did not exist before microprocessors. Programming allows the implementation of complex functions which could not be achieved with hard-wired logic. Changes are simple, and algorithms may be improved or changed with minimal or no hardware changes. Microprocessors have been used to control processes or flows—discrete or continuous—from traffic control to the distribution of liquids. These processors are capable of regulating virtually any control process.

A typical process control might be the regulation of a fermentation reactor.[2] Such a system would be equipped with sensors for temperature, pressure, and other parameters, such as pH or flow. Using the information supplied by the sensors, the system monitors the reactor and regulates the control parameters to optimize the reaction. It will control the temperature, pressure, and flow of the process, resulting in optimum performance. It will also improve the reliability of detecting or correcting malfunctions. Its data collection capability may result in an improvement of the processing strategy.

Microprocessor Impact

When a microprocessor is used for process control, the processor is available for other functions which were not previously provided for. This allows additions to the system such as a cassette recorder or a floppy disk memory which will enable it to log data continuously. During idle times, or at regular intervals, the microprocessor can not only monitor the state of the system, but record all the parameters in bulk memory for future analysis. It can also use this information for analysis. These techniques have been used in industrial controls which could afford to use a minicomputer. The essential point is that these techniques can now be used in microprocessor systems to improve the performance of the process system. This is sometimes called dynamic optimization.[3] The microcomputer can look up previous values of the control parameters which were found to be successful in improving the operation of the system and attempt to improve it further by trying additional alternatives.

Industrial applications are characterized by specific techniques which are almost universal. Most industrial control systems use status feedback for reliable operation. The microprocessor controls some output device and it must verify that the operation of this device is correct. When a command is given to the output device, such as "close relay $A9$," the microprocessor must verify that the relay $A9$ has been closed. Each control device can be monitored in this manner in order to provide information on its status. That information can be sent back to the microprocessor which will verify it, completing the status-feedback loop. In a typical system, the microprocessor will give the command to relay $A9$. Following a predetermined time after giving this command, it will read the status of the relay. If correct, the status bit will be true and the microprocessor will determine that the command has been correctly followed. Should the status not be true, this would indicate a malfunction. The microprocessor might then give the order a second and perhaps even a third time. If the relay then closes, the status information will tell the microprocessor that the order has been executed. The malfunction might be ignored as a random effect and execution could proceed. If this malfunction occurs repeatedly, the microprocessor might issue an alarm and request maintenance. If the relay should refuse to move, a number of alternatives might be considered. Soft-fail techniques would allow a progressive degradation of the system, rather than a complete failure when one of the components fails. The microprocessor might activate an alternate device or execute a backup algorithm, ignoring this device and sound an alarm.

When the values of input sensors are read by the microprocessor, it can determine that they are correct. Reasonable tests are used. A bracket is provided for every input parameter at any given time. For example, a system controlling traffic at an intersection will sense cars through magnetic loop detectors. It uses the information from the loop detectors to compute the speeds of the vehicles. A speed of 50 miles per hour in an urban area might be considered unreasonable. This may indicate a failure of the speed sensing system. In a similar manner, a process controller measuring temperatures can use unreasonable temperature levels to detect failures.

The usual procedure is simple: when there is a single occurrence of an unreasonable input value, it is ignored as noise. This technique thus performs a filtering of spurious indications. If the failure is repeated, it indicates a malfunction. A diagnostic can then be generated to have the device disconnected.

Should there be a temporary malfunction that can be tolerated, the microprocessor will keep checking the device. When the device gives reasonable indications for the required period of time, it can be reconnected to the system. Connecting and disconnecting the device need not be done physically in hardware; it can be normally accomplished by software.

There is also a weighing technique, where each sensor receives a confidence ratio or weight. Measurements are obtained from several sensors and then multiplied by the weights to compute the final averaged input value. Then the average can be compared with each sensor reading. For example, consider two temperature sensors. One might have a 60% weight, and the second one a 40% weight. The resulting temperature is the value of the first measurement multiplied by 6 plus the value of the second one multiplied by 4. If the first sensor fails, its weight is set to 0 and its value ignored. The input temperature is then derived from the second sensor. It would thus have been effectively disconnected by reducing its weight to zero. When the first sensor again gives reasonable values, it can be reconnected by reinstating a weight of 60% again.

Traffic Controllers

In the case of a traffic controller, another example of an unreasonable input would be a continuous speed indication of 0 mph by one of the detectors. This might occur because of a malfunction or because a car is parked directly on top of the loop detector. The processor can determine if a loop is giving an unreasonable value since all of the other loops may be indicating a speed of 35 mph. The faulty loop can be disconnected and a diagnostic generated. Minutes later, the microprocessor which is still monitoring this loop even though it may not use its results, will notice that the speed indicated is again 35 mph. After a period during which the loop behaves, it can be reconnected to the system. The fault may have occurred if a car stalled on top of the loop detector and was later towed away. The loop is reconnected to the system where in a less intelligent system this would have to be done manually.

The microprocessor has made it possible to replace most of the logic hardware modules with software equivalents. A typical microprocessor-equipped traffic control uses a standard microprocessor plus the required interface. All system functions are carried out by the program. The system illustrated in Figure 9.5 will now be considered. A microprocessor-based board provides the memory, I/O, and CPU facilities. Two modules are shown on the top of the illustration: they are the real-time clock, for precise timing of external events, and the power-fail restart unit for restarting the system after a power failure and for preserving data when a power failure is detected. Sensing and control are based on the information provided by the vehicle detectors. A rectangle is cut in the pavement and two or more loops of wire are deposited inside the groove. The loop is connected to an RC oscillating circuit. The frequency of oscillation will depend on the impedance of the loop. The presence of a large magnetic mass, such as a car, over part or all of the loop causes a change in inductance and oscillating frequency. The frequency shift is detected and converted into a discrete signal which is monitored by the microprocessor.

Loops are normally installed in each lane of an intersection. They detect the presence of a vehicle and can be used to measure the length of a line of vehicles. They are also being used to measure the speed of the vehicles.

The microprocessor's role is to measure the parameters and optimize traffic flow as a function of these indications. Optimization may be carried out

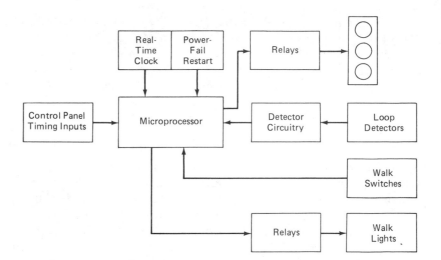

Fig. 9.5. Traffic control system.

with several different strategies. For instance, at certain times of the day it may be desirable to optimize the number of vehicles that pass through an intersection, or it may be desirable to optimize the flow of cars through certain streets in a network. In some cases, it may be desirable to guarantee a green light along a specified highway. When a car enters this highway and maintains the recommended speed, it can drive along the complete length without stopping at a traffic light. For a given urban network, a combination of these strategies might be needed. But they are mutually incompatible and cause great complexity in optimizing the flow of traffic over a given network.

Speed may be measured in several ways. One method is to compute the speed as $S = D/T$ where D is distance and T is time. The usual technique consists of two loop detectors, D meters apart. The microprocessor measures the time, T, separating the two successive pulses on each of the two loop detectors, and computes the speed. An alternate method uses a single loop and assumes an average vehicle size. The duration of the pulse triggered by a vehicle going over the loop is used to compute an estimated speed.

For monitoring traffic lights the microprocessor must light in sequence each of the bulbs in the traffic light: green, amber, and red. Because of the power involved, the switching is usually done with solid-state or mechanical relays. As in most other industrial control systems, status feedback is provided in order to verify the correct execution of command. This is accomplished with a status line from the load relay back into the microprocessor. Although the status of all three lights is usually monitored, green status is always done so. Each time the microprocessor attempts to turn the green light on, it will check a few milliseconds later to see that the relay has closed.

If not, the order will be repeated a number of times. If the failure is permanent, an emergency mode is entered. Using this feedback information, it is maintained that short of a microprocessor malfunction, no gross control problem may occur.

Microprocessor-based traffic control has become common for new installations in most of the United States and some parts of Europe. The techniques used to control the flow of vehicles are similar to the techniques used to control any continuous or discrete flow. Modified versions of these traffic controllers have been used for the flow-metering and control of water and other fluids in California and other locations.

MATERIAL CONTROL

Material control is concerned with the counting, sorting, and identification of raw materials and manufactured parts. We have already considered some of the characteristics and applications of low-cost microprocessor controls; now we will consider more specialized systems which may be utilized in the future in a wider range of material control or information systems.

Point-of-Sale Systems

One such material control application is the point-of-sale (POS) system which has been one of the most important applications of microcomputers. The POS terminal is an interactive device that processes sales information and stores it on a magnetic tape. There can be at least two possible inputs of data to the POS terminal:

1. Keyboard
2. Optical symbol reader or scanner.

As shown in Figure 9.6, these inputs are connected to the system data bus. Also attached to the data bus are the microprocessor, ROM, RAM, and the possible system outputs:

1. Displays
2. Printers
3. Tape cassettes
4. UART for serial transmission of data to a processing center.

The operator specifies the mode of operation: either keyboard or scanner by a program key on the keyboard. For keyboard operation, the POS terminal acts as a cash register, recording sales and providing a display for visual checking and a printed receipt. For operation with a optical scanner, encoding operations are required.

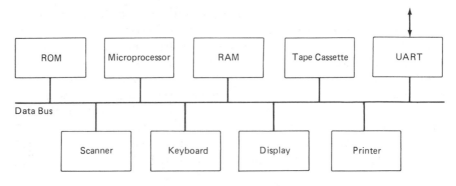

Fig. 9.6. Point-of-sale terminal.

With scanners for other kinds of POS terminal applications, it is useful to consider the specification of the Universal Product Code (UPC) symbol of the supermarket industry.[4] The UPC symbol provides an automated reading of product information in point-of-sale systems. The UPC symbol contains 10 digits of information divided into two 5-digit fields. The data in the fields are also represented as numerals below the symbol. In a specific representation, the left-hand 5-digit field contains the characters 12345, and the right-hand 5-digit field contains the characters 67890. In the grocery industry, the left-hand five digits will identify the manufacturer of the product, while the right-hand five digits will identify the product. The representation of a specific digit in the UPC symbol can be explained by Figure 9.7. Each character position consists of a region of seven bar positions. A dark bar represents a 1, while a light bar represents a 0. Thus the code represented by the character shown has bits 1000100. To decode this bit string, one uses the code shown below which indicates the decimal value 7.

There is a distinction between the characters in the left-hand 5-digit field, and the characters in the right-hand 5-digit field. This distinction permits the

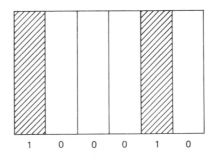

Fig. 9.7. UPC character.

DECIMAL VALUE	LEFT CHARACTERS	RIGHT CHARACTERS
	(Odd parity)	(Even parity)
0	0001101	1110010
1	0011001	1100110
2	0010011	1101100
3	0111101	1000010
4	0100011	0011100
5	0110001	0001110
6	0101111	1010000
7	0111011	1000100
8	0110111	1001000
9	0001011	1110100

symbol to be read in either direction. By encoding parity in the characters of the right and the left digit fields, the terminal can determine which way the symbol is being read and interpret the data accordingly.

Other characteristics of the UPC symbol are also of interest. For example, each character consists of two dark bands and two light bands. Each band is composed of one, two, three, or four bars or modules of the same color. On the far left-hand side of the symbol is a numeral that designates the code being used. A "0" refers to the UPC code presented above or a "3" refers to the National Drug Code.

The scanning hardware and microprocessor system is designed to handle the UPC or other symbol formats, using read-only memories containing the character look-up tables. Should the code need to be changed, for example, to read the National Drug Code, the user replaces the read-only memory with a new memory containing a different look-up table. The economic advantages and versatility of a microprocessor implementation for this type of system should not be overlooked for other similar applications in industry such as periodic inventory checking.

Remote Credit Checking

Another example of a system that may be adopted to a wider range of applications is the Transaction Telephone. The Transaction Telephone is a telephone set that permits one to check the validity of a credit card purchase through the telephone network. The Transaction Telephone differs from other credit validation systems in that it does not use a dedicated line to the central computer or an acoustical coupler with an ordinary telephone.

The Transaction Telephone was developed by Bell Telephone Laboratories, and used the Rockwell PPS-4 microprocessor with other Western electric components. The Rockwell PPS-4 (4-bit Parallel Processing System) was introduced in 1972 and marketed primarily to large OEM manufacturers, such as Western Electric. The PPS-4 is based on a 4-bit CPU and uses PMOS technology. It is packaged in a 42-pin flat pack.[5]

The Transaction Telephone user inserts a credit card into the card reader of the telephone system. The card reader senses the data on the magnetic stripe of the card and converts this data into digital signals. The microprocessor checks that the card has been read correctly by performing a parity check of the read information. If the card has been read correctly, the microprocessor interprets the data to control the touch-tone oscillators of the telephone set, sending the data over the telephone network to a computer. After the computer performs a credit check from the serial number on the card, a signal is sent back to the Transaction Telephone indicating if credit should be authorized. The microprocessor receives this signal and actuates a light on the telephone system to indicate to the user if the transaction is authorized. Although the Transaction Telephone was designed for retail establishments for credit validation purposes, other uses of the product have been utilized. Bank customers can automatically check their account balances by inserting their bank credit card into a Transaction Telephone system equipped with a numeric display. In addition, Electronic funds transfer may be done through a Transaction Telephone. Orders are placed by phone, and the caller's identity and credit authorization are checked remotely. The Transaction Telephone and similar industrial system applications of microprocessors can be expected to develop slowly, yet their importance will grow rapidly in the coming years.

Identification Systems

Identification systems are an important industrial area for microcomputers. Such systems can monitor or control the location of moving objects, such as parts, or vehicles, from a central location.[6] The operator may issue commands to control the flow or direction to groups of parts or a specific part or vehicle on the basis of the information which has been forwarded to the control station. A simplified block diagram of the system is shown in Figure 9.8. This diagram shows the system for communicating with the central control station. A receiver and transmitter are shown, but a transponder could be utilized equally as well. Communications are conducted through a UART and the I/O interface to the data bus of the microcomputer system. The system includes a microprocessor, RAM, ROM, a keyboard for entry of information by the operator, and a display for indicating information.

In systems such as these, complex filters may be required for image processing. These filters may also use microprocessors. Digital filters are useful devices that produce a predetermined digital output in response to a digital input. They find many applications in telephone, radar, and signal processing, and thus are an important area for the application of microprocessors.

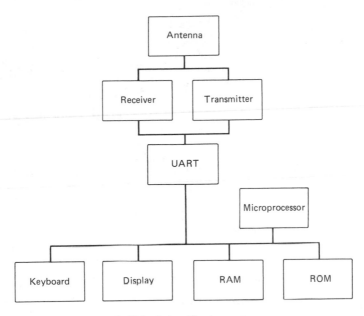

Fig. 9.8. Indentification system.

A digital filter may consist of elements for multiplication, addition, delays, and storage in order to obtain the desired transfer function. There are two types of digital filters: (1) recursive and (2) nonrecursive. A recursive filter uses a feedback path to provide input signals from the previously calculated outputs. A nonrecursive filter uses only the input to the filter to determine the output signal. Figure 9.9 shows how a microprocessor is applied to a recursive digital filter. The microprocessor and ROM replace the coefficient generator, multipliers, and adders of a hard-wired digital filter. The three microprocessors in this example are synchronized and connected by the I/O interface, along with a common data bus. The recursive data is applied to the three microprocessors as shown in the right-hand part of the diagram where particular parts of the circuit assume functional values $f(n)$, $f(n-1)$, and $f(n-2)$. In addition to the filtering functions, the microprocessor can be used for error checking, formatting, and other functions. The microprocessor allows changing the transfer function and other characteristics by a change in the stored program. This flexibility of changing the ROM for a change in filter function or characteristic is a major advantage with the microprocessor filter implementation.

VEHICULAR APPLICATIONS

There are many applications for microprocessors in vehicles. A list of potential applications as indicated by General Motors appears in Table 9.1, along with the development required for such systems.[7]

TABLE 9.1 Potential Automotive Applications For Microprocessors

SYSTEM	DEVELOPMENT				BARRIERS		
	TRANSDUCER	PROCESSOR	ACTUATOR	DISPLAY	COST	TECHNICAL	OTHERS
1. Automatic Door Locks			X		X		
2. Alcohol Detection Systems	X			X	X	X	X
3. Flasher Control Systems					X	X	
4. Programmed Driving Controls		X	X		X	X	
5. High Speed Warning			X		X		
6. High Speed Limiting			X		X		
7. Lamp Monitor Systems	X				X		
8. Electronic Horn					X		
9. Crash Recorder	X	X		X	X	X	X
10. Traffic Controls	X	X	X	X	X	X	X
11. Tire Pressure Monitor	X				X		
12. Tire Pressure Control	X		X		X	X	
13. Automatic Seat Positioner	X				X		
14. Automatic Mirror Control	X		X		X	X	
15. Automatic Icing Control	X				X	X	
16. Road Surface Indicator	X			X		X	
17. 4-Wheel Anti-lock	X		X		X	X	
18. Vehicle Guidance	X		X		X	X	X
19. Automatic Brakes — Radar	X	X	X			X	
Infrared	X	X	X			X	
Laser	X	X	X			X	
Sonic	X	X	X			X	
20. Predictive Crash Sensors — Radar	X				X	X	
Infrared	X				X	X	
Laser	X				X	X	
Sonic	X				X	X	
21. Electronic Timing					X		
22. Multiplex Harness Systems			X		X		

Feature	1	2	3	4	5	6	7
23. Electronic Transmission Control					X		
24. Electronic Cooling System Control					X		
25. Closed-Loop Emission Control	X				X	X	
26. Accessory Power Control	X				X		
27. Cruise Control					X		
28. Theft Deterrent Systems	X				X		
29. On-Board Diagnostic Systems	X				X		X
30. Off-Board Diagnostic Systems	X				X		X
31. Leveling Controls	X		X		X		
32. Radio Frequency Display							
33. Digital Speedometers				X	X		
34. Digital Tachometers				X	X		
35. Elapsed Time Clock				X	X		
36. Electronic Odometer				X	X		
37. Trip Odometer				X	X		
38. Destination Mileage				X	X		
39. Miles Per Gallon	X			X	X		
40. Miles To Go	X			X	X		
41. Estimated Arrival Time				X	X		
42. Trip Fuel Consumption	X			X	X		
43. Average Speed				X	X		
44. Average Miles Per Gallon				X	X		
45. Digital Fuel Gauge				X	X		
46. Service Interval				X	X		
47. Digital Temperature Gauges				X	X		
48. Digital Pressure Gauges				X	X		
49. Digital Voltmeter				X	X		
50. Digital Metric Conversions				X	X		
51. Acceleration Gauge	X				X		
52. Drunk Driver	X	X			X	X	X
53. E.K.G.	X	X			X	X	X
54. Sleep Detector	X	X			X	X	X

SOURCE: General Motors

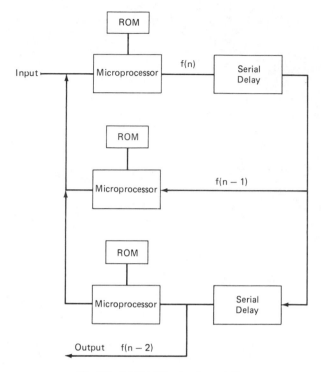

Fig. 9.9. Digital filter implementation.

Microprocessors can be used in cars for all of these functions. They might be used to monitor engine conditions and display them to the driver. They would also supply the diagnostics. They could provide management of the display panel from clock to digital speedometer, as well as monitor abnormal engine conditions. The reliability and performance of microprocessors in severe environments is sufficient for these applications. The essential problem is not the microprocessor, but the required sensors and displays. The cost of sensors is high and their reliability may not be sufficient in a severe environment. As a result, automobiles have refrained from using microprocessors in many of these applications since every dollar is significant in automobile costs. Still, it is only a matter of time until the required sensors and displays are developed.

The use of microprocessors for on-board vehicle control is one of the most important applications of microprocessors. (See Figure 9.10) Automotive electronics is in an active but early stage. The operating environment of the automobile engine has presented a challenge for many of the electronics system designs. In the past, both active and passive components have been widely used in automotive systems. An estimate of the number of discrete

Fig. 9.10. This chip, shown next to an ordinary needle and thread, is used in the Electronic Control Module (ECM) for GM's Computer Command Control (CCC) exhaust emission control system. The CCC was installed in nearly all 1981 GM gasoline-powered automobiles. (*Courtesy of General Motors Corporation.*)

electronic components used in some electronic systems in automobiles appears below:[8]

SYSTEM	ACTIVE	RESISTORS	CAPACITORS
Alternator	6	—	—
Voltage Regulator	5	5	1
Electronic Fuel Injection	—	160	10
Electronic Ignition	15	15	2
Windshield Wipers	5	5	2
Cruise Control	60	105	15
Wheel Lock Control	185	290	40
Traction Control	40	80	10
Headlight Dimmers	15	25	5
Climate Control	5	15	1
Digital Clock	200	220	35
Totals	706	1,020	136

SOURCE: General Motors

It can be expected that vehicles, like any other complex mechanical device, will be equipped with microprocessors creating a number of new functional and safety features in the future. As in the case of other applications, once microprocessors are installed in vehicles, the spare computing power available will provide a number of intelligence and convenience features which were not possible before.

Engine Control

A block diagram that shows the operations of a typical automotive microprocessor system is shown in Figure 9.11. The inputs to the microprocessor system are as follows:

1. Pressure.
2. Temperature.
3. RPM.
4. EGR (exhaust gas recirculation) valve position.

The inputs come from transducers or sensors located in the engine or EGR valve. One of the most difficult problems in the development of microprocessor systems for automotive applications has been in the design of low-cost transducers. As reliable transducers are developed, they will provide the input signals that are converted to digital values for use by the processor. These input signals may be temporarily stored in input latches until they are ready to be displayed or processed. The input latches are connected to the microprocessor through the system data bus. The outputs may be either to an actuator for performing engine control operations, or to a display for the

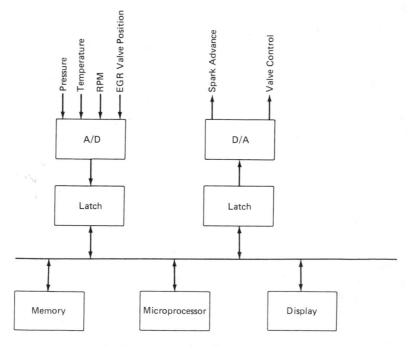

Fig. 9.11. Automotive microprocessor system.

monitoring of engine conditions and alerting of critical conditions. The actuator in Figure 9.10 indicates spark advance and EGR valve position adjustments. These adjustments will depend on the type of automobile and its operating environment and may be predetermined by the manufacturer and specified using parameters that are stored in a ROM. The microprocessor responds with the required engine adjustments on the basis of the stored information together with the current operating conditions sensed.

The following example will illustrate the essential advantages and features of using a microprocessor in automotive control. Another case will be presented which uses a custom-designed chip in a spark ignition control system.

In 1976, the Delco division of General Motors introduced a spark-timing system controlled by a microprocessor.[9] A diagram of the system appears in Figure 9.12. Sensors supply the microprocessor with the required information. Inputs include the engine vacuum, crankshaft position, reference timing, and coolant temperature. The main output is the timing signal to the distributor. The other two outputs of the system are status information. A special-purpose microprocessor was designed for this application. The system functions in a table-driven mode. There was no algorithm to determine the proper timing for the spark as a function of the input conditions.

With every engine type extensively tested, the manufacturer establishes tables which determine the desired timing as a function of the external parameters. The system implements an automated version of the table lookup mechanism, while a subset of the tables is stored in memory. For each set of external conditions measured by the system, the closest match in the tables are found. Interpolation techniques are used to compute the intermediate values. To do this, instructions are stored in the custom microprocessor.

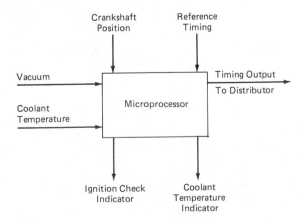

Fig. 9.12. Microprocessor spark-timing system.

This microprocessor also has input/output lines, as well as analog-to-digital facilities.

This form of microprocessor control offers a number of advantages. The most significant one is the reduction in pollutants. The precise control of timing results in significantly improved engine combustion and lower emission levels. Other advantages are some improvement in gas consumption and in engine responsiveness. An advantage of this technique to the manufacturer is that, through mass-testing of the programmed approach, the program can be improved and will result in better timing of the engine under most conditions. This results in improved gas economy as well as still reduced pollution. Following this innovation by General Motors, most other manufacturers have introduced similar devices, and many microprocessor manufacturers have made announcements of products specifically designed for automotive applications.

PROCESS CONTROL

A wide range of microprocessor control units are available for local and distributed control tasks. Examples are the Honeywell TDS–2000 and the EPTAK controller by Eagle.[10] Process systems employ microprocessors at all levels, ranging from simple display functions to actual local control.

Distributed Control Issues

We will outline some of the issues in distributed monitor/control systems. Typically, the cost-effective organization for distributed intelligence in process control applications is a hierarchical architecture (as shown in Figure 9.13). The main issue in the design of such a system is the distribution of intelligence within the hierarchy for a particular application. In some cases, it may be best to centralize the decision-making and control functions within

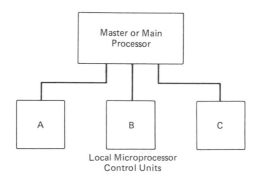

Fig. 9.13. Hierarchical process-control system.

the master or main processor. This scheme would place the local control units under complete control of the master, with an attendant increase in the communications and computation demands at that level. For other applications, it is conceivable that complete decentralization of control and monitoring functions is best. In those cases, the local control units would operate as independent agents performing local control. The trade-off between centralization and decentralization of intelligence in such a system is a key issue that affects the hardware and software design, and the trade-off is made from the identification of user needs and system requirements. Designing a heirarchical system without this knowledge reflects a bottom-up synthesis approach and can lead to shifts in the design at both the hardware and software levels. The goals of the system must meet the user's needs, and those needs must be specified before centralization or decentralization of microprocessors can be made.

After the system design has been specified, the other issues relating to the operational specifications can be considered. These fall into three categories: (1) communications, (2) the user interface, and (3) applications software.

Communications functions include:

1. The means of physical communication: direct wire, telephone link, microwave, and fiber optics.
2. The protocols for reliability, error checking, and security.
3. The rates that are compatible with system components such as printers, tape units, and CRTs.

The user interface should provide a range of capabilities, including the following: active reports, logs, alarms and interactive message communications, and a data base for analysis and record-keeping.

The system software should be designed to execute the control and monitoring tasks such as traditional control by event and by time, process control algorithms, and other applications software required by the system tasks. Many industry observers feel that fractionating column control is an art. Microcomputer technology offers the one opportunity to remove column control from this category.

Conventional Column Control

We will discuss the conventional methods of column control. A typical binary column with a steam reboiler, water-cooled condenser, and reflux drum is used as an example. Conventional single loop control is used. In this type of column, there are key variables which greatly affect the operation of the column. Some can be manipulated; others cannot. Among the manipulatable variables are column pressure, feed flow rate, feed temperature, energy input, energy removal, and product flow rate. Variables which cannot be changed are ambient barometric pressure, ambient temperature, feed composition, cooling water temperature, and inert vapor generation.[11]

The single-loop feedback control of the binary distillation column uses the principle of a single input and single output. The typical fractioning column is pressure-controlled.

Each loop is independently operated as a feedback device and no provision is made to compensate for any interaction among the controlled variables. The standard analog controller has an inherent internal interaction. When retuning of a controller becomes necessary, the variable on which this controller is applied can interact with other process variables, which necessitates retuning of these other variables as well. The application of a microcomputer to this system with conventional control is mostly ineffective unless the analog computer is replaced. Digital control can be applied with a microcomputer and can perform functions on the column. However, an economic and engineering study must be made prior to the implementation of a microcomputer on an existing conventional column control system.

Feedback control is the process of maintaining a controlled variable through using a device which compares the deviation between a set point and measurement of the controlled variable, and which tends to force that deviation to zero. Note that the error or deviation must exist before any corrective action can take place. Feedforward control is a technique where the magnitude of the error is anticipated and the corrective action is taken prior to the occurrence of an error.

Feedforward/feedback control uses a combination of both. This combining of both techniques results in the anticipation of an error and corrective action followed by readjustment. (Feedforward/feedback control is illustrated in Figure 9.14.) In the application of this concept to a column, the feedforward components of control might consist of a feed analyzer and feed flow transmitter.[12] These components analyze and sense the disturbances due to feed changes and composition. If the feed composition

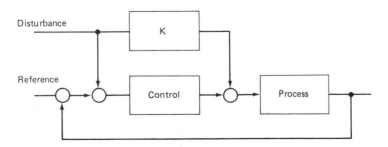

Fig. 9.14. Feedforward/feedback control technique.

changes, the output changes the product draw and bottom drain-off to approximately the correct or desired quantity. The product and bottom analyzers then correct the quantity of product and bottom draw to the desired quantity.

Many industrial process control applications over the last half-century are based on simple feedback or feedforward/feedback philosophies. Another way of describing this type of control is single variable or single input/single output control. The complexities of modern process technologies, however, combined with the requirements of closer constraints, smaller down times, higher throughput, and energy savings offer a challenge to the unit operator so complex that he cannot hope to cope with it using only conventional analog control. These factors, plus the realization that the control of one variable affects others, lead to the study of these interactions and how they can be controlled.

Multivariable Control

A multivariable control system uses built-in intelligence to simultaneously monitor many variables and to choose, based on the situation, the optimum of several programmed control strategies.[13] Consider the control of a column where such parameters as varying steam flow, differential pressure across the column, feed rate, bottom flow rate, and other variables such as product composition must be monitored. Each of these variables usually affects the others. These effects are defined as interactive, and conventional control systems can not compensate for the interaction among the variables. The complex requirements for control and operation, along with the interactive nature of the system result in a number of basic guidelines for applying microcomputers to column control:

1. Identify the areas to be improved.
2. Identify the variables which interact.
3. Develop a control philosphy not limited to the single input-single output type.
4. Identify the static and dynamic interactions of the variables.

In the binary distillation column, possible improvements are as follows:

1. Product quality.
2. Product flow rate or throughput.
3. Energy input.
4. Dynamic response to disturbances.

Typical variables which may interact are these: steam flow, differential pressure, pressure, feed rate, feed composition, and temperature.

The microcomputer design chosen for interacting variables may be difficult to institute because of the inertia of the single input-single output system. The microprocessor system should consider the following factors:

1. Heat and material balance requirements.
2. Product, flow rate, and quality controls.
3. Safety control.
4. Feedforward and feedback control.

Related to safety control are the requirements of the Clean Air Act for cleaner smokestack emissions. Here microcircuits have found a major use in the optical transmissometers for monitoring the opacity of smoke. In a typical instrument, a single light source is separated into a measuring beam and a reference beam.[14] The measuring beam is projected across the stack to a reflector unit, which returns the beam back to the detector. The beams are chopped alternately, and directed to a single photocell, and are made to match by moving a variable optical-density disk in the reference beam. The motion of the optical disk indicates the relative transmittance of the sample.

Process Chromatographs

A similar instrument that is used in continuous analysis in process plants is the process chromatograph.[15] The process chromatograph can be used to measure many components in the same stream. It can also be programmed to measure many streams, each with different concentrations. By the selection of appropriate columns and detectors, the process chromatograph may be used to measure the parts-per-million concentrations of impurities in gases.

The process chromatograph is limited to the analysis of gases or liquids that can be readily vaporized in the instrument. It is often called a gas chromatograph. (Figure 9.15 is a diagram of a gas chromatograph). The sampling system is more complex than that of an infrared analyzer, since many streams may be cycled to the analyzer, some of which may drop out liquid components if they are allowed to cool or drop too rapidly in pressure. Heat-traced sample lines are used in such sample systems, along with recycling lines from which a small side-stream is taken to the analyzer. The side-stream continuously passes through the loop of a sample injection valve. A measured sample of the stream is then injected into a chromatographic column, and the sample is carried through the column by the carrier gas, usually helium. The chromatographic column uses 3 to 10 feet of stainless steel tubing, $\frac{1}{4}$ inch in diameter, holding a porous solid on the surface of which a liquid has been adsorbed. Passing through the column, the sample is dissolved and then evaporated into the column space thousands of times. This is analogous to a distillation column operating with thousands of plates. The

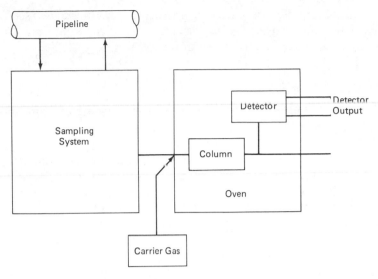

Fig. 9.15. Gas chromatograph system.

components of the sample are separated accordingly to their affinity for the liquid separating agent and they emerge from the column separated in time. A detector is then used to define the concentrations of the separated components.

A microcomputer system may program the gas chromatograph to efficiently use the outputs of the detectors. Instead of just recording the height of a peak as the composition of an ingredient, the microcomputer can integrate the area under each curve; multiply it by its calibration factor (which it also calculates) and sum the areas under the curve to determine the total. Then, dividing each area by this total, it can calculate a calibrated value for each component corrected for the component and the state of the instrument. It can even determine the area under peaks which are not separated, detect the areas over shifting base lines, and detect the base lines themselves. Alarms can be used when an unexpected change in concentration is detected or for undesirable conditions which may arise. The following alarms are available in a typical computerized gas chromatograph.

1. Out of calibration.
2. Base line drift.
3. Malfunction.
4. Power failure and automatic restart.
5. Limit check for components.
6. No information transfer to computer.
7. Expected peak does not appear.

A central computer can be used with a microprocessor that will scan all the analyzer units and convert and store the signals for use as required. (A block diagram of such a system is shown in Figure 9.16.)

Mass Spectrometers

At the time that the process chromatograph was being perfected in the 1960s, various instrument groups in the process industries were trying to perfect the mass spectrometer as a continuous process monitor.[16] Mass spectrometers had been used to measure the separation of uranium isotopes, and it was hoped a similar instrument could be used in process streams. But when this was tried, the fine capillary required for the process sample became obstructed by dust and dirt.

Then in 1978, several continuous process mass spectrometers were introduced, and proved to be successful in industry. One of the keys to their success is the microcomputer. But also important was that a very high vacuum and fine capillary were not required and durable ionization chambers were available.

In the mass spectrometer, charged particles of different atoms are separated by their mass-to-charge ratios. Separation takes place in a high vacuum to eliminate collision with other molecules. A sample is admitted and ionized under reduced pressure by an electron beam. The charged particles pass through a magnetic field to determine the mass-to-charge ratios. Spaced collectors pass the charges to an electrometer where they are amplified into voltages proportional to the compositions. A closed-loop control system compensates for any changes in sensitivity.

The use of a microcomputer makes the system self-calibrating and able to operate without human attention. To provide continuous operation, a dual filament, nonmagnetic ion source is used.

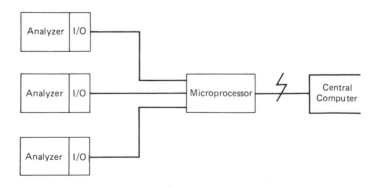

Fig. 9.16. Microprocessor-controlled gas chromatograph system.

Electrons emitted from the filament are focused on the input area of the gas sample, ionizing the particles with an energy of about 500 electron volts. The newer mass spectrometers use one of two inlet systems.

1. A capillary bypass inlet system, which uses a sample of 1 cm³/sec. The sample does not need to be pressurized; flow is maintained by a pump.
2. The flow-by inlet system which requires a sample of sufficient pressure to flow by the inlet and return back to the process at a lower pressure point. The sample is pulled into the analyzer by an internal pump, and sequencing is maintained by manual selection or a computer addressable switch.

Gases such as nitrogen, oxygen, and carbon dioxide are readily measured. In a test by Dow Chemical, carbon balances were maintained between 99.5 and 100.5%, and deviated only four times between 99.7 and 100.3%. Previous use of a gas chromatograph and oxygen analyzer for the same application provided a range of 98 to 102%, with three calibrations per month required for the chromatograph, and weekly calibrations for the oxygen analyzer.

To exploit the high speed of the mass spectrometer, a process computer is required. The microprocessor can be an optimizing controller for fractionation towers. The use of a high-speed mass spectrometer for analyzing feed, overhead, and bottoms streams can provide the means for feedforward control, which may improve tower efficiencies by 5 to 20%. Appreciable energy savings can also be achieved. The mass spectrometer can do what combined gas chromatograph, oxygen, and infrared analyzers do in ethylene cracking furnaces, enthylene oxide production, vinyl chloride processes, natural gas production, digestive sludges, and gasification control. In the latter application, the yield can be maximized by controlling the amount of oxygen for the fire.

Compressor Control

A compressor increases the pressure of a gas while delivering a quantity of this gas. A prime consideration in compressor operation is the prevention of surge conditions which, if not limited or acted upon quickly, could destroy the machine.[17] Various control systems can be implemented with a microprocessor configuration. The levels of involvement of the microcomputer are similar to those for a fractionating column. The greatest potential for the use of microcomputer technology in compressor applications is in the flexibility and adaptability of advanced control techniques for such systems. The operation of a compressor in a stable mode of operation requires the use of an adaptive control to compensate for changing characteristics of the process and compressor. This cannot be accomplished with conventional analog control equipment, but digital control systems such as microcomputers can do this by using control algorithms to perform the adaptive functions.

The microcomputer system may also provide communications for preprocessing data related to the detection of surge. The microcomputer can perform spectrum analysis of the noise generated as the compressor approaches the surge point. The microcomputer can then take corrective action. When the compressor is a factor in energy conservation, the microcomputer can become an integral part of the optimization system.

A number of installations using compressors contain units both upstream and downstream. Plant throughput is a function of all units and their operating efficiencies. In a multi-unit operation, it may be desirable to integrate compressor control as a part of the overall optimization strategy.

In multi-unit installations with compressors of different capacities and characteristics, one can distribute the load on each compressor so that total demand is satisfied, with the least possible energy consumption. This technique is similar to the utilities' distribution networks, where individual power-generation units contribute power such that the total energy consumed in the generation of all power is a minimum. Yet this method does not require that each compressor be at its lowest energy consumption level or at its greatest efficiency, but that all compressors operate such that *total* energy consumption is minimal.

In some installations, it is not feasible to optimize a single compressor because of interaction with the process. It may be feasible, though, to optimize the process with the compressor integrated into the microcomputer program.

Microcomputers with advanced control techniques have reached a degree of sophistication where the application of controls to prevent surge can be carried beyond empirical methods. These techniques, along with microcomputer technology, offer the potential of providing close control of compressor operation resulting in greater reliability and safety.

TELEPHONE SYSTEMS

The use of microprocessors in telephone applications is growing. There are a number of applications where the capabilities and low cost of microprocessors offer significant advantages. The applications that we will consider are switching systems and digital speech encoding.

Switched Telephone Systems

An important area for microprocessors is computer communications, using switched telephone systems. The application of microprocessors to data communications networks is more fully discussed in the section on computer networks (see pages 422–427).

A telephone switching system provides the communication links between lines in response to subscriber requests. Systems range in size from small private automated branch exchanges (PABX) with under 100 lines, to central office or tandem systems with tens of thousands of lines. A block diagram of a central office switching system is shown in Figure 9.17. The diagram shows the main elements of the system—the switching network and the processor. The switching network allows for selectively interconnecting the two-wire paths by internal junction circuits. The interconnections allow a path between a subscriber station and a trunk that connects to other central offices.

The applications of microprocessors in the telephone switching system are mostly the peripheral and administrative functions. Microprocessors can be used for special call facilities as a part of the system and to control administrative routines, which periodically perform the diagnostic checking throughout the system to determine the presence of malfunctions.

The central processor is the centralized data processing facility used to implement the various telephone, maintenance, and administrative functions of the telephone switching system.[18] The Central Processor can be divided into five elements:

1. Control system or main processor.
2. Program-store.
3. Call-store.
4. Signal processor (or auxiliary processor).
5. Signal processor call-store.

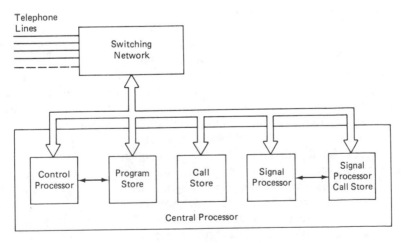

Fig. 9.17. Central telephone switching system.

The control system is composed of three functional parts: (1) data processing, (2) input and output communications, and (3) maintenance. The control system usually has two independent controls for reliability. The independent controls are arranged to perform all system actions, although in the usual mode both controls carry on the same functions on the basis of duplicate input information. This is called the in-step mode. Only one of the two controls may alter the system status or control the execution of telephone functions at a given instant. Thus, the two independent controls provide the control and maintenance information to the rest of the system on a mutually exclusive basis. The control system performs the data processing functions in accordance with the program orders stored in the control store. In response to the program order, the control system processes data obtained from the call store and generates and transmits signals for the control of the other system units.

The call-store is a word-organized random-access memory in which the more volatile system information is stored. Information is written into or read from the call store by the control system. Since information in the call store is changed at the normal system speed, the more volatile system information is stored here. This information may include:

1. Call signaling information.
2. Information relating to changes in directory number or line equipment number.
3. Changes in subscriber class.
4. System administration.
5. Subscriber and trunk busy-idle data.
6. Network path busy-idle data.
7. System work lists and queues.

Microprocessors can be implemented at various points in the control system to perform specific processing functions that were previously performed by a central processor on a periodic basis. By dedicating a single inexpensive processor to a single function, a certain amount of efficiency is gained. The signal processor is a special-purpose facility employed to carry out the repetitious input and output system functions which, if performed by central control, would limit the call handling capacity of the telephone system. The signal processor, although independent, is subject to the command of central control and communicates to the control information necessary to perform the data processing required for call processing and system maintenance. The signal processor call store is another word-organized random-access memory. The program for controlling the signal processor and the data upon which the processor operates are stored here. Each signal processor community of the system is associated with a separate call-store system. When more than one signal processor community is included in the system, a corresponding number of call systems is provided. The information in the signal processor call-store includes:

1. The program that controls the signal processor when the signal processor system is not responding to commands from central control.
2. The data generated and utilized by the signal processor system for its programmed operations.

The information stored in the signal processor call-store is a mixture of instruction words and data words. Among the types of data stored are:

1. Information relating to calls, such as the supervisory change of state information (which is received from the switching network) and miscellaneous administrative circuits of the switching system.
2. Information relating to calls which is received from the central control system for processing by the signal processor system.
3. System work lists and queues.

Microprocessors can be used to implement many of the functions of the signal processor, particularly the testing, supervisory, and administrative routines.

A number of bus and cable systems provides the communication paths for transmitting the control signals and information between the elements of the central processor and between the central processor and other sections of the switching system.[19] A bus system usually includes two duplicate busses termed bus 0 and bus 1. Each uses a number of pairs of conductors that are transformer-coupled between the sources and destinations. Data is transmitted over a bus in parallel in the form of short pulses that arrive at the destination at a common time. Multiconductor cables provide the bidirectional communications paths between the divisions of the central processor and other divisions of the switching system. The conductor pairs of the cables are either transformer-coupled or directly connected.

Digital Speech Encoding

Digital speech encoding may be an important part in the development of digital facilities in the switched telephone network. Digital transmission of ordinary voice telephone communications will become a major area of microprocessor applications. The use of digital facilities for voice transmission is a matter of economics and the volume of long-distance calls. There are basically two types of digital speech encoding used: (1) delta modulation and (2) pulse code modulation (PCM).

Delta modulation uses a comparison of the input analog signal with a reference signal on a periodic basis. Depending on the result of comparison, a 1 or 0 is transmitted. The reference signal is typically obtained by a feedback loop from the previous input signals. The basic delta modulator has a limited dynamic range, and a number of techniques are used to overcome this limitation, most of which increase the range by increasing the step size of the magnitude of the reference level each time that a comparison results in an answer similar to the one previously obtained. If the first comparison reference signal is less than the input signal, the reference level is increased by a certain step. On the next comparison, if the reference level is still less than the input signal, the step again is increased. This type of delta modulator is called a variable slope delta (VSD) modulator. The continuously variable slope delta (CVSD) modulator is a variation of the VSD type in which the comparison signal (which is an indication of the slope of the analog input signal) is sent through a low-pass filter with a band-width of 25 to 35 hertz.[20]

PCM uses a sampling of the input analog waveform at a predetermined rate, quantizing each sample, and coding it in terms of a sequence of pulses.

Microprocessors can be used in a delta modulation or PCM transmission system for control and monitoring functions. By storing the sampling, testing, and conversion functions in a program, the microprocessor eliminates considerable hardware and allows monitoring or testing operations.

COMPUTER NETWORKS

Large-scale computer networks are required by groups who work with large or distributed data bases. This market includes banks, financial institutions, insurance companies, manufacturers, retail firms, distribution outlets, and reservation systems, and the market for such applications is large and growing, both in terms of the number of users and the services expected. On the other hand, data processing requirements of smaller businesses may not require the transfer of data from one location to another, so the implementation of data processing capabilities for such users differs, including the use of microprocessors, machine specifications, and market characteristics. The typical data communication processing applications in the larger systems may include:

1. Message switching by the processing and communication of messages over limited channel capacity systems.
2. File management of the remote updating of a centralized file, or other file-handling and processing functions from a remote location.
3. Inquiry/response systems which are another form of a file-oriented system, in which a remote station makes inquiries of a centralized file but does not change that file.

4. Data collection by the use of a remote station to provide updated or current information to a centralized file.

To design a data communications system, the designer must integrate each of these technologies:

1. Transmission.
2. Communications.
3. Network structure.

The transmission technology is the means for transmitting the signals. In telephone communications, this entails the grade of the line: low-speed, voice, or broadband; or type of line: private, switched, or WATS. There are also a number of alternatives to telephone communications, including microwave and satellite transmission.

Data Communications

Data communication uses about 30% of the public telephone network, a percentage that is expected to grow.[21] Projections for special communications services, such as data communication or video-telephone have been optimistic, both inside and outside of the Bell System and other carriers. This growth has been affected by several factors:

1. Communications costs.
2. The variety of systems and procedures.
3. Alternative transmission technologies.
4. Regulatory and competitive factors.

There are two basic types of data communications: (1) direct data transmission and (2) concentrated data transmission. Direct data transmission is the use of a single line or channel for the transmission of data. This system is the simplest type and is suitable for handling a predetermined volume of messages. With direct data transmission, some form of multiplexing must be used, such as frequency-division multiplexing (FDM) or time-division multiplexing (TDM), whenever more than one user desires the communications line.

Concentrated data transmission uses store-and-forward techniques for handling the messages. These techniques include message switching and packet switching. Message switching is the accumulation of a message in a register or other storage device until a complete message has been assembled at which time it is then transmitted to the destination when a data channel becomes available. Message switching is thus different from channel switching in which no accumulation or storage takes place. In channel switching, if a line or data link is not available, the service request is repeated. Packet switching uses the formation of messages into a packet or group with a predetermined length.

The role of the microprocessor in data communications has been that of a communications processor. The microprocessor has been used as an interface, or front-end, to the host processor (as shown in Figure 9.18). Some of the functions of the microprocessor have been scheduling, data compression, polling, buffering, data link control, code conversion, and formatting.

Many of these functions were performed in the past by minicomputers, but dedicated microprocessors are much more efficient and cost effective in these applications. Moreover, microprocessors are used to perform a number of other functions in a data communication system, such as protocol handling, error code generating and checking, packet and message formation, receiver/transmitter control, synchronization, and automatic repeat request (ARQ) or forward error correction (FEC). They are also used for multiple access control in time-division, frequency-division, space-division, and code-division systems.

Packet Systems

An important microprocessor use in a communications system is the data-link interface processor in a packet communication system.

Packet communication is based on the transmission of message packets. There are two forms of packet communications: (1) packet switching and (2) packet broadcasting.

Packet switching uses the transmission of short bursts of data through a communication network to a predetermined destination.[22] These groups of packets use a destination address and are switched through the network until the destination is reached. Packet switches use a linked-node network.

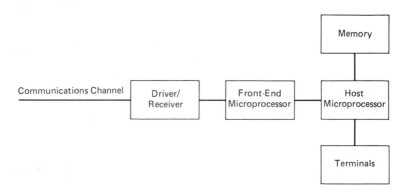

Fig. 9.18. Typical communications processor applications.

Packet broadcasting uses the simultaneous transmission of a packet to several remote stations. Each remote station is equipped with decoding circuitry to decode each incoming packet to determine if it is addressed to that station. Packet broadcasting is basically a radio broadcasting communication system.

A packet broadcasting system can also be implemented by means of a satellite transmission network. The increased availability and decreasing costs of satellite communications will play an important part in the growth of long-range data communications. Some of the advantages of satellite transmission are these:

1. Communication costs independent of the distance.
2. Data transmission using broadcasting rather than network switching.
3. Data rates to 30 megabits per second.

The drawbacks in satellite communication systems are the time delay as the signal is transmitted and the possible attenuation during precipitation and other conditions.

Packet broadcasting may also be done on wire channels. One packet broadcasting system uses ground-based broadcasting and satellite-based channels. Information is transmitted to the satellite from an earth station in bursts. The repeater on the satellite picks up the transmissions and broadcasts them over a region of the earth's surface. Ground stations in the region intercept the broadcasts, decode the address information, and select the packets labeled for their destination for further processing.[23]

We will now take a look at a microprocessor system in a packet-switched data communication network. This particular application is a data-link interface processor. A functional block diagram is shown in Figure 9.19. The communication processor links the transmission lines with the buffer store which is connected to the host processor. The user interfaces with the host processor through a CRT terminal. (The block diagram of the data link unit is shown in Figure 9.20.) The microprocessor is connected by the control, address, and data busses to the memory and interface units. The microprocessor data-link interface performs the following operations:

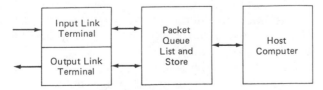

Fig. 9.19. Packet data-link interface.

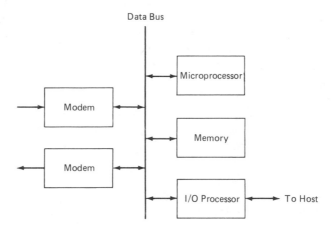

Fig. 9.20. Packet data-link processor.

1. Serial/parallel conversion.
2. Error checking, such as the arithmetic check sums and cyclic redundancy checks.
3. Encoding header and frame information on outgoing data and decoding header and frame information from incoming data.
4. Assembling data into packets.
5. Link and synchronization control.

The processor performs the packet handling functions based on a protocol flow chart. From the information in the flowchart, the system designer will code the program which performs the desired operation. The program may then be stored in a ROM to be called by system control or user command.

Figure 9.21 shows a prototype board used to develop the interface for a communications link processor.

NETWORK STRUCTURE

We have truly entered the era of distributed systems. These systems might be qualified as multimicroprocessor systems. There are multimicroprocessors involved, but they may not truly interact with each other for control purposes. With distributed systems, the intercommunication between a number of processors is reduced to a minimum. They may not interact in real time, but they will exchange data in words or blocks. Each processor is a direct controller that completely controls a process.

It is predicted that most microprocessor systems, in the future will involve a number of processors. For example, processors will be used in the peripheral chips of the system such as the PIO, the UART, or other system

Fig. 9.21. The interface functions for a bit-slice microprocessor used in a communications link system were developed on this board. (*Courtesy Siltran Digital.*)

chips. This may make the programming task more difficult, but more effective. Each of the chips that are used as interface devices will be fully programmable. Instructions will be sent to these devices by the control microprocessor. Thus, the processors residing in the peripheral devices will essentially act as slaves.

Multiprocessor Systems

A multiprocessor system is the use of more than one central processing unit in the system configuration. There are several reasons for multiprocessor systems:

1. Greater system efficiency and use of the system resources.
2. Increase in system capabilities in responding to real-time situations.
3. Improved fault tolerance; greater ability to deal with system malfunctions.

We may classify multiprocessor systems based on the following characteristics:

1. Types of processors; similar or different characteristics.
2. Interconnections between processors.

3. Relationship of the processors to memory and I/O.
4. Operating software for the processors and system.

Based on these characteristics, one can refer to certain processor structures as array processors, pipeline processors, parallel processors, ring processors, or reconfigurable processors.[24] One can also consider the system structure as being tightly or loosely coupled. Although microprocessors might be used for various functions in a multiprocessor system, the most interesting configuration is a multiprocessor system constructed of a number of microprocessors. The type of multiprocessor architecture that is particularly interesting is a reconfigurable architecture using microprocessors.

The configurable array processor is a system in which the processors are arranged in an array for processing data that have some geometrical relationship to each other. A two-dimensional array processor might operate on a two-dimensional representation of the data to be processed, such as calculations with respect to a set of grid coordinates. If the two-dimensional representation is changed to a different configuration of grid points, the system would reconfigure itself to another more suitable array configuration for the new task.

The compiler-based system configuration is organized on the structure of a language and operates by the direct execution or compilation of instruction sequences in that language. Compilation is done by translating instructions from a higher level language to instructions that are executed by the system. A reconfigurable system may arrange its configuration to conform with the program being compiled in order to expedite the compilation and execution steps. Microprocessors can be used to implement the system, based on a reconfigurable architecture. The system can be constructed in a multiprocessor array, along with supervisory and transfer functions controlled by other processors. The arrangement between the various processors determines the type of multiprocessor system. There are several types of configurations which may be used to create a reconfigurable system architecture, such as these: hierarchical, parallel, ring, and switched.

The hierarchical system (as shown in Figure 9.22) uses a master processor and two or more slave processors in a hierarchical-ordered relationship. The master processor controls or supervises the operation of the slave processors in either a tightly or a loosely coupled manner.

The parallel system (as shown in Figure 9.23) uses two or more processors which may operate on two or more data streams in parallel. The parallel system can also be configured to operate in parallel on a single data stream for high reliability processing applications.

The ring system (as shown in Figure 9.24) is an array of processors distributed along one or more rings or loops. Data are transferred around the ring or loop and used by a particular processor according to a predetermined address or tag.

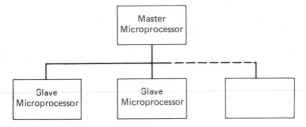

Fig. 9.22. Master-slave or hierarchical microprocessor system.

The switched system (as shown in Figure 9.25) uses an array of processors connected by crossbar switches that directly couple any one processor to any other processor.

In addition to these four classifications based on structure, additional functional classifications describing the nature or function of the processors are used. For example, one such classification might be used when the processors in the system have identical or special purpose functions. The particular classification defines a homogeneous or nonhomogeneous system.

Microprocessor Implementation

All of these multiprocessor systems can be implemented with microprocessors. Also, with the proper hardware and software structures to control and synchronize the multiprocessor configuration, a fully reconfigurable microprocessor architecture may be realized using many of the 16-bit microprocessors.[25] Conceptually, it is simple to interconnect in a network a number of microprocessors. This network then qualifies as a multimicroprocessor system. In cases where there is one main processor and a number of slave microprocessors, the system becomes a distributed system rather than a true multimicroprocessor system, for a multimicroprocessor system refers to a system where any number of processors may assume the role of a master.

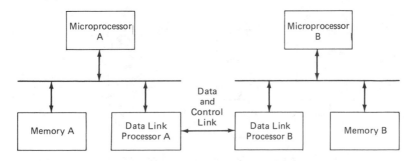

Fig. 9.23. Parallel or linked multimicroprocessor system.

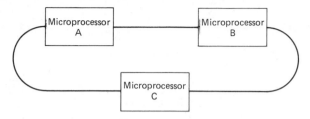

Fig. 9.24. Ring multimicroprocessor system.

This may involve a complex interconnecting operating system to synchronize the operation of the system.

It has been claimed that the philosophy of such a system runs contrary to cost-efficiency. The cost of developing complex operating systems capable of synchronizing a number of processors operating simultaneously has been demonstrated over past years to be overwhelming. It also implied a high unreliability for the system, as it can not be proven that the system will operate correctly under all circumstances. The cost and risk involved in developing complex software is large compared to the cost of the hardware. The usual philosophy is to simplify and allocate the hardware where needed for efficient software implementation. The implementation philosophy has been to use dedicated processors wherever they were needed and to synchronize their operation as loosely as possible to simplify the overall system operation. This resulted in lower costs, simplicity, and reliability. Some of

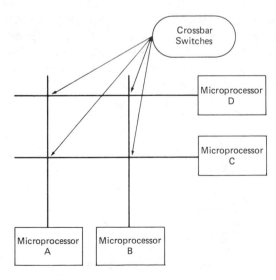

Fig. 9.25. Switched multimicroprocessor system.

the manufacturers of microprocessors have begun reducing these risks by providing operating systems for multiprocessing and multitasking system applications.[26] These operating systems are expected to increase the use of multimicroprocessor systems.

Reconfigurable Systems

The concept of reconfigurable data processing systems is not new. The elements of hardware and software reconfigurability are well known in multiprocessor systems, and the widespread availability of low cost central processing units in the form of microprocessors has allowed reconfigurable computer architectures to become economically feasible.

The multiprocessor computer system in its basic form consists of a number of processors, memory units, and I/O devices arranged in some predetermined configuration. At certain critical times, it may be desirable to change the configuration based on a particular internal or external event. A system which possesses the hardware or software capabilities to implement this reconfiguration is known as a reconfigurable system. The applications for reconfigurable systems include fault-tolerant systems, interactive multiprocessor systems, configurable-array processors, and compiler-based systems.

Fault-tolerant systems find their major application in high reliability systems, such as communications and telephone processing applications.[27] This equipment must perform the following fault processing operations: error detection, restriction of error propagation, and recovery from the fault or error. The system must reconfigure itself such that all data flow around the particular unit which is at fault, once that unit has been localized as the source of an error.

Interactive multiprocessor systems are systems used for the simultaneous processing by a large number of users running jobs with different characteristics. To increase the throughput, the reconfigurable system operates by allocating an optimum number of processors, memories, and I/O units to each respective user. Thus, the system reconfigures itself by partitioning the system into independently operating units, on a space- or time-division multiplex basis.

It is now reasonable to consider multimicroprocessor systems involving monolithic microprocessors for the reasons indicated. It is also reasonable and sometimes desirable to consider multiprocessor implementations using bit-slice devices. Bit-slice devices have been designed specifically to operate in parallel. It is possible to conceive and design novel computer architectures using a number of slices operating simultaneously on various instruction streams. This design philosophy will improve speed in any stream-processing system.

Any system which would be replicated a large enough number of times to distribute the cost of software over a large number of units produced is a candidate for a multimicroprocessor system. In this environment one should consider multimicroprocessor systems involving monolithic microprocessors.

REFERENCES

1. Intel, *Component Data Catalog,* Santa Clara: Intel, 1981.
2. Liptak, B. G., ed., *Process Control Instrument Engineers' Handbook,* Philadelphia: Chilton, 1969.
3. Skrokov, M. R., *Mini- and Microcomputer Control in Industrial Processes,* New York: Van Nostrand Reinhold, 1980.
4. Uniform Product Code Council, *UPC Symbol Specification Manual,* Alexandria, VA: Uniform Product Code Council, 1975.
5. Rockwell International, *Parallel Processing System (PPS-4) Microcomputer,* Anaheim: Rockwell International, Microelectronic Device Division, 1973.
6. Quigley, W. L., *Hoffman Electronics' Entry into the Security Market,* Los Angeles: WESCON, 1974.
7. McGlynn, D. R., *Microprocessors,* New York: Wiley, 1976.
8. Ibid.
9. Zaks, R., *Microprocessors,* Berkeley: Sybex, 1980.
10. Skrokov, M. R.
11. Liptak, B. G.
12. Skrokov, M. R.
13. Buckley, P. S., *Multivariable Control in the Process Industries,* Multivariable Control Systems Conference, Purdue, April 1975.
14. Skrokov, M. R.
15. Ibid.
16. Ibid.
17. Ibid.
18. McGlynn, D. R.
19. Ibid.
20. Ibid.
21. Ibid.
22. Kuo, F., ed., *Protocols and Techniques for Data Communication Networks,* Englewood Cliffs: Prentice-Hall, 1981.
23. Ibid.
24. Skrokov, M. R.
25. Tandem Computers, *Tandem 16 Non-Stop Systems Introduction,* Cupertino: Tandem Computers, 1975.
26. Intel, *The 8086 Family User's Manual,* Santa Clara: Intel, 1979.
27. Kraft, G. D. and Toy, W. N., *Microprogrammed Control and Reliable Design of Small Computers,* Englewood Cliffs: Prentice-Hall, 1981.

EXERCISES

1. A microprocessor oven controller is characterized by a simple control algorithm which has been traditionally implemented in electromechanical form. Discuss an

"intelligent" oven controller which uses reasonableness testing to reject any data considered unreasonable.

2. Two main types of medical applications have been developed which use microprocessors. Discuss system implementations which may be implanted in a human and system applications which are external.

3. Select one of the following as one of the most fruitful areas for microprocessor applications. Discuss the important aspects to consider.
   a. Large-scale communication networks for a computer.
   b. Telephone applications.
   c. Identification system applications.

4. Multiprocessor systems in large-scale data-processing applications with microprocessors for performing the processing functions, are important. The low-cost processing capabilities make the use of microprocessors attractive in larger-scale computer systems, but other factors may mitigate against their use. Discuss these other factors.

5. Discuss an industrial microcomputer implementation in each of the applications listed below.
   a. Supervisory or set point control.
   b. Direct digital control.
   c. Communications interface with a host minicomputer.
   d. Optimization with advanced control techniques.

10. System Development

MICROPROCESSOR SYSTEM DEVELOPMENT TECHNIQUES

In this chapter, we will consider the various stages of system development for microprocessors and the methods that may be applied during each stage. The topics include problem definition, program design, coding, debugging, testing, documentation and maintenance, and redesign. We will stress the variety of methods and trends rather than stress a single technique. A brief description of modern programming techniques is given, although no single method is widely used yet. Finally, some of the development systems and equipment that are available for microprocessors are discussed. System designers must be aware of the range of problems involved in microprocessor development, and they should be able to select the methods that seem the most effective for the application.

Many consider microprocessor system development to be mostly coding, which is the writing of a program in a language that can be loaded and used in the target computer. But coding is only a part of development.

The various tasks of system development are outlined below:

1. Product definition.   This stage is the initial definition of the task. It includes the specification of inputs and outputs and the processing and system requirements such as execution time, word length, response times, and error-checking. A basic flow chart showing the sequence of steps involved in the task should be formed.

The initial phase of any development is a design and evaluation phase, where a solution to the problem is designed, proposed, and evaluated. The design may involve the selection and assembly of the microprocessor system and the design of the software functions to be implemented on it. The essential consideration, at this stage, is the performance of the hardware and software system for the application.

2. Software/hardware system design.   This stage includes the design of a software package to meet the requirements of the problem definition. The techniques may include top-down design, structured programming,

434

modular programming, and flow-charting. Consideration should also be given to software design responsibilities and flow as well as the required development tools.

Hardware design and software design may be accomplished in parallel. This is a major difference when comparing microprocessor system development to other hardware development. The hardware design can be independent of the software development. The hardware design is simple when one uses standard microcomputer hardware. But it is more complex when it requires nonstandard interfaces. The most significant task is the software design. A number of development tools and systems for microprocessors are available which make it possible to design the software efficiently and independently of the hardware. One decision to be made by the designer is how many functions to implement in the form of chips and how many to implement in the form of software. This is sometimes called hardware/software partitioning. A major consideration is the quantity of systems produced. If the quantity is large, the number of hardware components should be minimized. As much as possible should be accomplished in software. If a small number of systems are to be produced, one should use more hardware as this will tend to decrease the complexity of the program. The evaluation becomes a matter of estimating the complexity of the software and the time and cost involved. When the decrease in software cost and required time is significant, then it becomes worth adding additional chips and board area.

3. Program development.   Developing the program involves coding the algorithm into a programming language. Coding is the translation of the program design into computer instructions. These instructions are the actual program or software product. We will discuss assembly language programming and alternative languages later in this chapter.

Good program design requires the precise formulation of the program logic and timing. Flow-charting, modular and structured programming, and top-down techniques are methods for formulating programs that can be easily coded, debugged, and tested. Good coding simplifies the later stages. The emphasis should be on clarity and comprehensibility. A simple program structure along with thorough documentation makes the program easy to debug and test. Later the designer can make the programs more efficient if desired.

4. Program verification and debugging.   This stage involves the discovery and correction of programming errors. Only simple programs run correctly the first time, so debugging is a critical and sometimes time-consuming task in system development. Editors, debugging software packages, simulators, emulators, logic analyzers, and other tools are useful during debugging. The types of errors that are most common in microprocessor programs, as well as some techniques to reduce their occurrence will be considered in this chapter.

System testing and program debugging are closely related. Testing is a later stage in which the program is validated by trying it for a number of test cases. Some of the test cases may be the same as used in the debugging phase.

5. System testing. This stage is the validation of the hardware and the program. Testing ensures that the program performs the required tasks in conjunction with the hardware. Important factors here include the selection of the test criteria from the specification and the development of the testing methods.

6. Evaluation and redesign. This stage may be an extension of the design for requirements in order to solve for problems beyond those described in the initial problem definition. The designers may want to take advantage of the programs and techniques for additional tasks. One should not consider any task completely in isolation from those tasks that may follow in improved product applications. Each stage of development affects the other stages. Problem definition may also include the consideration of a test plan, documentation and maintenance provisions, and the possible extension to other tasks. Program design should involve provisions for debugging, testing, and documentation. Coding, debugging, testing, and documentation are often concurrent activities.

PRODUCT DEFINITION

Many microprocessor-based systems are designed to carry out a number of operations rather than single tasks and thus require considerable definition effort. The use of a microprocessor to control an electrical or mechanical system such as a scale, CRT terminal, or card reader, requires a variety of calculations, and the device may generate a variety of outputs. The user may wish to solve a particular set of equations, find data records, or perform some other tasks. The initial stage of development must define the tasks to be performed and the requirements to be met.

Product Considerations

A major concern is the form of the inputs and outputs. For example, what devices will be attached to the microprocessor and in what form will they send and receive data? What are the required data rates, error-checking procedures, and control signals which the input/output devices use in order to indicate the availability of data or readiness to accept data. The word lengths, formatting requirements, and protocols must be decided. In most control tasks the input/output requirements are major factors in the definition phase.

Other questions involve the processing requirements. The designer must decide the sequence of operations on the input data and the order for all other tasks to be performed. The order of operations may be critical, if input/output signals must be sent or received in a particular time sequence. The system may have time requirements such as minimum data rates, mechanical or electrical delays, hold and settling times, recovery, enable, and disable rates. Latches and timing circuits can be used to satisfy some of these requirements, while memory limitations may control the amount of program and data memory or the size of buffers.

Paper-checks can be used for the check-out of the design on paper. This may be used both for the logic design and for the program. In a paper-checking exercise, one executes the program by hand, and fills out entries in a table corresponding to the values of the registers. The designer can then be assured that the results of the program are correct. This requires no development hardware but it is long and extremely tedious. Paper-checking can be accomplished at the flow chart level to verify the overall design, although it may not result in a reasonable evaluation of performance. In order to evaluate performance, development tools normally must be used. In many cases, paper-checks can be used to evaluate different microprocessors using a common benchmark program.

Benchmark programs, as discussed earlier in Chapter 3 are programs which are written in order to test the efficiency of a given microprocessor in a system. Manufacturer-supplied benchmark programs are programs, which for example, accomplish a block transfer or other operation. Often they are carefully optimized and may not be valid benchmarks. A valid benchmark must be written for the application. The benchmark should also be representative of the programmer's skill, if it is to be a true measure of the efficiency of the final program. One difficulty is that many applications cannot be characterized by simple programs and therefore require a mix of instructions to be executed. There may be no typical mix, and it is sometimes difficult to decide if a program has a true benchmark value in the evaluation phase.

The advantage of benchmarks occurs when the application is clearly defined. It is then possible to try a typical sample program using the execution times of different microprocessors and then decide which will be best for this type of application.

Documentation Concepts

Engineering embodies the creation, implementation, and documentation of products. Documentation allows product ideas to be produced and maintained.

Manufacturers may make control systems, instrumentation, or test equipment with conventional electronic or electromechanical components. The electronics senses external events through its inputs and causes a control reaction by driving an output line. Input signals may come from switch contacts or other sensing devices. Output loads can include relays, motors, and displays. The way the box functions when power is on is determined by the circuits used in it and the interconnects between the circuits. The internal circuits may include input and output drivers, timing, logic, arithmetic, and data storage. Circuits may be standard modules used in other systems. They are fully specified, documented, and tested apart from the system itself. Some circuits and interconnect wiring are usually designed solely for this system.

The use of the microprocessor in these systems introduces a new element: the control program. The microprocessor and its program replace many of the circuits and interconnects, which results in a reduction in hardware costs and an increase in system flexibility.

In logic design, the tools are block diagrams, schematics, assembly drawings, parts lists, and wire lists. For microprocessor designs it is necessary to use some of the old tools from logic design and additional tools and disciplines due to the abstract nature of the program design. These new tools are borrowed from the computer industry. Some simple examples are flow charts, memory maps, and program listings. The disciplined use of these tools, coupled with the techniques of partitioning, produces the design approach.

A block diagram is an essential tool. In most microprocessor designs the block diagram is the key link between the program and the hardware. It is at this level that partitioning of the problem begins. The block diagram serves several purposes. The main purpose is to condense the overall concepts of the design into a single drawing that should provide maximum communication with as little detail as possible. In the initial design, the block diagram provides the foundation for collecting and communicating the design ideas. In the production phase, the block diagram becomes a training tool for educating the test and service personnel. The designer uses the block diagram as a reference for the system resources. It shows all elements of the system and may be used for interfacing details such as port assignments and memory allocation.

The flow chart provides a visual statement of the solution of the problem with sequentially interconnected symbols which illustrate the program sequence. The flow chart serves to complement the block diagram. The block diagram illustrates the interconnection of the hardware and the flow chart shows the interconnection of the program flow. Flow charts are a key tool for program partitioning, reduction, and simplification.

In order to allow the sharing of system resources, the microprocessor accesses its resources by addressing, and to avoid addressing conflicts it is necessary to map out the resources available to the CPU and to make the allocation assignments as required. The resources such as registers, memory, or I/O must be allocated. To keep track of the allocation of those resources mapping is used. These are visual aids or maps to allow register, memory, or I/O space assignments as they are required.

A program listing is a step by step list of the program operation. The listing can be made up of the machine-language bit patterns, their numerical representations, or verbal assembly statements. The listing should include comments or other descriptive notation.

Flow charts have an advantage over program listings in that they do the following:

1. Show the order of operations and the relationships between sections of the program.
2. Are independent of a particular microcomputer or language.
3. Use a standard set of symbols (as shown in Figure 10.1).

Flow charts have the advantages of pictures over words, and they are a useful way for nonprogrammers and programmers to communicate. Several

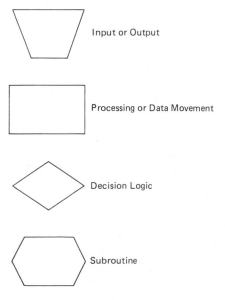

Fig. 10.1. Flow chart symbols.

levels of flow charts may be desirable—one showing the general flow of the program and the other providing details. Figure 10.2 shows a typical example using a simple editor program.

Too much detail makes a flow chart difficult to understand, and a very detailed flow chart has little advantage over a program listing. Flow charts may be helpful when general; however, they may have little connection to the actual structure of the data or the hardware. Flow charts may only describe the program flow; they will not show the relationships of the data structures or the hardware elements.

One should think first of the task the microcomputer has to do. After the task has been established, then consider the details of how the microcomputer carries it out. The design starts by figuring out what the task is and it continues with an analysis of a system which meets the requirements of the task and then proceeds to an implementation which accomplishes the result. We will consider a particular application in some detail. As we go through the design concept, we will apply relevant facts about microcomputers and how they are used so along with the design concept we'll consider the application characteristics which provide the design foundation.

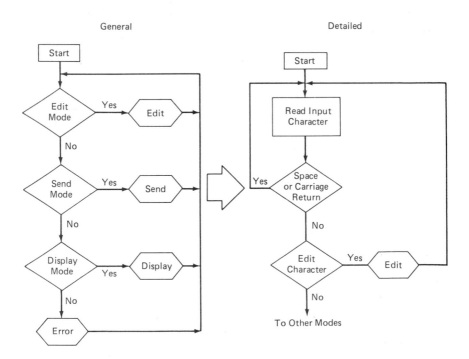

Fig. 10.2. Flow charts.

Functional Specification

The use of microprocessors for traffic light control was one of the first uses of microprocessors in an industrial environment.[1] The regulation of traffic lights at intersections had been accomplished using electromechanical control in simple situations and electronic control in more complex situations. The algorithms for controlling the flow of traffic in urban areas have grown in complexity, requiring complex logic facilities for sequencing the lights. Some of the functions performed by the traffic-light controller are as follows:

1. The sequencing of each group of traffic lights: red-amber-green.
2. The timing-cycle selection which may include cycles such as normal day sequencing, night-timing, rush-hour cycle, or others, depending on the time of the day or the traffic flow.
3. An initialization sequence—after the power is applied.
4. Facilities such as preemption by police or emergency vehicles.
5. Actuation by pedestrians or vehicles passing over loop detectors.
6. The computation of required traffic parameters such as density or volume.
7. Facilities for linking the controller to a central site or to other traffic controllers in a network (typically, a receiver, transmitter, and modem are used).

The major limitations of traditional electronic traffic-controllers are these:

1. Cost; a change in any of the functions required is expensive due to the rewiring and redesign required.
2. There are limitations in the complexity of the algorithms which may be implemented.
3. An adaption scheme is required for different intersections and different algorithms.
4. Low reliability of systems with high hardware complexity.

An important cost of previous traffic controllers was that each traffic controller had to be customized for the intersection.[2] The parameters of the customization are the geometry of the intersection and the number of phases and lights, as well as the combinations of algorithms which must be implemented. The various hardware modules are then combined in the traditional design such as volume counters, time-of-day sequencing modules, or pedestrian-actuation modules. The microprocessor replaces these hardware modules with software programs or subroutines. The required combinations of programs to accomplish the specified functions can easily be assembled and burned into PROMs which are then inserted into a standard control system. By having the customization occur at the software level, it allows one to produce identical standard traffic controllers. The adaptation and programming are done on a development system at the software level. Because of the production of identical hardware units, the hardware cost of the controller decreases significantly.

Another advantage is once the system is installed, its functions via the algorithms can be changed by inserting new PROMs. Other software features such as status monitoring can result in greater reliability through the detection of faulty relays or bulbs. The availability of programmed logic also allows the implementation of a variety of novel and complex algorithms. Complex green waves might be implemented. These allow a vehicle to proceed through all or most of the signals on a street without stopping. This may be accomplished by transmitting information from one traffic control microprocessor to the next in the network or coordinating the operation of the network from a central computer.

Alternate algorithms can be provided using alternate PROM chips rather than additional hardware modules. Typically, three modes of operations are used:[3]

1. The controller starts in the restart mode, where it assumes that no information is available. This is the power-up mode which is used until other system parameters become available. The essential input parameters are: a. the time of the day and b. the actual measurements.
2. The time-of-day programs are used during key segments of the day such as rush hour.
3. The parameter-actuated mode is used after the microprocessor has been in operation for some time. It uses traffic parameters such as the speed of vehicles, density, and the distance between vehicles.

The front panel provides the human interface. It includes the control switches for timing as well as the display information. The control switches are used to specify a number of parameters including, the timing intervals for amber and the selection between the various modes of operation. The status of the system, including the display of the traffic lights is also provided on the front panel. The system must also have manual actuation or preemption facilities for emergency operations, which are used by police when an accident occurs. The intersections are placed into specific modes or sequenced manually through push-buttons on the front panel. The manual override provided with this facility allows authorized personnel to place the intersection in alternating red and amber flashing modes.

All of the functional modules in the system have an impact on cost. Any communication facilities may entail a cost of several hundred dollars. The conflict monitor and flasher may also represent several hundred dollars. Load relays and loop detectors again can contribute hundreds of dollars to the system. The front panel may have a similar cost along with the metal cabinet. In this system, the cost of the microprocessor board is perhaps the smallest of any module. Because of the high cost of the various modules in such a system, the use of a microprocessor instead of hard-wired logic may not represent a significant savings in the production of a small number of units. But the savings are substantial for the production of a large number of units. The main advantage of the microprocessor is the intelligence capability in the implementation of the control algorithms, for it removes the limitations of hard-wired logic on the complexity of the algorithms that can be implemented.

It has been indicated that fail-soft facilities can be provided in case of hardware or software malfunction. This is done with a conflict monitor and its flasher unit. The green conflict monitor monitors the green status continually for all lights at the intersection. If two conflicting greens should ever be on simultaneously, the green conflict monitor can detect this, disconnect the microprocessor and turn on the flasher unit. The flasher produces alternate red and amber signals in the directions involved. This alleviates a situation that could have resulted in collisions.

If a software or hardware malfunction should occur which would result in a green conflict, the device will detect the condition and take action. The complete system is not disabled; only part of the functions are disabled by the malfunction. More refined techniques can be used in the microprocessor itself to diagnose and correct other possible error conditions.

Two back-up bypass lines are used to connect the transmitter and the receiver. These lines are used for loop-detector information and green status. They may be transmitted to a control center in a network of traffic control processors. All of these may communicate with the traffic control center. The information displayed at the control center may include the status of each intersection. The density of traffic may be evaluated at the control center for the synchronization of successive controllers along an arterial. If a malfunction should occur, another microprocessor could take over the functions if the system was equipped with additional software and connecting lines. When a significant flow of information may occur between the local controller and the control center, time-division multiplexing (TDM) can be used to encode the data for a single communication line. The microprocessor may be used to provide some TDM facilities in software, reducing the need for additional hardware.

In a completely dynamic self-optimizing system, the microprocessor starts in the time-of-day mode; then it switches to a parameter-actuated mode as the parameters become available, and then into a self-optimizing mode.[4]

SOFTWARE/HARDWARE SYSTEM DESIGN

Once the overall task has been defined, the next stage of development is the software/hardware design. Traditionally, system design has been linked with flow-charting. Flow-charting techniques are helpful when describing the program structure and in explaining the program, and they are also useful in documentation. But few programs ever result from a detailed flow chart which is then used to write the program. Drawing a detailed flow chart is as difficult as writing a working program—and less useful, since the program must then be derived from it.

Certain design techniques are useful in writing programs. They include the following:

1. *Modular programming.* A technique in which programs are divided into smaller programs or modules which can be designed, coded, and debugged separately and then linked together.
2. *Top-down design.* The overall task is first defined by generalized subtasks that, in turn, are more fully defined. The process continues down until all subtasks are defined in a form suitable for the microcomputer. The opposite is bottom-up design in which all subtasks are coded and then integrated into the overall design.
3. *Structured design.* This is a method in which programs are written according to specific defined forms. Only certain types of program logic are allowed, but routines may be nested within one another to handle complex situations. Structured programming often has program sections with a single entry and single exit.

These design techniques are considered in more detail in a later section of this chapter, but first let us consider some basic techniques for system development at the hardware level, the software level, and at the systems level. The major choices to be made are these:

1. Choosing the microprocessor or microprocessor board.
2. Performing the hardware/software partitioning.
3. Choosing the programming language.
4. Choosing the necessary development tools.

Basic Tasks

Selecting the microprocessor has been addressed in Chapter 3. This involves the selection of a product which has the performance sufficient for the application. Other considerations are availability of components and development support equipment and personnel.

The hardware/software partitioning task is based on the evaluation of the cost/performance aspects of the techniques to be selected. The techniques used to assemble the microprocessor system, as well as the software techniques used in the implementation facilitate this choice. Hardware/software partitioning is one of the most delicate tasks to be accomplished during the system design. The allocation should be re-evaluated throughout the design, and the trade-offs must be carefully considered. The partitioning has a major impact on the software design.

Throughout the design, a trade-off evaluation should be pursued (as exemplified in Figure 10.3). In order to reconsider the partitions that were made, it may become necessary to go from a polling scheme to interrupts, or to add hardware encoders. The system may also require other added circuitry in addition to the memory. Buffers, shift registers, latches, counters, level shifters, and interrupt control units are among the hardware that may be required.

Fig. 10.3. An expandable chassis such as this unit allows the microprocessor system to evolve as additional system capability is desired. (*Courtesy of the Intel Corporation.*)

In the past, designers tried to minimize memory usage and external hardware, since hardware and memory were more expensive than software. But, today the cost of memory and external hardware has been reduced. Tasks that once had to be done in hardware can now be done in software because of the reduced cost of processors and memory, and additional hardware which can substantially reduce the complexity of programming is also available at relatively low cost. Software costs are the same regardless of the number of units produced, but hardware costs are proportional to the number of units. So the trade-offs between hardware and software differ today from those of the days of expensive hardware.

The time and cost required to develop the software are important factors. Processors, memories, and other hardware are less expensive, but the cost of programming time rises. The change in the relative costs of hardware and software is a major reason for so much attention on techniques like structured programming that can increase programmer productivity. The proper design, debugging, testing, and documentation methods can reduce the overall development costs. Writing programs in high-level languages can increase programmer productivity and it makes many of the stages of development simpler. But there is a trade-off between software and hardware costs when using high-level languages; one can write and debug a program faster in a high-level language, but the final program requires more memory than one written in assembly language.

The product specification defines the problem, while the block diagrams break the problem into sections. The design and debugging is first done at the module level, then the subsystem level, and finally at the system level. Field trials can be used to verify the design solution in the application environment.

An important characteristic of the design is that it is modular. The first level of modules designed are circuit modules. The typical procedure is first to design the modules on paper; then the product can be built from the documents for testing. When the testing and debugging are complete, the documents can be updated for manufacturing.

Hardware Trade-offs

A number of hardware choices must be made when designing a microcomputer system. For example one may choose a single-chip microcomputer, which contains most of the elements in one package. Or one can start with a fully assembled board containing a microprocessor, which plugs into a chassis as shown in Figure 10.4. Performance and cost are key considerations, along with support hardware.

The evaluation of a microcomputer's performance often depends on the speed of its microprocessor. But speed is not the most important factor in

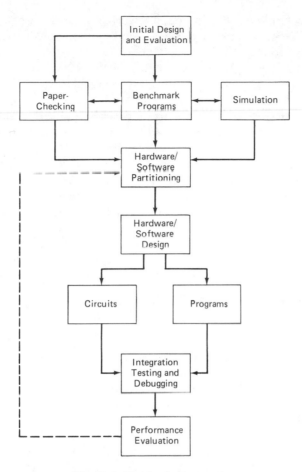

Fig. 10.4. The development cycle.

many applications: it should not be given a high priority automatically. Other important considerations are input and output lines, memory capacity, interfaces to other circuitry, and expansion capabilities as the system grows. In some applications, the processing requirements demand a fast microcomputer. Here, multiple microprocessors may be able to share the processing load. System expandability and support hardware allow one to add features and correct design problems without having to redesign the system or change to another microprocessor.

To consider the trade-offs between single-chip and single-board designs, we can compare a single-chip 8048 and a single-board 8080 system (iSBC 80/04).[5] The 8048 IC provides a CPU, ROM, RAM, and I/O in one dual inline package (DIP). Other ICs are added as needed. In the PC-board approach, much of the design has already been done. The 8048's pin-compatible EPROM version, the 8748, can be used for development and low-quantity production.

Assume that the application can be supported by either microcomputer system and that the program requires less than 1024 bytes. The cost of the system depends not only on the price of the parts; one must also include the design costs for nonrecurring engineering (NRE) and the production costs for each unit. The NRE costs include preliminary design, breadboarding, checkout, and other engineering costs for the first production unit. The initial design includes the clock, buffers, memory system, and the most critical design factor, the software.

After the hardware and software systems have been designed, they must be combined and checked out together. In this system-integration phase, problems occur from the new breadboard hardware and the new, untested software. If there is an error in the software, it may seem that the hardware is at fault. Development systems, in-circuit emulators, and high-level programming languages can reduce these problems during system integration. Once the system is complete, one must update the documentation: schematics, timing diagrams, program listings, flow charts, maintenance procedures, and the other support documents.

The NRE costs must be amortized over the production phase and recaptured within a certain time. When one includes the development expenses in the total system cost, we find that the NRE costs have little impact on the unit cost for a large production run of thousands, but the impact is enormous on a small production of systems.

One technique for minimizing the design cost is to use a pre-assembled microcomputer system in the final design. Even though both designs have about the same system capabilities, it's more expensive to completely duplicate the single-board computer. An 8085-based design would cost even more than the 8048 approach.

Support Considerations

Support comes in various forms. But, whatever the form, this support should be convenient at all stages of implementation. Initially, support is documentation and training. The more documentation, the easier it is to evaluate the system parameters affecting the application. Users' manuals, programming manuals, and application notes will help evaluate the capabilities of the microcomputer and aid in its design. Programming time can sometimes be reduced by commonly used software routines. A collection of user programs may be available, and many of these routines can be incorporated into the application program.

Seminars, workshops, and courses are also available. Moreover, personal contact with other engineers or consultants can help one to evaluate the cost trade-offs and the availability of components. One can use this additional help during all phases of design in order to discuss the advantages and disadvantages of prospective microcomputers and associated components in light of the project you're considering and to periodically review the design, which should optimize the end product.

Memory and I/O Expansion

After you've made the choice of microprocessor, you must evaluate the other components of the system: memory, input/output, and peripheral devices. Intelligent peripheral devices like floppy-disk controllers or CRT display controllers can help reduce the support circuitry. These devices will also simplify the programming needed for the peripherals.

For memories, the denser ROMs and RAMs will reduce the number of parts in the system as well as the system power consumption. EPROMs can be used during the development phase. By integrating memory, I/O, and other functions in a single chip, you can reduce the system complexity. For example, the 8155 has 256 bytes of RAM, 22 I/O lines, and a 14-bit timer.[6]

If you use pre-assembled boards, the system can expand easily (see Figure 10.3). Boards which are compatible with bus systems like the Intel Multibus, allow memory and I/O expansion, along with multiple microcomputers for added throughput. The Multibus is supported by over 90 different products from various manufacturers. This includes disk and tape controllers, IEEE-488 bus interfaces, switch boards, and wire-wrapped boards for custom interfaces.

The single board iSBC 80/04 has no built-in expansion bus, but it is hardware and software-compatible with the larger iSBC 80/05, which can be expanded to incorporate additional boards.[7] System expandability is important when choosing a single-board computer or selecting components for your own design. If one can upgrade the system, you do not have to change to another microcomputer for improved performance.

Program Design

The program design should also be a modular process. Just as shown in Figure 10.4 (see page 447), the design starts by breaking the design problem down into understandable modules and using flow charts which act as a tool for describing the sequence of events. Only two symbols are really necessary: a box for a process and a diamond for a decision. The number of levels in the flow chart is a function of the complexity of the program. Once the flow chart defines a module, the program can be started for this module.

When the program module or subroutine is designed and documented, it is integrated with other modules into one program. This integration is similar to the process of connecting circuits together into systems.

The three choices for a programming language are:

1. Direct binary or hexadecimal.
2. Assembly language.
3. High-level language.

Programming in binary or in hexadecimal does not require much support in terms of hardware or software. This method can be used on simple systems where the user communicates with the system with a hexadecimal keyboard and LED display. Instructions and data are put into the system via the keys in hexadecimal format. (See Figure 10.5) This is cost-efficient in hardware, but slow from the point of view of the programmer. Although one can design short programs and enter them into the system by this method, it is not advisable for longer programs in view of the alternatives available. But programming in binary or hexidecimal can be used when the user wants to change a few instructions in the memory. One does not need to go back to the editor to enter the changes, reassemble, load and then go into the execution mode. There has been the trend towards more powerful programming aids of increasing sophistication. One should not ignore them, unless the cost is prohibitive for the application.

Assembly-level language is a mnemonic or symbolic representation of the

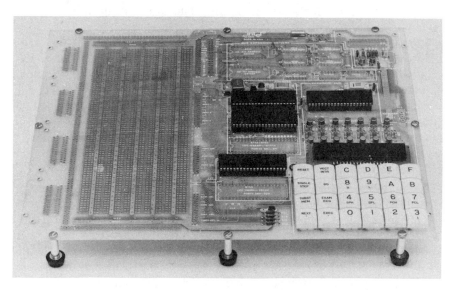

Fig. 10.5. Simple controller applications can be developed using a keyboard and LED display. (*Courtesy Intel Corporation.*)

binary code. In terms of efficiency of the user program, it is the most efficient method, but it requires manipulating registers along with a good understanding of the hardware structure of the system so as to result in the optimization of the program. The assembler converts the symbolic programs into an executable binary format. The assembler can also detect gross errors in syntax and flag them for the user. The major disadvantage is the tediousness of the programming in assembly language and the resulting programming time.

Assemblers produce either absolute or relocatable code. Absolute code must be loaded into a fixed location in memory, but relocatable code can be loaded at any point. Relocatability is an advantage because several program modules can be developed independently and then linked together by the linkage-editor program into one executable module.

A high-level language such as FORTRAN, PL/M or Pascal allows the programmer to use more powerful instructions to specify the algorithm. A high-level programming language is closer to the conventions used in the specification of the algorithm. It is then possible to code the algorithm in a shorter time. Programming in a high-level language can be ten times faster than programming in assembly-level language. This is true especially for long programs. The disadvantage is that most compilers used to produce the object code tend to be inefficient. It compiles a high-level instruction into a number of machine-level binary instructions; it does not optimize the use of registers, and this causes many unnecessary register transfers. A compiler can generate two to five times more instructions than would be generated at the assembly-level of programming. This results in additional memory requirements and in execution times two to five times slower. This may not always be an objection, however.

If the program is very complex, it might not ever get implemented correctly if it is programmed in assembly-level language. By programming it in a high-level language, it can be written and debugged fast. Later, one can produce a hand-optimized version. High-level languages allow a faster implementation of correct programs by more users.

Interpreters analyze source codes as a program is being executed so that no object code is needed. If an interactive interpreter is used, such as BASIC, the user can execute instructions one at a time and verify immediately if the syntax is correct with no errors in the instruction. The interpreter translates each instruction into binary code at once; thus, each part of a program may be executed as it is typed. This provides valuable diagnostics and results in faster debugging.

Many compilers let the user first develop a program in high-level language and then substitute assembly language modules within this high-level program. If the performance is insufficient or the memory utilization is too large, the user can recode sections of high-level modules using assembly language and substitute them into the program. Thus, one may code quickly in a high-level language and get the program to run correctly. The software is available to prove that the system will perform the required system tasks. One can then recode as many modules as necessary in assembly language. The efficiency of the program is improved, and the memory usage of the program is reduced. And this strategy introduces the product early. It can then be optimized before entering major production.

In deciding to use a high-level language or an assembly-level language, one must evaluate complexity and the resources available based on the number of units to be produced. The soft-ware cost will be the dominant factor for low production quantities. The software costs can be diminished by perhaps an order of magnitude using a high-level language. This can result in additional memory, but the cost may be small compared to the savings in programming time. For large quantities, the additional memory used is more significant and the programming costs are distributed over a large number of units. One can calculate the programming cost and divide it by the number of units for the software cost per unit. Then one can compare this to the hardware savings per unit from using assembly language.

SOFTWARE DESIGN METHODS

The last ten years have been marked by a number of new approaches to software design. The cause of this influx of software design methods is partly evolution and partly the increasing complexity of the problems involved. The availability of these many approaches has left many wondering which ones fit their class of problems.

Designers must think both intuitively and procedurally at the same time during a design effort. As the effort progresses, the emphasis shifts. At the outset, the designer initiates the ideas which set the design into motion. He may have an intuitive feel for the solution but suspects that it may be wrong. So he scrutinizes the ideas and makes some conclusions. The process can be characterized as divergence, transformation, and convergence.

The bigger problem is broken down into smaller problems, which is the basis of modular design. As in a modular hardware design, the modules isolate and separate functions, making designing, troubleshooting, and debugging easier. The advantages of program modules are that programming efforts may be distributed among several individuals; that the program modules can be run and tested separately before they are tied into the control program; and that modules designed with surrounding open locations allow for changes without affecting other parts of the program.

Modular Programming

Modular programming uses techniques in which programs are written, tested, and debugged in smaller units that are then combined. Top-down design requires modular programming, but modular programming is the older technique and it is often used independently of other techniques.

The modules are most often divided along functional lines. In microprocessor applications, this division can be most useful, since the modules can form a library of programs that can be used in later designs.

One disadvantage of modular programming is that it limits the size of programs to be debugged and tested, although it provides basic programs that can be reused and allows a division of tasks. Some other disadvantages include the additional program interfacing that may be required and the extra memory needed to transfer control to and from the modules, along with the need for separate testing of modules. And modular programming can be hard to apply when the strucure of the data is critical.

Modular programming can be used for developing the microprocessor software regardless of any other design techniques used. Some examples of typical modules might be as follows:

1. A program that signals an A/D converter to begin conversion, waits for the conversion to be completed, and then places the results in memory.
2. A program to read a keyboard and identify a key closure.
3. A program that multiplies two decimal numbers. This program could be used in any system which performs decimal arithmetic.

The designer can use a combination of techniques. Top-down design, structured programming, and modular programming are not mutually exclusive. The real task is to produce a working program, not follow the restrictions of any particular design method.

Top-Down Techniques

In top-down design, the testing and integration can occur along the way rather than at the end. Thus, incompatibilities can be discovered early. Testing can be done in the actual system instead of requiring driver programs. Top-down design tends to combine the design, coding, debugging, and testing stages of software development.

But top-down design sometimes forces the overall system design to take poor advantage of the hardware. It may require the hardware to perform tasks that it does poorly, and top-down design can be difficult when the same task occurs in several different places. The routine that performs the task must interface properly at each of these places. The proper stub can be difficult to write. Moreover, the program may not have the simple tree structures that mesh easily using the top-down approach. The sharing of data by different routines may also present problems, and errors at the top level may have major effects on the entire project.[8]

On the other hand, top-down design has improved productivity considerably in some applications. It should not be followed to such an extreme that it interferes with the development of reliable programs which allow the efficient use of a particular microprocessor.

A top-down design for A/D conversion might have the following steps:[9]

1. An overall flow chart is written (as shown in Figure 10.6). The initial program would call the A/D input routine which is a program stub, call the other routines or program stubs if the input data is not zero, and return to reading the A/D input.
2. The program stub which reads the A/D input is expanded to perform the following tasks (the input from the converter consists of three BCD digits that the CPU fetches one at a time):
   a. Send a START CONVERSION signal to the A/D converter.
   b. Check the CONVERSION COMPLETE line. Wait if the conversion is not complete.

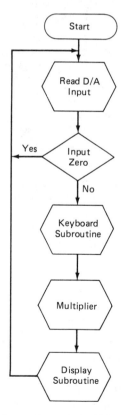

Fig. 10.6. Flow chart for A/D top-down design.

c. Fetch a digit.
d. Check the digit for zero.
e. Repeat *c* through *d* three times.
f. If all digits are zero, repeat starting with step *a*.
g. Check if the converter has reached the final value by waiting and then repeating steps *a* through *f*.
h. If the inputs are not equal, repeat step *g* until they reach to within the accuracy of the converter.
i. Save final input value.

Figure 10.7 is a flow chart of the partially expanded program stub. Steps *g* through *i* are not expanded. The procedure would continue by expanding each block until the detail was sufficient for coding.

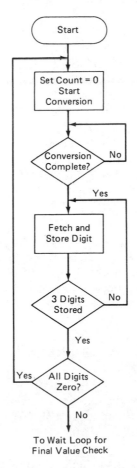

Fig. 10.7. A/D read preparation.

Structured Design Concepts

The structured design method consists of measures, analysis techniques and guidelines for following the flow of data through the system to formulate the program design. The data flow is traced by noting each data transformation, transforming process and the order of occurrence. The system specification is used to produce a data flow diagram, the diagram is used to develop the structure chart, the structure chart is used to develop the data structure and the results used to reinterpret the system specification. While the process is iterative, the order of iteration is not rigid.

Structured programming uses only simple logic structures. Three that are common are shown below:[10]

1. A sequential structure in which instructions or routines are executed in the order written.
2. A conditional structure of the IF–THEN–ELSE type; IF A THEN R₁ ELSE R₂ where A is a logical expression and R_1 and R_2 are routines consisting of the permitted structures. If A is true, the processor executes R_1; if A is false, the computer executes program R_2. R_2 is omitted if the computer is to do nothing if A is false.
   STRUCTURE EXAMPLE FOR *THEN AND ELSE*
   IF X ≠ 0, THEN Y = 1/X, ELSE Y = 0
   This structure ensures that the computer will never try to divide by zero and defines Y in the case where X is zero.
   STRUCTURE EXAMPLE FOR *THEN ONLY*
   IF CENTS ≥ 50 THEN DOLLARS = DOLLARS + 1
   This structure rounds DOLLARS to the nearest dollar. No action is taken if CENTS < 50.
3. A loop structure of the DO–WHILE type; DO WHILE A, where A is a logical expression and R is a routine consisting of the permitted structures. The processor checks A, executes R if a A is true and returns to check A again. The processor executes R as long as A is true.
   STRUCTURE EXAMPLE FOR *DO-WHILE*
   INDEX = 1
   DO WHILE INDEX ≤ MAX
      BLKA (INDEX) = BLKB (INDEX)
      INDEX = INDEX + 1
      END
   This structure moves the number of elements specified by MAX from memory locations in one array (BLKA) to the memory locations in another array (BLKB).

The structured program is written using only this set or some other set of structures. Figure 10.8 contains flow charts of the conditional and loop

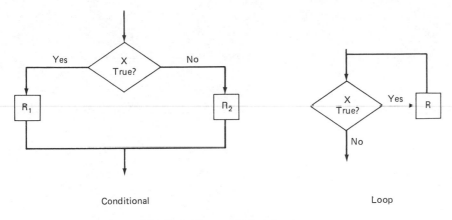

Fig. 10.8. Program logical structures.

structures. Each structure has a single entry and single exit. If an error oc-curred during the execution of R_2 in Figure 10.8, one would know how the processor reached that point. If the structure were as shown in Figure 10.9, the error might be in any of the sequences that led to R_2. A correction might affect one of the other sequences.

An example of the use of structured programming in the design of a simple editor program is now considered.[11] The program allows the user to space or backspace along a line on a CRT, delete or replace characters and end the edit by pressing the carriage return key. A structured program to perform the task follows:

TASK—SET POINTER TO FIRST CHARACTER IN LINE AND
      READ FIRST KEYBOARD INPUT
STRUCTURE—CHARACTER POINTER = 1
      READ INPUT
      Examine characters until carriage return found.
      DO WHILE INPUT ≠ CARRIAGE RETURN
      Move pointer if input is space and not already at end of line.
      IF INPUT = SPACE THEN
      IF CHARACTER POINTER = 80 THEN
      CHARACTER POINTER = CHARACTER
      POINTER + 1
      Move pointer if input is backspace and not already at start of line.
      ELSE IF INPUT = BACKSPACE THEN
      IF CHARACTER POINTER ≠ 1 THEN
      CHARACTER POINTER = CHARACTER

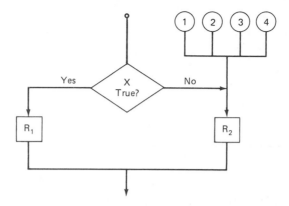

Fig. 10.9. Unstructured program example.

```
POINTER + 1
```
Delete character by replacing with space.
```
ELSE IF INPUT = DELETE THEN
     CHARACTER (CHARACTER POINTER) =
     SPACE
```
Replace with input character.
```
ELSE
     CHARACTER (CHARACTER POINTER) =
     INPUT
     IF CHARACTER POINTER ≠ 80 THEN
     CHARACTER POINTER = CHARACTER
     POINTER + 1
```
Read next input.
```
READ INPUT
END
```

The structured editor contains no unconditional **JUMP** or **GO TO** statements. The main loop is a **DO–WHILE** structure to examine the characters until it finds a carriage return. The loop will not be executed if the first character is a carriage return. The loop contains nested **IF–THEN–ELSE** statements. The indentation indicates the nesting levels. One can also use another **ELSE, ENDIF** to mark the end of the program.

The same structured design can be used even if the program is rewritten in a different language or for a different processor. Structured programming requires discipline, but the payoff can be substantial. In structured design, the key is the identification of the data flow through the system and the transformation that the input data undergo in the process of becoming output.

An example, though, of the problem with structured programs is tracing errors. One must first find all the statements that could cause a branch to the statement in question either by examining the entire program or by using a cross-reference table. Then one must determine which sequence of statements caused the error. The corrections must not affect other sequences that involve the altered statements.

Still, structured programs make the debugging, testing, and maintenance stages of software development much simpler. The major difficulties in using FORTRAN are the GO TO and IF statements. These can complicate the program structure since the programmer may not know how the program reached a particular point. Many advocates of structured programming do not use GO TO statements, which cause unconditional transfers of program control. The simpler flow of control produces clearer, more reliable, and more easily traced programs.

The results of structured programming in various applications have been rewarding. Many large programming projects use some variation of this technique. Improvements of 50 to 100% have been reported in programmer productivity, although many methods were actually used in most cases without careful controls.[12]

Microprocessor Design Considerations

What is the applicability of these techniques to microprocessor programming? Structured programming has primarily been used in large programming projects involving teams of programmers and tens of thousands of instructions. Structured programming techniques are most easily applied to programs written in high-level languages. Most microprocessor programs have been written in assembly or even machine language. But microprocessor programs are becoming longer. Techniques that make debugging and testing simpler will be in demand. Most microprocessor programs are written to be used as an integral part of the system. They must be tested, documented, maintained, and extended just like the hardware in the system hardware. Structured programming can help define the system software.

The process seems simple; but when one attempts to use it, difficulties can be encountered. Consistently identifying the transformations of data is not always easy. It is possible to be too detailed in some parts of the data flow and much less so in other parts. Identifying the incoming and outgoing flow boundaries is important in the definition of the modules and their relationships. The boundaries of the modules can be moved, leading to different system structures.

The structured design method can aid in the rapid definition and refinement of the data flows. This has been reported for military command and control applications.[13] But the technique used was not an integral part of the structured design method. The method and its graphics can reveal previously unknown properties of some systems, such as the generation of information already contained elsewhere in the system.

Few microprocessor designers have used languages that contain the actual structures of structured programming. The high-level languages based on PL/I such as Intel's PL/M and Motorola's MPL have the needed structures and can be used to write structured programs. But many programs are written with simple assemblers. Thus, structured programming could be used in the design stage, and the structured program could then be translated to assembly language because an assembly language program is hand-assembled into machine language.

Structured programs are often slower and require more memory than unstructured programs; however, execution time and memory usage may not be as critical as the time required for program development. The use of structured programming can substantially reduce overall program development time. The method is well suited to designs where a well-defined data flow can be derived from the specifications. Some of the characteristics that make the data flow well-defined are that input and output are clearly distinguished from each other and that transformations of data occur in incremental steps. Single transformations do not produce major changes in the character of the data.

In general, a software design method is a collection of techniques based upon a concept. Some other forms of design methods includes the following:

1. The Jackson Method.
2. The Logical Construction of Programs.
3. The Meta Stepwise Refinement (MSR).
4. Higher Order Software (HOS).

Each of these representative methods prescribes a set of activities and techniques intended to ensure a successful software design. Both the Jackson Methodology and the Logical Construction of Programs (also called the Warnier Methodology) advocate that the identification of the data structure is vital and that the structure of the data can be used to derive the structure and some details of the program.

The Jackson Method

The Jackson Method was popularized in England through the efforts of Michael Jackson.[14] In this method, the program is viewed as the means by which the input data is transformed into output data (as shown in Figure 10.10) and that paralleling the structure of the input data and output report ensures a good design. Other assumptions of this method are that the result-

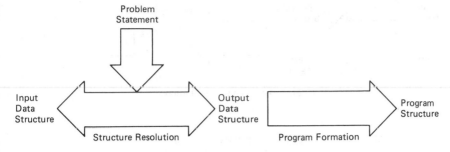

Fig. 10.10. The Jackson Method.

ing data structure will be compatible with a rational program structure; that only serial files will be used; and that the user of the method knows how to structure the data. Some features of this method that have been claimed are shown below:

1. It is not dependent on the designer's experience or creativity.
2. It uses principles by which each design step can be verified.
3. It is not difficult to learn and use correctly, so two designers working independently should arrive at nearly the same design.

The process appears simple, but difficulties include the supporting documentation and lack of some required structures for practical implementation. For example, error processing must be fitted in, since erroneous data do not exist in the structural sense. Also, various file accessing and manipulation schemes may not be acceptable. Much data structuring is dictated by the data base management system used, so there is a casual link between the data structure and the program. If this happens to be the case, the basic assumption may not be valid.

The LCP Method

The Logical Construction of Programs (LCP) Method (as shown in Figure 10.11) is similar in nature to the Jackson Method in that it also assumes data structure as the key to software design. But this method is more procedure-oriented in its approach. LCP uses the following guidelines:[15]

1. Identify and organize the input data in a hierarchical manner (files, records, entries, items).
2. Define and note the number of times each element of the input file occurs and use variable names to note the ratio of occurrences such as: N customer records.

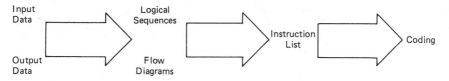

Fig. 10.11. The LCP Method.

3. Repeat steps 1 and 2 for the desired output.
4. Obtain the program details by identifying the types of instructions required in the design in a specific order: (1) read instructions (2) preparation and execution of branches (3) calculations (4) outputs and (5) subroutine calls.
5. Using flow chart techniques graph the logical sequence of instructions using **Begin Process, End Process, Branch,** and **Nesting** labels.
6. Number the elements of the logical sequence and expand each using Step 4. There are additional guidelines for data structure conflicts.

Many of the difficulties in the use of this method are similar to those found using the Jackson Method. It forces one to contrive a hierarchical data structure previously apparent, whereas it does not address such issues as run environment or file access methods. With the hierarchical data structure, we can get a pseudocode statement of the program rapidly, but the resulting program is not optimum.

The method is well suited to problems involving one or only a few modules, and where the data are tree-structured.[16] This leaves it susceptible to the same kind of problems as the Jackson Method.

Meta Stepwise Refinement

The Meta Stepwise Refinement (MSR) Method is based on the premise that the more times one does something, the better the final result is.[17] The designer assumes a simple solution to a problem and gradually builds in detail until the final solution is derived. Several refinements at the same level of detail are used by the designer each time the additional detail is required (as illustrated in Figure 10.12). The best of these is selected and more detailed versions are proposed. Only the selected solution is refined at each level of detail. The specific features of this method include:

1. It uses an exact, fixed problem definition.
2. It is language-independent in the early stages.

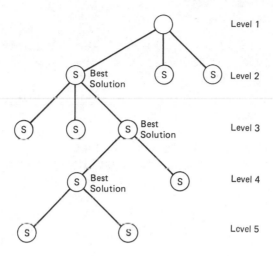

Fig. 10.12. Meta Stepwise Refinement.

3. The design is done by levels.
4. The details are postponed to lower levels.
5. The design is successively refined.

MSR is a combination and refinement of top-down design, the step-wise refinement concept, and level-structuring. It produces a tree-structured program using level-structuring concepts.

Through proper program organization, it is possible to separate functionally independent levels or layers into programs (as shown in Figure 10.12). The higher levels reflect the problem statement while the lower ones contain increasing amounts of implementation detail. The modules at a specific level invoke modules at the next lowest level.

In theory the method appears sound, but real applications require constant evaluation and modification since they are not stable. Because the solution at any one level depends on prior higher levels, any change in the problem affects prior levels, and a solution at any level is undermined until the changes are made. If one refuses changes until the design is complete, then the solution and the requirements are not synchronized.

The handling of multiple solutions is another problem. How to select the best solution can be difficult. Because of the number of times the problem will be solved, this approach is best on smaller problems. It can be useful where the problem specification is fixed and an elegant solution is required such as developing an executive for an operating system.

Higher Order Software `

Higher Order Software was developed on NASA projects as a formal means of defining reliable, large-scale, multiprogrammed multiprocessor systems.[18] Its basic features include:

1. A set of formal laws.
2. A specification language.
3. An automated analysis of the system interfaces.
4. Layers of system architecture produced from the analyzer output.
5. Transparent hardware.

This method is based on axioms which define a hierarchy of software control, where the control is a specified effect of one software object on another:[19]

1. A module controls the invocation of a set of valid functions on only its immediate, lower level.
2. A module is only responsible for elements of its own output space.
3. A module controls the access rights to a set of variables which define the output space for only each immediate, lower-level function.
4. A module may reject invalid elements from only its own input set.
5. A module controls the ordering of each tree for only the immediate, lower levels.

HOS has been used with an automated analyzer program to check the solution as expressed in the HOS metalanguage.[20] The analyzer is not inherent in the method, since one can use psuedocode in the method.

HOS seems to be useful in applications where the accuracy and auditing of the algorithms are major concerns such as scientific and detailed financial computations. HOS appears to ensure consistent reliability by the interface definitions and the attention to detail.

In most HOS software designs, the data base design has been addressed implicitly, since the structure of the code is the major problem. Large systems usually require the design of the code and data base to be synchronous in nature. A general summary of some of the software concepts discussed is shown in Table 10.1.

No single method exists which would be used in every design. Also, the assumptions made by each method are *assumptions* and can not be proved. Any of the methods can only contribute to the design effort. A design problem may be well suited to a particular technique but it may also be unique. The software design methods only assist in solving some of the routine

Table 10.1 Software Design Methods

	GRAPHICS	PROCEDURE(S)	COMPATIBILITY WITH OTHER TECHNIQUES	AREAS OF APPLICATION	EVALUATION CRITERIA
STRUCTURED DESIGN	structure charts for system architecture	iterative framework which guides the solution development	usable with any module design strategy	systems where data flow can be graphic	a well-defined set of design heuristics
THE JACKSON METHOD	tree-like charts for data structures	loosely defined guidelines	usable with other data structuring methods	systems with well-understood data structure(s)	compliance with basic assumptions
LOGICAL CONSTRUCTION OF PROGRAMS	Warnier charts for data structure	well-defined procedures at all levels of detail	procedural nature limits compatibility	systems with well-understood data structure(s)	compliance with basic assumptions
META STEPWISE REFINEMENT	tree diagrams for program	high-level guidelines	would benefit from design evaluation criteria	applications with well-understood, stable requirements	no specific guidelines
HIGHER ORDER SOFTWARE	structured flow charts for control structure	theoretical with limited operational details	would benefit from design guidelines	applications with high reliability requirements	automated analysis

aspects of the problem. Using a particular method only reveals the issues in a design problem and gives one more chance to address them.

Designing is problem solving, usually a fundamental, personnel issue. To some, design methods are resisted if imposed. The adoption of a method may require a fundamental change, an alternation in how certain problems are solved. Accomplishing the desired change can be difficult.

All of these methods are important but their successful application can occur only with a supportive management. The required elements of planning, scheduling, and control must also be effective. The balance between methods and environments is critical, and a merging of these may be the next evolution in software.

PROGRAMMING TECHNIQUES

Reliability and holding down programming costs are among the most important objectives in software development for microprocessors. A primary cost objective is to develop a program that works using a reasonable expenditure of time and money. Improvements can be made later if required, for some of the major cost in most projects is programming time; methods that can minimize the time required to complete a program are desirable. With the advent of larger memories and low-cost chips with faster processors, memory and hardware constraints are not critical in microprocessor software development as they have been in the development of software for larger computers.

The major emphasis in this section will be on how to write reliable programs in a reasonable time and how to document them. Some attention will also be paid to how to write shorter and faster executing programs for specific microprocessors. To begin with, we must have some criteria for evaluating programs. These criteria can help us determine the aims, methods, and relative importance of the various stages of software development. The followintg factors can be considered in writing programs for microprocessors.

The most important criterion for a program is whether it works reliably. The structure, the efficient use of time and memory, the short design time, and documentation are meaningless if the program does not work. The program should be checked to see that it works correctly under test conditions that reflect the actual operating conditions. The selection and execution of a test plan are not always simple tasks. The problem definition and program design stages must produce a test plan and a program that can be easily and thoroughly tested.

A program that executes tasks quickly will do more work than a slower one. Speed can determine if the program works at all, since critical timing requirements may exist. If the speed of the system depends on external factors, such as operator response time, input or output data rates of sensors, displays and/or converters, the program speed may not be as important.

Each chip needed for the program memory adds to the system cost. Also, extra read/write memory adds to the system cost. Additional memory requires additional interconnections, board space, decoding circuitry, and increased power. As larger semiconductor memories have become available, the importance of memory size has decreased. But memory size must still be considered, particularly in the smaller applications in which the cost of a single memory chip is significant.

A program which is easier to work with is more valuable than one that is relatively hard to use. Complicated data formats and unclear error messages can make a program difficult and expensive to debug, use, and maintain. Design and documentation are important factors in determining whether a program is easy to use. Human factors are often important when the program requires human interactions. Many microprocessor-based control systems are designed to simplify tasks for human operators.

A program that tolerates errors can be easier to maintain than one that does not. This requires that the program be designed to react in some way to errors whose occurrence cannot be foreseen. Error tolerance can be critical in situations where human operators can change the data or equipment. The program can make the operator or system element aware of erroneous inputs or malfunctions without shutting the system down.

The program that can be extended to tasks other than those for which it is specifically designed is superior over the long term to one that may be used for only one particular task. The design and documentation stages are again particularly important in meeting this objective. Modular programming can be useful in this area, although structured programming and other methods can also contribute to extending the program capabilities later.

Programming Style

We will next consider some specific hints on programming style that will be useful regardless of the particular language or processor involved. Other hints will be considered later for particular microprocessors.

1. Use names or labels instead of specific memory addresses, constants, or numerical factors.
2. The names or labels can suggest the actual purpose or meaning of the particular address or data.
3. Do repetitive operations outside loops.
4. Use short forms of addressing when possible. This may require that the data be reorganized.
5. Try to reduce jump statements. They use too much time and memory.
6. Take advantage of the addresses that are 8-bit quantities. This includes addresses such as the even multiples of 100 in hexadecimal.
7. Use stack addressing instead of direct addressing to move data between the memory and registers.

Program Optimization

Many of the same techniques listed above can minimize the execution time and memory size, since longer programs require more memory accesses and more execution time. Subroutines represent a memory savings at the cost of the execution time required for the call and return; loops represent a similar trade-off. When minimum execution time is required, subroutines and loops may be replaced by repeated copies of the same instructions; minimum memory requires the opposite. The gain from program optimization can result in a speed increase or memory reduction of about 25%. If larger gains are required, the following methods can be considered.

1. New algorithms can provide a larger increase in speed or larger decrease in memory use.
2. The use of microprogramming with a microprogrammable processor might help to execute the present program at significantly higher speeds.
3. The increasing of the clock speed will allow the processor and memory to run at a higher speed.
4. The use of external hardware such as multipliers can increase the throughput by relieving some of the processing burden from the CPU.
5. Parallel processing by two or more processors may be able to do the tasks at higher speeds without greatly affecting the system cost.
6. Distributed processing with two or more processors dividing the tasks can have the same effects as parallel processing.

If the microprocessor is presently pushed to the limits of its performance the techniques described above may be more helpful than will attempts to obtain large increases in performance by program optimization. Some general rules for increasing execution speed using programming techniques include the following:

1. Find the loops that are executed frequently by handchecking or testing the program. Try to reduce the number of instructions in these loops. Instructions that are used only a few times have little impact on program execution time.
2. Try to use register operations when possible since these operations are faster than any others. But they may require extra initialization. Among the register operations that can be used are the indirect jumps that are performed by transferring the contents of a register to the program counter.

Try to emphasize simplicity and comprehensibility. The main objective of programming is to write a program that works. Saving a few microseconds or a few memory locations is seldom critical. The coding can be optimized later. The initial program should always be obvious rather than clever. These are the practices to avoid: performing operations out of order, using multiple-word instructions for unrelated items, using leftover results to initialize variables or using them for calculations, and using parameters as fixed data. An example of a practice to avoid using the 8080 instructions is shown below:[21]

LSI   D, 280   :   INITIALIZE D TO 4, B TO 8

This next statement should not be used when A and B are unrelated. A better form is this:

```
MVI   A, 4  :  INITIALIZE A TO 4
MVI   B, 8  :  INITIALIZE B TO 8
```

Another example is this:

```
DCR   B
JNZ   STRT
MOV   A, B
```

This above sequence should not be used to clear *B*. A better form is shown here:

```
DCR   B
JNZ   STRT
MVI   A, O
```

The cost in memory is one word for the increased clarity.

Keep the modules short by dividing long modules into sections. A shorter module is easier to debug and correct, and it is more likely to be used again since its function is more likely to recur. One or two pages of code with 50 to 80 lines is a maximum size for a module. The modules can also be implemented as macros or copied into the program in order to avoid a large number of calls and returns. In microprocessors, the calls not only require extra time and memory but they can also overflow a limited stack for storing the return addresses.

Make the modules general. Modules that are too specific like one that sorts only 16 elements or searches for the letter *B* will find little repeated use; greater generality can often be achieved with little extra code. General routines that require large amounts of extra code such as a code conversion routine for both ASCII and EBCDIC characters should not be considered. Some simple ways to achieve generality have already been discussed: the use of names instead of specific addresses or data, the collection of definitions at the start of the routine, and the use of names that suggest the purpose or identities of the item. These techniques tend to produce a program that can be used frequently and that can be easily modified.

Program Documentation

Documentation is a stage of development that is often overlooked. Yet, it is not only useful in the debugging and testing stages, but it is also essential in the maintenance and redesign stages. A properly documented program can be used again when required. An undocumented program normally requires so much extra work to use that one might just as well start from the beginning. The techniques most common for documentation are flow charts, program listings with comments, memory maps, and parameter and definition lists. Structured programming and some of the other design techniques have developed some of their own documentation forms.[22]

Flow charts act as a visual aid for program documentation. A general flow chart can serve as a pictorial description of a program, and the more detailed programmer flow chart can be valuable to another programmer who must use or maintain the program.

Comments are a critical part of program documentation. A program with a clear structure and well chosen names can be almost self-documenting. The comments should explain the purpose of the instructions. They should not merely repeat the meaning of the instructions. Following is an example with comments that add nothing to the documentation for an 8080 program which finds the maximum of an array of elements starting in location BLK (the length of the array is in memory location LENG).[23]

```
             LDA LENG       :LENG TO A
             MOV B,A        :A TO B
             LXI H,BLK      :PUT BLK IN H
NEWMX:       MOV A,M        :M TO A
NEXTE:       INX H          :H TO H + 1
             DCR B          :B TO B - 1
             JZ DONE        :GO TO DONE IF ZERO
             CMP M          :COMPARE TO M
             JC NEWMX       :GO TO NEWMX IF CARRY
             JMP NEXTE      :GO TO NEXTE
DONE:        STA MAX        :A TO MAX
             HLT            :A TO MAX
```

Next is the same program properly documented.

```
             LDA LENG       :COUNT = LENGTH OF ARRAY
             MOV B,A        :COUNT = LENGTH OF ARRAY
             LXI H, BLK     :POINT TO START OF DATA
NEWMX:       MOV A,M        :ELEMENT IS NEW MAXIMUM
NEXTE:       INX H          :ELEMENT IS NEW MAXIMUM
             DCR B          :ELEMENT IS NEW MAXIMUM
             JZ DONE        :ELEMENT IS NEW MAXIMUM
             CMP M          :IS MAXIMUM LARGER THAN
                               CURRENT ELEMENT?
             JC NEWMX       :NO, REPLACE MAXIMUM
             JMP NEXTE      :YES, LOOK AT NEXT ELEMENT
DONE:        STA MAX        :STORE MAXIMUM
             HLT            :STORE MAXIMUM
```

The following general rules apply to comments.

1. Comments should explain the purpose of instructions or instruction sequences, not define the operational codes.
2. Comments should be clear but brief; avoid shorthand and obscure abbreviations. Complete sentence structure is not necessary.
3. The comments should be limited to the important points of program flow. Too many comments make the program difficult to follow. Standard sequences like loop controls do not need to be explained unless they are utilized in some unusual manner.
4. The comments should be placed close to the statements that they apply to.
5. Comments must be kept up to date. Comments that refer to previous versions of a program should be deleted.

Commenting is a tool that one should use properly. A designer must ask himself what explanation he would need to understand the program. Some comments, provided in a systematic manner, are helpful in all stages of the software development.

Memory maps list the memory assignments made for the program. These maps prevent different routines from interfering with each other, and they help in determining the amount of memory needed and as well as finding the locations of subroutines and tables. Memory maps are particularly important in microprocessor systems because of the use of separate program and data memory (ROM and RAM). The fact that addresses are assigned as part of the hardware design, the need to conserve memory usage, particularly for RAM, and the need to know the precise locations of parameters that may have to be changed are all important reasons for proper memory mapping.

Parameter and definition lists can also be a part of the documentation. These explain the function of each parameter and its meaning. The parameters may also be explained in the program.

Program forms describe the subroutines. The programmer should provide the purpose of the program, the form of the input and output data, the requirements for memory of the program, and a description of the parameters.

Proper software documentation should combine all or most of the methods discussed. The total documentation can include the following:

1. General flow charts.
2. Detailed programmer's flow charts.
3. A description of the test plan.
4. A written description of the program.
5. A listing for each program module.
6. A list of the parameters and definitions.
7. Memory maps.

Documentation is best performed simultaneously with the design, coding, debugging, and testing stages of software development. Good design and coding techniques make the program easier to document, and good documentation, in turn, simplifies the maintenance and any redesign required.

The redesign can involve adding new features or meeting changed requirements. The redesign should proceed through the previous design stages of software development. The process may also involve making a program meet critical time or memory requirements. This next section briefly describes methods for making programs faster or shorter.

8080 Family Software Hints

When increases of 25% or less in speed or reductions of the same order in memory are desired, the program can often be reorganized, but the program structure may have to be sacrificed. Such a task can require a large amount of time and should be avoided if possible. The use of names can reduce the confusion between addresses and data, as shown below:

```
P1TOP    EQU    255
MIN1     EQU    OFFH
```

This gives different names to the address 255 (P1TOP) and the number 255 (MIN1), since FF is -1 in two's complement). Meaningful names and labels can be helpful in documentation and maintenance as well as in debugging and integrating programs. The same 8080 block search program with and without meaningful names and labels is shown below:[24]

Program without meaningful names			*Program with meaningful names*		
	LXI	H,X		LXI	H,BLOCK
Z:	MOV	A,M	NEWMX:	MOV	A,M
W:	INX	H	NEXTE:	INX	H
	DCR	B		DCR	B
	JZ	Y		JZ	DONE
	CMP	M		CMP	M
	JC	Z		JC	NEWMX
	JMP	W		JMP	NEXTE
Y:	STA	V	DONE:	STA	MAX
	HLT			HLT	

The names should be simple and straightforward: MAX for the maximum value, START for the beginning of the program. The use of meaningful well thought out names can save the programmer time in all stages of software development. Try to group definitions at the start of the program; definitions that are grouped at the start of the program are easily located, checked, and changed. The example below also describes each definition with a comment.

RAM Locations

BUFR	EQU	257	:Teletypewriter input buffer
CLOCK	EQU	300	:Number of clock pulses
RFLAG	EQU	301	:Ready flag for TTY

Tables

SQU	EQU	606	:Table of squares
SSEG	EQU	520	:Seven-segment code table

Numerical Factors

MONE	EQU	−1	

Input/Output Devices

ADCON	EQU	4	:Input unit for A/D converter
KBD	EQU	3	:Input unit for keyboard
PTAPE	EQU	2	:Input unit for paper tape
TTY	EQU	1	:Output unit for TTY printer

Definitions that are scattered through the program can slow the debugging and documentation phases.

Distinctive names and labels can reduce confusion. The numbers *0, 1,* and *2* and the letters *O, I,* and *Z* can be confused as in MINI and MIN1. The chance for error here is great. Names like this which may confuse the programmer should be changed.

Obscure construction like the use of offsets from the program counter in computers that use many multiple-word instructions or use the complex conditional assemblies should be avoided or minimized. But at the same time one should make use of the power of a particular microprocessor's instruction set as shown in the examples which follow.

Some microprocessors like the 8080 use a subroutine call instruction for restarts (RST).[25] This instruction is the same as CALL i*8; where *i* = restart number, 0–7. The difference between the restart call and its equivalent subroutine call is that the subroutine call uses three bytes of memory and the restart call (RST) uses only one byte. Thus, an efficient way to use restarts involves converting the most frequently used subroutine calls to restart calls. Each conversion saves two memory bytes and six clock cycles. Restart choices are not limited to only 8 bytes because the called addresses lie 8 bytes apart; a jump can be used to continue the routine in the last three bytes of the restart area.

To optimize memory usage, one byte calls can be used to produce a large number of two byte calls. This is one byte longer than a restart but one byte shorter than a standard call. First create a table with the subroutine address.

```
TAB          DW          ROUT1
             DW          ROUT2
             DW          ROUT3
             •           •
             •           •
             DW          ROUTn
```

To call any of these routines, use the following:

```
RST      x                :restart call
DB       n*2              :n = routine number
```

With TAB positioned in the memory such that addition carry corrections are not required, the restart routine will transfer control to routine n in the table.

Arithmetic computations may be coded in the 8080 many ways.[26] Although the following examples apply to the 8080, the techniques may be applied to other microprocessors as well. Consider the problem of clearing a single register or a number of selected registers. One method for doing this requires the following three sequences:

```
SEQUENCE 1          MVI A,O      :Load accumulator with zero,
                                       A = O
SEQUENCE 2          LXI II,L     :Load register pair with zero,
                                       II,L = O
                    MVI E,O      :Load register with zero, E = O
SEQUENCE 3 LOOP •
                 •
                    DCR  B       : Decrement register
                    JNZ LOOP
                 •
                 •
                    MVI B,O      :Load register B with zero,
                                       B = O
```

These sequences all have inefficiencies.

SEQUENCE 1: The accumulator is loaded with zero; a faster method is to compute zero.
SEQUENCE 2: The register is loaded with zero; a better method is to move zero into the register, since H and L are already zero.
SEQUENCE 3: The loop is not required since the register already contains zero.

One method of computing zero is $A = A - A$ but an even faster way is $A = A$ XOR A. Many other arithmetic computations can be improved using the same type of critical analysis techniques.

The 8080 uses the following instructions to assist in binary coded decimal (BCD) arithmetic:

DDA   :Decimal adjust accumulator

This instruction has two shortcomings. It does not convert the accumulator from binary to BCD; it only adjusts the results. It can only be used with operations that automatically set the half-carry. The first limitation is illustrated below:

MVI A, 10   :Set accumulator to 10, A = 10
DDA   :Decimal adjust accumulator

This sequence will not convert the accumulator to the BCD value of 10. The assembler may be used to convert numbers to BCD. The number is first terminated with *H,* which instructs the assembler to store the number as a hexadecimal value; it is the same as BCD provided none of the digits exceeds 9.

The second limitation is shown below. Here, we attempt to add one to the BCD value in the accumulator.

INR A   :Increment accumulator, $A = A + 1$
DAA   :Decimal adjust accumulator

Since INR does not set the half-carry this sequence will not work and the following sequence must be used.

ADI A   :Add increment to accumulator, $A = A + 1$
DAA   :Decimal adjust accumulator

This sequence works since ADI sets the half-carry.

6800 Programming Hints

The 6800 has a software interrupt instruction (SWI) that may be used to decrease memory requirements. This instruction uses a subroutine address stored in the hexadecimal locations FFFC and FFFD. It is similar to an 8080 restart but its address is not fixed since it comes from the two hexadecimal locations. SWI can be used for the most frequently used subroutine instead of the BSR or JSR instructions. It may also be used to simulate hardware interrupts, which can allow debugging without special hardware. The following sequence can be used to call subroutines for the simulation:[27]

Create a table for the subroutine addresses

```
        TAB        FDB    ROUT1
                   FDB    ROUT2
                          •
                   FDB    ROUT2
```

To call a subroutine code, follow this sequence

```
        SWI              :Software interrupt
        FCB  N*2         :Where N = routine number
```

The software interrupt instruction fetches a subroutine from the table and transfers control to it using the following interrupt sequence

```
TSX                      :Transfer stack pointer, X = SP + 1
INC           6,X        :Increment to update return
LDX           5,X        :Load to get return
DEX                      :Decrement back to routine number
LDA   A O,X              :Load accumulator, A = routine no. *2
STA A TEMP + 1           :Store to transfer to index register
LDX           TEMP       :Load index register
LDX           TAB,X      :Load index register with target address
JMP           O,X        :Jump to routine
```

An RTI instruction is used to return control to the calling routine. Location TEMP must contain zero or be cleared. If the table is stored in a memory that can be modified, like a PROM, the PROM can be used to correct bugs. Once a bug is detected, the table in PROM is modified so that control for the detected subroutine goes to the PROM. Then the corrected subroutine is placed in the PROM and that subroutine returns control back to the main program.

Z80 Software Hints

The index registers in the Z80 are a useful method for addressing memory.[28] One limitation of the 8080 forced the memory locations to be addressed by (H,L) as the arithmetic operand. In the Z80, an index register can be used for the addressing of 256 locations. For example:

$$ADD   (IX + 10)$$

adds the contents of the memory location addresses by $IX + 10$ to the accumulator. The assembly time equivalence instruction (EQU) can be used for the same operation as shown below.

ABQ	EQU 10	:Assembly equivalence, $ABQ = 10$
	ADD (IX + ABQ)	:Add contents of $(IX + 10)$ to accumulator

The EQU instruction does not generate Z80 code; it only indicates to the assembler that label ABQ is the same as the constant 10. If EQU is used as follows,

VAR1	EQU	0	:VAR1 is byte 0
CON1	EQU	1	:CON1 is byte 1
VAR2	EQU	2	:VAR2 is byte 2
•	•		
END	EQU	255	:END is byte 255

then each variable or constant can be referenced. Memory space must be reserved for EQU since it does not generate code. To initialize the IX register so that it will address the reserved area of memory, use the following:

MEM	BSS	256	:Reserve 256 memory locations
	LD	IX,MEM	:Load to preset IX to location MEM

Then code

LD	A,(IX + VAR1)	:Load accumulator, $A = $ VARI
ADD	(IX + CON1)	:Add, $A = A + $ CON1
LD	(IX + VAR2),A	:Load, VAR2 = A

This sequence adds CON1 to VAR1 and places the result in VAR2. It replaces the following 8080 sequence that required 11 bytes:

LDA	MEM + VAR1
MOV	B,A
LDA	MEM + CON1
ADD	B
STA	MEM + VAR2

The two Z80 registers allow two groups of 256 locations to be accessed this way.

The Z80 has a group of instructions to move tables of data and locate entries within the tables. These are the four table-move instructions: LDI, LDIR, LDD and LDDR. Each one requires preset conditions for the registers:

1. (D,E)—address of destination.
2. (H,L)—address of source.
3. (B,C)—number of words to be transferred.

Each time the Z80 executes one of these instructions, the registers are updated. LDI and LDIR increment the (D,E) and (H,L) registers and LDD and LDDR decrement (D,E) and (H,L) after each move, and the four instructions decrement (B,C) after each move. LDIR and LDRR will continue to transfer data until (B,C) is equal to zero while the LDI and LDD transfer only one byte. If there are two tables, *TAB1* and *TAB2,* each with 100 bytes of data, then to transfer data between the tables we code:

```
LD    DE,TAB2      :Load, (D,E) = destination address
LD    HL,TAB1      :Load, (H,L) = source address
LD    BC,100       :Load, (B,C) = number of words
LDIR               :Transfer the data
```

The actual transfer is made by the last instruction in the sequence which uses 11 memory bytes and over 2,000 clock cycles. Without the LDIR instruction a loop must be used:

```
LOOP    LD    A,(DE)      :Load to get one byte
        LD    (HL),A      :Load to save the byte
        INC   DE          :Increment to update DE
        INC   HL          :Increment to update HL
        DEC   BC          :Decrement to update BC
        LD    A,B         :Load to test for BC equal to zero
        OR    C
        JP    NZ,LOOP     :Jump to LOOP and continue
                           until complete
```

Using this sequence, it takes about 5,000 clock cycles to move the same data in the 8080 as it did with the Z80.[29]

We have tried to emphasize defensive programming. This is programming in which changes can be made easily and in which misinterpretation and other errors are minimized. Defensive programming takes time and the programmer can never anticipate all the problems that might occur. But careful programming can result in fewer errors and programs that are easier to use and maintain. One may not always follow all the suggestions presented, but the use of these techniques can make software development for microprocessors much easier.

TESTING AND DEBUGGING

For a conventional electronic system design, the breadboard hardware is built up from assembly prints and tested to verify the engineer's assumptions described in the specification, schematic, and layout defined in the assembly print. In the debugging phase, the engineer may follow this approach, using the schematic and assembly print. He wires up the hardware and begins testing; with the discovery of an error, he follows this sequence: the schematic is first corrected by a redline in the circuit involved with the change. The assembly print is redlined and the breadboard reworked to reflect the change.

The debugging cycle is repeated many times during a normal design. The process requires no computer assistance and can be started and stopped at any point.

This design-debug style is employed first at the circuit module level, then at the subsystem level, and finally at the system level. At each level, the designer checks only a number of items. At the circuit level, he checks the interacting of the components which perform the circuit function, while at the subsystem level he checks the interaction of the modules. At the system level, the interaction of the subsystems is checked. This approach allows different groups of designers to work in parallel, as long as all groups follow the same documentation conventions.

Field trials are another part of the design cycle. They test the design in a real environment to the product specification. If the equipment can be modified in the field, then the field trials can proceed quickly.

A microcomputer system is most easily tested using the system in which it was developed—either a development system or a larger computer. The software testing should identify and correct many of the program bugs before the software is introduced into the hardware environment. If the software is to be loaded on a ROM, it must be thoroughly tested before the ROMs are programmed.

The program is then loaded into the system and a system checkout of both hardware and software is made. The critical items tend to be those concerned with the timing and synchronization between the processor and the other elements of the system.

A checkout of the peripherals is conducted next. These may be sensors, storage facilities, or actuators that provide the data or transmit the control response. Timing and synchronization fast and slow peripherals and the processor should be resolved in this phase.

The provision for field maintenance is important for continued product reliability. Diagnostic software can be provided on ROMs which are then plugged into the system in the field in the place of the ROM containing the system program. This diagnostic software can check the operation of the hardware and provide an error detection message when an anomaly is encountered.

Software Testing

The testing of microprocessor software can be a difficult and relatively lengthy task.[30] Testing can be carried out with specially built equipment along with some general-purpose software tools. Some rules that can aid in program testing follow:

1. Make the test plan part of the program design. Testing should be a consideration in the definition and design stages.
2. Check for trivial and special cases. These include zero inputs with no data, warning and alarm inputs, and other special situations. These simple cases sometimes lead to annoying and mysterious problems.
3. Select the test data on a random basis. This will eliminate any bias. Random number tables are available, and many computers have random number generator programs.
4. Plan and document the software testing.
5. Use maximum and minimum values for variables as test data. Extreme values can be the source of many special errors.
6. Use statistical methods for complex tests. Optimization techniques can be used to set system parameters.

Debugging Tools

The debugging of microprocessor programs can be difficult because of the inability to observe the register contents directly, the close interactions between the hardware and software, the dependence of programs on timing, and the difficulty of obtaining adequate data in real-time applications. Some of the tools that are used to debug programs are:

1. Simulators.
2. Logic analyzers.
3. Breakpoints.
4. Trace routines.
5. Memory dumps.
6. Software interrupts.

The simulator is a program which simulates the execution of programs on another computer. It acts as a programmer would to trace the effects of instructions. Usually the simulator runs on a larger computer for a smaller computer which lacks the facilities for convenient testing. Typical simulators are large programs. These programs are useful since the programmer can change data, examine the registers, and use other debugging facilities. Most simulators do not fully model the input/output or provide much help with timing problems. Sometimes the simulator is used to replace the real computer which may not have been built or delivered.

The logic analyzer is a test instrument that provides a digital bus-oriented version of an oscilloscope. The logic analyzer detects the states of the digital signals during a program cycle and stores them in a memory. It then displays the information on a CRT. Several events can be monitored and displayed at once. Triggered events can be defined and thresholds can be set. Logic analyzers provide a convenient display for changing parallel digital signals. Analyzers have the ability to trigger a particular instruction or sequence of instructions, recall previous data, and capture short noise spikes. Logic analyzers such as shown in Figure 10.13 can complement software simulators, since they may be used in solving timing problems.

A breakpoint is a place in the program at which the execution is halted to examine the current contents of registers, memory locations, or I/O ports. Most microcomputer development systems and many simulator programs have facilities for setting breakpoints. Breakpoints are often created with a TRAP instruction or a conditional jump instruction dependent on some external input that is controlled by the programmer. For example, the instruction JUMP ON NOT TEST causes a jump to itself until the TEST input is on. The contents of registers or memory locations may then be examined. Some microprocessors can place special status information on the buses

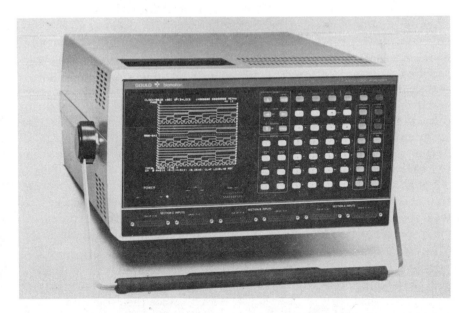

Fig. 10.13. A logic analyzer such as this can be used to solve timing problems during the debugging phase. (*Courtesy Gould Biomation.*)

while halted. This information can include the current contents of the accumulator, program counter, or other registers.

The trace is a program which prints information concerning the status of the processor at specified times. Many simulator programs and development systems use trace facilities. Sometimes the trace can print the complete status of registers and flags after the execution of each instruction. Other systems allow tracing of particular registers or memory locations only when the contents change. Traces can result in large listings unless the programmer can select variables and formats carefully.

A memory dump is a listing of the current contents of a section of memory. Simulator programs, development systems, and monitors can all produce memory dumps. A complete memory dump will be long and may be difficult to interpret. A memory dump is not an effective technique for debugging, but sometimes it is the only tool available. A complete memory dump is normally used when all other methods have failed.

A SOFTWARE INTERRUPT and TRAP instruction can be used for debugging. The instruction normally saves the current value of the program counter and then branches to a specified memory location. This memory location may be the starting point of a debugging program that lists or displays status information. The breakpoints are inserted with TRAP instructions.

As the 6800 executes a SOFTWARE INTERRUPT, it automatically saves the contents of all registers in the stack. The programmer may then observe the contents directly. The 8080 interrupt or RESTART instruction only saves the program counter in the stack.[31] The programmer enters a TRAP instruction into the program and provides the debugging routine if it is not part of the package. A monitor program that can place TRAP instructions at specified addresses can also be used.

Checklists are an obvious tool that may be used with flowcharts. The programmer checks that each variable has been initialized, that each flow chart element has been coded, that definitions are correct, and that all paths are connected properly. A good checklist can save time, but handchecking of long or complicated programs is not advised since the programmer is likely to make more mistakes when checking the program.

Loops and sections of programs can be handchecked to ensure that the flow of control is correct. In the case of loops, the programmer can check to see if the loop performs the first and last iterations correctly. They are normally sources of most loop errors. The program can also be handchecked for trivial cases, such as tables with no elements.

Error Checking

Checking and debugging should be done in a systematic manner. One should not assume that the first error found is the only one in the program. Some common errors are:

1. The failure to initialize variables, particularly in counters and pointers. Registers, flags, and memory locations can not be assumed to contain zero at the start of the program.
2. Incrementing of counters and pointers before it is required or not incrementing them at all.
3. Failure of the program with trivial cases, such as arrays or tables with no elements.
4. Inverting conditions, such as a JUMP NOT ON ZERO instead of on zero.
5. Reversing the order of operands, such as move A to B instead of B to A.
6. Jumping on conditions that may change after they are set. A common occurrence in assembly programming is using flags as jump conditions when they may be changed by intermediate instructions.
7. Lack of follow-through conditions, such as a data item that is never found in a table or a condition that is never met. This can cause an endless loop.
8. Failure to save the contents of the accumulator or other register before using the register again.
9. Inverting addresses and data, such as immediate addresses in which the data is part of the instruction, and direct addresses in which the address of data is part of the instruction.
10. An exchange of registers or memory locations without using an intermediate storage place

$$H = L$$
$$L = H$$

This sets both H and L to the previous contents of L, since the first statement destroys the previous contents of H. The following sequence will exchange the registers:

$$A = H$$
$$H = L$$
$$L = A$$

11. Confusing numbers and characters. ASCII zero or EBCDIC zero is not the number zero.
12. Confusing numerical codes like BCD 61 and binary 61.
13. Counting the length of a data block incorrectly; locations 20 through 28 have nine and not eight words.
14. Ignoring the direction of noncommutative operations as in the assembly language command SUB C which subtracts the contents of register C from the contents of the accumulator.

15. Confusing two's complement and sign magnitude notations.
16. Ignoring the overflow in signed arithmetic.
17. Ignoring the effects of subroutines which may change flags, registers, and memory locations.

Other errors may exist, but this list can be used to guide one where to look. An example of debugging is considered in the following task to find the length of a string of ASCII characters, which ends with a carriage return (OD hex).[32]

```
MBUF    EQU    40H
CR      EQU    00001101B
        LXI    H,MBUF      :Set memory pointer = start of string
        INX    H
CHK:    INR    B           :Character counter = character
                                               counter + 1
        CMP    M           :Next character carriage return?
        JNZ    CHK         :No, check again
        HLT
```

Here, the instruction INX H added one to the pointer before the data in the starting address was examined; thus, the carriage return character could never be recognized. Also, the accumulator and register *B* in the loop were never initialized. Correcting these errors, we have

```
MBUF    EQU    40H
CR      EQU    00001101B
        LXI    H,MBUF      :Set memory pointer = start of string
        MVI    A,CR        :Load carriage return for comparison
CHK     MVI    B,O         :Character counter = zero
        CMP    M           :Next character carriage return?
        JNZ    FIN         :Yes, finished
        INX    H
        IND    B           :No, increment character counter
        JMP    CHK         :No, increment character counter
DONE:   HLT
```

Now the instruction JNZ DONE is changed to JZ DONE to end the search when the carriage return is found. The INR B instruction increments the counter, but the program jumps to the MVI B,O instruction and sets the counter back to zero because the label CHKCR is on the wrong line. The correct program is shown below, which was produced by using several trial strings of characters.

```
MBUF    EQU    40H
CR      EQU    00001101B
        LXI    H,MBUF        :Set memory pointer = start of string
        MVI    A,CR          :Load carriage return for comparison
        MVI    B,O           :Character counter = zero
CHK     CMP    M             :Is next character a carriage return?
        JZ     FIN           :Yes, finished
        INX    H
        INR    B             :No, increment character counter
        JMP    CHK
DONE:   HLT
```

Debugging Programs

A debugger is a program which facilitates the debugging of a user developed program. It offers such facilities as these: stop at an instruction; execute instructions one at a time; display the contents of registers, or display the contents of memory in binary, hexadecimal, or symbolic form. Using a debugger, the contents of the register may be changed and the program can be restarted by the user.

Along with the software design and program coding, program debugging contributes a major part of the software-development costs as does generating the documentation necessary for maintaining and updating the software. For debugging, the listing produced by the assembler/compiler should be easy to follow and should provide line numbers, address, source, and object code on the same line. Error messages should be easy to read and understand. A good statement format is natural, unambiguous, and self-documenting. It can reduce coding errors produced by obscure mnemonics and eliminate the comments typically required to explain some mnemonics. The self-documenting and readability features also reduce program maintainance costs. The programmer generating the code doesn't have to explain how the program operates, or how to modify the code to perform a new function or modify an old one.

In program debugging, syntax errors can be flagged during the assembly process and the nature of the error indicated by an error message. A linked list of errors—the syntax error list—may also be provided so that programs can be scanned rapidly to locate all errors.

Program and data-memory allocation can be summerized by a load map produced by the linking loader. Program modules are listed in the sequence in which they are loaded, along with the absolute starting and ending memory addresses and the memory-address limits defined within each module, as shown below:

PROGRAM NAME	PROGRAM LIMITS	DATA LIMITS	
MAIN	0000 015A	2400	2468
ARITH	015B 02CF	2469	2477

A symbol cross-reference table of all identifiers or entry points used in the program modules can be provided by the linking loader. The identifiers may be listed in alphabetical order followed by the name of the module in which they are defined and by the modules referencing them. Combined with the assembler cross-reference listings, this table provides traceability of the identifiers and their references as shown below:

IDENTIF.	ADDR.	DEFINED	REFERENCED
ADD	015B	ARITH	MAIN
DIVIDE	01A6	ARITH	MAIN
MULTIPLY	023B	ARITH	MAIN
SUBTRACT	0270	ARITH	MAIN

The value of this traceability occurs when an error is detected within a subroutine. Before a correction is made to the subroutine, the effect of the correction may be traced to every program module that calls the subroutine. If the calling sequence to the subroutine is modified, the program modules affected by this change and the locations within each module may be determined from the symbol cross-reference tables. This prevents the same error from being debugged twice.

While the program is being debugged under the control of the debugger, the diagnostics will normally be printed on the printer or displayed on a CRT. Some corrections may then be possible. Otherwise, the user must go back to the beginning of the process, type-in the corrections, and reassemble.

One essential facility of the debugger is to provide breakpoints. These are addresses specified by the user where the program will stop automatically. The user can then examine the value of variables in the memory or the contents of registers. The program execution is suspended at these points by the user.

Program testing is more than a matter of exercising a program a few times. Testing of all cases is usually impractical. A simple routine that uses 16 bits of data to produce a 16-bit result requires 4 billion possible combinations of inputs and outputs.[33] Formal methods are only applications to simple programs. Most program testing requires a choice of test cases. Many microcomputer systems depend on real-time inputs which may be hard to simulate.

Debugging Techniques

A number of other tools are available to help with this task. This includes logic analyzers and software tools, including the following:

1. Input/output simulations which allow a number of devices to be simulated from a single input and a single output device. These simulations may also provide inputs for external timing and other controls. Most development systems have some facilities for I/O simulation, and many software simulators provide I/O simulation but not in real time.
2. In-circuit emulators allow the microcomputer prototype system to be attached to the hardware development system and tested. (See Figure 10.14)
3. Simulators provide read/write memory for programs with the timing characteristics of the ROM that will be used in the final design to execute the target microprocessor code. When the program is not executed on the real microprocessor, an emulator or simulator is used. A simulator is a program which runs on another machine like a 370 and executes 8086 code to simulate an 8086. The simulator cannot operate in real time because of the software interpretation involved. An

Fig. 10.14. An in-circuit emulator such as this unit for the 8086 allows access to the microprocessor bus and control signals in the application system. (*Courtesy Intel Corporation.*)

emulator is a simulator which runs nearly in real time. Emulation implies that the behavior is identical and not similar to the target.

4. Real-time operating systems or monitors to control real-time events, to provide interrupts, and to allow real-time traces and breakpoints.
5. Emulations that execute the instruction set at close to real time speeds.
6. Special interfaces which allow a computer or programmable controller to test the program by externally controlling the inputs and outputs.
7. Testing programs or exercisers that check branches in the program to find logical errors.

Memory Loading

After the program is completely debugged and its execution is presumed to be correct, the object code must be implanted in the actual memory which is usually ROM or PROM. During debugging, it was residing in RAM. To be placed in the PROMs, a PROM programmer is connected to the development system, and the binary contents of the program are transferred onto the PROM chips. The PROM chips are then inserted into the system. Stand-alone PROM programmers are also available (as shown in Figure 10.15).

For efficient program development, most of the above software facilities should be available for any program involving more than a few hundred in-

Fig. 10.15. A stand-alone PROM programmer for loading data programs into the microprocessor system. (*Courtesy Pro-Log Corporation.*)

structions; however, they are a necessity for any program involving several hundred or thousands of instructions. Using the support programs requires additional hardware facilities. The programs must be readily accessible, so they must be stored on a convenient medium which is easily accessible to the processor, which would suggest a general file system such as tape cassettes or floppy disks. Tape cassettes offer the advantage of low cost, but they are relatively slow since it can take several minutes to access information. The access to information on the cassette is sequential and if data is accessed at several points on a tape, winding and rewinding is involved.

An alternative is to use a floppy disk. This is a better storage medium, but the cost is higher. The floppy disk allows access to any location of the disk within milliseconds.

DEVELOPMENT SYSTEMS AND AIDS

This section considers the development systems that are used in writing software for microprocessors. A variety of systems are available that allow programs to be developed with the aid of special software and peripherals and later transferred to the actual microcomputer on which they will run. Among the techniques used are microcomputer development systems, timesharing services and development systems based on other computers. Some of the features of these systems have already been mentioned in earlier sections.

The microprocessor manufacturers, as well as many potential microprocessor users, quickly realized that the development of an operable microcomputer system starting with a microprocessor and a few associated parts can be a formidable task. To simplify the problem of hardware and software development, many of the manufacturers have packaged their products in ways which make the microprocessor more accessible and usable. These packages have the following forms: parts families, ready-to-assemble kits, prewired printed circuit (PC) cards, assembled kits, and development systems.

A parts family is a set of closely related and compatible IC components, such as a clock driver, microprocessor, RAM, ROM, and I/O chips. These are available as a kit and sold in single quantities at a special price by the manufacturer.

The ready-to-assemble kit consists of one or more PC cards and a set of ICs and discrete components for assembly on the cards. Once assembled, one has an operative microcomputer. These kits are also available in the form of factory-assembled systems. In some kits, program and data entry takes place using keyboard switches, while data output uses LED displays.

Kits or assembled boards are ideal for gaining familiarity with simple programming. Typically, they are not equipped with an assembler, so programming must be performed in hexadecimal. The resulting time limits the length of programs that can be developed on them to a few hundred instructions. The most widely used mass memory for such a board is the cassette recorder, which is interfaced to the board. Although such boards are a valuable educational tool, they cannot be used alone as a true development facility for a real program.

Many modular systems exist which allow the user to plug in additional boards and to build progressively a true development system. The main expense is not the processor board, but the peripherals.

Of the program development techniques, only one does not require any significant tools: hand-programming. For a program developed directly in binary or hexadecimal, all that is required is a hexadecimal keyboard and LED displays for the output. The more frequently used alternatives require powerful tools if one is to be efficient.

Prewired printed circuit cards, including a microprocessor and related interface ICs, are available from a number of microprocessor manufacturers for those who already have some microcomputer equipment, including RAM and ROM, and who wish to evaluate the microprocessor in their existing equipment.

Another method of developing microprocessor software involves the use of other computers. One technique is to purchase assembler and simulator programs for use on a local large or small computer. This technique is less expensive than using timesharing services over the long term, but it requires the purchase of software and perhaps its modification to meet the requirements of the local computer. The method depends on the facilities of the local computer, which may be much less extensive than those of a timesharing service. Working in the batch-mode without an editor and with limited storage space is considerably more difficult than using an interactive system.

Any computer may be used to execute these cross-programs. When an in-house computer is available, it may be possible to run the cross-assembler, cross-complier, and other programs on it. If the computer is used in the batch-mode, the program is submitted on cards, paper tape, or some other medium, and the results may be returned hours or days later. This can be a major obstacle to program development. Developing a program for a microprocessor may involve changes at the bit level, and it becomes intolerable to suffer delays of hours or days to perform these changes.

Some development software runs on mini- or microcomputers. These computers usually have a printer, editor, an interactive display terminal, and a large disk system. Such a minicomputer can be used almost as easily as timesharing. The computer I/O bus can also be interfaced so that the object code which the minicomputer generates may be transferred directly into the read/write program memory of the microcomputer being developed. Figure 10.16 is a block diagram of such a system.

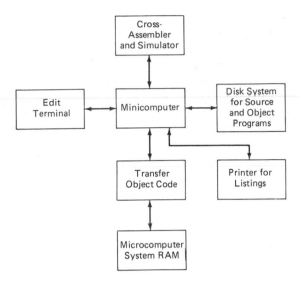

Fig. 10.16. Minicomputer-based development system.

Timesharing Systems

If an in-house system has timesharing capabilities, its advantages are the same as those above, except that like a timesharing system it does not allow any hardware checking capability or system integration. The only tool that allows both software and hardware debugging is the development system.

A timesharing system is a general-purpose computer used in the timesharing mode. Timesharing refers to the fact that a number of users are using the computer at the same time in an interactive mode where the system responds immediately, on-line. The service offered by a timesharing system is among the best that can be obtained. The dialogue with the machine is almost instantaneous since there is little or no waiting time. In addition, most timesharing systems have sophisticated peripherals and software, including powerful file systems and editors. The microprocessor program can be almost completely developed and debugged on such a system. The timesharing system may be equipped with a cross-assembler or a cross-complier for the 8086, the 6800, or any other MPU. Most commercial timesharing systems provide the cross-programs necessary to generate the code for many of the existing microprocessors. User programs can be generated and debugged efficiently on the system. But in order to execute the programs, it is necessary to use a simulator.

When programs are executed by a simulator, it is possible to debug the logic of the program, but it is not possible to check the input/output performance and to measure its timing. One may count the simulated duration of the instructions that are to be executed in the MPU. But one cannot simulate the actual architecture of the system or the input/output operations that will be performed. In addition, many input/output chips are becoming processor-equipped and they are also programmable. It would be necessary to simulate them, too, in order to have complete results of the program execution.

The timesharing system does offer the advantage of allowing several users to work at the same time. For many projects it may be desirable to have several persons working simultaneously on the same program.

In summary then, the timesharing system does allow for fast development of the program itself. But it does not allow any debugging in the area of actual timing, nor the verification of input/output functions. It can also be quite expensive. Most services have simulators and cross-assemblers for the popular microprocessors. They offer large amounts of storage, interactive facilities, and high-speed peripherals. Figure 10.17 shows the procedures for developing microprocessor software, using the timesharing services. The advantages are the software facilities, low initial cost, independence of a particular processor, fast mass storage, and access to high-speed peripherals. The disadvantages include high continuing costs, inability to test programs in the real computer environment, and the need to use facilities that are physically located at some distance and that may involve extra turnaround time. Timesharing is often a convenient way to get started on software development before other equipment is available.

Manufactured Development Systems

For those users who do not have any basic microcomputer equipment, the microprocessor manufacturers have provided a microprocessor development system. This system includes all of the basic hardware and software necessary for the development of a prototype microcomputer system.[34] The introduction of these development systems simplified the task for the system designer. As we have noted earlier, one of the key advantages of the microprocessor is its capability of replacing cost-recurring random logic hardware with noncost-recurring software. This advantage becomes less significant, however, when the system designer must build a hardware system for the software development. In order to simplify the software development, the

Fig. 10.17. Timesharing system operation.

microprocessor development system includes most of the hardware anticipated in any final system along with the software development aids. The system designer can then focus on the software capabilities of the microprocessor, and after the software has been developed and optimized, one can do the hardware design that is capable of implementing the software system. These microprocessor development systems are available from the chip manufacturers as well as from independent test hardware vendors at a variety of prices and capabilities.

Most of the microcomputer development systems consist of an actual microcomputer or an emulation of one with additional hardware and software for the development task. In general, these development systems have the following features:

1. A status display capability so that the programmer can observe the contents of registers and other memory locations.
2. A facility for changing the contents of memory locations.
3. A reset control to start the processor in a known state.
4. A single-step control which allows a program to be executed one step at a time for debugging purposes.
5. A run control to allow a program to be executed, beginning at a specific memory location.
6. RAM or PROM that can be used as an alterable program memory.
7. Interfaces for standard input/output devices, such as keyboards, displays, printers, and floppy-disk systems.
8. A bootstrap loader that enters the initial programs such as the loader into the microcomputer memory.
9. Utility programs that load the user programs into the microcomputer memory.

Development systems are normally constructed on a modular basis, with a number of plug-in printed boards for memory and I/O. The number of peripheral modules is an important factor to consider in determining the testing requirements of the prototype system that will be designed using the development system. A block diagram of a typical development processor module is shown in Figure 10.18. The various peripheral devices required by the system are connected to the I/O ports provided by the system. In addition, an I/O interface is also provided for program development on the system, although this interface would not be used in the final system since it is only used to develop software for the system. The usual interface is to a keyboard and CRT terminal in order to allow the user to do on-line programming and editing of the software.

The modular development system is popular since the user has the option of selecting the particular modules that are most particularly suited for his

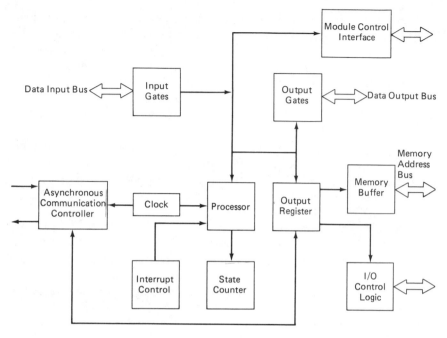

Fig. 10.18. Development system processor module.

application. A typical system might include the following hardware modules in addition to the processor:

1. Read/write memory.
2. Programmable read-only memory.
3. External event detection.
4. Monitor/control panel.
5. Prewired system backplane.
6. Power supply and reset circuit.

The entire system is connected together by means of a backplane. Physically, it looks like a traditional minicomputer. It is equipped with a simple front panel to facilitate debugging. When a development system is marketed by a manufacturer, it uses the manufacturer's microprocessor.[35] A variety of development systems are also available that use a microprocessor to produce code for several microprocessors.

These development systems offer the facilities that we have been considering as necessary. A development system should provide a file system, capable of connecting easily to a variety of peripherals. For software, it should have all the required programs, such as editor, assembler, and other support programs like utility routines for debugging. In addition, it may be desirable to have a high-level compiler or interpreter, if the system is planned to develop programs of any complexity.

In some development systems, the backplane can contain up to 14 modules. These may be necessary for added RAM or ROM or special input/output interfaces that will have to be inserted into the system. In addition to adding a number of boards to the chassis itself, it is also necessary to add the peripherals, which might include:

1. An input device such as a keyboard.
2. An output device such as a CRT display.
3. A printing device for hard-copy.
4. A mass memory for storing files such as dual floppy disks, which are necessary for merging files.
5. A PROM programmer for placing the program in the PROM memory chips.

Using the Development System

There are two basic methods of using a microprocessor development system in designing a system. One is to use the development system for software development. Once the software is developed, it is implemented on the hardware prototype system. The second, more common method, is to develop both the hardware and software at the same time while using the development system for control and diagnostics. The first method is suitable only for small systems where there is not a considerable amount of interaction between hardware and software. It can also be used for systems that are architecturally similar to the development system itself. The second method is suitable for more complex systems in which there are considerable interactions between the hardware and the software. In these systems, the development system can be linked by means of an umbilical to the hardware system being developed. (See Figure 10.19.)

When the basic hardware elements of the microcomputer system are provided in the development system, the designer can devote the majority of attention to the software design. Since a key advantage of a microprocessor system is its ability to replace hardware components by software, an optimum system design optimizes the software and coding. To aid the task of microprocessor program development, manufacturers have developed a number of software development aids for use in their development systems. These software aids include these items:

1. Assemblers.
2. Cross-assemblers.

Fig. 10.19. This development system can simultaneously debug four separate microcomputer systems. (*Courtesy Rockwell International.*)

3. High-level languages.
4. Editors.
5. Loaders.
6. Debuggers.
7. Simulators.
8. PROM programmers.

An assembler program converts the symbolic code written by the programmer into machine language instructions which can be executed by the processor. The assembler converts symbolic instructions such as ADD, SUB, and MULT into machine bit patterns. It also converts the labelled machine addresses designated by the programmer into real machine memory locations.

After the program has been typed into the development system, it is desirable to print it in order to verify that it is complete. A source program is printed which appears as a listing.

Assemblers

When the program is complete, we must proceed towards execution. Since the program is written in symbolic form, it must be translated into machine-executable format, which is what an assembler will do. The assembler translates the source code into the binary object program, which can then be directly executed by the machine. The assembler substitutes the actual addresses instead of symbolic ones; it substitutes the actual binary encoding of data instead of the symbolic names and the suitable binary code of instructions instead of their mnemonics. The object program is now created—a sequence of binary words, which may be directly executed by the processor.

At this point, it becomes necessary to execute the object program on the actual or simulated processor. It was not necessary to use the target microprocessor to develop the object program. The required functions provide the editing and the assembly facilities which any processor can do. Using a larger processor can result in improved system capabilities through powerful peripherals and sophisticated software facilities. Here the assembler acts as a cross-assembler. A cross-assembler is a program for one machine that resides on another machine. A cross-assembler for a 68000 is an assembler which will produce 68000 code, but which executes on a minicomputer or other larger machine.

The cross-assembler converts the symbolic code written by the programmer into machine language instructions that are executable not by the microprocessor but by another computer. A cross-assembler permits the programmer to design, develop, and refine the program on a larger, more familiar computer. Cross-assemblers have been written for minicomputers and even for large-scale computers.

Some assemblers have a macro capability, which allows one to associate an identifier with a block of text which is substituted every time the macro is invoked. Parametric macros allow a different parameter value to be used each time the macro is invoked, so the text can be varied.

An important trend is the use of high-level languages for use with development systems. The use of high-level languages greatly simplifies the task of the designer as we have discussed. It was noted that the efficiency of coding in a high-level language is less than what can be achieved using assembly language. But through the use of high-level languages, the development of microprocessor systems for commercial applications places less requirements on the software design. Generating the software is much easier when it is written in an Englishlike, high-level language like FORTRAN or PL/M. Compared with assembly language, the high-level language reduces the time to write and check out a program. With a compiler or assembler to translate the source language into machine code and a linker program to let one write software in small, easily manageable modules, one can even distribute the design among several different programmers working in different languages.

Editors

In order to modify the program for entry into the system, it is desirable to have an editor available. The editor is a program which allows the convenient manipulation of text. It allows the user to make textual changes in the program without reloading or rewiring the complete text. The editor performs the functions of adding or deleting a line or a character automatically. A simple typing error in a program would have to be corrected by retyping the entire program without the editor. With the editor, it is possible to command things like: go to line 8 and insert the following word; or look for $B2$ in the text and replace it by *B3*. A powerful editor is a function of the speed with which a program can be typed and modified once errors are located.

The debugger is a diagnostic tool that permits the user to analyze the program. The programmer can insert breakpoints in the program at critical points and obtain such information as register and memory dumps at desired points of the program execution. When the program detects an error, some debugger programs allow the user to make a modification and let the program continue to run. This essential feature of a debugger that allows examination of the contents of registers and changing them is accomplished by the debugger by either executing display instructions on the microprocessor or by executing them under the control of a simulator or an emulator, which then stores a copy of the value of the registers in memory.

The loader is a program which initializes the processor in order to allow the user program to begin execution. The loader is often used with the hardware facility for a reset. If the processor is halted, the user restarts the program by pressing a reset button. The reset circuit then interrupts the processor so that control is taken away from the program formally being executed and processing of the loader program begins. Some types of loaders permit separate groups of machine language code to be linked together and executed by the processor; these more sophisticated loaders thus act as linkage editors.

The simulator is a specialized program for performing analysis of user programs. A simulator will model or simulate the timing characteristics of hardware, such as peripherals, which may not be available for testing at the time the software is ready.

PROM Programmers

The PROM programmer is used with many development systems for the programming of ROMs. A PROM programmer simplifies the software development since the test programs can be placed on PROMs and run in the system without the loading of the program into RAM for each test. A PROM programmer may include such functions as program listing, manual keyboard, duplication, and verification.

The main role in some applications of the PROM programmer is to program the EPROMs or the PROMs on which the programs will reside. Many are equipped with a hexadecimal keyboard to allow the manual input of data.[36] They may also provide additional interfaces such as an RS232 connector so that the device can be connected to a microcomputer system.

Emulators

Another desirable device is the in-circuit emulator such as the Exorcizer. The addition of this device can result in a truly useful development system, adding convenience in programming, and resulting in gains in programming time. An in-circuit emulator will assist in debugging when the software is first integrated with the hardware (which will be in the early stages of debugging). Emulator devices with symbolic debugging capability can greatly reduce the hardware/software checkout time, and in-circuit emulators will let you operate the program in temporary RAMs prior to programming the PROMs. They allow monitoring of internal functions that may be otherwise inaccessible. The in-circuit emulator offers the capability of testing and debugging the actual system connected to the real input/output devices in real-time. This is one of the most powerful facilities that can be used for the debugging of the complete hardware/software system. It is a required device for the efficient debugging on any real-time system. In a typical microprocessor development system, the emulator executes about 10% slower than the actual microprocessor.

One of the important facilities of the in-circuit emulator is the trace capability, which can automatically record events during the previous machine cycles before the machine is stopped. Thus, the trace is analogous to a film of the events within the previous cycles of the system. When an error is diagnosed at a breakpoint, it is usually too late because the error has usually been caused by a previous instruction. The problem is to identify the instruction which has caused a wrong value at the point where it was first diagnosed. In most programs, a number of branching points exists, and it may be difficult to determine which branch was being executed prior to the detection of the error. It is therefore useful to record which path in the program was followed, up to the breakpoint. Then, either the problem instruction can be identified or an earlier breakpoint can be set. The other machine cycles can then be recorded until the error is traced to the erroneous instruction.

The microprocessor manufacturer's versions of an in-circuit emulator are typically used, but emulators are also available from independent vendors. In short, an in-circuit emulator is an essential facility to consider if one must integrate a hardware/software system in a short time.

Development Selection

A number of development systems are available from independent vendors, which have equivalent capabilities. Since they are not microprocessor manufacturers, these systems are microprocessor-independent. The same system may be used for an 8086, 68000, and others. They are general-purpose development systems, and they may be particularly attractive for a user who is reluctant to commit to a chip family. Many of the development systems, however, supplied by the manufacturers provide better software capabilities for the particular microprocessor considered, along with the prospect of continued improvements, and many of these development systems have cross-programs for other families of microprocessors.

Diagnostic aids are also available from a variety of sources, as well. The microprocessor analyzers, which have evolved from the digital analyzers, are useful for the tuning and debugging of complex hardware interfaces. Traditional design-support instruments like pulse generators, waveform analyzers, and oscilloscopes are useful when building a system with conventional logic components. They are less useful with microcomputer designs because much of the system activity takes place internally within the CPU, so it is unavailable for observation.

One should not forget the follow-on support or field service. While one could use a development system for field diagnosis, it's difficult to transport all the necessary components to some remote field locations. A portable test instrument that can duplicate some system capabilities is a good alternative. Some available equipment allows systems to be checked out in the field using an in-circuit emulator and a control panel.

In selecting a microprocessor development system, one must consider a few basic questions:

1. The complexity of the final system, in both hardware and software.
2. The configuration of the final system.
3. The amount of testing to be done.

The microprocessor development system is intended to simplify the most common hardware and software design problems by providing a suitable test vehicle, usually consisting of the following:

1. Microprocessor.
2. Random-access memory.
3. Read-only memory.
4. Clock and power supply.
5. I/O interfaces.
6. Console—including display of registers and instruction codes.
7. Panel switches for reset, stop, and single stepping.
8. Software packages for development.

Developing a microprocessor system involves both hardware and software techniques. The essential problem during development is usually the software debugging phase. This problem has been addressed, and the tools available described. The most efficient tool for both hardware and software development has been shown to be the microprocessor development system. Alternatives are timesharing systems, an inhouse computer, and kits. An excellent facility for debugging complex hardware systems, especially real-time systems, is in-circuit emulation. The investment required for a development system pays off rapidly in terms of reduced programming time and faster completion of a project. If you invest in an appropriate development system, one that expands with the product, it can pay for itself on the first project, because the development system can cut the design time and put the product on the market months sooner.

OPERATING SYSTEMS

An operating system (or OS) is a set of prewritten programs that reside in the memory along with the user-written application programs. An OS can allow (1) more efficient memory space by providing common services, (2) more efficient time utilization by permitting parallel activities to occur, and (3) more capability by providing services beyond the scope of the typical user program such as memory pool management.

The operating system is not dependent upon the application; the system might be used for accounting or controlling a complex process.

The microcomputer without an operating system can be used as a controller, but an OS can allow it to out perform some minicomputers. Operating systems may be small enough to fit in ROM, but for the flexibility needed for program development or multitasking, a floppy-disk is required. Operating systems act as managers on the system's resources: memory, terminals, communications links, and other peripherals. The OS contains a program or routine for each task and links the task programs together using other routines to perform the housekeeping operations (as shown in Figure 10.20).

There are two basic types of systems: (1) disk operating systems (DOS) and (2) the multitasking operating systems (MTOS).

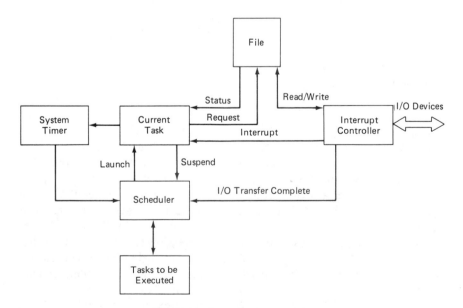

Fig. 10.20. Operating system tasks.

Disk Operating Systems

Some disk operating systems are designed to support users in preparing, debugging, testing, and running programs on another computer. This computer may be part of a standard development system, or it may be a larger, separate system.

When the DOS supports several peripherals such as two disks, a printer, several terminals, and required memory, it can have a fairly large program in memory at all times. The Intel ISIS-II, for example, uses 12K bytes. For many services additional programs are loaded into overlayed or common areas. The services provided by the DOS are accessed either from terminal hardware or from the user program. The terminal services, which aid the program preparation, are the text editing, assembling, compiling, linking, and loading functions. File manipulation functions include the copying, merging, deleting, and reformatting operations. Debugging aids may include inspecting and changing memory, setting breakpoints, and single-stepping.

A DOS-supported program usually starts with the initialization section. The variables such as pointers and flags are set to the appropriate starting values. The initialization usually involves some interactions between the user and the DOS program. After initialization, the typical DOS program enters a loop to read, analyze, and write the data.[37] It may read new information from a disk file with a terminal input.

After the initial data input, some calculations may require additional inputs to be completed. The overall loop is then repeated. Finally, a termination section outputs the messages or reports to the CRT terminal or the printer DOS to end the run. The DOS provides a means to open the files and read and write, and to close the files. It also handles the reading and writing of input messages along with the output of results to the printer. In addition, the DOS supplies utilities to load the program from the disk and to start the execution.

Multitasking

When several programs run in parallel on a system, the OS must handle multitasking. The MTOS provides the switching from one task to another. The OS assigns the various tasks different priorities. A line printer's I/Q driver would normally get a high priority because a line printer is relatively slow and in high demand. The high priority keeps the line printer busy as much as possible.

Several techniques are used to decide when a task is to run next. In the slice procedure, each task runs for a small fraction of CPU time. It is then suspended and the next task is started up. Event-driven systems change over when a significant event such as a completion flag or interrupt from a peripheral occurs. Some event-driven systems are interactive which allows one to send data to the program from the terminal during execution. As a prompt appears on the terminal, one enters a command and receives a response. Some typical commands are shown below:[38]

LOGON	Set the default disk and user name for the referencing of files.
NEWUSE	Create new file.
FILE	List the user's directory file.
RENAME	Change the name of a file.
PURGE	Delete a file.
RUN	Load a program file from disk and execute it.
EDIT	Run the Text Editor.
LINK	Run the Relocating/Linking Loader.
TIME	Display or set the current data and time.
ABORT	Terminate program.
RESUME	Resume execution of program.
SUBMIT	Change input from terminal to another device.
END	Terminate processing.

The time between the command entry and a reply is proportional to the difficulty of the task and the load on the system at the time of request.

The MTOS is desirable in applications which have significant random, asynchronous inputs. (An application of this nature is shown in Figure 10.21.) Most of these applications will have sections which are functionally similar with an overall organization that is structurally similar.[39]

The program illustrated in Figure 10.21 has eight subprograms or tasks. Each task is independent, with a beginning or entry point and one or more continuous paths to an end or exit point.

Operating Characteristics

In a DOS-supported program, a single execution point (the program counter) moves through the program from beginning to end. In the MTOS-supported program, each task uses an independent program counter to allow several tasks to be executed. The program for Figure 10.21 allows a parallel execution while the program for Figure 10.20 is designed for a single-path sequential execution.[40] Following the operation of the program for Figure 10.21, during startup, the OS resets itself and initializes the peripherals or other hardware in the system. All other tasks are deactivated as the OS activates the initialization phase. This task corresponds to the initialization section of the program for Figure 10.20. In addition to opening files and preparing data variables, the initialization phase may start up other tasks. When all this is done, the OS deactivates the initialization task. The initialization task requests the OS to start two tasks: (1) write the periodic reports and (2) update the panel display. Organizationally the tasks are similar. Each one per-

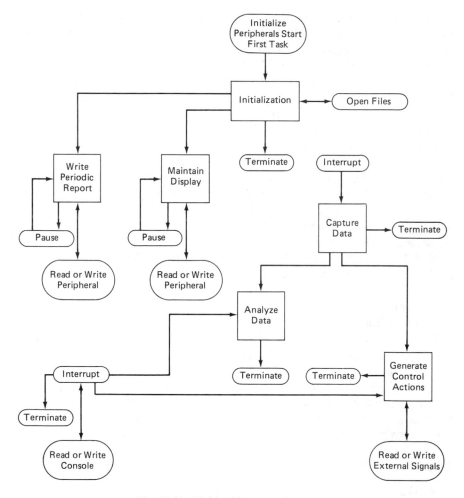

Fig. 10.21. Multitasking operating system.

forms calculations based on inputs from a peripheral or memory. It then outputs results to the printer or display and pauses for a set time period. When the pause is over, the cycle is repeated. The report writing and display maintenance proceed in parallel with the other activities. The parallel aspects of the system arise through a capture task which is activated when an external interrupt is received due to the arrival of data. The task inputs the data before it is lost. If any other task happens to be active at that time, it is suspended by the OS due to the higher priority data capture. The capture task may include an analysis of the incoming signals, and based on this examination, it may request the OS to activate one or more other tasks. (These are shown in Figure 10.21.)

The capture task may pass information in the form of arguments on to these secondary tasks to indicate the location in memory of the new data or the results of the analysis. The request to start the other task can also involve computing the priority in which that task will compete with the others for shared resources.

The program shown in Figure 10.21 has a task to handle the commands entered from the control panel. These commands arrive when the user hits a key switch as a message arrives. The OS activates the control processor task which then analyzes the message and selects a secondary task to carry out the request. Because of the random, asynchronous nature of the input data and control requests, some secondary tasks may be already busy with the previous input. Therefore, the OS must manage these requests by queuing them until the desired tasks are available. Since many tasks must proceed simultaneously, new data must be captured or they will be lost, and some activities must be suspended and resumed when time is available. If high priority data arrive while low priority data are being analyzed, the low priority task has to yield.

With only one CPU and program counter, only one task can be executed at any given time. The OS gives the CPU the highest priority task that is ready to be executed. If the task reaches a pause such as waiting for disk access, the next-highest-priority task is given a chance to continue as long as it can, during the pause. In switching from task to task, the OS swaps the program counter and other registers. This keeps the CPU busy while moving the tasks along in parallel. This juggling is invisible to the individual task programs.

This dynamic management of the CPU distinguishes the MTOS from a DOS. The MTOS functions in a real-time, on-line environment, often on hardware dedicated to a specific application. The services provided through an MTOS include the starting and coordinating of tasks, controlling the pauses, and centralized I/O handling. Control panel servicing is usually limited to debugging, determining the system status, and passing the requests and commands on to a user task.

Real-time Applications

Applications that can benefit from the use of an MTOS are normally real time, as opposed to applications in which the physical time is unimportant. Thus, an MTOS is also a real-time operating system or RTOS.

Real-time applications can be developed on general hardware using a DOS with the MTOS as a part of the applications program. The application program can then be transferred to the dedicated hardware and run under the MTOS alone. Operating systems and application programs are not always distinct levels of software. The distinction is often blurred because there is no universal agreement on which functions should be included at the OS level, and which at the user level.[41] The division between an MTOS and application program is often ill-defined. If one has a real-time application and needs some multitasking, but the application is small, one may consider writing a special MTOS which does not waste overhead on features not needed. Usually one is better off using an available general MTOS except for the most trivial jobs; it takes man-months to design, code, and debug a MTOS, even one of limited size because of the subtle timing bugs and priority conflicts. If a real-time application is successful, it will expand as new requirements arise, and then the small MTOS becomes a patchworked program. A general MTOS may use time and space almost as efficiently as a special OS. Most of the features available in a general MTOS are found in an equivalent form in the special OS. Because of the many common subprograms, only a little memory is wasted by including extra MTOS facilities.

Another type of operating system called an executive, is a real-time system that is reconfigured for each application. One example is Intel's RMX/80, which is composed of relocatable program modules.[42] After the software has been developed on a development system, it is linked with the desired system modules and stored in ROM, PROM, or RAM. A disk-driver module gives the system file-management capability.

File Management

In order to manage information storage and retrieval, an OS uses a file system. Some systems treat all the peripheral devices, including the line printers, CRT, terminals, and disk drives, as files. Here the programs treat all I/O in a similar fashion with no concern for the particular characteristics of a device. For example, to print on the line printer the system routine for File Open (FOP) is called to open the line printer file. FOP allocates the line printer to the user if no other program is controlling it; then it issues a form feed. File Write (FWRIT) is called to issue each line. Then the user program calls File Close (FCLOS) to deallocate the line printer. A list of the typical routines a user program may call follows:[43]

FOP-Controls access to a particular file. Files are opened for read only, write only, or read and write. The program may specify shared or exclusive access and the physical device on which the file exists.

FREAD/FWRITE-Allows a read or write of the file. The application program uses this interface for all I/O functions. Access can be either sequential or random.

FCLOS-Releases access to a file. The file is either kept or deleted. If the file is a disk file, any unused disk sectors may be released.

TERMINATE-Indicates to the operating system that the execution of the program is terminated.

CURRENT TIME-Gives the current date and time.

FILE DESIGNATOR-Decodes an ASCII string and builds the block needed by FOP for specifying the file to be opened.

Applications Programs

Most microcomputer development systems use a variety of general-purpose applications programs that may be associated with an OS. These can include editors, assemblers, language compilers, linkers, loaders, debuggers, and utilities. Some are written as subroutines that can be linked with the application program. Others are used as separate programs, handling the user programs as input.

An interactive editor can simplify the software development greatly. Programs are put into the system through the terminal keyboard and stored in a disk file. The file is modified using editor commands such as ADD, DELETE, COPY, FIND, LIST, and REPLACE as shown below:

ADD	Add lines entered from the terminal into the text file.
DELETE	Delete lines from the text file.
LIST	List lines on the terminal or line printer.
FIND	Find a character string or line.
REPLACE	Replace a character string with a new character string.
MODIFY	Modify character strings with subcommands.
COPY	Copy lines or a block of lines.
TEXT	Read a block of text from disk or tape.
KEEP	Store a block of text on disk or tape.

The editor assigns line numbers to the stored text so that the individual lines can be identified and accessed. Some editors renumber the lines each time new ones are added or deleted. Others use incremental line numbers. For example, a line added between lines 102 and 103 could be numbered 102.1.

An OS can handle a mixture of languages, including assemblers and high-level languages.

Assembly language is efficient in terms of speed and memory since each instruction corresponds to a hardware instruction. The programmer manipulates the registers and allocates memory space. The assembler mnemonics are sometimes hard to remember since each computer manufacturer uses a different set of mnemonics. To make the program understandable, a comment may be needed on nearly every line.

High-level languages like FORTRAN and BASIC allow the programmer to forget about allocating registers or memory space because the compiler or interpreter takes care of such details. High-level programs can be machine-independent, but they are slower than assembled programs because the interpreter's code is not as efficient. High-level programs use fewer lines of source code and require less detailed comments than assembler programs. Since the programmer can concentrate on the application more, the program takes less time to code, debug, and maintain. Languages such as Algol, Pascal and PL/I use control structures with syntaxes that make it easier to follow the flow of a program. Such constructs as IF-THEN-ELSE, BEGIN-END, and DO-WHILE encourage structured programming by eliminating go-to loops. Languages such as Pascal are available on some microcomputers. FORTRAN, which was the first high-level language, lacks these transfer-of-control structures, but it is still widely used.

REFERENCES

1. Zaks, R., *Microprocessors,* Berkeley: Sybex, 1980.
2. Ibid.
3. Ibid.
4. Ibid.
5. Benson, T., Microcomputers: Single-chip or Single-board?, *Electronic Design* 13, June 21, 1978.
6. Intel, *Component Data Catalog,* Santa Clara: Intel, 1981.
7. Intel, *Systems Data Catalog,* Santa Clara: Intel, 1981.
8. Leventhal, L.V., *Microprocessors: Software, Hardware, Programming,* Englewood Cliffs: Prentice-Hall, 1978.
9. Ibid.
10. Ibid.
11. Ibid.
12. Peters, L. J., and Tripp, L. L., Comparing Software Design Methodologies, *Datamation,* November, 1977.
13. Ibid.
14. Jackson, M. A., *Principles of Program Design,* New York: Academic Press, 1975.
15. Warnier, J. D., *Logical Construction of Programs,* Leider: Stenfert Kroese, 1974.
16. Peters, L. J., and Tripp, L. L.
17. Ibid.
18. Ibid.
19. Hamilton, M., and Zeldin, S., Higher Order Software—A Methodology for Defining Software, *IEEE Transactions on Software Engineering,* March 1976.
20. Peters, L. J., and Tripp, L. L.
21. Hordeski, M. F., *Microprocessor Cookbook,* Blue Ridge Summit: Tab, 1979.
22. Ledgard, M. F., The Case for Structured Programming, *Bit* 13, 1973.
23. Leventhal, L. V.
24. Ibid.
25. Hordeski, M. F.
26. Ibid.
27. Ibid.
28. Ibid.

29. Ibid.
30. Hordeski, M. F., Selection of a Test Strategy for MPU Systems, *Electronics Test,* February 1982.
31. Hordeski, M. F., *Microprocessor Cookbook.*
32. Leventhal, L. V.
33. Ibid.
34. Intel, *Systems Data Catalog*
35. Ibid.
36. Pro-Log, *PROM User's Guide,* Monterey: Pro-Log, 1979.
37. Burzio, G., Operating Systems Enhance uCs, *Electronic Design,* June 21, 1978.
38. Ibid.
39. Ibid.
40. Ibid.
41. Ibid.
42. Intel, *Systems Data Catalog.*
43. Burzio, G.

EXERCISES

1. Discuss the problems involved in designing a railroad crossing monitor with a microprocessor. The system input is a switch that is closed by the weight of the train. The outputs activate warning lights, sound alarms, and lower the crossing gates. Describe the input, output, processing and accuracy requirements, memory, and error-handling. The crossing gates remain closed until the train has passed the crossing. The system must allow cars and people to leave the crossing before the gates are lowered. What are the time considerations if the switch is 0.7 miles from the crossing and the train travels at 60 miles per hour?

2. Consider the problems involved in designing a digital stopwatch with a microprocessor. The system uses inputs from a keyboard and counts down time on a LED display. Describe the input, output, processing and accuracy requirements, memory, and error-handling. The timer displays seconds and tenths of seconds and is activated by a START key.

3. Define the requirements in designing a digital thermometer using a microprocessor. The system inputs are an A/D converter connected to a resistive temperature sensor. It displays the temperature in degrees Celsius on an LED display. Describe the input, output, processing, and accuracy requirements, memory, and error-handling. The thermometer displays temperatures to the nearest degree over a 0 to 60°C range. What type converter would be used and how often will the temperature be sampled? What would be needed if a switch determined if temperature is displayed in degrees Celsius or Fahrenheit?

4. Draw a general flow chart for the following task. The microprocessor examines an input port. If the value at the port is not zero, the microprocessor waits 1 ms and samples the port again. If the value is the same, the processor must turn on an alarm light. Otherwise, the processor discards the first result and repeats the delay and sampling process. When the value at the port reaches zero again, the light is turned off.

5. Draw a general flow chart for the following task. The microprocessor reads an

ASCII character from an input port. If the character is not ETX, the microprocessor waits 2 ms and reads another character; if the character is ETX, the microprocessor performs a message-handling routine and starts the read process again.

6. Discuss the basic sequence of steps necessary for developing a microprocessor system. Consider the problems involved in each of these steps and present some typical solutions along with devices which have been developed to facilitate the implementation of these solutions at the various steps.

7. If microprocessor programming is to be accomplished quickly, three essential tools are available. Discuss the respective merits of a (1) time sharing system, (2) an in-house computer, and (3) a development system

8. Assuming that a 2K program is being developed and that no disk file system is available, how can the user-program as well as the support-programs be stored?

9. A large-scale computer is available with a cross-assembler. Discuss the execution, testing, and debugging of a 10K program using the cross-assembler versus a microprocessor development system.

10. If the microprocessor system itself does not possess all the facilities to fully analyze each program step, how might the detection of critical breakpoints be handled?

11. Some microprocessor development systems suffer from the low speeds, limited software, and peripherals that are usually available and their limitation to a single processor. External interfaces can be used, but they may complicate system development because they depend on facilities present in the development system but not in the final product. Discuss how more advanced and flexible microcomputer development systems may solve many of these problems.

12. The documentation of a program is intended for those who must use and maintain it, and who can understand it and extend it for further applications. Discuss how flow charts, comments, and memory maps are used as documentation techniques.

13. The maintenance stage allows the updating and correcting of the program to account for changing conditions or field experience. Discuss how the proper testing and documentation can reduce the frequency and extent of maintenance required for a microprocessor system.

14. An object program is to be placed in the memory of the system in which it will execute. Discuss the loading phase when the loading is accomplished by a loader program.

15. In the case of complex programs, the complexity of coding in assembly-level language may be unreasonable and inefficient. The reasonable solution becomes the use of a high-level language. If the program is that complex, the programming cost will be high and it may not be reasonable to consider a microprocessor. Discuss this argument.

16. There are some errors that may be found in the late stages of program or field testing. Equality cases within loops and conditional jumps are sources of these errors. The problem here is usually which value of a flag to use as the jump condition and what action to take when a variable is equal to a threshold rather than above or below it. Discuss some techniques for checking these troublesome cases.

17. Show how it is possible to trigger an external scope if fine debugging is needed for complex hardware interfacing.

18. Advocates of the Meta Stepwise Refinement (MSR) state that if the problem is solved several times, each solution is more detailed and complete than its predecessor. What are some drawbacks in applying this philosophy?
19. Supporters for Higher Order Software (HOS) provide a set of axioms which must be used. Discuss some problems in applying these axioms.
20. Discuss some applications where simple hand-testing can provide enough insight into program logic as compared with sophisticated debugging tools. Debugging real-time systems can be more difficult and requires more equipment. Discuss how an operating system can aid here.
21. If the microprocessor must interact in a very precise manner with a large and complex system, how can the necessary data be generated and presented to the microcomputer? Show using a general flow diagram.
22. A useful file-system feature is a user directory. It allows one to group files on each disk into several directories. When referring to a file, you specify the disk number, directory name, and file name. If only the file name is specified, the OS will use the default-directory name set up at log-on time. Devise a routine to obtain the proper file under these conditions.

Additional Readings

Abbott, R. A., Regitz, W. M. and Karp, J. A. A 4K MOS dynamic random access memory, *IEEE J. Solid State Circuit,* V.SC-8, October, No. 10. (1973). Reports on one of the first 4K Memories.

Abramson, N., and Kuo, F. F., Eds., *Computer-Communications Networks,* Englewood Cliffs: Prentice-Hall, 1973. A collection of articles on network systems.

Abrons, J. W. and Gardner, R. D. Interaction of technology and performance in COS-MOS integrated circuits, *IEEE J. Solid State Circuits,* V.SC-5. (1970). Considers some of the trade-offs in CMOS technology.

Amelio, G. E. et al. Experimental verification of the charge coupled device concept, *Bell Syst. Tech. J.,* V.49, (1970).
—Charge coupled imaging devices-design considerations, *IEEE Trans. on Electronic Device,* V.ED-18, (1971).
Early articles on practical CCD devices.

Allison, D. R., A Design Philosophy for Microcomputer Architectures, *Computer,* Vol. 10, No. 2, February (1977). Architectural considerations for microcomputers.

Altman, L. Charge couple devices move in on memories and analog signal processing, *Electronics,* V. 47, (1974). Reports on the initial impact of CCD devices.
—ed., *Microprocessors,* New York: Electronic Magazine Book Series, 1975. A collection of articles on early microprocessor applications.

American Micro-Systems, Inc., *MOS Integrated Circuits,* New York: Van Nostrand Reinhold, 1972. A basic reference on MOS technology.

Baker, W. D. Oxide isolation brings high density to production of bipolar memories, *Electronics,* V.46, March, (1973). Reports on the effect of oxide isolation on bipolar memory devices.

Barna, A., and Porat, D. I. Integrated Circuits in Digital Electronics, New York: John Wiley & Sons, Inc., 1973. Integrated circuit technology, design considerations.

Barrett, J. C., Bergh, A., Horank, T. and Price, J. E. Design considerations for a high speed bipolar read only memory, *IEEE J. Solid State Circuits,* V. SB-5, No. 5. (1970). Presents some of the factors in high speed memory design.

Baumgart, G. E. and Jones, D. W. Modular Approach Speeds DC Drive System Build-Up, *Control Engineering,* Vol. 25, No. 1, January (1978). Motor control application factors.

Barjanac, V. Architectural Design Theory: Models of the Design Process, in *Basic Questions of Design Theory,* W. R. Spillers, editor. New York: American Elsevier Publishing Co., Inc., 1974. Architectural considerations for designers.

Bell, C., and Newell, A., *Computer Structures,* New York: McGraw-Hill, 1970. A summary of architectures for computers.

Benedict, R. P., *Fundamentals of Temperature, Pressure and Flow Measurements,* New York: Wiley, 1969. One of a number of instrumentation basic references.

Bentchkowsky, Frohman, D. An integrated metal-nitride oxide silicon (MNOS) memory, *Proc. IEEE* V.57, June, pp. 1190–1192. (1969). Reports on an early MNOS device.

Bernhard, R., Bubbles take on Disks, *IEEE Spectrum,* May (1980). Reports on the potential impact of bubble memories.

Brooks, F. P. An Overview of Microcomputer Architecture and Software, *Micro Architecture,* Euromicro 1976 Proceedings (1976). Summarizes microcomputer architectures in use.

Burton, D. P. and Dexter, A. L. Handle Microcomputer I/O Efficiently *Electronic Design,* 13, June 21, (1978). I/O design considerations.

Burzio, G. Operating Systems Enhance uCs, *Electronic Design,* June 21, (1978). Shows how operating systems function.

Camenzind, H. R., *Electronic Integrated System Design,* New York: Van Nostrand Reinhold, 1972. Integrated circuit design considerations.

Considine, Douglas M. (ed.), *Process Instruments and Controls Handbook,* New York: McGraw-Hill, 1967. A collection of articles on process instrumentation.

Childs, R. E., Multiple Microprocessor Systems: Goals, Limitations and Alternatives, Digest of Papers *COMPCON* Spring 79, (1979). Spells out some of the issues in multimicroprocessor systems.

Cragon, H. G., The Elements of Single-Chip Microcomputer Architecture, *Computer,* Oct. (1980). Considers the issues involved in the architecture of commercial single-chip microcomputers.

Cushman, R. H., The Intel 8080: First of the Second-Generation Microprocessors, *EDN,* Vol. 19, No. 9, May 1 (1974). An early article on the 8080.

Cutler, H., Linear Velocity Ramp Speeds Stepper and Servo Positioning, *Control Engineering,* Vol. 24, No. 5, May (1977). Motor control application issues.

Davis, S., Selection and Application of Semiconductor Memories, *Computer Design,* Vol. 13, No. 1, January (1974). Presents some guidelines for using semiconductor memories.

Doherty, D. W. and Wells, E. J. Digital Power Drive Dynamics are Characterized by ROMs, *Control Engineering,* Vol. 25, No. 1, January (1978). Motor control techniques using ROM.

Eckhouse, R. H., Jr., *Minicomputer Systems,* Englewood Cliffs: Prentice-Hall, 1975. Minicomputer system design issues.

Enslow, P. H., Jr., ed., Multiprocessors and Parallel Processing, New York: John Wiley, 1974. A collection of early articles on multiprocessing.

Foster, C. C., *Computer Architecture.* New York: Van Nostrand Reinhold Company, 1970. An early work on computer architectures up to that period.

Frankenberg, R. J., *Designer's Guide to Semiconductor Memories,* Boston: Cabners, 1975. Presents the technology of, and considers the use of, semiconductor memory families.

Franklin, M. A., Kahn, S. A., and Stucki, M. J., Design Issues in the Development of Modular Multiprocessor Communications Network, *Sixth Ann. Symp. Computer Architecture,* April, 23–25 (1979). Considers the issues in the design of multiprocessor communications networks.

Fung, K. T., and Torng, On the Analysis of Memory Conflicts and Bus Contentions in a Multiple-Microprocessor System, *IEEE Trans. Computers,* Vol. C-27, No. 1, January (1979). Treats some of the problems in a multimicroprocessor system.

Garland, H. *Introduction to Microprocessor System Design,* New York: McGraw-Hill, 1979. Brief treatment of microprocessor types, technology and interfacing.

Greene, R., and House, D., Designing with Intel PROMs and ROMs, *Intel Application Note AP-6,* Santa Clara: Intel Corporation, (1975). Useful article on the application of ROMs and PROMs.

Gutzwiller, F. W., ed. *SCR Manual,* Syracuse: General Electric, 1969. A useful work on SCR motor controls.

Halsall, F., A Microprocessor Controlled Interface for Data Transmission, *The Radio and Electronic Engineer,* Vol. 45, No. 3, (1975). Reports on an early communications application of microprocessors.

Hall, J. Flowmeters—Matching Applications and Devices, *Instruments and Control Systems,* February (1978). A useful article on basic flowmeter characteristics.

Hamilton, M., and Zeldin, S., Higher Order Software-A Methodology for Defining Software, *IEEE Transactions on Software Engineering,* Vol. SE-2, No. 1, March (1976). Defines the HOS methodology.

Harris, J. A., and Smith, D. R., Hierarchical Multiprocessor Organizations, *Fourth Ann. Symp. Computer Architecture,* March, 23–25 (1977). Considers the hierarchical multiprocessor issues.

Hordeski, M. F., Digital Sensors Simplify Digital Measurements, *Measurements and Data,* May–June (1976). The use of digital instruments in control systems.

—When should you use pneumatics, when electronics? *Instruments and Control Systems,* November (1976). Pneumatic/electronic instrument considerations.

—Guide to digital instrumentation for temperature, pressure instruments, *Oil Gas and Petrochem Equipment,* November (1976). A summary of temperature and pressure instrument characteristics.

—Digital instrumentation for pressure, temperature/pressure, readout instruments, *Oil Gas and Petrochem Equipment,* December (1976). Includes instrument readout characteristics.

—Innovative Design: Microprocessors, *Digital Design,* December (1976). Discusses issues in the application of microprocessors.

—Adapting Electric Actuators to Digital Control, *Instrumentation Technology,* March (1977). Considers the issues of converting to digital control.

—Balancing Microprocessor-Interface Trade-offs, *Digital Design,* April (1977). Considers a number of analog and digital interfaces with different hardware/software mixes.

—Digital Position Encoders for Linear Applications, *Measurements and Control,* July–August (1977). Reports on a linear encoder for digital control applications.

—Future Microprocessor Software, *Digital Design,* August (1977). Discusses some issues on the future of microprocessor software.

—Process Controls are Evolving Fast, *Electronic Design,* November 22 (1977). Presents some digital control techniques for process and manufacturing systems.

—The Human Interface in ATE Design, presentation at the ATE Seminar, Los Angeles, January 30, 1978. Considers the operator factor in test equipment design.

—Fundamentals of Digital Control Loops, *Measurements and Control,* February (1978). A treatment on digital control analysis and testing.

—Using Microprocessors, *Measurements and Control,* June (1978). Presents some basic considerations on using microprocessors in industrial applications.

—*Illustrated Dictionary of Micro Computer Terminology,* Blue Ridge Summit, PA: Tab, 1978. Includes many microprocessor concepts and technology relations.

—*Microprocessor Cookbook,* Blue Ridge Summit, PA: Tab, 1979. A summary of commercial microprocessor hardware, software, and application techniques.

—Selection of a Test Strategy for MPU systems, *Electronics Test,* February (1982). Considers the issues in testing microprocessor systems.

Hnatek, Eugene R., *A User's Handbook of Semiconductor Memories,* New York: Wiley, 1977. Presents the characteristics and guidelines for the use of semiconductor memories.

Intel Corp., *8086 User's Guide,* Santa Clara, CA: Intel Corporation, 1978. A programming and hardware interface manual for the 8086 family.

—*4004/4040 Assembly Language Programming Manual,* Santa Clara: Intel Corporation, 1974. A programming guide for the 4004 and 4040 microprocessors.

—*8080 User's Manual,* Santa Clara: Intel Corporation, 1975. A programming and hardware interface guide to the 8080 family.

—*8080 Assembly Language Programming Manual,* Santa Clara: Intel Corporation, 1975. A programming guide for the 8080.

Jackson, M. A. Principles of Program Design, New York: Academic Press, 1975. Defines the Jackson software design method.

Kolk, W. R., PPM—Control Candidate in Energy Limited Systems, *Control Engineering* Vol.

24, No. 10, October (1977). Shows how pulse-frequency modulation can be used to save energy in control systems.

Leventhal, L. V. *Microprocessors: Software, Hardware, Programming,* Englewood Cliffs, N.J.: Prentice-Hall, 1978. Program-oriented treatment with strong minicomputer basis.

Lorin, H., *Parallelism in Hardware and Software,* Englewood Cliffs: Prentice-Hall, 1972. Considers issues in parallel systems.

Liptak, B. G. and Venczel, K., eds. *Instrument Engineers' Handbook on Process Measurement,* Radnor, PA: Chilton, 1982. Extensive collection of instrument techniques for process systems.

Martin, Donald P., *Microcomputer Design,* Chicago: Martin Research Ltd., 1975. Considers a number of early microprocessor applications along with hardware implementation.

Mazur, T., Microprocessor Basics. Part 4: The Motorola 6800, *Electronic Design,* July 19, (1976). Considers the features of the 6800.

McGlynn, D. R., *Microprocessors,* New York, Wiley, 1976. Basic treatment of microprocessors, their technology, and applications.

Moss, D., Multiprocessing Adds Muscle to uPs, *Electronic Design II,* May 24, (1978). Application of multiple microprocessors to simple systems.

Motorola Semiconductor, *M 68000 Microprocessor User's Manual,* Austin, TX: Motorola. Hardware and software features required by 68000 users.

—*M6800 Microprocessor Applications Manual,* Phoenix: Motorola, (1975). A collection of 6800 applications.

—*M6800 Programming Manual,* Phoenix: Motorola, (1975). Programming techniques for the 6800.

—*MECL Integrated Circuits Data Book,* Phoenix: Motorola, (1972). Useful for ECL technology characteristics.

Muth, S., *Synchro Conversion Handbook,* Bohemia, NY: ILC Data, 1974. Contains many circuits and techniques for converting synchro data to digital format.

Myers, Glenford J., *Advances in Computer Architecture,* New York: Wiley, 1978. Summarizes the trends in architecture.

National Semiconductor, The NS16000 Family of 16-Bit Microprocessors, Santa Clara, CA: National Semiconductor. Describes the features of the 16000 family.

—Digital Integrated Circuits, Santa Clara, CA: National Semiconductor. 1973. Contains characteristics of the early National microprocessors.

Nick, J. R., Using Schottky 3-State Outputs in Bus-Organized Systems, *Electronic Design News,* Vol. 19, No. 23, December 5, (1974). Presents design techniques for using 3-State buffers in microprocessor systems.

Norton, H. N., *Handbook of Transducers for Electronic Measuring Systems,* Englewood Cliffs: Prentice-Hall, 1969. Good treatment of transducer characteristics for most devices.

Noyce, R. N. and Hoff, M. E. Jr., A History of Microprocessor Development at Intel, *IEEE Micro,* February (1981). Good background material for understanding the microprocessor evolution.

Palmer, R., Nonlinear Feedforward Can Reduce Servo Settling Time, *Control Engineering,* Vol. 26, No. 3, March (1978). Considers the application of feedforward in motor control.

Patel, J. H., Processor-Memory Interconnections for Multiprocessors, *Proc. Sixth Ann. Symp. Computer Architecture,* April 23–25 (1979). Considers a number of configurations for multiprocessor systems.

Peters, L. J., and Tripp, L. L. Is Software Design Wicked?, *Datamation,* Vol. 22, No. 6, June (1976). Considers if software design methods are really useful.

Peuto, B. L. and Shustek, L. J., Current Issues in the Architecture of Microprocessors, *Computer,* February (1977). Presents a number of considerations on microprocessor architecture.

Sheingold, D. H., *Analog-Digital Conversion Handbook,* Norwood, MA: Analog Devices, 1974. Contains many useful circuits and techniques for conversion.

Sigma Instruments, *Stepping Motor Handbook,* Braintree, MA: Sigma Instruments, 1974. Contains useful material on stepper motors and drive techniques.

Skrokov, M. R., ed. *Mini- and Microcomputer Control in Industrial Processes,* New York: Van Nostrand Reinhold, 1980. A collection of articles on mini- and microcomputer applications in industrial control.

Soucek, B. *Microprocessors and Microcomputers,* New York: Wiley, 1976. Considers the hardware characteristics of early microprocessors.

Stevens, W. P., Myers, G. J., and Constantine, L. L. *Structural Design,* New York: Yourdon, 1975. Considers some elements of the structured design method.

Stone, H. S., *Introduction to Computer Architecture,* New York: McGraw-Hill, 1975. A basic text on general computer architectures.

Texas Instruments *TMS 9900 Microprocessor Data Manual.* Dallas: Texas Instruments. Contains 9900 microprocessor hardware and software features.

—*The TTL Data Book for Design Engineers,* Dallas: Texas Instruments, 1978. Contains TTL family and device characteristics needed by the designer.

Thurber, K. J., and Masson, G. M., *Distributed Processor Communication Architecture,* Lexington, MA: Lexington, 1979. Considers distributed architectures for communication systems.

Toong, H. D., and Gupta, A., A Architectural Comparison of Contemporary 16-bit Microprocessors, *IEEE Micro,* May (1981). Considers the differences in a number of 16-bit microprocessors.

Torrero, E. A., Focus on Microprocessors, *Electronic Design,* September 1, (1974). A collection of early applications of microprocessors.

—ed., *Microprocessors: New Directions For Designers,* Rochelle Park, NJ: Hayden Book Co., 1975. A collection of articles on early microprocessor applications along with design techniques.

Yourdon, E., and Constantine, L. L., *Structured Design,* New York: Yourdon, (1975). Defines the structured design method.

Zaks, R., *Microprocessors,* Berkeley, CA: Sybex, 1980. A good general treatment on microprocessors, technology and system design.

—and Lesea A., Microprocessor Interfacing Techniques, Berkeley, CA: Sybex, 1979. Concentrates on interface chips and typical application interfaces.

Zilog Corp., *Z8000 User's Guide,* Cupertino, CA. 95014. Contains the hardware and software documentation for the Z8000 family.

Index

FEB 2 8 1986 DEC 1 3 1993	DATE DUE	